THE MAKING OF EARLY ENGLAND

The Making
of Early England

D. P. Kirby

SCHOCKEN BOOKS · NEW YORK

Dedicated to
E. E. KIRBY

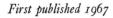

First published 1967

© D. P. Kirby 1967

Made and printed in Great Britain
by William Clowes and Sons Ltd, London and Beccles
for the publishers B. T. BATSFORD LTD
4 Fitzhardinge Street, London W1

Contents

CONTENTS

Illustrations

Acknowledgments

I wish to acknowledge the generous help received in the writing of this book from many scholars and friends.

Dr. J. N. L. Myres very kindly read and commented on my chapters on The Anglo-Saxon Conquest and The Heptarchy, and Dr. Dorothea Oschinsky that on Agriculture. Mr. R. N. Bailey gave me the benefit of his deep familiarity with the artistic and cultural development of Anglo-Saxon England. I am particularly grateful to Professor A. R. Myers who read the complete typescript of the book, and to Mr. H. R. Loyn who read the book at proof stage. I know that I have profited from the interest and advice of these two distinguished historians. Any inaccuracies which remain, and the interpretations offered, are entirely my responsibility.

Finally, though they may not have been directly associated with the preparation of this volume, I would not like to close without remembering all who taught me over the years the early history of the British Isles. I hope that this book is in some measure worthy of them.

The Author and Publishers would like to thank the museums, libraries and photographers particularised on pages 7 and 8 for permission to reproduce individual illustrations.

1 Map of Anglo-Saxon England

Book one

1 THE PRE-VIKING PERIOD

Chapter one

The Anglo-Saxon Conquest

Prehistoric archaeology has reconstructed a picture of successive waves of invasion across Europe in the centuries before recorded history, culminating in the invasions of Celtic-speaking peoples from *c.* 500 B.C. It was a western Europe dominated by a Celtic aristocracy which the Romans conquered in the first centuries B.C. and A.D. Historians of Celtic society have been known to express regret that the Romans repressed an emerging Celtic culture, but it is by no means certain that Celtic society in its entirety would have survived for long had the Romans not intervened. When Julius Caesar conquered Gaul, the Celts were already under attack from Germanic-speaking tribes across the Rhine. Once the Pax Romana finally crumbled in the west in the fifth century A.D. the Germanic peoples swept across Europe. Land-hunger, population pressure, and the movements of tribes in eastern Europe, particularly the Huns, are believed to have set the Germanic peoples in motion. In the fifth and sixth centuries, therefore, the west was caught in the grip of a recurring phenomenon of invasion; and, as the imperial administration at Rome failed increasingly to cope with the problems of governing the western Empire, Goths, Vandals, Franks and Saxons settled within its confines. In the place of a Europe which was Celtic and Romanised, they created a Europe dominated by a Germanic aristocracy and infiltrated by a Germanic peasantry. The Vandals established themselves in Africa, the Goths in Italy, southern Gaul and Spain, and the Franks in northern Gaul, inheriting in varying degrees a legacy of imperial administration and culture. The Angles, Saxons and Jutes of north Germany and Denmark formed the majority of the invaders who crossed to Britain; and it is important to remember that what occurred in Britain was but part of a pattern of change common to the whole of western Europe.

The End of Roman Britain and the Narrative of Gildas

During the third and fourth centuries A.D. Roman Britain was subject to periodic attacks from the Picts of Scotland and the Irish—or Scots—of Ireland, attacks which primarily affected the east and west coastal districts of Britain and the northern frontier of Hadrian's Wall. The Irish were seeking footholds along the west coast, for example in Wales, and they succeeded by the late fifth century in establishing the Scottish kingdom of Dalriada (Argyll). Irish pressure on the Picts may have been one of the causes of the Pictish attacks on North Britain. Pictish and Scottish restlessness was symptomatic of the tide of migration which was moving throughout the barbarian world beyond the frontiers of the Roman Empire. From the mid-third century, raids along the eastern and southern coasts of Britain by Saxon pirates paralleled the Pictish and Scottish attacks. These fair-haired, blue-eyed raiders, in their 'sea-steeds' or 'wave-horses' as they called their ships, were feared for the speed and ferocity of their attacks not only in Britain but also on the Continent. Despite periodic crises, however, at the beginning of the fifth century Britain still appeared secure and a part of the Roman Empire which was expected to last for ever. Informed Romans saw no reason why the Empire should not continue to absorb its assailants as it had done in the past. The Germanic tribes appeared to have no wish to destroy the Empire, only to share in its supposed benefits. To many Romans the actual benefits of life within the Empire were being seriously mitigated by the crushing effects of increasing and heavy taxation to pay for the imperial administration, but probably the majority of educated and thinking citizens believed that the Empire was experiencing only temporary difficulties. In Britain, town life may not have been flourishing as vigorously as in the second century, but villa economy, on the other hand, was still thriving, and the diocese of Britain had been divided into four or possibly five administrative provinces, two of which were centred on London and Cirencester and a third probably on York. In addition, the military organisation of Britain was in the process of revision and by the early years of the fifth century there had been appointed a Duke of the Britains in charge of the northern frontier, a Count of the Britains in command of a field army, and a

Count of the Saxon Shore commanding the forts and defences of the coastal regions. Further, though the requirements of frontier defence on the Continent necessitated the withdrawal of troops of the imperial army from Britain from time to time, to a certain extent these losses were apparently compensated for by the emergence of new British states in north and west Britain which could shoulder some of the work of defence. At some point in the early fifth century, a British leader, Cunedda, is traditionally reported to have crossed from north-east Britain to North Wales to oppose the attacks of the Scots in those regions.

The defence of Roman Britain was primarily geared to the fundamental assumption that the greatest danger to the security of the land came from the north. This had been so particularly since the advance of the legions had been terminated at the line represented by Hadrian's Wall. The conviction that the Picts and Scots were the great menace to security was so strong that during the late fourth century Anglo-Saxon mercenaries were settled along the east coast to be used as reinforcements against them. It was traditional Roman policy so to use barbarian forces against an existing enemy, and it is clear that despite the Saxon raids there can have been little indication in the late fourth and early fifth centuries that the Anglo-Saxons were to constitute the greatest threat of all. The Scottish attack may have been much more intense than historians have allowed; but it is clear that while Britain appeared to be securely defended it was actually in the difficult position of being open to potentially serious attack from the east as well as from the north and west. So far as the Romano-Britons were concerned there existed a reasonable balance between themselves and what was left of the Roman army, between the Picts and Scots and the Saxon mercenaries. In 383, however, the Britons had been deserted by a usurping emperor, Magnus Maximus, and the Roman army stationed in Britain; and again in 407 the Roman army in Britain set up a rival emperor, Constantine III, to the Emperor Honorius at Rome and crossed to Gaul. By 410 the Britons were assuming responsibility for their own defence, and Honorius was urging them to continue to do so. Honorius was in great difficulties himself, for not only did he face an imperial rival but the Germanic tribes had flooded across the Rhine, and Italy was a battlefield. It is at this point that the darkness of the Anglo-Saxon Conquest descends.

Though it is possible to exaggerate the deficiencies of the literary records which are really better than might have been expected from this confused period, it is of course essential to realise that we possess no comprehensive account of the Conquest, only a few pieces of evidence which spotlight particular aspects of the invasion or specific areas of activity and which require to be illuminated further in the light of archaeological and place-name evidence. The only writer of the time who attempted any survey of the Conquest as a whole was a British monk, Gildas, who wrote his account of the *Ruin of Britain* about 540. This was a work of moral exhortation to the kings and clergy of the Britons, deliberately calling attention to the evils of British society as Gildas saw them and prefaced by what was intended to be an account of the Anglo-Saxon Conquest down to the time of a great battle at Mount *Badon* (unidentified) which checked the Saxon advance. Recent attempts to prove, on the basis of chronological arguments, that this account of the Conquest was really written in the eighth century are completely unsound, and the narrative of Gildas may still be taken as that of a sixth-century commentator. Unfortunately, the often hysterical tone of Gildas has not always commended his historicity to modern historians, but he does describe a sequence of events which can be divorced to a certain extent from the gloss he put upon them. This sequence of events must form the basis for any study of the course of the Anglo-Saxon Conquest.

Gildas states that when the Britons were deserted by Magnus Maximus in 383 they appealed to Rome for aid against the Picts and Scots and received it. When the Picts and Scots had been repulsed and the troops from the Continent had withdrawn, further attack ensued, another appeal was sent to Rome, and again a Roman army returned. On this occasion, after the defeat of the invaders, the Romans left Britain as men never to return. When the Picts and Scots renewed their attack, an appeal was sent to Agitius, usually identified with Aetius, in his third consulship (*i.e.* in the period 446–54), but Aetius was evidently preoccupied in Gaul and could give no help. The Britons rallied and defeated the enemy themselves, and a period of prosperity followed during which tyrants came to power and rival princes rose and fell. Eventually it was heard that the Picts and Scots were planning another assault, and the British rulers, led by a proud tyrant (unnamed), took the disastrous course of admitting the Saxons to repel them, settling the Saxons in the eastern part of the island. More and more barbarians crossed to Britain, finding the land rich and inviting. Eventually, after a dispute with the Britons over monthly food supplies, the Saxon mercenaries rebelled and a terrible wave of destruction followed which was only checked by Ambrosius Aurelianus, called the last of the Romans, in a resistance which culminated in the British victory at *Badon*. Gildas attempted to date this battle, but it is not clear whether he originally wrote that *Badon* was fought in the forty-fourth year after the arrival of Saxons or that he was writing in the forty-fourth year after the battle. It has recently been suggested that he meant that he was writing in the forty-fourth year after the rise to power of Ambrosius.

Gildas shows that the Britons continued the Roman policy of using barbarians against barbarians and he describes how a great Saxon revolt occurred, but it is difficult to date the events to which he refers or to equate his account of the last stages of Roman occupation with independently recorded incidents. It is the problem of what Gildas meant by the departure of the Roman army for the last time which is at the heart of the matter. Most historians have argued, on the basis of the absence of archaeological and sound literary evidence to the contrary, that the Romans never returned to Britain after 407. Nevertheless, the revisers of the *Notitia Dignitatum*, a complicated Roman military document, even after as late as 425, continued to include the British section. Following the settlement of the Visigoths in Aquitaine in 418, there were no more violent upheavals in Gaul for twenty years and during the first half of the fifth century Britain's links with Gaul remained close. The Saxons believed that in 418 the Romans were in Britain burying treasure and taking other valuables back to Gaul. More important, in 429 Germanus, bishop of Auxerre, came to Britain. Germanus held posts of civil and military responsibility in North Gaul, and during his visit he led the Britons to a great victory over their enemies. Tradition about such an event might well have reached Gildas in terms of a return of the Romans. Gildas certainly seems to have thought of Britain as within the sphere of Roman influence until the time of the appeal to Aetius.

Historians have hitherto challenged Gildas's description of an evidently lengthy period of prosperity after the appeal to Aetius in 446–54. A Gallic chronicle recorded for the year 442–3 (*i.e.* 441–2)[1] that Britain came under the control of the Saxons, while Bede, in his *Ecclesiastical History of the English Nation*, written in 731, and the *Anglo-Saxon Chronicle* A, compiled *c.* 890–2, both drawing on Kentish dynastic tradition, date the arrival of the Saxon mercenaries who were to lead the revolt to 449. Whichever source is the more correct chronologically, an insufficient time interval is left for Gildas's period of prosperity. Con-

---

[1] Several of the dates in this chronicle appear to be inaccurate by one year.

sequently, historians have placed the years of prosperity after 410 rather than after 446–54. The period 441–2 for the conquest of the Britons by the Saxons, however, is generally incompatible with all other literary evidence for the Anglo-Saxon Conquest and there is no reason to assume that what happened in 441–2 represents anything other than one in a series of agreements between the Britons and Saxon mercenaries. The Anglo-Saxons remembered an appeal for aid from the Britons which they dated to 443. There are no grounds for assuming that the early dates given by Bede and the *Chronicle* are necessarily correct. Dating by the Incarnation did not become the fashion in England until the eighth century. Dates had then to be calculated on the basis of regnal lists, which gave the names of successive kings and the number of years they each reigned, and on folk-traditions that a given event had occurred in a certain year (*e.g.* the seventh) of a particular king. These pieces of evidence and tradition provided a sliding scale for working out dates, but it appears that Incarnation dates so established, especially very early ones, could be wide of the mark and many years too early. Regnal years could be incorrectly transcribed and kings who reigned jointly could be listed as having ruled successively. Such mathematical calculations cannot be set against the story Gildas tells, and a possibility remains that the years of prosperity did occur after *c.* 450. In this case, the arrival of Saxon mercenaries at the invitation of the British tyrant could date to some time after the appeal to Aetius, *i.e.* to *c.* 460–70. If the Romans really did leave Britain for the last time in 407, it is perhaps unlikely that the rise of tyrants did not occur until after *c.* 450, but while the possibility of Roman military expeditions from Gaul after 418 remains so does the possibility that the Anglo-Saxon Conquest did not begin until *c.* 460–70. This would mean that Romano-British society survived longer than was originally thought, an important point in the consideration of that society on the eve of conquest.

The Emergence of the Anglo-Saxon Kingdoms

The *Anglo-Saxon Chronicle*, first put together *c.* 890–2 at the court of Alfred the Great, king of Wessex, is a primary English source for the Conquest. Though the dates in the *Chronicle* are unreliable for this period of history, there is no reason to suppose that the traditions of the Conquest, which the *Chronicle* preserves, are unhistorical. Brief references to battles represent the dim memories preserved by Anglo-

Saxon dynasties of their royal ancestors who defeated the Britons and carved kingdoms for themselves. The *Chronicle* does not preserve memories of English defeats. Only if a dynasty could trace its ancestry back to the Conquest would it preserve traditions of the period, but most Anglo-Saxon royal lines took their origin in the mid-sixth century or after. This is one of the reasons why the records of the Conquest are so uneven. If no records survive for a given region this is not necessarily because no fighting took place there, but rather because no traditions were handed down. The *Anglo-Saxon Chronicle* is based essentially on West Saxon dynastic tradition, and, therefore, has little to say about the early history, for example, of Mercia or Northumbria.

Details from Kent survive in the *Chronicle* of the first phase of conquest. In this instance the account in the *Chronicle* can be supplemented by traditions included by Nennius in his *History of the Britons*, written in Wales *c.* 825. A further set of annals survive in the *Chronicle* for Sussex. The dates in the *Chronicle* for events in Sussex are no more reliable than those for Kent, but tradition evidently indicated to the chronicler that the conquests of Kent and Sussex took place at about the same time. The Northumbrian scholar, Bede, paraphrased Gildas's account in his *Ecclesiastical History* (written in 731), and using Kentish tradition named the proud tyrant as Vortigern. Vortigern was a fifth-century British chieftain, regarded in Wales as the ancestor of the kings of Powys. Bede names the leaders of the Saxon mercenaries who revolted as Hengest and Horsa, the conquerors of Kent. Hengest and Horsa fought Vortigern at *Ægelesthrep*, usually though not certainly identified with Aylesford, where Horsa and Cattegirn, son of Vortigern, are said to have been slain. Though Hengest and Horsa came to be regarded as the leaders of the Saxon revolt it cannot be emphasised too strongly that they and their men represented only a fraction of the Saxons in revolt. Archaeological evidence reveals a screen of Saxon mercenaries all down the east coast. Nennius mentions that the son and nephew of Hengest were settled by the Frisian sea, possibly the Firth of Forth, and Bede records that the Saxons allied with the Picts and Scots when they revolted. Similarly, though Vortigern's name means 'chief lord' and he came to be regarded as the proud tyrant, it remains possible that the tyrant and he were distinct from one another. If Vortigern's rule extended from Wales or the Welsh border to Kent, however, he must have been very powerful indeed.

The conquests of Kent and Sussex were evidently violent. In a subsequent battle in Kent 12 British chieftains perished and the Britons fled in great fear to London. The reference to London is particularly interesting, for the fate of London at the hands of the Saxons, like that of all the Roman cities, is obscure. London was eventually annexed by the East Saxons and did not pass to the men of Kent; it became the site of the bishopric of the East Saxons. The Kentish royal line made its capital Canterbury, an old Roman centre which shows signs of occupation by mercenaries from the mid-fifth century. In Sussex, Chichester, another Roman site, may have become an important early centre for it is called after Cissa, the name of a son of Ælle who conquered Sussex. Most of the recorded battles of the Conquest seem to have taken place on the sea-shore, by woods, and at strategic river crossings rather than at fortified centres, but an exception is provided by the career of Ælle. The *Chronicle* records that Ælle sacked *Anderida*, the Saxon Shore fort of Pevensey, and slew all who were inside, a grim reference to the violence of conquest. There is no reason to assume that Ælle was exceptionally brutal, but he so distinguished himself as a military leader that he was remembered as the first of the English *bretwaldas*. In the seventh century a *bretwalda* was an overlord who had asserted his supremacy over his royal neighbours. It is not clear how extensive Ælle's overlordship was but it probably embraced Kent, Surrey and the earliest settlers along the Thames valley, and may even have extended over the very earliest settlers in Wessex. It must have been a remarkable achievement, and if any of the leaders of the Anglo-Saxon Conquest approached the position of commander-in-chief over a wide area, that leader would seem to have been Ælle of Sussex.

What checked the rise of the kingdom of the South Saxons and thrust it back into narrow confines is not yet clear. It used to be thought that it was the South Saxons who came up against the Britons at *Badon* but in the absence not only of a certain identification of the battle-site but also of a sound chronology this must remain conjectural. Nevertheless, it is difficult to resist the conclusion that the South Saxons in particular were adversely affected by the British resurgence which *Badon* represented since they had most to lose in view of Ælle's position. It is most unfortunate that the British background to the Anglo-Saxon Conquest is not known in greater detail. Nennius records that a civil war occurred among the Britons between Ambrosius Aurelianus and a rival who may have been a kinsman of Vortigern, in the eighth year after the arrival of the Saxons. This may have strengthened the position of the invaders and facilitated the conquest of Kent and Sussex and adjacent districts. But the Britons certainly had their champions. The rise of Ambrosius witnessed the beginning of a series of British victories. And, though Gildas does not mention Arthur, Nennius preserves a list of 12 victories attributed to him, culminating in that at *Badon*. Out of this list, however, only two battle-sites can be positively identified, one at Chester and one in the great wood of Caledonia north of Hadrian's Wall, and the inclusion of Chester could be by confusion with a later battle of Chester in *c*. 615. There is a possibility that the battle of *Camlann*, in which Arthur perished, was fought at the fort of Birdoswald on Hadrian's Wall, so that what indications there are suggest that Arthur devoted part at least of his attention to military concerns on the northern frontier. It must be emphasised that the Britons were probably fighting on two fronts during most of the Conquest, and that the distraction of continuing conflict with the northern tribes may have been a fundamental factor in the defeat of the Britons by the Anglo-Saxons.

The narrative of Gildas shows that whenever and wherever the battle of *Badon* was fought it ushered in a period of peace. It is known that *c*. 531 the Anglo-Saxons were returning in large numbers to the Continent, possibly as a result of the British victory at *Badon*. Gildas wrote during this period, but it is clear from the *Chronicle* and Nennius that a second wave of attack by the Anglo-Saxons began in the mid-sixth century. The *Chronicle* places the arrival of a group of invaders under Cerdic and his son, Cynric, in Southampton Water in the year 495 but this date has even less to commend it than 449. Chronological evidence suggests that Cerdic and Cynric date rather to post-550— Cynric, for example, was an older contemporary of Ceawlin, who belongs to the late sixth century—and that the West Saxon advance which they led from the New Forest through Wiltshire to Old Sarum belongs to the second phase of conquest.[1] The capture of Old Sarum made Cynric master of the Wiltshire area, and in what was probably the 580s he is found fighting the Britons in alliance with Ceawlin. By the late seventh century Ceawlin was regarded as a son of Cynric but the earliest traditions do not so describe him. The name of Ceawlin's father is not given in the annals of the Conquest. Ceawlin's activities radiated out from the Thames valley. In the last decades of the sixth century he defeated three kings in one battle and mastered the cities of Bath,

---

[1] For a discussion of these dates, see the article 'Problems of Early West Saxon History' cited in the bibliography, p. 285.

Cirencester and Gloucester, and he campaigned possibly into north Oxfordshire or into Warwickshire, where, at the battle of *Fethanleag*, he suffered some set-back and is said to have returned in anger to his own country, though with great spoil. His brother, Cuthwulf, broke up what must have been an important British enclave by his capture of Limbury, Aylesbury, Bensington and Eynsham. Invaders had poured into the Thames valley from the earliest days of the Conquest either along the Thames itself or down the Icknield Way from the east coast and across the Chilterns, settling particularly on the south bank of the river. The Thames valley Saxons came to form an important element in the emerging kingdom of Wessex. That anything is known of Cerdic and Cynric from the *Anglo-Saxon Chronicle* is probably due to the fact that when Cædwalla, a descendant of Ceawlin, finally subjected the Wiltshire Saxons in the 680s a genealogical link was established between Ceawlin and Cynric which enabled Cædwalla to pose as the descendant of both princes, thereby uniting the divergent strains of early Wessex. The evidence suggests, however, that in the sixth and early seventh century the Wiltshire and Thames valley Saxons were two distinct peoples, and that Ceawlin was a leader of the Saxons of the Thames valley who came into contact with Cynric only as the latter advanced north from Old Sarum. Ceawlin's attack on Cirencester must have been of particular significance for this city had been one of the late Roman administrative centres of Britain. Ceawlin was remembered as the second *bretwalda*, indicating that he was able to impose his overlordship upon the settlers of southern England. Though there are alternative possibilities of origin, it may be that sections of the Wansdyke, a great linear defence work part of which defends north Somerset and north Wiltshire, were utilised by the Wiltshire Saxons against those of the Thames valley; and a series of dykes in Cambridgeshire, across the routes via the Icknield Way and the Chilterns from the Thames valley, may have been constructed by the East Angles with the primary purpose of frustrating the expanse of the Thames valley Saxons.

It is to the second half of the sixth century that the development of the historic kingdom of East Anglia can be traced. Fifth-century settlement in East Anglia was primarily in Norfolk, along the many waterways flowing into the Wash and, found as they often are in association with Roman sites as at Caistor-by-Norwich, some go back to a period before the Saxon revolt occurred. But archaeological evidence suggests that a second wave of invaders, exhibiting strong Swedish affinities in a culture which seems to have reached East Anglia from northern Denmark, struck into south-east Suffolk in the course of the sixth century. An East Anglian dynasty emerged, known as the *Wuffingas*, because descent was claimed from an early warrior chief named Wuffa. Nennius records that Wehha, father of Wuffa, first conquered East Anglia, by which he meant that Wehha was the first king of the *Wuffing* dynasty to reign in East Anglia. By allowing 30 years to a generation and counting the number of generations in the East Anglian royal pedigree between Wehha and Rædwald, the first securely dated king of East Anglia, an estimated date *c.* 500–25 has been obtained for Wehha; but all that can be said is that Wehha could have lived as early as 500 or as late as 550. The probability is that he belongs like Cerdic and Cynric to the second period of conquest following the years of peace after the battle of *Badon*. In the case of Mercia, the march-land or the land of 'the boundary folk' who were otherwise known as the Southumbrians because they dwelt south of the Humber mainly along the Trent, the kings were the *Icelingas*, taking their name from an ancestor, Icel. They may have advanced inland from East Anglia and the basin of the Wash. Icel appears to date to *c.* 500. The genealogical links between Icel and Penda, the first king of Mercia in the pedigree to be securely dated, are numerous and not of certain reliability, but no writer claims that Icel was the first king of the Mercians and he, himself, may never have come to Britain. Archaeological and place-name evidence reveals no substantial settlement in Derbyshire and beyond until at least the middle of the sixth century. This suggests that the unification and expansion of the peoples of the Trent into the kingdom of Mercia also occurred in the second phase of the Conquest.

The Northumbrians came to be so called because they were the settlers north of the Humber. The plain of York, the nucleus of the southern part of Northumbria, was known as the kingdom of the Deirans; it was settled in the mid-fifth century in part at least by Saxon mercenaries established there before the revolt. The accession of the first securely dated and well-attested king of Deira, Ælle, was as late as *c.* 558. Nennius preserves a tradition that Soemil, ancestor of Ælle in a Deiran pedigree given by Nennius, first separated Deira from Bernicia. Bernicia was that part of the later kingdom of Northumbria north of the Tees, ruled by its own dynasty. From his position in the pedigree Soemil has usually been dated to *c.* 450, to the hitherto estimated time of the Saxon revolt. But whatever Soemil's actual date, there is uncertainty as to the place he should occupy in the Deiran pedigree, and it is possible that he represents an earlier line of conquerors in Deira. A point of considerable interest is that Ælle's accession may have coincided in time with the descent of Ida, ancestor of the Bernician kings, on the coast of Northumberland. Bede dates Ida's arrival to 547, but there are chronological grounds for placing Ida's attack on the Britons of the far north in 558.[1] The simultaneous appearance of these two Northumbrian rulers indicates that a political transformation of some magnitude affected the Anglo-Saxon settlements above the Humber in the years after c. 550.

In contrast to the progress of the Conquest in East Anglia and Mercia, the wars of Ida and his successors in Bernicia against the Britons are relatively well chronicled. Nennius has preserved what appears to be a seventh-century British account of the struggle. Ida (558–70) made Bamburgh his stronghold and fought a British chieftain, Outigern. Hussa (579–86), of uncertain parentage, and Ida's son, Theodoric (586–93), faced a powerful coalition of British states to destroy their emerging kingdom, led by Urien of Rheged and Rhydderch of Strathclyde. The kingdom of Strathclyde was centred on Dumbarton, Rheged probably on Carlisle and in particular the Eden valley. The surviving North British genealogies enable the development of such kingdoms to be traced back in outline to the late fourth century. The ancestors of Urien and Rhydderch had probably long been involved in a struggle with the Picts and Scots, but it is primarily in their wars with the Angles of Bernicia that Urien and Rhydderch appear in the early records. Theodoric was besieged three days and three nights on Lindisfarne (Holy Island), but the British attack broke up when Urien was assassinated by a rival chieftain, Morcant, through jealousy because Urien was acclaimed the greatest of all the military leaders of the Britons at that time. Urien of Rheged has a particular interest for historians because a group of bardic poems, composed at his court by the poet Taliesin, has survived to throw valuable light on the court of Rheged and on the wars of Urien and his son, Owain, with the Bernicians, particularly with an Anglian leader known as Flamebearer who may be Theodoric. These panegyrical poems naturally represent the Britons as victors, pursuing the enemy as wolves chasing sheep. The poet claims that the men of *Lloegr* (the Angles) obtained from the

[1] For a decision of this date, and other Northumbrian dates (*infra*, pp. 40 ff.), see the article 'Bede and Northumbrian Chronology' cited in the bibliography, p. 286.

British leaders death, frequent vexation, the burning of homesteads and great suffering. This is an interesting picture of the hazards confronting the early Anglo-Saxon settlements. Not every conflict described by the poet was against the Angles; evidently some occurred within British territories, for example, at Dumbarton. A few are apparently mere skirmishes during the course of a cattle raid. At one point Urien is described as the ruler of *Catraeth*, which is an intriguing reference because another British poet of roughly the same period, Aneirin, in his epic poem the *Gododdin*, describes how an expedition of first-class warriors from Celtic lands, directed by 'the Mountainous One of Great Wealth' from Edinburgh, descended upon the men of Deira and Bernicia only to be defeated at *Catraeth*. The battle of *Catraeth* is usually placed *c.* 600. It was probably fought when Æthelfrith was ruling in Bernicia (593–605). Æthelfrith was a descendant of Ida, the son of a nephew of Theodoric, and Bede records that he ravaged the Britons more terribly than any of his predecessors. There is some doubt as to where *Catraeth* was fought, and an identification with Catterick which would place it in Deira is not universally accepted. If the campaign were directed specifically against Æthelfrith it would be readily intelligible in view of Bede's remark, and the association of Urien with *Catraeth* perhaps suggests the context of the British wars with the Bernicians. The situation in Deira *c.* 600 is obscure, but it should be noted that a poem by Taliesin to another British chieftain, Gwallauc, probably ruler of the kingdom of Elmet in the neighbourhood of Leeds between the rivers Aire and Wharfe, refers to a battle at *Ybrot*, which could be York, so that fighting in Deira at this late date is not impossible. So grave a threat was Æthelfrith considered to be, however, that in 604 Aedan, ruler of the Scots of the Irish settlements of Dalriada, launched a further mighty coalition directly against Æthelfrith who was still at this time ruler only of Bernicia. The coalition was crushed at *Degsastan*, possibly in Liddesdale. Bede claims that after this defeat no king of the Scots dared to attack the Northumbrians. In 605 Æthelfrith mastered Deira and reigned over a united Northumbria until his death. In *c.* 615 he campaigned as far afield as Chester, where he came into conflict with North-Welsh princes. Twelve hundred monks from the not far distant monastery of Bangor-is-coed are said to have been slain by Æthelfrith in this battle because he believed that they fought against him when they prayed against him to their God. In 617 Æthelfrith was slain in battle against the East Angles, and his sons were driven into exile among the Picts and Scots by Edwin, son of Ælle of Deira, who made himself king of Northumbria (617–34).

The battle of *Degsastan* and the expedition to Chester suggest that Northumbria, and in particular Bernicia which was the spearhead of the Anglian attack in the north, rapidly developed into a powerful military state, breaking up the British resistance across a wide area of northern Britain. It is at this point in time that the North British royal pedigrees begin to terminate, and there are indications that the British kingdoms of Rheged and Strathclyde retreated on the defensive from a violent Anglo-Saxon attack. Future archaeological and place-name studies may enable this process to be traced in greater detail. It is important to remember, however, that, despite the ravages of the invaders, quite substantial British enclaves could survive. The British kingdom of Elmet was overthrown only in the early years of the reign of Edwin.

The general character of the Anglo-Saxon Conquest

It is a disadvantage in the study of the Anglo-Saxon Conquest that more is not known of British society on the eve of and during the Conquest period. Celtic hanging bowls of fifth- and sixth-century date cannot be safely used as the basis of a study of British art until it has been firmly determined whether or not they are of Irish origin. They reflect a revival of older pre-Roman Celtic art forms. It appears unlikely that the Romano-British peasantry had any great knowledge of Latin and traces of Latin culture were no doubt confined to members of the Church and the aristocracy. Ambrosius Aurelianus, described by Gildas as the last of the Romans, was probably a Romano-British administrative official. His contemporaries in Gaul were Aegidius and Syagrius of Soissons, who opposed the advance of the Franks. It must be remembered in any study of the strategy of the Conquest that the Britons were still living within the geographical framework of the cities and roads established by the Romans. The references in the early sources, for example, to London, Pevensey, Cirencester and Chester provide a useful indication of this. Though they entered by the riverways of Britain, the invading Anglo-Saxons would be naturally drawn into campaigns fought out along Roman roads and directed at Roman towns. There can be no doubt that Romano-British society in southern Britain enjoyed a higher civilisation than the invading Anglo-Saxons, but as the Church broke up before the Saxon advance so Latinity was

extinguished. The undoubted violence of the Conquest, in certain
regions at least, and the loss of extensive territory to the invaders must
have broken down the administrative and economic bases of Romano-
British society. In the north and west, from the late fourth century
onwards, there was a swift reversal to Celtic tribalism. The late
sixth-century poems of Taliesin present a harsh, barbaric, albeit Christian
world, indistinguishable in its heroic values from pagan Anglo-Saxon
society. These poems reflect the same type of martial society as the
Anglo-Saxon epic poem *Beowulf*, which depicts the metallic character
of the life of the Germanic warrior band around the mighty chief.
There are some charming poetic touches in Taliesin: Urien, the golden
king of the North, dwelt in beautiful *Llwyfenydd* (probably Lyvennet,
Westmorland) by the fresh water and among the blossoms of Easter
time, attended by a host with diadems and fair thrones. But Urien was
waging a deadly conflict with the Angles, his supporters divided and
weakened by jealous strife and he can have had little time for genteel
refinements of manners and culture.

A further disadvantage in the historical study of the Anglo-Saxon
Conquest is the unevenness of the English evidence which makes precise comparison between one area and another almost impossible.
Whereas the literary evidence for the emergence of Kent and early
Wessex is considerable, relatively speaking, it is not so for Mercia or
East Anglia; for Kent the archaeological material is substantial, but not
for Wessex; for East Anglia there is the evidence both of archaeology
and place-names, for Essex or Lancashire virtually only that of place-
names; in Northumbria we are dependent primarily on archaeological
evidence for Deira, on literary evidence for Bernicia.

Bede describes the Angles as coming from *Angulus* (modern Angeln,
southern Denmark), the Saxons from Old Saxony (between the Elbe
and the Weser), and the Jutes from north of the Angles (modern Jutland, not certainly named after the Jutes). Bede says that so completely
was *Angulus* abandoned that it remained deserted up to the time of his
writing. He goes on to describe how the Jutes became the ancestors of
the men of Kent, the Isle of Wight and part of south-east Wessex
opposite the Isle of Wight. The Saxons became the ancestors of the
East, South and West Saxons, and the Angles of the East and Middle
Angles, the Mercians and the Northumbrians. This passage has provoked a weighty amount of criticism, both with regard to where Bede
places the homelands of the invading tribes and his description of the

settlement pattern in England. Not all this criticism has been soundly based. Material from cemeteries on the continent and in England has suggested to many that the cultures of the various tribes were so inter-mixed that it must have been very difficult to say that one group was Angle rather than Saxon; but this is to assume that a shared culture obliterated folk distinctions. Archaeological evidence indicated that the Jutes must have spent some time among the Franks of the Rhineland before crossing to Britain. Recent archaeological study, on the other hand, has revealed the certain presence of Franks among even the earliest invaders of Kent which, together with subsequent trade con-tracts, goes a long way to explain the Frankish element in Kentish grave-finds. In fact, artistic affinities have been traced which link an Anglian culture of northern and midland England with the district of Schleswig (Bede's *Angulus*), a distinct Saxon culture of southern England with the lands between the Elbe and Weser, and even early elements in the culture of Kent with that of early Jutland. The account of Bede is strengthened by such affinities, and it receives not incon-siderable support from the names and traditions of the several king-doms. Not without good reason can the settlers north of the Thames have become known as East Saxons and their neighbours north of the Stour as East Angles. The poet Taliesin knew the Bernicians as *eigyl*, Angles. The East Saxon dynasty traced its ancestry back to Woden through Seaxnot, a traditional deity of the continental Saxons, while the Anglian dynasty of Mercia traced its ancestry back to Woden through Offa, a king of Angeln in the pre-Migration period. And there is no doubt that the Jutes were believed by many to have played a part in the conquest of Wessex. The West Saxon mother of King Alfred was of Jutish descent on her father's side, and in the eleventh century the New Forest region of Hampshire was still known as the territory of the Jutes.

No archaeologist or historian would deny, of course, that the picture of settlement in England remains incredibly complex. Already there has accumulated a vast amount of varied material from pagan Anglo-Saxon graves (swords, spear-heads, buckles, jewellery, brooches, pendants, wrist-clasps, pots, etc., buried with the deceased) all of which can only be dated by analogy and on the basis of typological development. A great deal of the work of cataloguing and classifying remains to be done. And though it is possible to define in England a northern region which is primarily Anglian in culture and a southern which is primarily Saxon, between the basin of the Wash and the valley of the Thames stretches a cultural pattern which can only be described as Anglo-Saxon. Whether an early stratum of Saxon invaders here was subsequently overrun by Anglian invaders remains uncertain. What can be said is that the counties of the east midlands, the region subsequently known as Middle Anglia, were particularly subject to diverse influences and became a melting-pot of Conquest England. It is also evident that the Angles, Saxons and Jutes were not the only peoples to invade Britain in the fifth and sixth centuries. Archaeologists have detected the presence of Franks in Kent. Procopius, a mid-sixth-century Greek writer, describes the Britain of *c.* 540 as divided between Britons, Angles and Frisians. No other early source places the Frisians of the lower Elbe among the invaders of Britain during the period of the Conquest, but linguistic and archaeological links between England and Frisia confirm the truth of Procopius' statement. Nennius refers to the Frisian sea in Britain, possibly the Firth of Forth. Surviving pieces of pottery suggest that some at least of the settlers in northern England, even in northeast Kent, came immediately from Holland rather than from Schleswig. It is possible that at the time of the Conquest the Frisians and Saxons were tending to merge into one people, which would account for Bede's failure to mention Frisians specifically, but it would seem that Frisians were mixing not only with Saxons but also with Angles and Jutes.

In this century it has become possible to approach a general outline of the Anglo-Saxon Conquest on the basis of a new, scientific study of place-names. The study of British and Anglo-Saxon place-names can show the density of Anglo-Saxon settlement, and by implication, therefore, those regions most affected by the Conquest. Anglo-Saxon place-names are particularly thick, and British conspicuously absent in eastern England, south of a line from the Yorkshire Wolds to Southampton. The most Romanised part of Britain was clearly the hardest hit. Even between the Yorkshire-Southampton line and the uplands of Cumberland and Westmorland, the Welsh border and Devonshire British place-names remain few, usually being applied to natural features. Only in the Celtic regions of the west do Celtic place-names become the norm. It has been possible to isolate from early English place-names a group of apparently early names, containing an Anglo-Saxon personal name coupled with -*ingas* ('people of', 'descendants of') as in Hastings ('people of Hæsta') and Reading ('people of Reada'). They suggest a group of people associated together under a single leader and, since the personal names are often archaic and failed to become popular in England, they possibly date to the days of the Conquest. They may not all derive from the period before *Badon*, but they do reveal a pattern established in the primary phase of settlement in eastern coastal regions from Yorkshire to Sussex, coinciding in a striking manner with those districts in which archaeological traces of early Anglo-Saxon invaders have been most numerous. Place-names containing the elements -ham, -tun (ton), -worth, -field, etc., but without an original *-ingas*, which is in effect the great majority of English place-names, belong to a subsequent, secondary phase of settlement spread out over many more decades. To the historical geographer, place-name evidence reveals a great deal of information regarding the type of region in which the Anglo-Saxons preferred to settle. Upland forest regions of heavy clay soils were avoided as were sandy and gravelly heathlands. Sandy and gravelly soils at lower altitudes, however, often containing a proportion of clay, along great rivers and their tributaries were particularly favoured. Settlements had to be on soils which afforded an accessible and constant water supply, and it was the pattern of the waterways which largely determined the settlement pattern of Anglo-Saxon England.

In this formative period of widespread invasion and settlement a fundamental problem concerns the extent to which the Anglo-Saxons destroyed Romano-British society, the degree to which the invaders were influenced by that society. The issue of continuity as opposed to discontinuity underlies the whole study of the Conquest. The view to dominate historical writing in the first half of this century has been that, although conquest may have been more peaceful than violent in certain areas (this has been repeatedly stressed), there did occur a decisive break between Roman Britain and Anglo-Saxon England when a Romanised British society was effectively displaced by a non-Romanised Germanic society. In very recent years some scholars have been tending to revert to an older nineteenth-century view, though using new arguments, that much of Romano-British society did in fact survive to shape Anglo-Saxon, and there are signs that this interpretation will become more common. The issue cannot be resolved here, but the outlines of approach may be indicated.

First, the case for a break in continuity. Some of the evidence for the violence of the Conquest has already been mentioned. The most complete picture of destruction is provided by Gildas who describes the Britons as slain, enslaved or expelled, their towns and houses sacked and destroyed. Attempts have been made to present the statements of

Gildas as simply those of an hysterical critic of British weakness, but his story is not without supporting evidence. The villas of Late Roman Britain were almost universally abandoned in the course of the Conquest, and their names, unlike those of the villas in Gaul where continuity from Roman to Frankish Gaul is very marked, did not survive. There is no linguistic evidence that the Anglo-Saxons came into contact with a Latin culture at this period. The organisation of the Romano-British Church was destroyed in the regions settled by the Anglo-Saxons, and the Anglo-Saxons are not known to have inherited a Late Roman civil administration as the Frankish kings did. Anglo-Saxon Law was Germanic Law, untempered by Late Roman influences. The Britons, at a less advanced cultural stage than the Gallo-Romans, put up a sturdy resistance when the Gallo-Romans peacefully capitulated, and consequently they provoked retaliation. The British language had such a negligible effect on English, and British place-names are so conspicuously lacking in the areas of primary Anglo-Saxon settlement that it may be argued that the Britons can hardly have remained a cultural and social force among the Anglo-Saxons. There are valid reasons to suppose, therefore, that the Romano-British aristocracy was slain or dispersed during the Conquest and Romano-British society shattered.

A case for marked continuities is not yet so well established, but it is gaining in strength. Not all arguments have been well founded, however, and a good example is the view that the invading Anglo-Saxons must have been numerically few because their ships were small. But an average ship of the time could perhaps carry upwards of 60 to 80 persons and if a great many ships made a great many crossings an infinite number of men and women could be transported to Britain. Bede's statement that Angeln was depopulated is substantiated by a gap in the archaeological evidence from Angeln. One Anglian chieftain, unfortunately unnamed, is said by Procopius to have sent his sister with a military expedition of 400 ships and 100,000 warriors to the Continent c. 535. These figures may be excessive but the memory of a sizeable attacking army seems to lie behind them, which would represent only a fraction of the chieftain's military strength. That women accompanied their menfolk to Britain is amply demonstrated by an intense Germanic female culture revealed by innumerable pagan Anglo-Saxon cemeteries. There can be little serious doubt that the Conquest was indeed a mass migration of whole peoples. Similarly, art historians have sometimes traced the influence of British art on Anglo-Saxon ornament, but such influences have been either insufficiently marked or too uncertain for this to be generally acceptable. A minimisation of British artistic influence is more common.

The village community has been seen in the past as an Anglo-Saxon introduction into Britain, but a possibility exists that there could be some degree of continuity between Romano-British settlements and Anglo-Saxon villages. Knowledge of Romano-British agricultural communities is based on upland sites, where the Anglo-Saxons did not settle, and which were essentially pastoral communities centred on isolated farmsteads. How the Romano-Britons lived in and farmed the fertile land of the valleys, where the Anglo-Saxons did settle so preponderantly thus obscuring older patterns, is the fundamental issue. If it could be shown conclusively that in the valleys the Romano-Britons lived not in isolated farmsteads but in some kind of village communities, this would be of crucial importance in the study of continuity. It used to be argued that the Anglo-Saxons brought with them the heavy plough, enabling them to farm a greater extent of arable land than possible hitherto, and that this, together with the introduction of new crops, for example barley as opposed to wheat, opened up a very different era in agriculture to that which had gone before. But the history of the plough is a little obscure; it is likely that the heavy plough was to be found in Roman Britain. The agricultural history of the sixth and seventh centuries is certainly too ill-defined to permit generalisations in the matter of crop changes. Villa names may not have survived but what we need to know is the scale on which estates of Romano-British villas were taken over directly by the Anglo-Saxons. This may be a more open question than many historians will allow. It is reasonable to suppose that much of the land belonging to the great villas and to Romano-British communities did come under Anglo-Saxon cultivation. On the Continent, agricultural continuity is so striking a feature of the invasion period, because only new techniques and new implements could transform existing patterns, that similar continuity, even if to a lesser degree, becomes highly probable in England. The future study of the agricultural history of Britain from the beginning of the fifth to the seventh century may well throw valuable light on the Romano-British legacy to the Anglo-Saxons and it is perhaps in this field that exponents of the idea of continuity will achieve most success. A recent stimulating suggestion, that in some instances Anglo-Saxon estates and elements in Anglo-Saxon royal taxation—and, therefore, elements in royal administration—may well go back to Romano-British origins, emphasises the importance of tenurial continuity.

There is certainly evidence for the survival of Britons in the Anglo-Saxon kingdoms. Intermarriage clearly took place in the royal families. Cædbæd, a seventh-century king of Lindsey (Lincolnshire), and Cædwalla of Wessex (685/6–8) have names containing Celtic elements, and Cædbæd might be an English version of a completely Celtic name. Oswiu, king of Northumbria (643–71), a son of Æthelfrith, married the British princess Riemmelth, a descendant of Urien of Rheged, probably c. 640. Oswiu had a son, Alchfrith, old enough to fight in a battle in 656, and who was said to be commemorated on the famous Bewcastle cross (Cumberland), close to the old kingdom of Rheged. He may have been Riemmelth's son. Unfortunately, the inscription on the Bewcastle cross is not now legible. On a lower social level, Cædmon, the seventh-century poet of the monastery of Whitby, had a partly Celtic name. It is likely that British women at least tended to survive the violence of the Conquest, passing into the hands of victorious war bands, and that in this way a British strain entered Anglo-Saxon society. There can be little doubt, however, that an enslaved Briton, whether male or female, was a better commercial proposition than a dead Briton. The utilisation of slave labour would be a natural economic asset to emerging kingdoms, particularly on the great estates of kings and nobles. The laws of Æthelberht of Kent (early seventh century) refer to a *læt*, in social status above the slave but below the free peasant or ceorl, who may have been of British extraction, and in the laws of Ine of Wessex (688–726), compiled 688–94, references occur to a Welsh rent-payer, a Welsh landowner, and the king's Welsh horseman, the latter evidently some sort of royal servant. Free, land-owning Welshmen (*i.e.* Britons) are mentioned in a tenth-century Northumbrian document, the *Law of the North People*.

The whole issue of continuity from Romano-British to Anglo-Saxon society, therefore, is now much more open to debate and varying interpretations than it was a few years ago, and the matter is a vital one to the proper understanding of Anglo-Saxon England.

Offa, 757–96

Æthelwulf, 839–58

Alfred, 871–99

Athelstan, 924–39

Æthelred, 978–1016

Cnut, 1017–35

Edward the Confessor, 1042–66

Harold II, 1066

2 Anglo-Saxon portrait-bearing pennies (enlarged)

3 Visored iron helmet—Sutton Hoo,
seventh century

4 Iron sword,
ninth–tenth century

5 Procession of warriors bearing swords and axes,
Lindisfarne stone slab: probably ninth century

Chapter two

The Conversion

The Celtic Background

It is generally regarded as certain that the Anglo-Saxon Conquest destroyed the territorial diocesan organisation of the Romano-British Church in the lowland regions which became the primary zones of Anglo-Saxon settlement. There is only a limited amount of evidence for the British Church on the eve of the Conquest. It is known to have been seriously affected by the heresy of Pelagianism. Pelagius, from the British Isles and probably from Britain, was said to have taught that a man could achieve salvation through his own merits, a doctrine condemned by St. Augustine and the Roman Church. In 429 and again in the 440s, Germanus, bishop of Auxerre, was sent to counteract this heresy among the Britons. It has been argued that Vortigern was a secular leader of the Pelagian party, but there is no real evidence of for this. In the mid-sixth century, when the British Church reappears clearly in the records of the time, it was still under severe criticism, this time from Gildas. By this time Pelagianism appears to have been a thing of the past, and Gildas was concerned with laxity of morals, neglect of duty, and the foolish and shameful conduct of the clergy, the priests of the Britons. He does not paint a very attractive picture. What he does say, however, must be the basis of any study of the British Church in the sixth century.

Gildas was a monk and, though his views were not those of an extremist but of a moderate ascetic, it is likely that his writings were part of a programme of a monastic reform party which was to transform the character of the Church in Celtic lands. When the British Church appears in the records of the fifth century it is a Church in close contact with the Continent, where monasticism was gaining a hold. Monasticism spread from the eastern Mediterranean to Italy and Gaul. In the second half of the fourth century, St. Martin of Tours established an influential monastic centre at Tours. In Britain, in the first half of the fifth century, St. Ninian is traditionally credited with having established what must have been one of the earliest British monasteries at Whithorn (Dumfriesshire), possibly—but only possibly—on lines adopted by St. Martin at Tours. Monasticism must have reached Britain through many channels; for example, Lupus, bishop of Troyes, who visited Britain in 429 with Germanus of Auxerre, is known to have had links with the important South Gallic monastery of Lérins, and an eighth-century document claims that Germanus and Lupus introduced the rule of Lérins into Britain. British ecclesiastics are known to have visited the Continent in the fifth century and it is highly probable that they met monastic leaders in the Gallic Church and were influenced by them. The break-up of the Romano-British Church in the late fifth century, therefore, chanced to coincide with the introduction of monasticism, which may have been an important factor in the survival of an effective Christianity in Celtic regions. There are indications that the growth of monasticism in Britain constituted a tremendous revolution in the Church, the details of which are unfortunately lost to us. There survive, however, a great many later *Lives* of the saints of the western British Church, who lived in the sixth century, and a handful of earlier *Lives*, the analysis of which may yet yield further information. Taken together, the sources suggest the presence in the sixth-century British Church of a moderate monastic party, represented by such men as Gildas, and a more extreme group represented by men like St. David of Wales. The Church in Celtic lands, where there were no Roman towns and often no diocesan traditions, under the influence of the monastic movement came to be dominated by monasteries. Bishops became subordinate to abbots, attached to particular monasteries and with authority not over a territorial diocese but simply over a chain of dependent monastic communities. It is possible that this development was not as swift as once thought and further research may possibly clarify the process of change, but the general outlines of the transformation are not likely to be seriously contested. Whatever ecclesiastical organisation the British missionary, Patrick, had envisaged for Ireland in the course of his mission in the late fourth or fifth century, the Irish sources for the sixth century show that by this period the Church in Ireland was largely monastic. St. Ninian is said to have converted the Picts of what is now southern Scotland, and if this is true he was probably compelled to set up an ecclesiastical organisation centred primarily around monastic communities. When Columba went from Ireland to work in self-imposed exile among the Scots of Dalriada in 563 it was as abbot of the monastery he founded on Iona that he was known and it was a monastic Church which he introduced among the northern Picts. The dominant influence of monasticism in the Celtic Church tended to make it more ascetic in character than the Roman Church, in which monasticism was but one of many elements, and Celtic saints became famous in the west for the austere and disciplinary nature of their lives.

There is no question but that the Church in Celtic regions developed along different lines from the continental Roman Church. Monastic as opposed to diocesan bishops were only one peculiarity. By the seventh century there were differences in the shape of the monastic tonsure and important variations in liturgy and ritual. Less is known of such variations, however, than about the differences over the true date of Easter, with which contemporaries were particularly preoccupied. The Celtic Church dated this major movable Christian festival by the 84-year cycle for calculating the date of Easter which Rome had observed before 343. In 457 Victorius of Aquitaine worked out a new cycle of 532 years and this was accepted by the Roman Church. As the Victorian cycle began to secure a hold in southern Ireland in the early seventh century, Rome switched to the 19-year cycle of Dionysius Exiguus. These changes in cycles meant that Easter was celebrated at varying dates, depending on which cycle was followed. The issue became the fundamental debate between the Roman and the Celtic Churches, though it also symbolised a wide divide in a variety of ecclesiastical matters. In the course of the late seventh and eighth centuries the Celtic Church was brought into conformity with the Roman. Bede's monastery of Monkwearmouth and Jarrow in Northumbria exerted an important influence on the Pictish Church and on Adamnan, abbot of Iona, who persuaded the Irish to adopt the Roman Easter, but the distinctive character of the Celtic Church was not substantially changed until the advent of Norman might and influence in the twelfth century. These peculiarities of Celtic Christianity are of great importance to the history of Anglo-Saxon England because of the major part taken by the representatives of the Celtic Church in the conversion of England in the seventh century.

Missions to the Anglo-Saxons

When the Anglo-Saxons conquered Britain in the fifth and sixth centuries they brought with them their worship of gods whose cults derived from the forests, heaths and marshes of the Germanic homeland; their gods were the ancient protectors of men, the bestowers of gifts, the divine ancestors of princes. Bede mentions the goddesses Hretha and Eostre, the latter probably a goddess of light, who gave their names to the Anglo-Saxon months of March and April, but little is known about them. The more important gods by the time of the Conquest, it seems, gave their names not to the months of the year but to the days of the week, Woden (Wednesday), Thunor (Thursday) and the lesser known Tiw (Tuesday), and Frig, wife of Woden (Friday). Tiw was a god of war, but by the sixth century he was being eclipsed by Woden, god of death and battle and regarded as the divine ancestor of the Anglo-Saxon dynasties. Woden's great festival was at Yuletide (mid-winter). His cult was subsequently introduced, probably in the ninth century, into Norway where he was known as Othin; much of what Norse tradition tells about Othin is applicable, therefore, to Woden, though by the thirteenth century, when Norse tradition was committed to writing, Othin was coming to be identified with the Christian God as a great All-father who created mankind and was the father of Balder the Beautiful; Balder was accidentally slain and imprisoned in the misty regions of Hel, goddess of the underworld, but in a final and great conflict between All-father and the powers of evil, Balder was to return to rule an eternal kingdom. There is no evidence, however, that the Anglo-Saxons knew of Balder, and their conception of Woden was rather as a grim figure of the dead; he delighted in broken oaths and conflicts between kinsmen, and men and beasts were offered as sacrifices to him. The favoured beasts of Woden were the horse and the wolf, his favoured bird the raven. The horse was a symbol of fertility and possibly of death, the wolf and raven scavengers of the battlefield. The Anglo-Saxons knew of his wælcyrians, bloody witches of the battlefield, who may have selected the dead to dwell with Woden, in the same way as the valkyries or shield-maidens of later Norse mythology selected the dead heroes to feast with Othin in Valhalla, hall of the slain: but there is no indication that the Anglo-Saxons had any developed concept of Valhalla, and they seem to have possessed only the haziest ideas about life after death.

Thunor was more the god of farmers, of fertility and the elements, maintaining order in the universe with his magic weapons, particularly his hammer. Little is known of Thunor, and even less of Frig. There is no doubt that much of the mythology of the sixth century is lost to us. The East Saxons claimed descent from Woden through Seaxnot, a god known to have been worshipped among the continental Saxons, but apart from deducing that he was a god of battle his cult is indiscernible. One of the greatest gods of the early Germanic tribes on the Continent, whose cult is described by Tacitus, was Nerthus, Mother Earth, a pre-eminent goddess of fertility. Woden, Thunor, Tiw and Frig have left their traces in English place-names, but Nerthus has not: nevertheless, it is known that her cult crossed to Britain for an Anglo-Saxon incantation to ensure crop fertility has survived which actually invokes her.

Men's lives were subject to the caprice of the three Fates, Past, Present and Future, who were superior to the gods in their supernatural nature and who were constantly seeking to frustrate the plans of the gods, weaving a web of destiny which would destroy both man and gods. It is clear also that belief existed in a whole galaxy of lesser gods and spirits, of the family and households, and of natural features. Elves, possibly originally conceived as dead men, dwelt in mounds or hid in marsh-mists and made men ill by their poisonous elf-darts. The very air was alive with spirits, and the countryside of the Anglo-Saxons was peopled by supernatural monsters and dragons, who lurked in lonely caverns or haunted lakes, and of whom men went in great dread.

When the Anglo-Saxons settled in Britain they built temples and offered sacrifices to their gods. *Hearg*, meaning 'temple', survives, for example, in Harrow (Middlesex), and *weoh*, meaning 'sanctuary', in Weedon (Bucks). Harrow (Middlesex) was originally the temple of the *Gumeningas*. Even individuals sometimes had their own private shires. Judging from the name Manshead (Bedfordshire), human sacrifice may not have been entirely unknown. On Harrow Hill, Angmering (Sussex), large numbers of ox-skulls suggest that here was one site where cattle were slaughtered as a sacrifice. Bede records that sacrifices were made in November, the month in which cattle were slaughtered before winter and which was known as 'blood-month'. Gregory the Great in a letter to the Kentish missionaries in 601 mentions the sacrifice of oxen. A pagan priesthood is known to have officiated. A temple at Goodmanham, near York, was destroyed by Coifi, chief priest of Edwin, king of Northumbria, when Coifi abandoned the gods he had served.

The strength of paganism lay not so much in its philosophical content as in its daily practical application in the lives of men. Incantations and spells were used to ensure good crops and to prevent sickness or cure disease. The various phases of the moon regulated the actions of men and certain activities might be absolutely prohibited on specified days of the moon. And in the same way as a Christian king would pray for divine aid in battle, so the pagan King Penda of Mercia was said to be victorious in battle through diabolical arts. At one and the same time as the missionary Paulinus offered thanks to Christ for the safe delivery of the Northumbrian queen, King Edwin gave thanks to his gods. Christian missionaries poured scorn on the worship of idols made by the hands of men, but the Anglo-Saxons no more worshipped these idols than the Christians worshipped representations of Christ; they worshipped the gods whom the idols represented, and these gods touched the lives of men at so many points that they could not be lightly set aside. The subtleties of a Jewish faith, clothed in sophisticated Greek thought and transmitted in the context of a Latin culture were not going to be quickly grasped by an Anglo-Saxon audience. Even princes could fail completely to understand the significance of Christian ritual. One occasion at least is recorded when the peasants of Tyneside jeered at the monks and wished them dead because they said they had robbed men of their old ways of worship and how the new worship was to be conducted no one knew. These words do not refer simply to the conduct of church services, but to a whole world of ritual and incantation to be practised by the ordinary man to ensure fertility of crops and good health. A great social and psychological crisis is reflected in them.

There can be no doubt that much pagan belief was translated into a Christian context during the process of conversion. As the goddess Eostre gave her name to Easter, so the great heathen festival of Midwinter's Day, 25 December, was recognised as the Nativity of Christ. As the glorious King of Hosts, the Lord of Life, the Giver of victory, the Rising Sun, the Author of light, the Lord of the harvest, the Young Hero, Jesus Christ evidently absorbed many of the features of the pagan gods, while the Virgin Mary, the most blessed of maidens, led a noble host through the bright realms of the Glorious Father, the Guardian of Heaven. The pagan wælcyrians found a parallel in the angels who bore the souls of holy men to Paradise, while sinful men went to Hell, not a goddess now but a place of torment. The sign of the Cross was seen rather as a magical charm affording protection against evil, and by the

670s Christian houses were distinguished, in some instances at least, by crosses upon their doors. The missionaries sought to displace the spirits of the Anglo-Saxon countryside by the devils and demons of Christian mythology who could literally scare the wits out of the English, noble and peasant alike. But the first king even to begin to prohibit the worship of idols, as paganism was described, was Earconberht of Kent (640-64), and throughout the Anglo-Saxon period it remained necessary to forbid the worship of the spirits of trees, wells, and stones by royal and ecclesiastical legislation. Little is known of the pagan beliefs of the Anglo-Saxons because Christian writers had no desire to describe them, and there is no doubt that our understanding of the conversion of the Anglo-Saxons by Roman and Celtic missionaries is limited in consequence. The presence, however, of a great many pagan place-names in England, particularly east and south of a line from Ipswich to Stafford and Stafford to Weymouth, testifies to the strength of paganism in England on the eve of the conversion.

While it is possible that enclaves of British Christians, and particularly Christian British slaves, survived among the Anglo-Saxon communities, it has not been generally believed that British missionaries were at work among the pagan English. Bede says that the Britons would not and did not preach to the Anglo-Saxons, but this statement probably needs modifying. The materials for the British Church in the second half of the sixth century relate only to the western regions, and certainly no *Life* survives of a saint who worked among the pagan Anglo-Saxons. St. Beuno is represented in his *Life*, in an incident which appears to date to *c*. 620-30, as deliberately withdrawing inland from the west bank of the Severn to avoid contact with Anglo-Saxons on the east bank. But this incident, if historical, may have been not so much the consequence of having nothing to do with the English as the result of a recent breakdown in relations between the Church in Wales and the newly established Roman mission at Canterbury under Augustine. Augustine was sent to Britain by Pope Gregory the Great in 596 and arrived in Kent in 597; a premature and possibly mismanaged meeting of Augustine with representatives of the British Church, probably somewhere on the Severn, to discuss the Easter question, was a fiasco. It was in connection with Augustine's mission that Pope Gregory had written to the Frankish rulers that the clergy in the neighbourhood of the Saxons were making no effort to convert them. This is particularly interesting because, while Gregory was referring to Frankish clergy in

Gaul, the statement could have been taken to refer to British clergy, and it is not impossible that it ultimately forms the basis of Bede's remarks concerning the failure of the Britons to preach to the English. Even if this is not so, the British part in the conversion of the Anglo-Saxon kingdoms must be reconsidered. Particularly in border districts of Northumbria, Mercia or Wessex, where there would be present a considerable British element in the population, British clergy must have found it difficult to ignore completely the Anglo-Saxon settlers. Recently attention has been drawn to the existence of British monasteries in west Wessex, not simply at Glastonbury (Somerset) but further to the east at Shaftesbury and probably Sherborne (Dorset). A striking example of British missionary activity is to be found in the kingdom of Northumbria. Bede provides a detailed account of the conversion of Edwin, king of Northumbria (617–34), by Paulinus, a member of the Roman mission to Kent, but Nennius was told by two British bishops in the early ninth century that Edwin was baptised by Rhun, son of Urbgen, the latter usually being identified with Urien of Rheged. It may be that Rhun's achievement has been magnified, but possibly he did work among the Bernicians. It is difficult to set the testimony of Nennius entirely aside. Several years later, Chad, appointed bishop of York c. 665, was able to find two British bishops to assist the bishop of Winchester at his consecration.

In so far as the records of the conversion of the Anglo-Saxons survive, however, they relate in the main to the activities of Roman or Irish (Scottish) missionaries. Roman missionaries, led by Augustine, landed on Thanet in 597 and appear to have speedily converted Æthelberht, king of Kent. In this they must have exceeded their wildest expectations, for rumours of the fierceness of the Saxons were so strong that Augustine and his companions turned back at one stage of their journey. One Scottish missionary is known to have failed completely among the Northumbrians in the 630s, returning home to protest at their barbarism. The letters of Pope Gregory to the Frankish rulers, however, state that requests for missionaries had actually been made (to the Frankish clergy) by the English, presumably by pro-Christian circles already established in Kent, and that it was in response to these requests that Gregory had decided to send Augustine. Æthelberht of Kent was married to a Christian princess from Gaul, Bertha, who was attended in Kent by her own chaplain, Liudhard, also from Gaul, and it is often suggested that Bertha may have disposed Æthelberht to receive the new faith. But Frankish princesses were not always distinguished for their piety, and so far removed from Christianity was Æthelberht that he is said to have received Augustine in the open air, lest the missionaries should gain an unfair advantage over him indoors with the aid of evil spirits. Pro-Christian communities are perhaps more likely to have derived from Liudhard's influence. What is important is that they existed though Bede knew nothing of them.

There are indications that the kings strove to make an intelligent response to the challenge of the new faith, that they were aware of the responsibility of changing the traditional beliefs of their people. An old ealdorman used philosophical arguments to convince King Edwin that he ought to accept Christianity, reputedly on the grounds that paganism taught nothing clearly about life after death. Æthelberht withdrew to consider Augustine's words at length. No doubt political and prestige considerations entered into the royal deliberations. The Anglo-Saxon rulers, who were anxious for nothing more than present military glory and posthumous fame, responded well to the teaching that Christ was a more powerful support in battle than Woden. Æthelberht became an active convert and it was put to him in a letter from Pope Gregory that Christ would bestow a fame upon him beyond that of any of his predecessors. There are chronological indications that the *bretwalda*, Ceawlin, ruler of the Saxons of the Thames valley, survived until *c.* 600, which gives added point to Æthelberht's acceptance of Christianity. Æthelberht succeeded Ceawlin as *bretwalda* and it was this position which enabled him to organise the conference between Augustine and the British clergy. It also enabled him to impose Christianity on his subject kingdoms, on his nephew Sæberht, king of the East Saxons, and on Rædwald, king of the East Angles. Rædwald was converted at Æthelberht's court, but evidently under pressure for in his own kingdom he did not cease to maintain an altar to pagan gods.

It was Pope Gregory's intention that Augustine should establish his archiepiscopal see in London, with a northern counterpart at York. London was in the kingdom of the East Saxons, and Augustine, who was dependent on Æthelberht of Kent, was compelled to settle at the Kentish royal city of Canterbury. An old church of Romano-British origin, at some stage in its history dedicated to St. Martin of Tours, was given to the missionaries. It had been used by Queen Bertha, and parts of the original chancel can still be seen. With the baptism of the king, Augustine received yet another Romano-British church which he made his permanent residence, dedicated to Christ and subsequently known as Canterbury Cathedral. Such churches must be presumed to have survived elsewhere, but not everywhere; Pope Gregory told the missionaries not to hesitate to reconsecrate heathen temples as Christian churches, presumably in districts where no older Christian buildings survived. Augustine and his companions were monks and they quickly took advantage of Æthelberht's patronage to found a monastery dedicated to SS. Peter and Paul, in the eastern part of the city of Canterbury, subsequently known as the monastery of St. Augustine and the burial place of Kentish archbishops and kings. Before Augustine died (c. 604) a further bishopric was established in Kent for West Kent, at the Roman site of Rochester, and Æthelberht had probably issued the first Christian codification of Kentish Law. Through the authority of Æthelberht, the influence of the church at Canterbury was extended into Essex and East Anglia, and a bishopric established at London for the East Saxons.

When Æthelberht died in c. 618, a pagan reaction swept through Kent, Essex, and apparently East Anglia. In Essex, the sons and successors of Sæberht, judging from a recorded fragment of conversation in Bede's account, were completely at a loss to understand Christian teaching about the Mass. They expelled Mellitus, bishop of London, and his fellow-workers. In Kent, King Eadbald, son and successor of Æthelberht, was a pagan who came near to forcing the mission at Canterbury to leave the kingdom. Laurentius, archbishop of Canterbury, proved himself a determined opponent of the king and succeeded in bringing about his conversion. The conversion of Eadbald, just as the community at Canterbury was about to break up, avoided what could have been a long delay before the process of conversion began again in southern England. Laurentius's success determined that the influence of the Roman Church and Mediterranean culture would remain formative elements in the early development of Anglo-Saxon civilisation. It has sometimes been said that the Augustinian mission was a failure. In that the whole of England was not converted immediately, perhaps it was; but it is unlikely that any informed missionary seriously expected an instant transformation. When Gregory planned that York be immediately established as an archiepiscopal see, he probably had little conception of the pratical problems involved. How the success of Augustine is viewed depends on our assessment of the strength of Anglo-Saxon paganism. The example of Essex and East Anglia, which reverted to paganism after Æthelberht's death and were not immediately reconverted, revealed that instant conversion could be a dangerously superficial phenomenon. At least the Augustinian mission had established an important and essential foothold in Kent, together with the necessary administrative organisation of bishoprics and monasteries; and it had behind it the manpower of the continental Church and the spiritual and cultural force of Rome and the Mediterranean world. No time was lost in educating and training native Anglo-Saxons for the Christian ministry; and probably by 619 the Church in Kent embarked on the conversion of Northumbria.

When Edwin, king of Northumbria, sought in marriage Æthelburh, sister of Eadbald, the opportunity was taken to send north with the Christian princess a chaplain, Paulinus, a member of the Canterbury mission, probably with the intention from the outset that he should establish a see at York. Paulinus was aided by a companion, James the Deacon. Bede's chronology for Northumbrian affairs in the early seventh century requires modification and hence many of the following Northumbrian dates differ by a year from those actually given by Bede. It would seem that it was in 626 that Paulinus was consecrated bishop of York, before Edwin had been converted. Edwin's baptism did not take place until 628, but it appeared to be a great triumph for the Roman mission. Edwin established himself as *bretwalda*, dominating all the kingdoms of southern England except Kent. According to the usual pattern, Eorpwald, son of Rædwald and king of East Anglia, accepted Christianity at Edwin's court. When Eorpwald was slain shortly afterwards, East Anglia relapsed again into paganism until the early 630s when Eorpwald's brother, Sigeberht, became king. Sigeberht had lived in exile on the Continent, and on his accession was already a Christian. He permitted Felix, a missionary bishop from Burgundy, to establish an episcopal see at Dunwich, developed close contacts with Canterbury, and founded schools on the models of schools in Gaul with help from Canterbury. The permanent success of the Church in East Anglia was offset by disaster in Northumbria. In 634 Edwin was killed in battle by the combined forces of Cadwallon, king of Gwynedd (North Wales), and Penda, heathen king of Mercia. Northumbria was savagely ravaged by the invading armies and Paulinus withdrew with the queen and royal children to Kent. James the Deacon remained behind in a village near Catterick. He lived on in Northumbria to attend the Synod of Whitby in 664. Paulinus was made bishop of Rochester and never returned to Northumbria. Eanfrith, son of Æthelfrith, re-turned from exile with his Christian brothers to lead Bernician resis-tance. He relapsed into paganism, as did Edwin's cousin and successor in Deira, Osric, presumably preferring to place faith in the older gods of war. Both were slain by Cadwallon. The Mercian forces probably departed into Middle and East Anglia, however, where Penda even-tually slew King Sigeberht in 636. Cadwallon was on his own when he perished in battle against Oswald, son of Æthelfrith, in 635. Oswald became king of Northumbria and set about his task of reconstruction. The papacy at Rome evidently resolved to redress the balance by attempting the conversion of the Mercians. Birinus was despatched to England, c. 636, but on his progress into the hinterland came first to the pagan Saxons of the Thames valley. He converted the king, Cynegils, probably a grandson of Ceawlin, and with Cynegils several members of the royal family, and he was given Dorchester-on-Thames as the site of his bishopric.

It should be emphasised that the activities of Birinus are not known to have extended beyond the Thames valley. How the Saxons of Wilt-shire, for example, were converted is unrecorded; but Malmesbury was the home of a seventh-century Irish missionary, Maildulf, and it is possible that Irish or Scottish influence in the West Saxon area was considerable. There are indications that Irish pilgrims used the land route across Britain from the Bristol Channel to a Kentish port as their main approach to the Continent, which must have brought a constant stream of Irish clergy into southern England. An Irish pilgrim, Fursa, founded a monastery at Burgh Castle, in East Anglia, in the reign of Sigeberht, and his fellow-countryman, Dicuil, was working among the South Saxons from a base at Bosham in the 670s. But the records of the widespread activities of Scottish monks came from the kingdom of Northumbria. Oswald, king of Northumbria, had been educated among the Scots of Dalriada, and on his accession he sent for missionaries not to Canterbury but to Iona. Aidan was sent and a bishopric established on the island of Lindisfarne, not far from the royal Bernician stronghold at Bamburgh. To Bede, Aidan appears to have been a model bishop in his devotion to his pastoral duties. Bede greatly admired his humility, his love of peace and charity, his industry, diligence and authority; his tenderness in defending and comforting the poor and the afflicted made him the very father of the wretched. Because Bede's account of Aidan is so relatively detailed, the activities of his mission can be studied in some depth. Aidan organised his episcopal see not wholly on Celtic lines for as bishop he did not submit himself to the authority of an abbot, but the austerities of the monks on Lindisfarne reflected the traditions of the Celtic Church. At first Aidan had to preach through an interpreter, at court King Oswald himself. His essential need was manpower, and he purchased slaves so that he might free them and train them for the ministry. Extensive preaching tours by Aidan served to bring Christianity, albeit infrequently, to the more remote regions of the kingdom. He appears to have done a great deal to establish monastic communities for men and women throughout Northumbria. Melrose and Gateshead monasteries dated to his lifetime; he consecrated Heiu, first Northumbrian to become a nun, who founded a monastery at Hartlepool. Hild founded monasteries at the mouth of the Wear and at Whitby, and Aidan used to instruct her in monastic discipline. Some of these foundations were double monasteries, established for the benefit of both monks and nuns who lived in separate communities within them. Whitby was a double monastery; though presided over by Abbess Hild it was the training centre for many later bishops, among them three bishops of York. Aidan was not insensitive to the Roman mission in England. York church, founded by Paulinus, was rebuilt by Oswald and Aidan, and in his lifetime Aidan was highly thought of by Honorius, archbishop of Canterbury, and Felix, bishop of Dunwich. The only criticism that Bede could make was that he celebrated Easter incorrectly, according to the traditions of the Celtic Church.

Oswald (635–43) and Oswiu (643–71), his brother and successor, both established themselves as *bretwaldas*, and the influence of the church of Lindisfarne expanded with the authority of the Northumbrian king. Oswald attended the baptism of Cynegils, king of the Saxons of the Thames valley, and stood godfather to him. Possibly this was an attempted alliance against a mutual foe, Mercia, but in 643 Oswald was slain by Penda of Mercia while attacking his kingdom. Oswiu had to consolidate his position before he could acquire his brother's prestige. His son, Alchfrith, had married Penda's daughter, and when Penda's son, Peada, sought to marry Oswiu's daughter the opportunity was taken to influence him towards Christianity. Peada was no insignificant prince; his father had made him ruler of the Middle Angles, by this date an important subject territory of the Mercians. In 654 Peada was baptised by Aidan's successor, Finan, bishop of Lindisfarne, in Northumbria and returned to Middle Anglia with four priests, among them Cedd, from Lindisfarne. To much the same period dates the conversion of Sigeberht, king of the East Saxons, at the court of Oswiu. Oswiu is said to have told Sigeberht that objects made by the hands of men could not be gods; God was invisible to human eyes and of incomprehensible majesty. Cedd was detached from the Mercian mission and sent back with the king to Essex. When Oswiu defeated and slew Penda in battle in 656, Diuma, one of the four missionaries sent to Middle Anglia, was appointed bishop over both the Mercians and the Middle Angles; Bede says that it was the shortage of men which compelled one man to administer two provinces. The assassination of Peada at Easter 657, reputedly by the treachery of his Northumbrian wife, did not affect the influence of the Scottish mission in Mercia for Oswiu remained master of the kingdom. But in 659, Wulfhere, son of Penda, seized power. Wulfhere's first bishop was Trumhere, an Englishman but ordained among the Scots, so that Scottish, if not Lindisfarne, traditions were continued. Among the East Saxons, Cedd enjoyed so much immediate success that he was consecrated bishop by Finan of Lindisfarne and established two missionary centres at Bradwell and Tilbury. The kingdom of the East Saxons, however, provides an instructive example of the thin line between success and failure. Sigeberht was assassinated because he was too apt to forgive his enemies, an aspect of his character which his own kinsmen took as a sign of weakness. And after Cedd's death in the plague of 664, and as a result of this plague, a pagan reaction swept the kingdom. Essex was reconverted by Jaruman, bishop of the Mercians, at the command of Wulfhere who had asserted his authority over the kingdom.

By 664 the Northumbrians were beginning seriously to question the support they were giving Scottish missionaries. In that year a council was held at Whitby, subsequently known as the Synod of Whitby, on the orders of King Oswiu and presided over by him, to determine whether the Northumbrian Church should continue to observe the Celtic as opposed to the Roman Easter. In 665 the dates of the Victorian and Dionysian Easters would diverge widely and there was probably a general concern, among the Roman party as much as among the Celtic, to determine the calculation to be adopted once and for all. The issue was of immediate importance to Oswiu because his queen, Eanflæd, daughter of Edwin, had been brought up in Kent and followed the Roman reckoning, and his son, Alchfrith, had been won over to the Roman side by the young monk, Wilfrid, subsequently to have a stormy career as bishop of York. That we know so much of Wilfrid is because his *Life* was written by a companion, Eddius Stephanus, in the early years of the eighth century. Wilfrid had been educated on Lindisfarne, but a visit to Rome had confirmed his dissatisfaction and he was the spokesman of the Roman party at Whitby. Not only personal antipathy to the austerities of Celtic religious life animated Wilfrid; he was inspired also by a desire for closer union with the Church of Rome as the acknowledged head of all the Western Churches and with the Graeco-Latin legacy of the Ancient World which it represented. Though the date of Easter was the focal point of the debate, it was the whole range of the peculiarities in the life and custom of the Scottish monks which was being challenged. Wilfrid emerged victorious and Oswiu declared himself in favour of the Roman Easter. His final decision is surprising in a way, for he had been brought up since the age of three in accordance with the practices of the Celtic Church. Historians have generally suspected, however, that political difficulties determined his decision, for Oswiu may have feared internal disunity in Northumbria if matters were not resolved. Rather than conform to the Roman Easter, which clearly meant conformity in every aspect of religious life, many of the Scottish monks, led by Colman, bishop of Lindisfarne, returned home. Those who did remain, and those of the English educated in Scottish ways, managed to preserve much of Celtic traditions of discipline and asceticism, so that there was no instant transformation of the Northumbrian Church. But in time, such men and women died out and Scottish influence weakened with the passage of the years. Though there were always Irish and Scottish clergy wandering through England in later centuries, they were never favourably regarded by the established Church, which questioned the validity of their Orders, and they were never permitted again to become a powerful religious force.

Organisation and reform

By 664 the authority of the see of Canterbury over the Church in the English kingdoms other than Kent was virtually non-existent. The years between the late 630s and the late 660s were a period of almost total decentralisation in the English Church. Only at Dunwich, in East Anglia, was a succession of bishops maintained who were in touch with Canterbury and who received consecration from the archbishop.

Elsewhere, kings like Oswald of Northumbria created bishoprics as they wished and appointed whom they wished. In Mercia and Essex a series of bishops owed primary allegiance to the bishop of Lindisfarne. In Wessex, in the period *c.* 660–4, Cenwalh, king of the Thames valley Saxons, disliking his bishop, Agilbert, who was a Frank, appointed an Englishman, Wine, as bishop, and a see was created for him at Winchester in Hampshire. An immediate consequence of the Synod of Whitby in Northumbria was the revival of the see of York, intended by Alchfrith for Wilfrid but by Oswiu for Chad, brother of Cedd and more Celtic in temperament. Chad was installed during Wilfrid's absence in search of consecration on the Continent. At this particular moment there was a vacancy at Canterbury. Oswiu conferred with Egbert, king of Kent, but the man they sent to Rome died whilst he was there, and the pope sent in his place an aged monk, Theodore of Tarsus. The work of ecclesiastical centralisation and reform took its origins in the policy of the church of Canterbury to the other bishops as developed by Archbishop Theodore (669–90), generally placed among the greatest of the Anglo-Saxon archbishops.

Theodore was determined to make his authority felt throughout England and to secure for Canterbury the dominant position in the English Church. There does not seem to have been any talk of Gregory the Great's plan to make York an archbishopric; this was not to happen until 735. Theodore began by removing Chad from York, confirming Wilfrid as bishop and appointing Chad to be bishop of the Mercians with his see at Lichfield. He intended that there should be many more bishoprics to enable more satisfactory administration of less sprawling dioceses. The Synod of Hertford (672) ordered their creation, for the dioceses of Northumbria, East Anglia, Mercia and Wessex were clearly far too vast for one man. Hæddi, who became bishop of Winchester in 678 and who was the only bishop in Wessex, for Dorchester had been lost to Mercia, successfully resisted any partition of his diocese until his death in 705, when a separate see was created at Sherborne for west Wessex under Aldhelm of Malmesbury. Wilfrid, bishop of York, was less successful. In 678, taking advantage of a quarrel between Wilfrid and Ecgfrith, son of Oswiu and king of Northumbria (671–85), Theodore divided the kingdom of Northumbria into four dioceses, with additional sees to those of York and Lindisfarne at Hexham, one of Wilfrid's monastic foundations, and at *Syddensis* (unidentified) for the subject province of Lindsey. Lindsey was almost immediately annexed

6 Gold buckle—
Sutton Hoo

7 Gold clasps—Sutton Hoo

8 The Kingston brooch

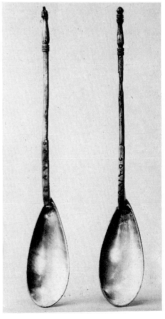

9 Pair of silver spoons—
Sutton Hoo

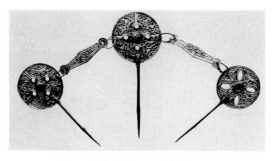

10   Silver linked pins, eighth century

12   Silver disc brooch:
the Fuller brooch,
ninth century

11   Gold ring of Æthelwulf,
King of Wessex

13   Silver bowl—Sutton Hoo

14   The Alfred jewel

by Æthelred, son of Wulfhere and king of Mercia, and became a suffragan bishopric in the diocese of Lichfield. Wilfrid resisted with all his power, appealing to the pope at Rome more than once, but his position was seriously weakened by the persistent hostility of Ecgfrith. Similarly, though eventually restored as bishop of Hexham (686/7–8) and then of York (688–91/2), Wilfrid was unable to agree with Ecgfrith's brother and successor, Aldfrith (685–704). After a second expulsion and a second restoration he ended his days as bishop only of Hexham (705–9). In the 680s Theodore created two new bishoprics in Northumbria: Ripon, another of Wilfrid's monastic foundations, and Abercorn, on the Firth of Forth, the latter to serve the Pictish provinces then subject to the Northumbrians. Neither survived long. Ripon disappears from the records in the 690s, and Abercorn was abandoned after the Picts defeated and slew Ecgfrith in 685. Yet another Northumbrian diocese was created c. 720, after Theodore's death, at Whithorn in Wigtownshire, the site of Ninian's church, to serve the Anglian settlers in the district and the subject Britons. Otherwise the diocesan administration of Northumbria was on the lines established by Theodore.

Theodore's policy of reorganisation also affected Mercia. In c. 675 he deposed Wynfrith, bishop of Lichfield, for disobedience, and c. 675–9 Mercia was divided into five sees: Lichfield for Mercia itself, Leicester for Middle Anglia, Dorchester-on-Thames for the Thames valley, Worcester for the people of the *Hwicce*, and a bishopric for the *Magonsæte* beyond the Severn, later known to be situated at Hereford. Wilfrid was bishop of Leicester for a time, while in exile in Mercia (691–7), but it was not until 737 that the see was permanently established. The Mercian bishopric of Dorchester was of brief duration in the pre-Viking period, Leicester constituting the only see for the eastern midlands in the eighth and early ninth centuries. The East Saxon kingdom was reorganised as a diocese around the old bishopric of London, and in East Anglia, when Bisi, bishop of Dunwich, became too infirm, Theodore appointed two bishops, one to Dunwich and the other to North Elmham (Norfolk).

It is a little strange to think of all this work of reconstruction going on while part of southern England was still pagan. The by now isolated and petty kingdom of the South Saxons was only converted and a bishopric established at Selsey c. 681–5 by Wilfrid, during his exile from Northumbria; and the permanency of his work was threatened when Æthelwalh, king of the South Saxons, was slain during an invasion of

Sussex by the pagan Cædwalla, a descendant of Ceawlin and king of Wessex from 685/6 to 688. Wilfrid is said to have become one of Cædwalla's counsellors. The king abdicated in 688 and went to Rome for baptism, dying shortly after. The events of South Saxon history in this period are in striking contrast to the more settled conditions of other parts of England; in contrast to Northumbria, for example, where the young Bede was already an inmate of the monastery of Monkwearmouth and Jarrow, so well stocked with books and paintings collected on the Continent by its founder, Benedict Biscop. By c. 680, pagan Sussex was an anachronism. The emphasis of the Church was now not so much on missionary activity as on organisation, even reform.

Theodore's work of centralisation was to be paralleled at a lower level within each diocese. An urgent need was for the bishop to establish his authority over the Christian communities of his diocese, particularly the monasteries. Of the monasteries and nunneries founded by saints and pious laymen in the seventh century, only a few appear to be mentioned in contemporary sources, some referred to only in passing. A great many monasteries can have left no trace of their existence. Not all survived, as did the great seventh-century fenland monasteries of Peterborough, Ely, and Ramsey, for example, to become important Benedictine houses throughout the Middle Ages. The early bishops, with so much pastoral work to undertake, left most of the founding of churches and monasteries to the enthusiasm and initiative of local converts. Often the founders were members of a royal family. Abbess Hild of Whitby was a daughter of a nephew of King Edwin. Æthelthryth, ex-queen of Ecgfrith, king of Northumbria founded Ely. But influential members of the nobility doubtless played the greatest part. Occasionally a monastery developed from a hermitage, as did Crowland in the eighth century, the cell of Guthlac, a Mercian nobleman. The rules of life in such foundations must have varied immensely, usually dictated solely by the personal tastes of the abbot. Cuthbert, the saintly hermit of Farne (d. 687), who was first provost of the monastery of Lindisfarne and then (685–7) bishop there, was probably largely responsible for the blend of Benedictinism and Irish asceticism which seems to have prevailed in that monastery by the early eighth century. Two *Lives*, from the early eighth century, survive of Cuthbert, one by a monk of Lindisfarne and one by Bede, and hence a great deal is known about him. As bishop of York, however, it was primarily Wilfrid who championed the Rule of St. Benedict in Northumbria. In the sixth century in Italy,

Benedict of Nursia drew up a monastic rule of life which, by its order and simplicity, rendered itself applicable in different ages and different societies. It was only over many centuries that Benedictinism became the usual monastic discipline in Western Europe, but the fact that Wilfrid cited his support of the Benedictine Rule in his own defence suggests that it was highly favoured by the ecclesiastical authorities in England by the beginning of the eighth century. One of the main pre-occupations of the English Church in the early eighth century was to combat lax discipline in the monasteries. The Synod of Hertford (672) had been concerned to preserve the freedom of monastic communities from episcopal intervention, but by the time of the Council of *Clofesho* (unidentified) (747) bishops were being urged to supervise monasteries and nunneries to ensure strictness. The monasteries were of great importance to the early Church in England because, apart from being centres of learning, they were often units in diocesan administration. Monasteries were otherwise known as minsters, and could serve as parish churches, not ministering to the small parishes of a later century but to extensive tracts of territory. As more and more churches were built, and parishes divided and subdivided, the role of the monastery as minster-church was eclipsed, but there can be no doubt that in the conditions of the seventh century monastic communities were natural centres of local administration.

It may be questioned that there was any decline in religious standards between the contrasting ecclesiastical legislation of 672 and 747. The view that there was a golden age in the early English Church from the mid-seventh century to *c.* 700 is the result of Bede's approach to the history of the Church. Bede set out in his *Ecclesiastical History* (731) to exhort his contemporaries to better lives by holding up to them the image of a pure and noble Church during the years of the Conversion. There is every likelihood that many of the missionaries were saintly and devout men, earnestly labouring to overcome great practical difficulties; but it is equally probable that the leading figures of the past had come to assume heroic proportions. Bede was writing primarily about the period of time in which he had not lived or was too young to remember distinctly, and he was deliberately selecting traditions about virtuous men. Of the Church in his own day he had considerable reservations and chose not to write about it. In his letter to Egbert, archbishop of York, written in 734, Bede complains that dioceses were still too vast for effective pastoral work, that monks and clergy were often ignorant of Latin (and therefore of the services of the Church), that some bishops did not live in a sober or a becoming fashion, that many monasteries failed to observe a regular rule of life, that some abbots were scornful and many monks rebellious, and that some monasteries were lay establishments designed by a local lord simply as a means of tax evasion. The Council of *Clofesho* (747) confirms that paganism was still prevalent and that priests were in need of instruction in the Roman rites and liturgy, in the Creed, the Lord's Prayer, and the sacramental words of Mass and Baptism; bishops are exhorted to travel through their diocese, not to be more engaged in secular affairs than in affairs of God, given to abstemious virtues and works of righteousness rather than to looseness in living and tardiness in teaching; the fasts of the Church year are to be observed uniformly and in accordance with the rites of the Roman Church; Church alms are to be gladly given, and kings and great men are not to envy and covet the possessions of monasteries and churches. These shortcomings in the Church certainly existed, but there is room for doubt that the situation in 734 or 747 was worse than it had been previously. The impression given by the decrees of the Synod of Hertford (672) is of a chronic absence of control. Canon Law was cited to forbid a bishop to intrude himself into the diocese of another; monks were prohibited from wandering round from one monastery to another as fancy led them, priests from deserting their own bishop to serve another. It was certainly not unknown in the seventh century for a bishop to be deposed or for a monastery to be regarded as a home of sin. It is more probable that the reform and reorganisation of the Church in England by Theodore and his successors was a natural consequence of the decentralised and haphazard process of conversion rather than the result of a sharp decline in the standards of Christian life once the task of conversion had been accomplished.

Criticism of the Church continued throughout the eighth century. Boniface, the English missionary to Germany, wrote to Cuthbert, archbishop of Canterbury, in 747 urging him to check drunkenness among the bishops. Boniface leaves little doubt in his letters to English kings and bishops that he considered the Church in danger of becoming depraved through evil habits. Towards the end of the eighth century, Alcuin, the Northumbrian scholar at the court of Charlemagne, never lost touch with the leaders of the English Church whom he criticised for addiction to vain styles of dress, immoderate habits of feasting, and undue pleasure in hunting. In 786 two papal legates were sent to

England, and provincial synods were held in southern England and Northumbria, which decreed that two councils meet annually, that bishops travel round their dioceses and that only suitable priests be ordained. It is probable that there were many in the Church whose standards were too low but who have escaped criticism. Bishop Daniel of Winchester (705–44), however, who, so far as can be seen from narrative and epistle sources—he offered advice on missionary tactics to Boniface—was an excellent prelate, was held in such disrespect at the monastery of Much Wenlock (Shropshire) that a monk had a vision of a numerous wailing company of infants who died without baptism, especially in the time of Daniel. Daniel is known to have been ill for a time before he resigned, and evidently his infirmity had practical consequences in diocesan administration. But shortcomings in the Church are not the whole story. The eighth century was the time when Anglo-Saxon missionaries, supported by the enthusiasm and practical aid of the English Church, were tackling with particular success the conversion of the continental tribes of Frisia and Germany. The surviving correspondence of Boniface (*d.* 754) and his companions and successors reveals the wide range of his contacts and supporters in English monasteries and churches from Thanet to Whithorn. Not only did Boniface accomplish much among the tribes of Bavaria, Hesse, and Thuringia, but he embarked also on the reform of the backward Frankish Church in 742. The vitality and vision of the English Church in the eighth century precludes the view that it was then itself in serious need of reform.

Chapter three

The Heptarchy

The seven major kingdoms of pre-Viking England[1], which dominated the political development of the country, have become known to historians as the Heptarchy. The several activities of their successive rulers make up a complex pattern of political events, and as it is with the actions of these rulers that early English sources are primarily concerned the historian is necessarily obliged to turn to them in some detail. The political evolution of these early and primitive English kingdoms, however, provides a theme of considerable historical interest. And, although every king pursued his individual interests, a constant rivalry for a position of military and political suzerainty affords a common factor amidst the bewildering array of aims and objectives. The most powerful ruler in his day sought the position of *bretwalda* or 'ruler of Britain' which involved the establishment of his overlordship upon subject kingdoms from which tribute could be exacted. Ælle of Sussex and Ceawlin of the Thames valley Saxons held this position during the period of the Conquest. In the Christian period suzerainty passed in turn to one or more of the kings of Kent, East Anglia, Northumbria, Mercia and Wessex. The seventh century was essentially the age of Northumbrian domination, the eighth century that of the Mercian, and the ninth century that of the West Saxon. Bede lists the *bretwaldas* down to his time of writing, and the *Anglo-Saxon Chronicle* adds Egbert of Wessex, omitting the Mercian kings out of simple jealousy. Bede describes the title of *bretwalda* as signifying authority over all lands south of the Humber, but it must be remembered that Bede was a Northumbrian and that for him Northumbrian overlordship would involve exactly this. A Mercian or West Saxon *bretwalda* would not hesitate to assert his authority north of the Humber if the chance

[1] *i.e.* the kingdoms of Northumbria, Mercia, Wessex, East Anglia, Essex, Kent, and Sussex.

presented itself. The rise and fall of a *bretwalda* naturally involved a great deal of warfare between the kingdoms of the Heptarchy, particularly in the seventh century. The conflicts and skirmishes of these years may not have affected more than the small proportion of the population actually involved in the battle, that is to say the king and his war band; but when the Anglo-Saxon poets pictured the terror of war, the crashing of shields, flying arrows, the blowing of trumpets, the unfurling of banners, golden helmets, gleaming spears, the press of men, the slaughter of hosts, the song of victory, and the human carrion on the field of battle, they were describing a not infrequent scene in Anglo-Saxon England.

The Anglian Kingdoms

The Angles penetrated into Britain via the waterways of the Wash and the Humber, and gave rise to the kingdoms of East Anglia, Middle Anglia which was quickly absorbed by Mercia and has no separate historic existence, Lindsey, Mercia, and Northumbria.

Though there were settlers in East Anglia throughout the fifth century, the dynasty which successfully welded these settlers into a single kingdom probably took its origin as late as *c.* 550. The *Wuffingas* dynasty from south-east Suffolk is thought to have advanced along the Icknield Way to subdue the northern settlers on the Ouse and its tributaries. All the evidence suggests that the Icknield Way was a main thoroughfare from north Norfolk to the Berkshire Downs. Control of this prehistoric trackway may have been fundamental to the imperium of Rædwald of East Anglia. On the death of the *bretwalda* Æthelberht of Kent, *c.* 618, Rædwald, previously one of several subject kings, imposed a transitory overlordship upon his neighbouring rulers. His major recorded political action was the defeat of Æthelfrith, king of Northumbria, and the placing of Edwin, son of Ælle, on the Northumbrian throne in 617. Eorpwald, son and successor of Rædwald, was unable to stand against Edwin. He was baptised at the Northumbrian court *c.* 628–30, by which time Edwin was master of the southern kingdoms except Kent. The major external threat to East Anglia, however, came not from Northumbria but from Mercia. The educated Sigeberht, brother of Eorpwald and king of East Anglia (*c.* 632–5), resigned the kingdom to his kinsman, Ecgric, and entered a monastery but before long he was compelled to fight beside Ecgric against Penda, king of Mercia (*c.* 634–56). Because of his monastic vows, Sigeberht refused to bear arms and both the East Anglian leaders were slain. The most distinguished East Anglian king of the seventh century was Anna (636–55), nephew of Rædwald. He owed his reputation to his personal character as a devout Christian and to the fact that many of his daughters became saints of the Anglo-Saxon Church, but he also perished while resisting a further attack by Penda of Mercia. It was as an ally of Penda that Anna's brother and successor, Æthelhere, fell the next year at the battle of *Winwæd*, fought against the Northumbrians and in which Penda also was slain. After this period, East Anglian history sinks into obscurity. Because of the lack of documentary evidence it is not possible to trace the relations of subsequent East Anglian kings with the powerful eighth-century rulers of Mercia. It is generally held that the native dynasty died out with King Ælfwald in 749, on whose death the kingdom was divided between Hun, Beonna and Alberht (Æthelberht). It is unlikely that the latter is the Æthelberht, king of East Anglia, whose execution at the command of Offa of Mercia in 794 forms the one central event of late eighth-century East Anglian history. The names of the East Anglian kings of the first half of the ninth century are known only from surviving coins. This is an unfortunate deficiency of sources for the East Anglians played a particularly important part in the overthrow of Mercian supremacy in this period.

The early ascendancy of East Anglia in the time of Rædwald may have rested not only on control of the Icknield Way but also on sea power, and the domination of the southern coastal waters. Interest in East Anglian history was intensified with the excavation in 1939 of the ship burial at Sutton Hoo, situated on the river Deben in south-east Suffolk and not far from a recorded royal centre at Rendlesham. Virtually every scrap of recorded East Anglian history has at one time or another been made relevant to the study of this ship burial and brought to bear upon it. The burial of a ship, loaded with treasure but containing no body, was designed as a cenotaph to an important East Anglian personage, generally believed to have been a king. At first it was thought that this was Rædwald's cenotaph, but a hoard of Merovingian gold coins indicated a date *c.* 650–60 for the burial, and opinions have tended to vary between Anna and Æthelhere as the king commemorated. It has now been suggested that these coins should really be dated to *c.* 625, which again places the burial in the time of Rædwald. The ship burial was primarily a pagan monument and the body of the king had either been lost or given a burial, possibly a Christian burial, elsewhere. The cenotaph reflects the maritime character of the East Anglian kingdom in this period and it shows something of the wealth of and influences on the royal court. The ship itself was some 85 feet long and some 14 feet wide; it had evidently been a fine vessel. A chamber in the middle of the ship contained the treasure, including what seems to have been a royal standard, a ceremonial whetstone, the remains of a helmet, a shield, and a purse, a bronze hanging bowl, the remains of a harp and several drinking horns, a great Byzantine silver dish and what are regarded as two silver christening spoons inscribed 'Saul' and 'Paul', other bowls, iron-mounted buckets, bronze cauldrons, a mail coat or corselet, an iron throwing-axe, clasps, buckles, a sword, a ring, and various spear-heads. The foreign element in this unique collection of goods implies contacts, though not necessarily direct, with Sweden, Gaul and Byzantium. The very nature of the boat burial has suggested Swedish affinities to many archaeologists. East Anglia was the home of a rich culture with far-flung continental links, and Mercian interest in the kingdom is readily understandable.

The settlers north of the Humber came to be known as the Northumbrians. A great deal is recorded of Northumbria during the period of the Heptarchy; Bede was particularly concerned with Northumbrian development in his *Ecclesiastical History* and a set of admirable Northumbrian annals has survived for the eighth century. Northumbria was originally two units, Deira south of the Tees and Bernicia north of it. The Bernician royal house under Æthelfrith (593–617) succeeded in annexing Deira and in creating a united Northumbria. Edwin, son of Ælle of Deira, was driven into exile and spent some time among the North Welsh, the Mercians and the East Angles before Rædwald of East Anglia restored him to his inheritance in 617. Edwin drove the sons of Æthelfrith into exile among the Picts and Scots and governed Northumbria as a single realm. His reign, however, was but a brief interlude in Bernician mastery. When Edwin was slain in 634 by Cadwallon of Gwynedd (North Wales) and Penda of Mercia, Deira and Bernicia fell apart. They were reunited by Oswald, son of Æthelfrith, who slew Cadwallon in 635. From this date until 759, though the task of holding Deira and Bernicia together often proved difficult, a single Bernician dynasty dominated the kingdom of Northumbria.

The seventh century was the period during which the kings of Northumbria achieved their greatest influence. Æthelfrith campaigned as far afield as Chester, but Edwin was the first Northumbrian ruler to acquire the position of *bretwalda*. What became of Rædwald is unknown, but Edwin began his rise to power by annexing the petty British kingdom of Elmet and in 627 he was strong enough to attack Wessex and slay five kings. His position as *bretwalda* was no doubt assured when he turned against Cadwallon of Gwynedd in *c.* 629, conquering Anglesey and Man and driving Cadwallon across to Ireland. There is no doubt that sea power must have been an essential element in Edwin's success. These early rulers may have been sea kings to a degree now difficult to comprehend. It may be that the struggle with Gwynedd was intended to assert Northumbrian overlordship of the Britons of north-west Britain, and it certainly provoked a savage reaction from the king of North Wales. Following the death of Edwin in battle, Cadwallon severely ravaged Northumbria and Bede implies that he was attempting mass extermination. As soon as Oswald had slain Cadwallon at the battle of Heavenfield (near Hexham), however, Northumbrian power was speedily restored. Very early in his reign, Oswald stood as godfather to Cynegils, newly converted king of the Thames valley Saxons. This relationship may reflect a common hostility to the emerging kingdom of Mercia under Penda, who was attacking his neighbours on all sides. In 638 the Irish annals record the siege of Edinburgh, which probably marks the date at which the Northumbrians succeeded in pushing the Bernician frontier to the Firth of Forth. It was at about this time that Oswiu, brother of Oswald, married Riemmelth of Rheged, thereby confirming Northumbrian lordship of this western region. In 643 Oswald was engaged in an attack on Mercia, and had driven Penda into Wales, when he was surprised by combined Welsh and Mercian forces and slain at *Maserfelth*, at the fortress of Old Oswestry. The initial failure of Oswiu (643-71) to retain control of Deira, which fell first to Oswine, son of Osric, assassinated by Oswiu in 652, and then to Æthelwald, son of Oswald, left Oswiu on the defensive. The great turning point of Northumbrian history was the battle of *Winwæd*, fought somewhere in the vicinity of Leeds, when Oswiu defeated and slew Penda of Mercia despite the assistance given to Penda by the kings of Gwynedd and East Anglia and by Æthelwald of Deira. The immediate cause of the conflict is obscure, and Æthelhere, king of East Anglia, surprisingly is held primarily responsible by Bede. The battle marked the end of effective Welsh interference in Northumbrian affairs, and Oswiu emerged strong enough to establish himself as *bretwalda* and even to impose his own administrators on Mercia for some three years.

It is at this point that Northumbrian history takes an unexpected turn, deflecting itself out of the mainstream of English political development. Instead of concentrating on the mastery of the southern English kingdoms, where Northumbrian suzerainty was successfully challenged by Wulfhere, son of Penda (659–75), Oswiu turned to attack the Picts. Oswiu had been brought up among the Scots of Dalriada, and his brother Eanfrith was the father of one Pictish king and the ancestor of others. Oswiu evidently preferred to participate in Celtic politics rather than English, and his military activities after 656 confirmed his attentions north of the Forth. It is not known just how extensive Oswiu's conquests in Pictland were, and the evidence suggests that in 685 the Northumbrians were not used to advancing north of the Tay. If the southern Picts were attacked and subdued, however, it is not impossible that the northern Picts simply acknowledged Oswiu's overlordship. It is recorded that in 673–4 innumerable tribes of the Picts came to attack Oswiu's son and successor, Ecgfrith (671–85). Ecgfrith defeated this rebellion, and it is probably to the years following 673–4 that the recognition of Northumbrian overlordship by the Scots and the Strathclyde Britons should be dated. In 679 Ecgfrith's decisive defeat on the Trent by Æthelred of Mercia clearly indicated the limitations upon Northumbrian political influence in southern England, but in north Britain there is no doubt that Ecgfrith's influence was paramount. In 684 he outraged educated opinion by actually sending a fleet to ravage Meath in Ireland, for Ireland had long afforded a home for English scholars and students. The attack on Meath is generally understood as the prelude to the attack on Pictland in 685, possibly designed to nip a second rebellion in the bud. It was in the course of this invasion of Pictland that Ecgfrith was slain at *Nechtanesmere* (near Dunnichen) by Brude, son of Bile, king of the Picts and Ecgfrith's second cousin. This Pictish victory marked the disintegration of Northumbrian supremacy. Though further Northumbrian-Pictish conflicts occurred in 698 and 711, and in 711 the Northumbrians stabilised their frontier on the river Carron, there was no reassertion of Northumbrian supremacy. Ecgfrith's brother and successor, Aldfrith (685–704), enjoyed a reign not seriously disturbed by external or internal difficulties. Under his immediate successors, Northumbrian-Pictish relations were distinguished by their peaceful nature as the Pictish Church was brought to accept the Roman Easter partly at least through the influence of Bede's monastery of Monkwearmouth and Jarrow (c. 710–16). The Picts do not appear to have exhibited any consistent determination to subdue Northumbria, and the Pictish ascendancy of the eighth century was confined to Celtic lands. Only one of the later kings of Northumbria is known to have been an important influence in northern politics, namely Eadberht (737–58), who took advantage of the death of a king of Strathclyde and civil warfare in Pictland to annex the plain of Kyle in modern Ayrshire (c. 752). Some four years later he joined with the most powerful Pictish king of the eighth century, Angus son of Fergus, in a successful attack on Dumbarton, capital of Strathclyde, but immediately after—how we are not told—Eadberht's army was unexpectedly destroyed.

Aldfrith, king of Northumbria, was succeeded by his seven year old son, Osred, though not without a civil war. On Osred's death in 716 the accession of Cenred, a representative of a hitherto obscure line of Bernician aristocrats claiming descent from Ida, set the pattern for the eighth century in Northumbria when it became common for noble families to contend violently for the kingship. Eadberht made an attempt to rid himself of his Bernician rivals, but in 759 his son and successor, Oswulf, was slain by a certain Æthelwald Moll, whose strength lay in Deira. Northumbrian history in the eighth century provides the classic example of the way in which dynastic strife could affect the stability of an Anglo-Saxon kingdom. In 789, for example, King Ælfwold, son of Oswulf, was slain by his nephew, Osred; Osred was driven out the next year by Æthelred, son of Æthelwald Moll, who consolidated his position by drowning the young sons of Ælfwold. Such instances could be multiplied. These men were not necessarily more murderous than their contemporaries, but their passions were allowed a freer rein by the absence of a strong kingship. Some, among them Æthelwald, became abbots after deposition. Eadberht's brother, Egbert, became archbishop of York and a great one. Ælfwold was remembered as a just and pious ruler. The Northumbrian court took an interest in the continental mission field. The second half of the eighth century, however, was increasingly an age of isolation for Northumbria. The Picts were not interested and the Mercians pre-occupied with southern England. The various Northumbrian factions were temporarily quelled by Eanred (c. 809–41) but they reappeared after his death to tear Northumbria to the eve of the Viking attack. The military strength of the later Northumbrian kings, however, must not be underestimated. King Eardwulf, father of Eanred, did not shrink from challenging, not unsuccessfully, the powerful Cenwulf of Mercia in 801; and mid-ninth-century Northumbrian kings are said in a later source to have provided the Picts with support in the wars with Kenneth son of Alpin, king of Dalriada, evidently to little avail for the Pictish kingdom was ultimately destroyed.

The rulers of the sprawling kingdom of the Southumbrians or Mercians, based on the valley of the Trent, were the most successful of all the kings of the Heptarchy in establishing a prolonged military domination over their neighbours. Much of the history of Mercia, however, remains obscure because no Mercian narrative source for the pre-Viking period has survived and what is known of Mercia is known indirectly from Northumbrian, Welsh or West Saxon sources. The most useful guides for reconstructing the age of Mercian domination have not been chronicles at all but charters, records of land grants which reveal some of the territories in which the Mercian kings had influence; charters, on the other hand, no more give a comprehensive picture than do chronicles, and, for example, it is not possible to describe Mercian dealings with the East Angles from charters for none survive from East Anglia.

Mercia does not appear clearly in the early records until the time of Penda (c. 634–56), the enemy of Edwin, Oswald and Oswiu. But very early in his career Penda secured Mercian control of the Severn from the Thames valley Saxons and it is clear that Northumbria was not his prime concern. Penda seems to have been dominated by the kings of Gwynedd and it was as an ally of the Welsh that he attacked Northumbria. From an obscure reference by Nennius it appears that Penda may have incurred Northumbrian animosity because until his time the Southumbrians had existed in some sort of dependence upon the Northumbrians. Penda broke this dependence. His own interests, however, led him to concentrate on securing a route to the sea for his inland realm, particularly across Middle Anglia to East Anglia and contact with continental trade routes. Probably as early as c. 635 and certainly by 654 at the latest, when he made his son Peada their prince, Penda had conquered the Middle Angles. This was his most substantial conquest. He constantly harassed East Anglia and the kingdom was evidently subject by 656. By 665 the kingdom of the East Saxons was subject to his son,

Wulfhere (656–75). In *c.* 661 Wulfhere harried as far south as the Isle of Wight, and there can be no doubt that Wulfhere was the most powerful king in southern England for most of his reign. It was probably in the early 660s that the Mercians slew Cynddylan, a Welsh prince of the kingdom of Powys, and destroyed his palace at *Pengwrn* (not certainly identified but probably at Shrewsbury). This event was subsequently commemorated as a lament for Cynddylan in Welsh bardic poetry. It is the only reference to a Welsh–Mercian conflict before the reign of Cenred (704–9), but as the Mercians did not use gentle means of advancement in southern England they are hardly likely to have done so against the Welsh: and Cynddylan himself was remembered by the Welsh as a great warrior who had campaigned as far east as Lichfield. To the reign of Wulfhere also belongs the permanent annexation of the plain of Cheshire. Along the Severn in modern Worcestershire the kingdom of the *Hwicce* was developing as a part of the kingdom of Mercia, a frontier state facing Wessex, and beyond; and across the Severn the petty tribe of the *Magonsæte* in modern Herefordshire was formed as a similar buffer against South Welsh aggression. So securely established were these two kingdoms by 675–9 that they were given their own bishoprics. In 679 Lindsey was finally made a part of Mercia by Wulfhere's brother and successor, Æthelred (675–704). Æthelred did not hesitate to ravage Kent in 676. It is the outward expansion at all points of the compass of the inland realm of Mercia which provides the key to much of the development of the Heptarchy.

There is a hint of internal strife in Mercia in 697 when Æthelred's queen, Ostryth, sister of Ecgfrith of Northumbria, was assassinated, but Peada, Æthelred's brother, had been slain it was said by Ostryth's sister, his own wife, so that this may have been a blood-feud slaying. Æthelred abdicated in 704 and his successor, Cenred, son of Wulfhere, went to Rome in 709. Ceolred (709–16), son of Æthelred, appears to have been subject to fits which his contemporaries regarded as madness and a retribution for dissolute morals, but he was also a warrior who fought and defeated Ine of Wessex in 715. He was the last prince, however, to be descended from Penda. The great Mercian kings of the eighth century were descended from Penda's brother, Eowa, who fell in the same battle as Oswald of Northumbria. With the reign of Æthelbald (716–57), grandson of Eowa, the history of Mercia and southern England entered a new phase. Æthelbald was seen as a grossly immoral ruler in certain ecclesiastical circles and his ultimate fate was assassination by his own retinue, a violation of heroic standards which does suggest a rather unsavoury personality; but he began his career as a landless exile in the fens around Crowland and by 731 had made himself overlord of all southern England. In 740 he attacked the Northumbrians while Eadberht was engaged against the Picts, but no outcome of the campaign is recorded. He appears to have used the services of two successive kings of Wessex, Æthelheard and Cuthred, against the South Welsh. In 752 Cuthred rebelled, but Cynewulf of Wessex (757–86) appears to have acknowledged Mercian overlordship only a short while before Æthelbald's assassination at Seckington (near Tamworth). A contested succession threatened Mercia's position and when Offa, Æthelbald's cousin, finally became king in 758 he had to begin again the work of his predecessor. But the foundations had been laid and the pattern of Mercian supremacy established. Offa was in control of Essex almost from the beginning of his reign and of Kent by c. 764, and in 771 he was campaigning in Sussex against the men of Hastings. The degree of West Saxon independence under Offa is uncertain, but in 779 Offa won a victory over the West Saxons at Bensington which may have given him a measure of authority. Cynewulf's successor, Beorhtric (786–802), was certainly dependent on Offa for aid against a rival, Egbert, and Beorhtric's marriage to a daughter of the Mercian king no doubt set the seal on his subjection. In 792 Æthelred of Northumbria married another of Offa's daughters, and again some submission to Offa is thereby implied. The charters of the period reveal clearly the extent of Offa's authority in the kingdoms of the East Saxons and the South Saxons, Kent and the territory of the *Hwicce*; and they throw light on some of the day-to-day implications of the Mercian hegemony. Offa was able to control the internal administration of subject territories as he thought fit, taking revenues for himself; he was quite strong enough to depose and appoint kings. In 794 he ordered the execution of Æthelberht of East Anglia. By 774 he had taken the title of *rex Anglorum*, reflecting a primitive conception of a kingdom of all England, and so influential did he make himself that he sought to treat on equal terms with the great ruler of the Franks, Charles the Great. Though Charlemagne did not become emperor during Offa's lifetime, he was without question the dominant personality on the Continent. In c. 789, however, Charlemagne's offer that his son should marry one of Offa's daughters fell through when Offa insisted in return that his son, Ecgfrith, marry one of Charlemagne's daughters. This dispute led to the closing of continental ports to English trade until a new trade settlement was negotiated by Charlemagne and Offa in 796 to regulate and define the trade between the two realms.

Offa's Mercia drew its wealth from the royal control of the trade of south-east England. Possession of the rich province of Kent was essential to the Mercian position. On the death of Offa, followed in a matter of months by that of his son, the kingship passed to a distant relative, Cenwulf (796–821), whose early years were primarily occupied with the suppression, in an evidently savage manner, of a revolt in Kent. Eadberht Præn, king of Kent, was blinded and mutilated. The efforts of Offa and Cenwulf to create a new archbishopric at Lichfield which would guarantee the ecclesiastical independence of Mercia and displace the primacy of Canterbury may have been a factor in the rebellion. In 788 Hygeberht, bishop of Lichfield, was recognised as archbishop by Rome but in 798 Cenwulf intimated to Pope Leo III that London should be established as the southern metropolitan see, intending this as a compromise between Lichfield and Canterbury. By 801–2, however, Cenwulf had reasserted his authority in Kent and was prepared to restore Canterbury to its ancient position.

From the second half of the eighth century onwards the survival of Welsh annals makes it possible to fill in to some extent the history of the Welsh-Mercian border. The Welsh annals record a battle at Hereford in 760 between Britons and Saxons, and a harrying of Dyfed (south-west Wales) by Offa in 777, followed by another campaign in 783. It is probably to the years after 784 that construction of the great earthwork known as Offa's Dyke should be dated. An earlier earthwork, known as Wat's Dyke, to the east of Offa's, may have been constructed by Æthelbald, but to Offa the great dyke is specifically attributed by the Welshman, Asser, in his *Life* of King Alfred. Offa's reign certainly provides an understandable context for such a massive construction which runs virtually the whole length of the border, from near Rhuddlan to near Chepstow, though for some distance the river Severn itself forms a continuation link. The dyke appears to mark the boundary which the Mercians desired should separate Wales from Mercia. It was not a final solution to frontier difficulties and in 796, the very year of Offa's death, there was a battle at Rhuddlan. Cenwulf campaigned in Wales on a considerable scale. In 798 Caradog, king of Gwynedd, was slain by the Saxons, while in 816 Snowdonia was ravaged and the little North Welsh kingdom of Rhufuniog, between the Clwyd and the Elwy, was annexed by the Mercians. In 818 Cenwulf ravaged Dyfed and if, as a late source records, he died at Basingwerk he may have been engaged in a further campaign in the year of his death. Certainly, the culmination of the Mercian attack followed immediately. In 822, in the reign of Cenwulf's brother, Ceolwulf (I) (821–3), the ancient Welsh fortress of Degannwy was destroyed and the kingdom of Powys brought under Saxon rule. The precise details are unknown, but there can be no doubt that the Mercian conquest of Powys was a striking military achievement. But while Mercian power was being so effectively demonstrated against the Welsh, undercurrents of restlessness among subject or overshadowed English kingdoms were beginning to threaten the foundations of Mercian power.

The Saxon kingdoms and Kent

The Saxon kingdoms of Sussex and Essex, and the so-called 'Jutish' kingdom of Kent do not play a particularly conspicuous part in the political history of the Heptarchy in the period following the Anglo-Saxon Conquest. Their history relates primarily to their subjection to Mercia. By contrast, West Saxon dealings with Mercia are obscure and the main interest of West Saxon history lies in the internal developments of the kingdom.

The kingdom of the East Saxons was probably the most insignificant of those kingdoms which are regarded as making up the Heptarchy. A heavily wooded region, its most important centre was London and once control of London was lost to the Mercians the kings of Essex withdrew into obscurity. It was not at first apparent that Essex would fail to expand into an influential kingdom. By c. 600 the East Saxons had annexed the territory of the Middle Saxons (Middlesex) and Pope Gregory intended that London should become an archbishopric. Æthelberht of Kent checked East Saxon development, however, and when expansion was resumed on Æthelberht's death by the two pagan kings, Sæweard and Seaxred, not only did they expel the missionaries from London, thereby destroying any chance of London replacing Canterbury, but they proved unequal to the task of challenging the Thames valley Saxons against whom they fell in battle. Hemmed in by more powerful conglomerations of tribes, the East Saxon rulers generally appear henceforth as satellites of some greater power.

Sigeberht the Good (*c.* 652–*c.* 660) was converted through the influence of Oswiu, king of Northumbria, Suithelm (*c.* 660–4) was baptised by the Northumbrian missionary, Cedd, at the court of Æthelwald, king of East Anglia, and Sighere and Sebbi, who succeeded jointly in 664, were subject kings of Wulfhere of Mercia. East Saxon charters for the late seventh and eighth centuries reveal the continued dependence of Essex on Mercia. It was probably the reign of Æthelbald of Mercia (716–57) which witnessed the detachment of London from East Saxon control, together with the province of the Middle Saxons. With London secure, the Mercians could afford to ignore the petty princes of inland Essex, the very succession of whom is imperfectly known.

Following the reign of Ælle, South Saxon history is poorly documented. No royal genealogy survives for the kingdom, and little in the way of annalistic record. In *c.* 610 Ceolwulf, king of Wessex, fought the South Saxons. In 661, after harrying the Isle of Wight, Wulfhere of Mercia gave the island and the Jutish province of the *Meonware* (on the river Meon, Hants.), hitherto within West Saxon territories, to the South Saxons. It was probably at this time that Æthelwalh, king of the South Saxons, was baptised at the court of Wulfhere, on the occasion of his marriage to a Christian princess of the *Hwicce*. This Mercian-South-Saxon alliance is most interesting and explains the hostility of Cædwalla of Wessex to Æthelwalh. When Wilfrid, bishop of York, arrived among the South Saxons as an exile in the early 680s he succeeded in converting them but his mission was interrupted by Cædwalla's invasion of Sussex and the slaying of Æthelwalh. The king's death may have marked the end of the native royal line in Sussex for Bede records that the king's ealdormen, Berhthun and Andhun, assumed the government of the kingdom until Cædwalla slew Berhthun and subdued the South Saxons (686–7). Sussex appears to have remained subject to Wessex throughout the reign of Ine of Wessex (688–726), for not only does Ine confirm grants of land in Sussex made by King Nunna but the *Chronicle* records that in 710 Ine and his kinsman, Nun, fought against the Cornishmen. After a period of obscurity, Sussex is found as one of the subject territories of Offa of Mercia from *c.* 770, and a decisive stage in Offa's conquest of east Sussex must have been reached in 771 with the war against the men of Hastings. In the late eighth century men who had formerly ruled in Sussex as kings appear only as *duces*, implying a sub-royal position not far removed from that of ealdorman.

It is possible to study West Saxon history in greater detail because the *Anglo-Saxon Chronicle* is primarily concerned to provide an account of the kings of Wessex from Cerdic to Alfred. The material is patchy, and the chronicler assembled much more information on the period before 754 than on the years 754–815, but the *Chronicle* is nevertheless a substantial record and provides a basis for more detailed study. There was probably no doubt in the mind of the chronicler that Alfred was descended from Cerdic, but, though Alfred's ancestry can certainly be traced back through Cædwalla to Ceawlin, there is a strong possibility that the link which made Ceawlin a son of Cynric son of Cerdic was a genealogical fiction of the time of Cædwalla, when that pagan prince sought to master the whole of Wessex. During the time of Cenwalh, probably a great-grandson of Ceawlin and king of the Thames valley Saxons, Mercian pressure along the Thames was such that the Thames valley Saxons began to move into Hampshire in the 650s and 60s. Winchester became their ecclesiastical centre. In Wiltshire, however, they faced the successors of Cerdic and Cynric, and though Cenwalh achieved some sort of hegemony his position was lost at his death (*c*. 672–5). For a while, the Wiltshire rulers gained the upper hand. Centwine (678–85) was strong enough to put the Britons to flight as far as the sea, evidently marking an important stage in the conquest of Devon. The annalistic records are clearly incomplete at this point for Aldhelm of Malmesbury states that Centwine fought three great battles against his enemies. These enemies are unnamed, but one battle may have been against Cædwalla. Cædwalla began his career as a royal exile in the Chilterns and the Kentish Weald, but when he attacked Wessex he had already tested his strength against the South Saxons. Of the details of his rise to power in Wessex nothing is known, though Aldhelm may be understood to imply that Centwine retired into a monastery. What is clear is that a permanently unified kingdom of Wessex dates to the reign of Cædwalla (685/6–8). His invasion of the Isle of Wight was a violent process; the royal house was exterminated. Secure in Wessex, Cædwalla flung himself on Kent, but he received such serious wounds during the Isle of Wight campaign that he abdicated in 688 to seek baptism and death at Rome. His successor and cousin, Ine (688–726), completed the fusion of the older folk-groups by promulgating a code of law to be applied to the whole kingdom.

Ine's achievement was to preserve the work of Cædwalla. The *Chronicle* reveals that there were many claimants to the kingship, all of whom he managed to suppress without seriously endangering the new unity of the kingdom. He retained control of Sussex, enjoyed prestige in Kent, and kept the Mercians at bay. It was in his time that the conquest of Devon was completed, and his defeat of Geraint, king of the Cornish Britons, in 710 undoubtedly represents an important West Saxon advance. Ine abdicated in 726, however, and his kinsman and successor, Æthelheard (726–40), became subject to Æthelbald of Mercia. Cuthred (740–56) was restless under Mercian domination and in 752 he defeated Æthelbald in battle. Though Cynewulf (757–86) seems to have made submission to Æthelbald shortly before the latter's death, it is not until 772 that he is found in the entourage of Offa. His possession of Mercian territory in Berkshire and Oxfordshire suggests that he more than held his own against the Mercians. In his own kingdom he is known to have fought more than one campaign against the Britons of Cornwall. In 786 he fell a victim to internal discord, and the account of his death provided the chronicler with a classic piece of Anglo-Saxon prose. Cynewulf had come to power by the deposition of King Sigeberht (756–7) and in 786 he was slain in a surprise attack by Sigeberht's brother, Cyneheard. The devotion of the men of Cynewulf and Cyneheard to their lords affords some of the best evidence for the martial values of eighth-century Anglo-Saxon warriors. All preferred to die rather than abandon their chiefs. The death of Cynewulf provided Offa with the opportunity to assert his influence more noticeably in Wessex by marrying his daughter to Beorhtric (786–802), the new ruler of Wessex. Accidentally poisoned, it was said, by his wife in 802, Beorhtric was remembered as a pious king. He was opposed by a rival, Egbert, whom he succeeded in driving into exile with the assistance of Offa of Mercia.

Egbert was descended from Ingild, brother of Ine, and his father, Ealhmund, is generally identified with an Ealhmund who was ruling as king in Kent in 784. The kingdom of Kent passed into eclipse under Eadbald, son of Æthelberht. Though Eadbald managed to retain his independence during Edwin's imperium, Kent never again achieved a position of political influence. Eadbald's grandson, Egbert (664–73), came to power through the assassination of his cousins, one of whose sons, by name Oswine, seized power in 673 and plunged Kent into civil war. Egbert's brother, Hlothere (674–85), vainly fought against Oswine, against external attack from Mercia and Essex and particularly against Swæbheard, a prince of Essex, and against his own nephew

Eadric who attacked with South Saxon support. Hlothere eventually died of wounds and Eadric found himself under attack from Cædwalla of Wessex. Both Hlothere and Eadric resumed the codification of Kentish law, begun by Æthelberht, but it was not until the reign of Wihtred, son of Egbert, that order was restored (692–725). Wihtred continued the legislative activities of his predecessors and granted important privileges to the churches of Kent. His second queen, Werburh, has a Mercian name, so that Mercian influence in Kent in his time is possible, but the full subjection of Kent to Æthelbald probably occurred after Wihtred's death. The royal family of Kent survived until the death of Wihtred's son, Æthelberht, in 762, but after this date appear kings of unknown origin, usually as Mercian dependants, and from 764 at the latest Offa was in firm control. The various kings of Kent in the late eighth century do not usually appear in the scanty annals of the period, but there are indications that Kent was not easily integrated into the Mercian empire. In 776 the men of Kent fought with Offa at Otford, and this would seem to have been a Kentish victory for Offa's series of Kentish charters temporarily ceases. A reassertion of Mercian authority occurred, however, and in 785 Offa's Kentish charters recommence. In 784 Ealhmund was reigning, and the *Chronicle* claims that the men of Kent were wrongfully forced away from Egbert's kin. It is possible that Ealhmund may have been the leader of the men of Kent at Otford. The events in Kent certainly throw light on Offa's hostility to Egbert, son of Ealhmund, in Wessex. Offa is said to have hated the men of Kent and his death was the signal for the Kentish rebellion of 796 which was so ruthlessly suppressed by Cenwulf. Following the suppression of the revolt, Cenwulf appointed his own brother, Cuthred, as king in Kent so that his control should be more effective. On Cuthred's death in 807, Baldred, of unknown origin, was appointed king. Mercian control of the province must have seemed very secure in the early years of the ninth century.

The West Saxon and Mercian struggle

On the death of Beorhtric of Wessex in 802, Cenwulf of Mercia does not seem to have made any determined effort to prevent the succession of Egbert, son of Ealhmund. On the very day that Egbert succeeded, a force from the territory of the *Hwicce* invaded Wessex to be defeated by the men of Wiltshire under Ealdorman Weohstan, Egbert's brother-in-law, but otherwise Egbert's accession was unchallenged. Egbert appears to have remained very quiet during the lifetime of Cenwulf. An attack on the Cornish Britons in 815 is his first recorded military action. He had spent part of his exile in Gaul, and may have had the opportunity to observe Charlemagne at close quarters, possibly even to learn from him. In Wessex he had acquired a firm basis for military aggrandisement; whereas Mercia was now ringed in by restless dependencies and enemies, Egbert had the security of a long seaboard to the south and to the north the protective barrier of the downland ridge across Berkshire and Wiltshire. His wars with the Cornish Britons were of inconsequential significance compared to the Welsh preoccupations of the Mercian rulers. The *Chronicle* claims that the men of Kent, Sussex and Essex regarded him as lawful king. His political and dynastic position made him an obvious potential danger to the security of the Mercian kingdom.

The fragmentary evidence suggests that a reaction occurred in Mercia against an aggressive Welsh policy. Despite Mercian successes in Powys, Ceolwulf was deposed in 823 and replaced by Beornwulf, of unknown ancestry, who was clearly resolved to concentrate on the preservation of Mercian authority in the richer provinces of southern England. In 825 he marched on Egbert, to be defeated at *Ellendun* (Wroughton). The battle of Wroughton was not the end for Beornwulf; it might have been but a temporary check, comparable to Cuthred's defeat of Æthelbald or Offa's defeat at Otford. But Egbert transformed the situation by taking advantage of existing discontent outside Wessex. From the battlefield itself he sent his son, Æthelwulf, and Ealhstan, bishop of Sherborne, into Kent. Baldred was driven out and the men of Kent, Surrey, Sussex and Essex immediately submitted to Egbert. An unnamed ruler of East Anglia appealed to him for aid. It is not known whether aid was received, but when Beornwulf marched on the East Angles in the same year he was defeated and slain. It is significant that it was not against Wessex but against East Anglia that Beornwulf's successor, Ludeca, launched his attack in 827. For the second time the Mercian army was defeated by the East Anglian and the Mercian king slain. The prominence of East Anglia in these events is particularly striking. The swift collapse of the Mercian hegemony, despite the recent Welsh successes, is one of the most surprising developments in the history of the Heptarchy. The rapid succession of three kings in six years, a probable reorientation in policy, and the loss of men in three major battles was apparently too much for Mercian administration and military strength.

Two years later, in 829, Egbert attacked Ludeca's successor, Wiglaf, and expelled him, conquering Mercia and receiving acknowledgement from all peoples south of the Humber as overlord. He led his army as far north as Dore, in north Derbyshire, and received the submission of the Northumbrians under King Eanred. One account describes him as ravaging Northumbria and exacting tribute. It is impossible not to be impressed by Egbert's meteoric rise to power after years of quiescence. In 830 Egbert is said to have received the submission of the Welsh, but the Welsh annals do not record this incident. The expedition to Wales, on what ever scale it was carried out, marked the high-water mark of Egbert's career. Henceforth, the records of his military activities relate to wars against the Cornish Britons and the Danes on the coast of Wessex. It should not be thought that Egbert permanently established the supremacy of Wessex. His imperium showed every indication of being but a temporary interlude in Mercian overlordship. In 830 Wiglaf recovered his kingdom and, once in power again in Mercia, he consolidated his authority in Middlesex and the regions bordering the Thames to the north, and even asserted his influence in Berkshire. London remained in Mercian hands and a Mercian assembly held in 836 reveals that Wiglaf was claiming authority over the southern episcopate. There can be little doubt that the return of Wiglaf terminated Egbert's overlordship of Northumbria and probably also over East Anglia. But Kent, Surrey, Sussex and Essex were retained and when Æthelwulf became king of Wessex in 839 he entrusted them to his eldest son Athelstan. Wessex and Mercia were now pretty evenly matched and an uncertain equilibrium of power was maintained. The Mercian king, Beorhtwulf (c. 839–52), preserved Wiglaf's position except that he lost Berkshire to Æthelwulf, c. 845. It was he who assumed responsibility for the defence of London when the city was attacked by the Danes in 851. In 853 his successor, Burgred, sought and obtained the assistance of Æthelwulf against the North Welsh who were subdued to Burgred, and in 855 Burgred married Æthelwulf's daughter. According to William of Malmesbury, it was the opinion of Bishop Ealhstan that Æthelwulf was not the warrior he should have been, and this may have been a factor in the Mercian recovery. It is difficult to say whether the king of Wessex or the king of Mercia had the edge of supremacy over the other or how relations between them would have developed had not the Danish invasions intervened to destroy the *status quo*.

2 THE POST-VIKING PERIOD

Chapter one

King Alfred the Great
and his Successors

Viking raids and invasions in the pre-Alfredian period

The history of the Scandinavian lands remains shrouded in obscurity until the late eighth century. At that point in time the Scandinavians irrupted into European society, their activities ultimately ranging from the Black Sea and south Russia to Greenland and beyond, probably even to North America. From the time that Charlemagne commissioned an extensive system of coastal defences in the last years (810–14) of his reign to guard his northern frontiers, their activities become more discernible. Denmark was Charlemagne's immediate concern for the Danes were his neighbours, but beyond the Danes were the Swedes and the Norsemen, men of Norway. The agricultural worth of their lands may not have been great and it is possible that population pressures were at work. The Swedes were drawn south in a trading and colonising movement which was to play a part in the evolution of Russia around the centres of Novgorod and Kiev, linking the Scandinavian lands with the trade of the east Mediterranean. It is easy to forget that the Scandinavians of what has become known as the Viking period were traders as well as raiders and settlers. The Danes developed an important trading centre at Hedeby, and Norway took its name from the North Way, the trade route to the White Sea.

The meaning of the word Viking is uncertain. It could signify 'creek warrior' or it could possess the sense of a sea-warrior who went away from home on distant expeditions. The term has become synonymous with Scandinavian sea-pirates of the ninth and tenth centuries, and it is largely as angels of death and destruction that the Vikings are represented in contemporary sources. The men who led the Viking armies were ferocious and violent, seeming even more terrible to west Europeans because as pagans they had no respect for churches. Some of the warriors were known as wolf-coats, because of the way they dressed and because they howled like wolves in battle; others were known as *berserks* because they fought without protective armour, often in a kind of frenzy. Such warrior types may not have been unknown in the British Isles. Nevertheless, there can be little doubt that the Scandinavian lands were largely outside the main stream of civilisation at the beginning of the ninth century, and not infrequently verging on anarchy. Only one ruler, Horik of Denmark (827–54), came near to establishing order and control in his kingdom before he, too, fell a victim to internal strife. Norway remained without a strong ruler until the ascendancy of Harold Fairhair from *c.* 872 onwards. There existed, therefore, in Denmark and Norway an undisciplined warrior aristocracy which might react to pressures of over-population and land-hunger by seeking booty and land elsewhere. Such economic factors would compel the peasant cultivators to form the rank and file of Scandinavian armies in the hope of securing a better livelihood. It must be recognised, however, that any deeper sociological motivating forces behind the Viking movements may lie hidden from us, as in the case of the migrations of the fifth and sixth centuries, by the limited contemporary evidence. Vikings fought Vikings and Norse migrants even raided their own homeland from Britain.

By the ninth century the Scandinavians had surpassed west Europeans in the development of ships possessing not only oars but sails and strong keels carved from single oaks. These Viking ships were no larger than those of west Europe but they were so technically superior that they gave the Scandinavians the advantage at sea. Without this technical superiority the Viking Age would probably have been impossible. To their supremacy at sea the Vikings added a grasp of the value of fortified land bases or fortresses. Viking forts at first baffled their opponents and eventually changed the nature of land fighting in many of the later campaigns of the Dark Ages. Finally, what was probably a more liberal distribution of helmets and mail-shirts, the use of long and kite-shaped shields as opposed to round shields, and skill in the manipulation of long-handled and vicious battle-axes, transformed the Scandinavian warriors into the storm-troopers of their day.

There were two main westward routes for the Vikings. The Norse expeditions sailed across to north Britain and, via Orkney and Shetland, to Ireland and the Isle of Man. The Danes were drawn to the mouth of the Rhine, one of the trading arteries of Europe, and from there down the Channel to England and north Gaul. Norse raiders on their way round Scotland were probably responsible for the sack of Lindisfarne in 793 and Jarrow, Bede's monastery, in 794, though Danes may have participated. Alcuin wrote to Hygebald, bishop of Lindisfarne, who was evidently stunned by the catastrophe, promising to see if Charlemagne could do anything for those led into captivity. The Norse at this period were primarily occupied with Scotland and Ireland. They were carving a kingdom for themselves in Ireland by c. 840, with an important centre at Dublin, and c. 850 Kenneth son of Alpin, king of the Scots of Dalriada, took advantage of a Scandinavian attack on the Picts to subject much of southern Pictland at least to his own rule. In the ninth century it was the Danes who attacked and settled in England. A raiding party slew the reeve of Dorchester in the reign of Beorhtric of Wessex (786–802). A series of sporadic raids along the West Saxon coast occurred in the early years of the ninth century, probably of quite limited significance. Egbert of Wessex was defeated in what could have been a sea battle at Carhampton in 836, but in 838 he overthrew a combined Danish and Cornish force on Hingston Down. In c. 843 Æthelwulf, king of Wessex, was also defeated at Carhampton, but in 851 he and his son, Æthelbald, won a great victory at *Aclea*. The same year Æthelwulf's son, Athelstan, who disappears from the records at this point, won what was certainly a naval conflict at Sandwich, the most important of the Kentish ports in the Anglo-Saxon period. It should not be thought that the west Europeans did not possess ships, albeit technically inferior ships, and that they did not use them against the Vikings. Charlemagne constructed a fleet, a king of Dalriada fought a naval engagement in 839, and the West Saxons, certainly in 851 and several times in the early years of the reign of Alfred, were prepared to fight at sea. Anglo-Saxon poets, in the period before the Vikings, delighted to describe their ships on the sea as ocean steeds skimming over the waves of the sea road. King Alfred subsequently rebuilt the West Saxon fleet, or part of it, c. 896, but he by no means created it.

By the fourth decade of the ninth century there were indications that the Danish raids could become more serious. In 841 East Anglia and Lindsey were ravaged, and c. 844 Rædwulf, king of Northumbria, was slain in battle by the Danes. Perhaps this was the conflict (c. 844) that the Frankish annals say was waged for three days. In 851 Beorhtwulf, king of Mercia, proved unable to protect London, and in 855 the Danes wintered for the first time in England on the island of Sheppey in the Thames. In 860, though it was subsequently defeated, a raiding party managed to storm Winchester. There is no evidence that the kings of Mercia or Wessex as yet felt any serious alarm. Æthelwulf's sons and successors, Æthelbald (858–60) and Æthelberht (860–5) do not appear to have taken the field against the Danes, though in 865 the men of Kent had to buy peace from the Vikings on Thanet. But during the years 865–74 the Danish attack acquired sufficient momentum and magnitude to transform the political map of England.

In 865 a great Danish army led by Ivar and Halfdene, reputed sons of Ragnar Lothbrok, a famous Viking warrior, arrived in East Anglia, possibly from the Seine where there had been fighting between Danes and Franks. We do not know the numerical strength of this army but we do know that the East Angles were sufficiently overawed by it to make immediate peace and to provide it with horses. From East Anglia the Danish army attacked Northumbria, and York was captured on 1 November 866. This was a most substantial achievement. Ragnar Lothbrok was said later in legend to have been previously put to death by Ælle, king of Northumbria. Ælle now united with his Northumbrian rival, Osberht, to expel Ragnar's sons, but on 21 March 867 both kings were slain when they attempted to recapture York, Ælle in a most barbaric manner by the sons of Ragnar. The kingdom of Northumbria had crumbled before a well-directed Danish army, and for a time the Danes even appointed puppet kings beyond the Tyne. In late 867 the Danes moved into Mercia and wintered at Nottingham. Mercia was still a strong kingdom. As recently as 865 the Mercians had successfully invaded Gwynedd and attacked Anglesey. Nevertheless, Burgred, king of Mercia, despite the aid of Æthelred, king of Wessex (865–71), and his brother Alfred, was now unable to dislodge the Danes from their fortress. The Mercians made peace and the Danes returned to York. In late 869 they moved into East Anglia, to winter quarters at Thetford, and slew Edmund, king of East Anglia, at or near Hoxne. Edmund is said to have been shot to death with arrows: he became one of the principal saints of the Anglo-Saxon Church.

The Danish leaders were now masters of much of eastern England and in a position to strike at Mercia or Wessex. Making a base at Reading in late 870, they defeated the army of Berkshire and repulsed Æthelred and Alfred. It was only when they advanced along the ridge of the Berkshire Downs in early 871 that Æthelred and Alfred were able to defeat them at Ashdown. But Ashdown proved only a temporary success. A fortnight later the West Saxons were defeated at Basing and two months later in April, at Easter, King Æthelred died, not impossibly from battle wounds. The very day that Alfred attended his brother's funeral at Wimborne, the Danes won another victory at Reading, and after prolonged conflict throughout the first year of his reign Alfred was forced to sue for peace. At London the Danes permitted the Mercians to make peace also, and returned to York to suppress rebellion in Northumbria. Secure again in Northumbria, they invaded Mercia and from a base at Repton in 874 expelled King Burgred. In his place, probably over west Mercia, they appointed a puppet king, Ceolwulf (II), who would govern Mercia for them and be prepared to serve the Danes if summoned. In the space of some eight years, three of the major kingdoms of the Heptarchy had been shattered. Any survey of the Danish wars in England which fails to attach very considerable weight to this central phenomenon will be incapable of placing the wars of Alfred with the Danes in a sound historical context.

In 874-5 the invincible Viking army divided. It was probably this division which saved Alfred and his kingdom of Wessex. Halfdene went to the Tyne, whence he ravaged Bernicia and even attacked Pictland and Strathclyde. The community of Lindisfarne, led by Bishop Eardwulf, fled in fear with the relics of St. Cuthbert, attempting at one point to sail to Ireland. In 876 Halfdene is said to have shared out the land of the Northumbrians, and the Danes proceeded to plough and to support themselves. The evidence suggests that this division of land only affected Deira, but it gives the measure of security the invaders had achieved in Northumbria as a whole. The other half of the army, led among others by a king, Guthrum, moved to Cambridge whence it aimed at the overthrow of the kingdom of Wessex.

Alfred the Great (871–99)

By 875 Alfred was the sole adult ruling representative of the Old English dynasties. He was also the youngest and the only surviving son of King Æthelwulf. At the time of his accession in 871 the sons of his older brother, Æthelred, were set aside because they were too young and there was no rule of primogeniture in Anglo-Saxon England. Alfred was about 23 at his accession, but since the age of 19 he had distinguished himself as his brother's right-hand man. At the battle of Ashdown, his eagerness for battle and his sense of generalship led him to attack the enemy while Æthelred was still hearing mass. Though a devout Christian himself, Alfred appreciated that heathen Danes would not wait for a Christian service. It is probable that he saw the Viking wars as a Divine scourge. As a soldier, Alfred was trained in a hard school. At Ashdown the Danes had the advantage of a hill-top position and the battle raged into the night. The scale of campaigns had assumed a magnitude unknown in the eighth century. In 876 the Danish army left Cambridge for Wareham in Dorset. Alfred made peace on condition the Danes left Wessex, but instead they moved to Exeter. Leaving Exeter in the summer of 877 they passed through Gloucester into Mercia, where they shared out the land, giving some to Ceolwulf (II). East Mercia seems to have been firmly retained in Danish hands, and by the early tenth century Lincoln, Nottingham, Derby, Stamford and Leicester, for example, had become important Danish army bases.

After Twelfth Night in 878, the Danes surprised the royal vill of Chippenham in Wessex, and the *Anglo-Saxon Chronicle* records that they occupied the land of the West Saxons, driving men across the sea and conquering others. The army can hardly have been strong enough to take over the whole of Wessex; but there is no doubt that Alfred was abandoned by many men, that one ealdorman, Wulfhere, made a traitorous pact with the Danes, and that the West Saxons submitted to the leaders of the Danish army. Alfred escaped, however, into the marshes of Somerset, and with the aid of the loyal Æthelnoth, ealdorman of Somerset, was able to make a fortified base on the Isle of Athelney the centre for incessant guerrilla warfare against the Danes at Chippenham. To this period in Alfred's life belongs the charming though later story of the burning of the cakes. From his hideout on Athelney Alfred was able so to co-ordinate the movements of the West Saxon armies from Somerset, Wiltshire and Hampshire that they all met with him on the same day in the seventh week after the Easter of 878 at Egbert's Stone. Egbert's Stone was west of the forest of Selwood, somewhere at the foot of the Wiltshire Downs, possibly in the neighbourhood of Kilmington Common. Within two days Alfred had led his regrouped forces along the downs as far as Edington where he encountered the Chippenham army under Guthrum. It may be that Alfred raced the Danes to Bratton Camp, an Iron Age fortress above Edington, but however the armies were positioned victory went to

Alfred who pursued the Danes and besieged them for a fortnight in Chippenham. The Danes promised that they would leave Wessex, and Guthrum that he would receive baptism. Three weeks later, with 30 of his leading men, Guthrum came to Alfred at Aller and there his baptism took place. He was given the name of Athelstan and stayed 12 days with Alfred, evidently at Wedmore. The Danish army did not withdraw immediately, but stayed a year (878-9) at Cirencester before returning to East Anglia where they shared out the land. In 881 part of Guthrum's army crossed to Gaul to join battle with the Franks.

Historians have generally seen the battle of Edington as probably the most important turning point in the wars between Saxon and Dane at this time, the victory by which Alfred saved the West Saxon kingdom and guaranteed the survival of a Christian Anglo-Saxon culture. We do not know, of course, precisely what would have happened in Wessex had Alfred perished. The measure of his achievement in the military sphere depends partly on the strength of opposing Danish forces. The conventional view that Alfred faced an enemy running into thousands has been challenged in recent years by the hypothesis that Danish armies should be reckoned rather in hundreds. The density of Scandinavian place-names in the Danelaw has been shown to be an uncertain basis for arguing the numerical strength of the Danish invasions for the ninth century. Not all such place-names, for example those ending in -by, necessarily go back to the ninth or even early tenth century. Viking ships and forts were small and it would be difficult in the ninth century to maintain a very large army in the field for long. But size and strength are relative quantities, and the Danish army of 865 was clearly well-nigh invincible. Alfred was probably fortunate in that this great army had split up before the invasion of Wessex in 877-8, and particularly in that he was on the fringes of Danish activity. Subject to raids and attacks he may have been, but a Danish army operating from a base at Chippenham was a long way from home. Guthrum settled in Suffolk and died in 890 at Hadleigh. In the 880s Alfred fought a series of petty skirmishes with this East Anglian army and captured London in 886, at which time he made a treaty with Guthrum acknowledging the frontiers of Danish territory to be along the Thames and the Lea, then in a straight line to Bedford, up the Ouse to Watling Street and along Watling Street. But even Guthrum's East Anglian settlements by no means represented the real core of the Danelaw, the territory of the Danes. Place-name evidence reveals that Suffolk was not a region of

15 The Chi-Rho page of the Lindisfarne Gospels (*B.M. Nero D.IV*)

16 David the Harpist and attendant musicians: eighth century
Canterbury Psalter (*B.M. Vesp. A.I*)

dense settlement, and that the heaviest concentration was certainly in Leicestershire, Nottinghamshire, particularly Lincolnshire, and Yorkshire. Probably the most powerful Danish king in England was Guthred of York (883-95), a Christian and possibly of part-Anglian descent from the King Ælle who was slain in 867. Guthred was in a position to control the major Danish settlements, and c. 886 he made an alliance with Anarawd, king of Gwynedd.

The defeat of the Danes in 878, however, was but the first step in Alfred's attempted restoration of Egbert's imperium. About 883 Æthelred, ealdorman of (west) Mercia, rose to power and showed himself a formidable warrior. He was the heir to a long tradition of Welsh-Mercian strife which had but recently flared in 878, when the Saxons slew Rhodri the Great of Gwynedd, and in 881 when the Welsh avenged this slaying. These border conflicts suggest that Mercian military strength was not nearly so non-existent during the early Danish wars as might be supposed. Æthelred was so great a menace to the princes of South Wales that to escape his depredations, and those of Anarawd, son of Rhodri the Great, the South Welsh rulers submitted to Alfred and sought his aid. This was probably between 883 and 886. In 886, having recaptured London, Alfred returned it to Mercia, that is to Æthelred to whom he also gave his daughter, Æthelflæd, in marriage. The *Anglo-Saxon Chronicle* records that at this point all the English people, including therefore the West Mercians, not under subjection to the Danes submitted to Alfred. Facing a ring of hostile or potentially hostile enemies, namely the Mercians, the South Welsh and the West Saxons, Anarawd of Gwynedd made his alliance with Guthred of York. This alliance gave Guthred a contact beyond west Mercia which opened up additional routes of contact with the Scandinavians of Ireland and Dublin, and it was an alliance from which he is said to have profited most. These two coalitions faced each other when the second Danish invasion during the reign of Alfred occurred in 892.

The invading Danish army, returning from Gaul under its leader Hæsten, struck at Kent and then sailed up the Thames to a base at Benfleet in Essex. Alfred was evidently in a sufficiently strong position to take oaths from the Northumbrian and East Anglian Danes that they would keep the peace, though as it happened these oaths were to no avail. Within his own kingdom Alfred so reorganised the army, ordered the construction of forts (a most unpopular measure because of the labour involved), and commissioned the building of ships twice as large as the Danish, that during these years the Danes were unable to make much headway in Wessex. Their attack, however, may have been more deliberately directed at west Mercia, against Æthelred. Though the *Anglo-Saxon Chronicle* naturally gives most information about West Saxon campaigns, the new invaders, with Northumbrian and East Anglian support, appear to have campaigned primarily between their East Saxon bases and the Mercian-Welsh border. The major battle of these years was fought against the Danes by the Mercians and West Saxons, led by Æthelred of Mercia and Æthelnoth of Somerset, at Buttington on the Severn (893). Whereas in the campaigns of 871–8 Alfred was very much a petty downland general seeking to protect his own territory and folk, in the years 892–9 his forces operated on a much wider scale and he, himself, engaged in far-flung diplomacy. Though the details of how he did it are lost, it is clear that he succeeded in breaking the alliance between North Welsh and Northumbrian Danes. In 894 Æthelnoth of Somerset actually went to York. It may be that Guthred's control of the Northumbrian Danes was weakening from 892 onwards, with the arrival of new leaders. In 893 a Northumbrian pirate, Sigeferth, harried the coast of Wessex, and a king Siefred (Sigeferth?) ruled at York after Guthred. Guthred may have felt it advisable to come to terms with Alfred. In 895 Guthred died; Northumbrian sources assert that the Northumbrians established peace with Alfred who was given the disposal of the Northumbrian kingdom. Any period of uncontested authority in the north on the part of Alfred must have been of short duration, for coin evidence reveals that King Siefred (Sigeferth?) reigned at York *c.* 895 and a king Cnut *c.* 897–900, but there is no evidence that these men were very formidable figures and in 900 the Danes at York were again without a king. There can be little question that Alfred succeeded in making his influence felt in the north. Faced with this striking West Saxon ascendancy, Anarawd of Gwynedd came to the court of Alfred and made his submission. The West Saxons may still have been engaged in conflict with the Danes when Alfred died in October 899, but the tide of victory had turned markedly in favour of the English.

And we must not get the warfare with the Danes out of perspective. The *Anglo-Saxon Chronicle* states that in 896 the English people (probably meaning in particular the West Saxons) were more afflicted by a mortality of cattle and men than by the Danish army. Such natural scourges would affect the Danes too. Behind the warrior host of heroic saga came the rank and file of the refugees from Scandinavia. The Danish armies included women and children, and shortage of food, with its attendant hazards of malnutrition and disease, must have been a constant problem. In 914, many Danes, in what was only a raiding party, died of hunger because they were driven off to the island of Steepholme and could not procure sufficient food.

The reconquest of the Danelaw

On the death of King Alfred (899) the security of Wessex was threatened immediately by a divided succession. Æthelwold, son of Æthelred I, Alfred's brother, opposed the succession of Edward, son of Alfred. He first led an unsuccessful revolt in Wessex and then fled to Northumbria where he was accepted as king by the Danes of York. Sailing south in 901 he received the submission of the East Saxons and in 902 won the allegiance of the Danish army of East Anglia. Mercia and north Wessex were harried in the course of 903. Edward collected an army and harried between the Cambridgeshire dykes and the river Ouse. When Edward returned home, the Kentish contingent lingered behind, and it was with this petty force that the Danes joined battle. Though the Danes gained the victory, however, Æthelwold was slain, and with him perished Eohric, Danish king of East Anglia. This victory no doubt placed Edward in a stronger bargaining position when he negotiated peace with the Northumbrian and East Anglian Danes at Tiddingford, near Leighton Buzzard, in 906, but as the *Chronicle* admits that it was from necessity that he came to terms it would seem that the revolt of Æthelwold had seriously weakened the authority of the king of Wessex.

In 909 Edward sent a raiding party into Danish territory, and in 910 the Northumbrian Danes responded by ravaging Mercia as far south as the Gloucestershire Avon. On their return home, they were intercepted by a combined West Saxon and Mercian army at Wednesfield (Staffordshire). In the subsequent battle, three Danish kings, evidently from Northumbria, were slain, which no doubt hastened the disintegration of the Danish kingdom of York. The death of Æthelred, ealdorman of Mercia, in the following year further strengthened Edward's position by enabling him to secure control of the Mercian lands of London and Oxford. From this point onwards, Edward, together with his sister Æthelflæd, who succeeded her late husband as ruler of the Mercians, embarked on the construction of a series of fortresses which were to change the character of the Danish wars. The Danes had always made great use of fortified bases, and it is clear from the records of Edward's reign that the Danish armies were concentrated at certain strategic and fortified centres, in particular Bedford, Cambridge, Huntingdon, Northampton, Leicester, Derby, Nottingham, Stamford and York. It remained for Edward and Æthelflæd to shatter this military network. Alfred had grasped the value of English fortresses by the 880s at the latest. These fortresses or *burhs* (later boroughs) were earthwork constructions with ditches and ramparts. Whenever possible the outlines of a prehistoric fortress would be used, as at Eddisbury (Cheshire). Though they later developed in the majority of instances into urban centres, and though they had nearly always been the sites of markets, their primary purpose in the early tenth century was defensive and military. Either Alfred, or Edward in the first years of his reign, constructed fortifications within Wessex at such places as Bath, Exeter, Wareham, Portchester, Wallingford, Cricklade and at Chichester in Sussex. Where possible old Roman walls were used, otherwise rectangular earthworks were constructed. Within a year of coming into possession of Oxford and London, Edward ordered the construction of fortresses at Hertford, one on the north and one on the south bank of the river Lea, and at Witham in Essex. Instant submissions followed in Essex. From his base at Hertford, Edward advanced to Buckingham in 914, spending four weeks there building a fortress, during which time he received the submission not only of Thurcetel, earl of the Danes at Bedford, but also that of many of the men of Northampton. In late 915 Edward advanced to Bedford, received the submission again of the Danes there and spent four weeks constructing a fortress of his own. The following year he built fortresses at Maldon, Towcester and *Wigingamere*.

Meanwhile, Æthelflæd had been far from idle in Mercia. The West Saxon annals in the *Chronicle* record nothing of her activities, but fortunately for the study of these years certain texts of the *Chronicle* have preserved a set of Mercian annals, known as the Mercian '*Register*'. From this source it is known that Æthelflæd fortified Chester in 907 and in 910 built a fortress at *Bremesbyrig*. In 912 she built *Scergeat*, and fortified the old and favoured Danish base at Bridgnorth on the Severn. In the following year Tamworth and Stafford were fortified, and in 914 Warwick and Eddisbury, in 915 Runcorn and Chirbury. In 917

Æthelflæd was able to capture Derby, almost certainly because the Danes of Derby were away on a campaign with the armies of Leicester and Northampton against the forts of Edward. It was in the fighting of 917 that the work of Edward was put successfully to the test. Though the combined Danish armies attacked Towcester on Watling Street, they were unable to capture it. A second army from Huntingdon, having abandoned Huntingdon and moved south to Tempsford whence it could better attack Edward, joined with the East Anglian army and besieged Bedford, again without success. Edward retaliated by attacking Tempsford with what was described as an immense host and not only captured the base but slew the king of East Anglia. While a Danish army failed to capture Maldon, a second English force took Colchester. From this point Edward entered into a triumphal progress. While supervising the construction of a stone wall at Towcester, he received the submission of Thurferth, probably earl of the Danes at Leicester; in 918 Æthelflæd peacefully obtained possession of Leicester. The leaders of the army from Northampton also submitted to Edward. The king advanced to take Huntingdon, receiving the submission of the Danes there, while at Colchester he received the submission of the men of Essex and East Anglia, followed in the same year by those of Cambridge. Moving into the more northerly Danish territories in 918, he made himself master of the Danish strongholds at Stamford and Nottingham. The death of Æthelflæd in the same year, shortly after she had received the submission of the men of York, left Edward in command of Mercia and secured his authority over the whole of England south of the Humber. Not content with this alone, he protected his left flank by receiving the submission of the rulers of North and South Wales. Æthelflæd is known to have attacked the kingdom of Brecknock in South Wales in 916, and between them Edward and his sister were evidently able to preserve their father's influence in these Welsh regions.

It is fortunate that the *Anglo-Saxon Chronicle* preserves so detailed an account of the systematic way in which Edward and Æthelflæd carried out their assault on the Danish territories over this period of some eight years. There can be no question that they both displayed a high standard of generalship, and that the construction of opposing English fortresses was an essential, if not the essential, cause of the Danish collapse. By 917 a long line of forts, stretching from north Cheshire to Essex, formed a defence against Danish bases, blocking important routes, harassing communications, launching raiding parties and providing jumping-off points for more extended campaigns.

Edward's military offensive was now to be primarily directed north of the Mersey-Humber line. The subjection of the northern Scandinavian territories proved particularly arduous for the West Saxon dynasty. It is clear from the evidence of place-names that in the early tenth century Norsemen, as opposed to Danes, were crossing from Ireland and the Norse kingdom of Dublin in large numbers and flooding into Cumberland, Westmorland and Lancashire. Pushing eastwards across the Pennines into the North and West Ridings of Yorkshire they turned the north into chaos and may well have deflected the attention of the Northumbrian Danes from the attack of Edward and Æthelflæd on the Danelaw. In 914 what was probably a Norse raiding party, having crossed from Brittany and ravaged south Mercia, was repelled by the men of Hereford and Gloucester and sailed away to Ireland. There is no doubt, however, that it was Northumbria which felt the real force of the Irish-Norse movements, and Æthelflæd's fortresses at Chester, Eddisbury and Runcorn were intended to protect the north Mercian frontier. In 914 a Norse Viking, Rægnald, attacked Northumbria and made himself king of York by 919. That year Edward fortified Thelwall on the Mersey and sent a force into Northumbrian territory to repair and man the fortress of Manchester. In 920 he constructed a second fortress at Nottingham, on the south side of the river, and built that at Bakewell in the Peak District. Though this year witnessed the destruction of Davenport in Cheshire by Rægnald's cousin, Sihtric, it also saw the acknowledgement of Edward's overlordship by a galaxy of northern potentates. At Bakewell there submitted to Edward all who dwelt in Northumbria—English, Danes and Norse—led by Rægnald, king of York and Ealdred, earl of Bamburgh, and in addition the king of Strathclyde and Constantine II, king of the Scots. Ealdred represented a line of Bernician aristocrats who had made themselves masters at Bamburgh and who resisted the attacks of Danes and Norse to the south and Scots to the north. It is probable that the kings of the Strathclyde Britons and of the Scots, and Ealdred himself, had much to gain in seeking an ally against the Scandinavians in the victorious king of Wessex, even if this meant an acceptance of Edward as suzerain. By coming to terms himself, Rægnald avoided attack by this coalition and secured possession of York, where Edward was evidently prepared to leave him. When Edward the Elder died in 924, therefore, he had attained a position of pre-eminence un-equalled by any previous king in England.

Edward's last days were clouded by a revolt in Mercia, centred on Chester, which he had just suppressed when he died. West Saxon rule may have been unpopular at first in Mercia, but the accession of Edward's son, Athelstan (924–39), brought up in Mercia by Æthel-flæd and first acclaimed king there, temporarily healed the breach. Athelstan was one of the mightiest of West Saxon kings but, in contrast to the records of Edward's reign, those of his are so slight that it is not possible to describe Athelstan's actions in detail. He began by marrying his sister in 925 to Rægnald's cousin and successor at York, Sihtric. When Sihtric died in 927, Athelstan invaded Northumbria, captured York and drove out Sihtric's son, Olaf, king of York, and Olaf's uncle, Guthfrith, king of Dublin. Guthfrith found refuge among the Scots who, following the conquest of Northumbria by Athelstan, appear to have seen the greatest threat to their security as coming from the West Saxons. Athelstan demanded that Guthfrith be handed over to him, and, though Guthfrith himself escaped, Athelstan received recognition of his overlordship from Constantine, king of the Scots, Owen the Bald, king of Strathclyde, Hywel the Good, king of Dyfed and Ealdred of Bamburgh at Eamont, near Penrith (927). Athelstan went on to confirm his lordship over the Welsh princes at a meeting at Hereford, when he imposed an annual tribute. At about the same time he expelled the Cornish Britons from Exeter, confining them west of the Tamar, and it is at this point that the succession of Cornish kings appears to cease. When Constantine broke the treaty of 924, Athelstan was able to imple-ment his authority to the extent of taking Welsh princes with him on campaign against the king of the Scots in 934. This campaign gives some indication of the military strength of the West Saxon king, for Athelstan's land army advanced probably as far as the great natural fortress of Dunnottar while the English fleet ravaged Caithness. Caith-ness, by this date, was more Scandinavian than Pictish or Scottish. The far-flung campaign of 934 provoked the organisation, by the king of the Scots, of what was perhaps the greatest coalition which ever opposed a king of Wessex. Constantine directed an alliance which not only em-braced the Scots and the Strathclyde Britons but also the naval and military resources of Dublin, led by Olaf, son of Guthfrith and by now king of Dublin, and Olaf, son of Sihtric, by now Constantine's son-in-law, with reinforcements from Limerick and the western isles of Scotland.

Constantine probably desired to annex Bernicia to his own kingdom and the Scandinavians must have sought the reconquest of York for the Dublin princes. It is one of the misfortunes of Anglo-Saxon military history that the movements of the opposing forces cannot be traced. A tradition survived that the Scottish and Norse army sailed into the Humber, but the actual battle-site, though it is known by the two ancient names of *Wendun* and *Brunanburh*, and possibly also by that of *Vinheath*, cannot be positively identified. Athelstan and his 15-year-old brother, Edmund, defeated their assailants with heavy losses on both sides in what must have been a titanic struggle. The compiler of the *Anglo-Saxon Chronicle* included an epic poem on the battle for the year 937, while the Irish annals describe the conflict as lamentable, terrible and savage. Five kings perished, among them a son of King Constantine. It left no doubt of Athelstan's supremacy.

From Alfred's victory at Edington to Athelstan's at *Brunanburh* (878–937), though there had been occasional setbacks, the West Saxon kings had steadily and seemingly remorselessly asserted their influence in and authority over the Celtic and Scandinavian regions of Britain. Though in practice this may at times have meant little more than a formal recognition of their pre-eminent position, not only was tribute exacted in the case of Wales but all the Scandinavian settlers in England had been deprived of their own rulers and compelled to accept the king of Wessex as lord. It is hardly surprising that even before *Brunanburh* Athelstan could describe himself as 'most glorious king of the Anglo-Saxons and Danes', 'king of the English, elevated by . . . the Almighty . . . to the throne of Britain', and 'emperor' (*i.e. bretwalda*). Athelstan was accustomed to holding great assemblies of lay and ecclesiastical potentates from north and south at which subject princes were sometimes to be found. It was at such assemblies that he invoked these grand titles.

Athelstan died prematurely in 939. His brother and successor, Edmund (939–46), was only 18 at his accession. Though an experienced fighter, as Alfred at his accession had been, Edmund faced an immediate Northumbrian revolt, supported by Wulfstan, archbishop of York, which placed Olaf, son of Guthfrith, over both the Norse kingdom of York and the five Danish army bases of the east midlands—Leicester, Lincoln, Nottingham, Derby and Stamford—known by now as the Five Boroughs. With this revolt Edmund proved unable to cope. Olaf died in 941 to be succeeded by Olaf, son of Sihtric. It was not until 942

that Edmund was in a position to overrun Mercia and recover the Five
Boroughs, chasing Olaf and Wulfstan out of Leicester and capturing
also Tamworth. Olaf came to terms with Edmund who stood sponsor
at his baptism in 943. Later in the year Edmund stood sponsor at the
baptism of Rægnald, son of Guthfrith, who seems to have been sharing
the northern kingship with Olaf. When Archbishop Wulfstan changed
sides the next year, Edmund was able to invade Northumbria, driving
the two Norse kings out of York, but the position in the north remained
so unsettled that in 945 Edmund found it advisable to grant Cumbria,
in this case probably the land south of the Solway (Cumberland and
Westmorland), to Malcolm I, king of the Scots, on condition that
Malcolm became his helper by land and sea. Edmund was slain by a
common criminal in 946 and his brother, Eadred (946–55), succeeded.
Though king of Wessex, however, it was necessary for Eadred to
secure separate recognition from the Northumbrians at Tanshelf in
947. Even so, in 948 the Northumbrians, with the renewed support of
Archbishop Wulfstan, accepted Eric 'Bloodaxe', pagan son of Harold
Fairhair, as king at York. Eadred invaded Northumbria, and in the
course of his attack Ripon minster was burnt down. On the way home,
Eadred's army was surprised at the difficult river crossing at Castleford
by an army from York and destroyed. Though Eadred threatened
vengeance and though the Northumbrians abandoned Eric and paid
compensation, the next year Olaf, son of Sihtric, became king again at
York. Eadred captured Wulfstan in 952 and imprisoned him, and the
same year the Northumbrians expelled Olaf and accepted Eric for a
second time. It was only when Oswulf, earl of Bamburgh, betrayed Eric
to Maccus, son of Olaf (probably one of the Norse kings of York of that
name), and Eric was slain on Stainmoor, that Eadred was able to secure
recognition as king over Northumbria in 954. Eadred rewarded Oswulf
with the earldom of all Northumbria and felt secure enough to re-
instate Archbishop Wulfstan. It is not easy to account for these
Northumbrian vacillations, but there was clearly a complex political
ferment in the north, among Angles, Danes and Norse; and the internal
rivalry of political and dynastic factions was played out against a background of hostility to West Saxon overlordship. For 10 out of 14 years
in the period 940–54 Scandinavian kings reigned at York, hostile to the
kings of Wessex. This cannot but have broken West Saxon influence in
the north at a crucial moment when the West Saxon dynasty should

have been integrating Northumbria into an Anglo-Danish state dominated by Wessex.

Eadred spent the last years of his life a chronically sick man. When he died at an early age in 955, Edwy or Eadwig, son of Edmund, was accepted as king of Wessex, to be opposed in 957 by his younger brother, Edgar, in Mercia. Both princes were young—Edgar was 13 in 957—and pawns in the rivalry of opposing parties and royal factions, with dissension serving only to weaken the influence of the West Saxon monarchy. After he became king in Wessex following Eadwig's death (959), Edgar took steps to reassert the authority of his tenth-century predecessors. He is known to have ravaged Glamorgan, and is said to have possessed a vast fleet which annually patrolled the waters around the British Isles. Because of the brevity of the *Chronicle* for his reign, however, the details of his ascendancy cannot be traced, so that his measure of success is difficult to define. After a grand ceremonial coronation at Bath in 973, Edgar received at Chester a pledge of help by land and sea from some six kings, including Kenneth II, king of the Scots, Donald, king probably of the Britons of Strathclyde, a Scottish prince—Malcolm of Cumbria, and Iago, king of Gwynedd. These kings are said to have rowed Edgar on the Dee, which is generally construed as an acknowledgement of his overlordship; but it may be that, although according to him a position of primacy, they did not so much submit to Edgar as enter into an alliance with him to protect the peace of the British Isles as a whole. The Scandinavian attack was in temporary abeyance during these years and there cannot have been the same pressures on these rulers to submit to Edgar as there had been on those who earlier had acknowledged the suzerainty of Edward and Athelstan. Kenneth II was much stronger than Constantine had been, and Edgar actually ceded part of Lothian to him. The fact that the Scottish rulers appear to have done homage to the king of Wessex for Cumbrian and Lothian lands did not materially affect the balance of power. And whatever degree of personal pre-eminence Edgar achieved, it was the internal English situation which was to be crucial. Edgar was able to divide Northumbria again in 966 by re-creating a separate Deira, but he could not really check the growth of the over-mighty ealdorman in the great territorial units of Northumbria, East Anglia and Mercia. Edgar assumed responsibility in southern England for merchants from York, but for any systematic administration of more northerly regions by West Saxon officials—in the same way, for example, as Oswiu of Northumbria had ruled Mercia for a time—there is no evidence. On the contrary, Edgar had to make concessions to regional differences, acknowledging the existence of a separate body of legal custom amongst Scandinavian settlers. It is unlikely that any alternative course of action would have been practical, and the struggle with the Danes must have been an exhausting one for the West Saxon monarchy. Edgar, of course, cannot have known the reign of his son, Æthelred II (978–1016), would witness not only a renewed Scandinavian attack but also the conquest of England and Wessex by the Danish kings, Swein and his son Cnut. Nevertheless, the collapse of England under Æthelred cannot be entirely explicable without a fair measure of responsibility for military and administrative oversights on the part of the successors of Athelstan. The final break-up of the Norse kingdom of York in 954 is sometimes looked upon as an important turning point in English history; but in that Swein and Cnut were able to secure the allegiance of the Danelaw with the ease of an Olaf or an Eric, it is clear that there was no subsequent transformation on any scale of the confused and restless situation in north England.

The English Church and the tenth-century Monastic Revival

The English bishops and their pastoral cares

There can be no doubt that the Viking invasions did disrupt ecclesiastical organisation in the areas most affected by the attack. The records are so imperfect for much of eastern England that the fate of the East Anglian Church is completely unknown. The line of bishops ceased altogether at Dunwich and the see of North Elmham is not known to have been revived before 956; prior to this revival it is possible that the diocese was administered by the bishops of London from a centre at Hoxne in Suffolk. The bishop of Leicester in the 870s seems to have fled to Dorchester-on-Thames, but there is no evidence for a continuous succession of bishops at Dorchester-on-Thames before *c.* 909 and the authority of the tenth-century bishops is unlikely to have extended far into the Five Boroughs (which included Leicester) before the mid-950s. Oscetel, bishop of Dorchester, from *c.* 951 to 956, when he became archbishop of York, was of Danish extraction, however, and a bishop, Leofwine, of a revived see of Lindsey can be traced back to 953. In 956 Leofwine became bishop of Dorchester. This was following the final submission of the northern regions to Eadred, king of Wessex, and Leofwine's diocese evidently embraced Lindsey and Leicester. It may be that the formal amalgamation of these several dioceses in one belongs to the reign of Edgar in Mercia (957-9).

More is known of the Church in Northumbria than of the Church in the eastern Danelaw, due to the survival of Symeon of Durham's *History of the Church of Durham*, put together 1104-9 and using older traditions; but by contrast almost nothing is known of the church of York in the ninth and tenth centuries. For seven years (865-72) Wulfhere, archbishop of York, lived in virtual hiding at Addingham in

Wharfedale. In 875 the community of Lindisfarne abandoned their island bishopric to wander round Northumbria with the relics of St. Cuthbert for seven years (875–82), straying even into the vicinity of Whithorn in an unsuccessful attempt to cross to Ireland. When they eventually returned to Northumbria they settled not at Lindisfarne but, with the permission of Guthred, Danish king of York, at Chester-le-Street and it was from Chester-le-Street that they moved in 990 (with the support of Earl Uhtred) to the more defensible position of Durham. The community of St. Cuthbert was fortunate. The bishopric and community at Hexham ceased to exist in the second half of the ninth century, and by the tenth century the bishopric and community of Whithorn also. The absence of detailed information prevents a proper study of this process of disintegration. The ravages of war undoubtedly took their toll. In 947 it was the army of Eadred, king of Wessex, which burnt Ripon minster. Attempts were made to revive religious life at such centres as Ripon and Hexham as the tenth century proceeded, but there had clearly been a serious breakdown which was not easily remedied. The kingdom of Northumbria was probably the first to attempt diocesan reorganisation. King Athelstan placed the district of Nottingham under the control of the archbishops of York, and during his reign (924–39) bishops of unknown sees make an appearance, who may in many instances have been from Northumbria. It is apparent from the innumerable bishops of unknown sees who witness tenth-century charters that our knowledge of the Anglo-Saxon episcopate in this period is far from complete. In the case of those unknown bishops who seem to be of Northumbrian origin, there is no evidence that they were followed by a regular succession; it may be that the revival of old or the creation of new sees in Northumbria proved to be impracticable, as it did in some instances in Wessex.

The process of diocesan reorganisation began in Wessex in the reign of Edward the Elder. In c. 909 new bishoprics were created at Ramsbury (for Wiltshire), Wells (for Somerset), and Crediton (for Devon and Cornwall). For a time in the early tenth century Berkshire may have had its own bishopric at Sonning, but otherwise Berkshire was attached to the diocese of Ramsbury. Small dioceses proved economically weak. In the eleventh century, Herman, bishop of poverty-stricken Ramsbury, sought to move to Malmesbury without success, though he did succeed in uniting Ramsbury and Sherborne at Sherborne in 1058. King Athelstan created a separate diocese for Cornwall in 926 at St. Germans, but in 1050 Leofric, bishop of Crediton, reunited St. Germans and Crediton in a new diocese centred at Exeter. Even before the Norman Conquest, therefore, certain bishops felt that their bishoprics were sited unsatisfactorily. Herman continued to be dissatisfied with Sherborne and planned to move to Old Sarum, a move which was effectively carried through by his Norman successor, Osmund. The Normans objected in several instances to the placing of bishoprics in mere villages. Consequently, the bishopric of Dorchester was transferred to Lincoln, that of North Elmham to Thetford and then to Norwich, that of Selsey to Chichester, that of Wells to Bath, and that of Lichfield first to Chester and then to Coventry. This shifting of bishoprics did not seriously modify the diocesan framework which had been established before the Norman Conquest, and between the changes outlined above and the Henrican Reformation only two new sees were created in England, at Carlisle and Ely.

It is the development of these dioceses which provides the continuous basis for the study of the Anglo-Saxon Church. The history of each individual bishopric might not be known in detail, and there exist no episcopal registers or parish records for the pre-Conquest Church; but the bishop's see was the geographical and administrative focal point within the diocese, around which the life of the diocese revolved to a greater or lesser extent. It is in the nature of Anglo-Saxon historical records, most of which were written in monasteries and not in busy episcopal writing offices, that most of our information relates to the monasteries. But monastic sources generally deal with affairs of only local importance, for it was not the monasteries, however rich and influential, which directed the daily administration of the diocese. To the bishop and his staff fell the responsibility of supervising the religious life of the whole diocese, in all its aspects.

In the 890s Pope Formosus wrote to the English bishops reproaching them for not having converted the Danes more speedily. Very little is known, in fact, of the progress of conversion within the Danelaw. The Church in Northumbria found an evidently Christian Danish king, possibly of Anglian descent, in Guthred of York, who died in 895 and was buried in York minster. In East Anglia, Guthrum, who died in 890, was at least a nominal Christian. Pagan Danes and Norse, however, worshipping Othin and Thor, were continuously arriving on English shores in the first half of the tenth century, and this must have protracted the work of conversion. The pagan followers of Rægnald, king of York, c. 920, scoffed at Cuthheard, bishop of Chester-le-Street, and seized Church lands; and, though in 924 Athelstan demanded the abandonment of paganism from subject Danes, it is clear that most of the Scandinavian kings of York down to 954 were pagans. An epic poem was composed on the orders of the widow of Eric Bloodaxe, describing how Eric was received into Valhalla with his slain host by Othin. The laws of the later kings of Wessex provide clear evidence for what must have been fairly widespread pagan beliefs among the settlers in the Danelaw down to the eleventh century. Roseberry Topping, in the North Riding of Yorkshire, was originally Othin's Hill. A veneer of Christianity could obscure but not conceal the continuing vitality of ancient pagan practices and beliefs.

It is the diocesan legislation of the late tenth and early eleventh centuries which illuminates for the historian the broad outlines of diocesan work in this period. Basically, the problems facing a bishop in his diocese were still the same as in the eighth century. The battle against continuing pagan practices was still being waged, waged with greater intensity as a consequence of the Scandinavian invasions, but not so much through the dramatic missions of the seventh century as through the unceasing routine of parochial activity. It was probably the late Old English period which witnessed the evolution of that parish system which has remained an essential feature of the Church in England. The parish system was present in England by the twelfth century and, though its origins are obscure, several factors appear to have contributed towards its growth in the Anglo-Saxon period. From an early date, the bishop in the head-minster or cathedral assigned priests to specific areas, sending them out from a dependent minster or monastery. While some minsters may have been monasteries, they were primarily administrative centres. The names of such centres survive in places like Beaminster, Axminster, Warminster and Ilminster. In time the areas they served would tend to become fragmented as still more dependent churches were founded, and the local lords who founded churches for their own convenience on their estates would accelerate this process of fragmentation. Many parish churches by the time of the Norman Conquest were controlled by a lord, sometimes the king, very often a nobleman. This is what is known as lay patronage. The lord appointed the priest to his church. The parish priest, for his part, had a primary administrative responsibility to collect the church taxes from his parish. From the earliest times the Church had been supported by several taxes, church *scot* (offering), soul-*scot*, and plough-alms, paid in kind. It was not until the reign of Edgar (959–75) that the payment of tithes or a tenth of income to the Church was made compulsory with penalties for non-payment. Part of the tithes went to the minster, part to the lord and part to the parish church itself. It may well have been the exaction of tithes which stimulated the growth of the parochial system in the tenth century. This parochial system rapidly became an essential element in the organisation of the English Church, not simply as a financial organ but also as a pastoral. Churches were classed as head-minsters (cathedrals), ordinary minsters, lesser minsters (parish churches) and field chapels, probably to facilitate diocesan administration and the more effective application of reform principles. Over the priests of the lesser minsters the bishops generally kept a watchful eye. The canons of the Anglo-Saxon Church of the late tenth century and early eleventh, closely modelled in content on continental canonical collections, show that there was a great deal in the parish which did require constant supervision. Priests were to possess at ordination a mass-book, a Gospel-book, an epistle-book, a psalter, a pastoral book, a reading book and a penitential. They had to be celibate and were to sing regularly the canonical hours. On Sundays, the mass-priest had to explain the Gospel in English and, as often as he could, the Creed and the Lord's Prayer. He had not to neglect the baptism and education of children, nor the shriving of sinners, and holy oil always had to be ready for the sick. Mass vestments had to be clean and in good condition, and the altar cloth similarly. A priest was forbidden to get drunk, to frequent taverns, or to carry weapons. He was advised to learn a handicraft. Priests were liable to fines if they omitted to perform the necessary services of the Church, or if they fought and behaved generally in a drunken, dissolute manner. It is not known how effective such injunctions were. Married clergy survived down to the Norman Conquest and beyond. Nevertheless, it is difficult to believe that the activity implied by the scale of such legislation was not matched by equal assiduity in enforcing what had been decreed.

The bishops were always being urged to visit their dioceses, and an Anglo-Saxon prelate must have been regularly engaged in visiting tours if he were to perform his duties diligently. Oda, archbishop of Canterbury in the reign of Edmund I, instructed his bishops to go on annual diocesan visitations. Pastoral care was very much a matter of deep concern in the Old English Church. Ælfric of Eynsham, for

17 New Minster Charter: King Edgar offering the charter
to Our Lord (*B.M. Vesp. A.VIII*)

18, 19 Embroidered vestments from
the tomb of St. Cuthbert,
tenth century

20 St. Cuthbert's Pectoral Cross,
seventh century

example, wrote a letter of pastoral advice to Wulfsige, bishop of Sherborne, c. 994, urging him to stand firm against secular attacks, while the *Institutes of Polity*, probably to be ascribed to Wulfstan II, archbishop of York (1002–23), state that a bishop must be a good man, wise and prudent in instructing his flock, and in upholding righteousness and justice.

Bishops in England were sometimes assisted in their diocesan labours by *chorepiscopi* or assistant bishops. Though unpopular with ninth-century papal reformers on the Continent, *chorepiscopi* survived in England until the Norman Conquest. There was a succession of such bishops at the church of St. Martin's, Canterbury, assistants of the archbishop of Canterbury, at least until 1016. They must have been an obvious help in the conditions of the Anglo-Saxon Church. In addition, from the earliest times, bishops were aided by deacons, that is by men who took initial Orders in the Church but who did not proceed to the priesthood. They devoted themselves rather to the administration and legal affairs of the diocese. James the Deacon had assisted the missionary bishop, Paulinus. By the tenth century in England the head deacon or archdeacon was appearing as the bishop's right-hand man. In the diocese of Canterbury, where the archbishop's commitments must have been very heavy, a multiplicity of archdeacons occurs by the ninth century. Wulfred, archbishop of Canterbury (805–32), had himself been an archdeacon. By the eleventh century the archbishop of York had at least one archdeacon, probably more. It was to the archdeacon that the parish priest was made immediately responsible, and it was the archdeacon's duty to visit the parish churches and assure himself of their efficient running. In so far, however, as the number of archdeacons probably remained small, by contrast with the Continent, it cannot be said that there is evidence for really significant advance in the organisation of diocesan administration in England before 1066.

William of Malmesbury's *Life* of Wulfstan, bishop of Worcester (1062–95), based on an earlier *Life* by a contemporary, depicts Wulfstan as exemplifying the ideal pious, rather ascetic bishop of the Anglo-Saxon Church, preoccupied with simple pastoral cares and devotional exercises. Down to 1042 almost all the English bishops were native born, and the great majority had taken monastic vows and lived in monastic communities before their election. In this they contrasted with the normal diocesan of west Europe at that time, and so powerful an element was monasticism in the Old English Church that between 960 and 1066 considerably more than half the English bishops certainly, and possibly as many as three-quarters or more, were monks. Wulfstan, bishop of Worcester, had been a monk of Evesham and Peterborough and abbot of Pershore before succeeding to the see of Worcester. This cannot but have lent a strain of asceticism to the Old English episcopate, giving it a character quite different from anything on the Continent and suffusing it with a spirit possibly still closer to that of the Celtic Church than to that of France or Germany. Particularly between 1042 and the mid-1050s, however, and again after the Norman Conquest, the bishops of Wulfstan's type were tending to be replaced by men trained in the king's household as royal clerks. It may be that the interest of such bishops in reforming the communities of cathedral canons in the last years of the Old English state was stimulated by the papal exhortation to all clergy to lead a regular and canonical life at the great reform council of Rheims in 1049. Bishop Duduc of Wells attended this council and in 1050 Ealdred, then bishop of Worcester (subsequently of York), and Herman, bishop of Ramsbury, were at Rome. Edward the Confessor ordered that whatever was done or said at Rheims should be written in English and a copy kept in the royal treasury. In general, however, the papal reform movement of the mid-eleventh century seems to have come too late to have any direct or considerable influence on the Old English episcopate. The few continentals from Lotharingia who were appointed to English bishoprics in the reign of Edward the Confessor—Herman of Ramsbury, Giso of Wells, and Leofric of Exeter who, though probably a Cornishman, had been educated in Lotharingia—appear to have found themselves a little out of sympathy with the slower tempo of English Church life and largely obstructed in their reforming aspirations by it. Nevertheless, it was not so much that the Old English Church needed reform, though unquestionably, in common with the whole of west Europe, there must have been areas of Church life which did need reform or development; it was partly that two different conceptions of the episcopal office and the form that diocesan administration should take were coming into conflict, one essentially monastic, devotional and pastoral, the other rather more sensitive to the administrative responsibilities of office, more practical in its outlook, on the whole possessed of a deeper familiarity with the ways of the secular world.

The communities of canons in the Old English Church

In the seventh and eighth centuries a great number of monastic houses, both large and small, flourished in Anglo-Saxon England. It is clear, however, that many communities describing themselves as monastic were not monastic at all but communities of clerks or priests. The distinction is that, whereas the members of a monastic community lived according to a specifically monastic rule, having no personal possessions and following a life of devotion and contemplation, communities of priests—or, as they became known, of canons—lived together but worked in and spent much of their time in the world and were supported individually by a prebend, a portion of the revenue of the minster to which they were attached. The tenth century, following a period of apparent monastic decline, witnessed a great revival of monastic fervour in England, severely critical of canonical communities. As it was in the monastic houses that virtually all the historical writing of the time was undertaken, the Church in England in the tenth century is seen almost entirely through monastic eyes and very little is known of the canonical communities of the same period. So far as diocesan administration is concerned, however, it is the communities of canons, not the monasteries, which had a continuing importance, experiencing towards the end of the Anglo-Saxon period their own reform and revival.

While there is no doubt as to the great administrative importance of communities of canons, we can state little in detail concerning their activities. The seventh century seems to have seen small distinction between monks and canons, and, though canons appear more clearly in the records of the eighth century, it remained possible for a community itself to be uncertain whether it was monastic or canonical. At Christ Church, Canterbury, and at Crediton, for example, quasi-monastic communities appear to have embraced both monks and canons, and such a state of affairs was probably not uncommon. It was communities of canons which served the great cathedrals on the Continent and probably, by the eighth century, the greater and lesser minsters of England. Such groups of canons were regarded as members of the bishop's family and they organised the work of the Church at a local level throughout the diocese, detaching one of their members every so often to work in an evolving parish. And, just as other elements in the life of the Church needed periodic reform, so did these communities of canons. There was a recurring tendency to laxity in discipline, to marriage and the actual holding of property and houses by individuals. In c. 755 Chrodegang, archbishop of Metz, imposed a stricter rule of life, based on that of St. Benedict, on the clergy of his cathedral, and the great council at Aachen in 817 sought to impose Chrodegang's rule on all clergy whether living in a community of canons or not. In the legatine council of 786, held in England, all canons were ordered to live canonically, that is, according to the prescribed rule of life for such communities. In the early ninth century, Wulfred, archbishop of Canterbury (805–32), though he did not altogether suppress the holding of individual houses, imposed the rule of Chrodegang on the clergy of Christ Church and built for them a dormitory and refectory.

The early tenth-century kings of Wessex were not unfavourable to canonical or quasi-monastic communities. The community of New Minster, Winchester, founded by Edward the Elder but planned by Alfred, was probably from its very beginning composed more of canons than monks. King Athelstan gave Abingdon, evidently a clerical community, to a priest, Godescalc, probably from Germany, and in 944 Edmund gave Bath to refugee clerks from the monastery of St. Bertin in Flanders, fleeing from monastic reform. It was claimed by later monastic writers that Edmund introduced clerks into Evesham and Eadwig clerks into Malmesbury. Clerks were to be found at many religious centres otherwise known as monasteries, but it is probable that some at least of such communities were canonical rather than monastic from their creation—for example, the early community of St. Andrew at Rochester, founded by Æthelberht of Kent, and that of St. Albans, founded by King Offa.

It cannot be over-emphasised that, although overshadowed by the great reformed monastic houses of the tenth century, canonical communities remained an essential part of Church life in England throughout the Anglo-Saxon period. King Æthelred, c. 1008, ordered canons, whether their endowments enabled them to have a refectory and dormitory or not, to maintain celibacy and a regular canonical life in their foundation or risk losing their prebends. At about the same time he urged canons as well as monks to return to the proper discharge of their duties and to live according to their rule, an injunction reiterated by Cnut. Not all canons measured up to the desired standard. The best glimpse of an Anglo-Saxon community of canons is provided by Symeon of Durham's account of the episcopal church of Durham, though this account was written in the early years of the twelfth century by one who was a Benedictine monk and at a time when memories of the pre-Conquest community were probably growing a little dim. The clergy of St. Cuthbert were usually married men, claiming descent from members of the ninth-century community, living in their own houses and possessing hereditary estates but maintaining a monastic type of service in the church of Durham. Though their way of life would not commend itself to the reformers of the tenth or eleventh centuries, they appear to have maintained quite a high standard in pastoral work. Bishop Ealdhun, who founded the see of St. Cuthbert at Durham in 990, was highly thought of by the inhabitants of Durham and an account of his merits was handed down from father to son. His successor in the reign of Cnut, Edmund, was similarly remembered, as a man who never gave occasion for evil surmise in the whole of his life and who was energetic in the management of the church. It was said that Eardwulf, bishop at the time of the founding of the see at Chester-le-Street in 883, bestowed as much pastoral care on the remote districts of the diocese as upon the immediate vicinity of his bishopric. Bishop Ealdhun was so heartbroken at the destruction of so many of his flock at the battle of Carham (1018) that he died soon after, as was his earnest desire. At Durham, certainly by the eleventh century, a school was maintained for the education of clerks, a keen interest was taken in the relics of Northumbrian saints and consequently in the *Lives* of the saints, and an almost continuous tradition of historical writing was maintained. The devotion of the community to their patron saint, Cuthbert, was such that Cuthbert's reputation spread even to Winchester and Sherborne. By tradition, all the bishops of St. Cuthbert took monastic vows at their election. After the death of Ealdhun, no priest was willing to assume monastic orders; the canons, who appear as sensible and level-headed men concerned with the interests of the church, finally elected Edmund, a priest, and Edmund accepted office after prolonged heart-searching. He sought advice and guidance on the monastic life from Æthelric, a monk of Peterborough. Æthelric became bishop in 1042 but, probably because he was from a reformed Benedictine community, proved extremely unpopular with many of the clergy and resigned in 1056 to return to Peterborough. His brother and episcopal successor, Æthelwine, was equally disliked. Though charges of avarice and peculation were made, their basic unpopularity no doubt derived from an attempt to carry the clergy over to a more thorough-going monasticism. It is very likely that the community of St. Cuthbert had its ecclesiastical short-comings, but, on the whole, the impression conveyed by the pages of Symeon is a favourable one. Durham, however, probably compared well on the eve of the Norman Conquest with the more impoverished and more imperfectly organised chapters of cathedral canons at Selsey, Rochester, Ramsbury and Lichfield.

The community of St. Cuthbert experienced no reform along canonical lines until after the Norman Conquest when Walcher, a secular clerk of Lorraine and appointed bishop of Durham in 1071, instructed the clerks at Durham to adopt canonical usage in their daily and nightly offices, and to refrain from imitating monastic customs in these matters. Certain other communities of cathedral canons experienced reform a shade earlier, probably across the very years of Conquest. Ælfric, archbishop of York (1023–51), had founded a community of clergy following a regular canonical life at the ancient minster of Beverley; and Ealdred, archbishop of York (1060–9), himself like Ælfric a monk, endowed colleges of canons with refectories, cloisters and dormitories at York, Ripon and Southwell, as well as developing that at Beverley. It seems possible that the Norman bishops of London, Robert (1044–51) and William (1051–75), established prebends for the canons of St. Paul's, while Leofric, bishop of Exeter (1046–72), and Giso, bishop of Wells (1060–88), both imposed a more canonical rule of life on their cathedral clergy. When Earl Harold founded his community of canons at Waltham in Essex he was evidently in sympathy with contemporary ecclesiastical trends.

Throughout this period the rule of Chrodegang of Metz remained *par excellence* the rule to be adopted by enlightened canonical communities. Leofric is said specifically to have introduced the rule of Chrodegang at Exeter. It was not until the twelfth century that the Augustinian Order, based on ancient precepts going back to the time of St. Augustine of Hippo, was formally established for canonical communities.

The monastic reform movement of the tenth century in England

By the time of Alfred the Great (871–99) monasticism seems to have been regarded as virtually extinct. Asser, Alfred's biographer, considered the increased luxury of the eighth and ninth centuries as prejudicial to the monastic life, the seizure of monastic lands by secular lords and the ravages of the Vikings may also have adversely affected the monasteries. But it is important not to misconstrue Asser's words. He says that regular monastic life had ceased throughout England and many other nations, though many monasteries remained. It is not that monasteries no longer exist but that the regular monastic life no longer survives. It is essential to appreciate exactly what Asser meant by this.

By Alfred's time, the Carolingian renaissance on the Continent, and the reinterpretation of the rule of St. Benedict of Nursia by Benedict of Aniane at the council of Aachen in 817, had established St. Benedict's Rule of life as the primary and most perfect guide for monastic communities. Though the Carolingian empire disintegrated in the course of the ninth century and much of the work of Benedict of Aniane was undone, his revision of St. Benedict's Rule remained the fundamental source of inspiration to monastic reformers both on the Continent and in England. Prior to the work of Benedict of Aniane, however, the Rule of St. Benedict had been simply one of a great many in west Europe, all perfectly acceptable to the early Church. There were almost as many rules as there were monastic houses. In the ninth and tenth centuries, such rules were compared unfavourably with the Rule of St. Benedict, communities which followed them being no longer regarded as monastic in character by Benedictine reformers. When Alfred founded his monastery of Athelney he appointed as abbot John the Old Saxon, possibly from the great reformed Benedictine monastery of Corvey in Saxony. The *Dialogues* of Pope Gregory the Great, which Alfred had translated, is an important source for the life and Rule of St. Benedict.

It is to the reigns of Athelstan, Edmund and Eadred in particular that the origin of the movement for monastic reform on Benedictine lines can be traced, a movement essentially of West Saxon origin and one which was to flower in the reign of Edgar (959–75). The principal advocates of monastic reform appear to have been Dunstan (*c.* 909–88), Æthelwold (*c.* 910–84) and Oswald (*c.* 920–92). Their reform movement is important for its effect upon the Anglo-Saxon Church as a whole, and because it seems to have been primarily responsible for that revival of literature and art in England which has become known as the tenth-century English renaissance. The reformers determined the ecclesiastic and cultural development of England down almost to the Norman

Conquest. This is not to say that they enjoyed unqualified success. They undoubtedly represented a stern, ascetic and at times unscrupulous element within the English Church. The reformers were unable to influence every sphere of ecclesiastical life, and communities of canons, to which they were opposed, not only survived the attack but experienced that revival of their own way of life in the eleventh century which has already been described. Despite the dedicated enthusiasm of men like Æthelwold and Oswald, it seems probable that the total number of reformed houses by c. 1000 was far less than the number of monasteries which had existed—and no doubt to some extent still did exist following individual rules—in the pre-Viking period.

A useful pointer to the success of the reform movement, which provides something in the way of a statistical background to the study of the monastic records of the time, is the number of reformed foundations at a given time. Some 28 houses are known to have been reformed by the death of Edgar in 975, but only about 20 between 975 and 1066. This means that more reformed centres were created in some 18 years than in the following period of 91 years. The figures show clearly that the reign of Edgar in particular was the great age of monastic reform, after which the movement evidently suffered a serious setback. Similarly, there are indications of a check to the process of acquiring land for the reformed houses after 975.

The leaders of the monastic reform movement in the reign of Edgar had very often been—as in the case of Æthelwold—astute businessmen, managing to combine a detached unworldliness with a sound and methodical approach to financial transactions. So far as Æthelwold's foundation at Ely is concerned, the records of Ely show that no transaction, no sale of land and its possible purchase by himself, was too small to be beneath his notice. The Ely records are remarkably full, and there is no reason to doubt that the policy of Æthelwold in providing adequate territorial endowment for his monastery was not common practice among the reformers. The reign of Edward the Martyr (975–8) witnessed something in the nature of an anti-monastic reaction from certain secular lords, led by Ælfhere, ealdorman of Mercia, and Æthelwine, ealdorman of East Anglia. In part, their trouble-making was political, related to the opposition around the young Æthelred to Edward, king in Wessex; but, nevertheless, they appear to have been reacting also against the excessive territorial acquisitions of the reformed monasteries. It is important to bear in mind this arrested development of the movement after 975 when approaching the sources for the principal monastic reformers.

The three fundamental sources for the monastic revival in the tenth century are the first *Lives* of Dunstan, Æthelwold and Oswald, all compiled *c.* 1000, that is to say when the monastic movement was already on the wane. These *Lives*, however, were written at monastic houses which were closely associated with the reformers and in which zeal for their reforming policies evidently remained intense. The best example of this is provided by the earliest, anonymous, *Life of Dunstan*. Dunstan became archbishop of Canterbury in 960. The writer of the *Life of Dunstan* was a priest, but the *Life* is dedicated to Archbishop Ælfric of Canterbury (995–1005), who was the first to introduce a substantial community of monks into Christ Church cathedral. Such an action was unquestionably the mark of a zealot. The introduction of monks into cathedral chapters was unknown on the Continent and happened only rarely in England. Æthelwold, who became bishop of Winchester in 963, expelled the canons and introduced monks into Winchester cathedral. Oswald, who became bishop of Worcester in 961, permitted the gradual introduction of a monastic community at Worcester cathedral *c.* 974–7. The last time before the Norman Conquest was when Wulfsige, bishop of Sherborne, introduced monks at Sherborne, *c.* 1000. The men who acted thus represented the most extreme element among the monastic reformers. Communities of monks, whose lives were subject to the demands of monastic discipline, were not the most satisfactory bodies to administer cathedrals and dioceses. The earliest *Life of Dunstan*, therefore, was written for an archbishop whom many churchmen would no doubt have regarded as a fanatic. What is probably the earliest *Life of Æthelwold* was written by that great literary figure of the late tenth century, Ælfric, abbot of Eynsham. Ælfric, who sent Wulfsige, bishop of Sherborne, a pastoral letter when he became bishop and was therefore in close touch with the reform movement at Sherborne, was an ex-pupil of Æthelwold; he dedicated his *Life of Æthelwold* to Cenwulf, bishop of Winchester (1005–6), ex-abbot of Æthelwold's revived foundation at Peterborough. Ælfric and Cenwulf clearly remained devoted to the memory of their saint, and Ælfric was well placed to gather material about Æthelwold. The earliest, anonymous, *Life of Oswald* was written before 1005, for Archbishop Ælfric is described as still living, and was probably put together at the monastery of Ramsey, revived by Oswald. Later *Lives* of Dunstan, Æthelwold and

Oswald add some additional information, but essentially they are based on the *Lives* considered above.

As a result of the continuing interest of what seems to have been the vanguard of monastic reformers *c.* 1000 in Dunstan, Æthelwold and Oswald, a fair amount is known of these men. It must be emphasised, however, that this does not necessarily mean that they alone were responsible for the monastic revival. It is highly probable that there were several monastic reformers in the second half of the tenth century about whom nothing is recorded because they did not become bishops or because their monastic houses lacked the necessary biographer and the right incentive. It would be helpful to know more, for example, of Sideman, tutor to the young Edward, son of Edgar, whom Edgar made abbot of Exeter in 968 and bishop of Crediton in 971; or of Thurcetel, abbot of Bedford in 971 and kinsman of Oscetel, archbishop of York (d. 971), whose kinsman also was Oswald of Worcester. Thurcetel was identified in the traditions of Crowland monastery with Thurcetel, abbot of Crowland in the second half of the tenth century. The monastery of Crowland is an excellent example of an important missing piece of evidence. For its development we are largely dependent on what little can be made of the history of pseudo-Ingulf, compiled in the later Middle Ages by a man who represented himself as writing in the late eleventh century, mainly out of forged documents and fabricated detail. There is the further difficulty that a number of monasteries founded or revived in the tenth century may have left no records, and dissolved by 1066. This could certainly happen to monasteries even at the end of the Anglo-Saxon period. A monastery at Exeter, for example, seems to have virtually ceased to exist by 1066, and neither was there a community at Bedford by that date. What could happen to a monastery can be seen from the example of Oswald of Worcester's foundation at Westbury-on-Trym; an account of the fortunes of the monastery states that, after Oswald's death, it was so laid waste by evil men and Vikings that there was but one priest left who seldom sang mass. The same is true of nunneries. Much less is known of Anglo-Saxon Benedictine nunneries than of the monasteries. Those of which anything is known are primarily the West Saxon foundations, as at Wilton, Wherwell, Shaftesbury and Amesbury, patronised by West Saxon noble ladies, princesses and queens. But it is clear that there must have been many more of which nothing is known. There was an important nunnery, for example, at Wareham, where the body of Edward the Martyr rested before its eventual translation to Shaftesbury. Shaftesbury had been founded originally by Alfred the Great, but of the origin and ultimate fate of Wareham nothing is known. There is no trace of it by 1066. If Wareham nunnery could so disappear, how much more so is this a possibility in the case of lesser foundations.

It is clear from the *Lives* of Dunstan, Æthelwold and Oswald that they did not of themselves conceive the revival of monasticism. They drew on the inspiration and hopes of an older generation. This older generation is largely lost to us, because the writers of the *Lives* of Dunstan, Æthelwold and Oswald were concerned with it only incidentally in so far as it related to the Dunstan era. The casual references that do survive, however, show how Dunstan and his contemporaries were influenced by their elders. The two older bishops about whom we know most and that is very little—were Oda, archbishop of Canterbury (942-58), kinsman of Oscetel, archbishop of York, and uncle of Oswald, and Ælfheah, bishop of Winchester (934-51), kinsman of Dunstan. The early tenth century on the Continent witnessed a monastic revival and reform movement on Benedictine lines as pioneer reformed houses were founded at Cluny in Burgundy, at Fleury-on-the-Loire—reformed under the influence of Cluny—and at St. Omer and Ghent in Flanders. These reformed houses adhered to a strict observance of the Rule of St. Benedict and were strongly opposed to secular control of the Church. The continental monastic reform movement antedates and underlies that in England, and when Oda became archbishop he sent to Fleury and requested the monastic habit. He became a monk, but without monastic training as such. This was a significant step. It shows that Church leaders in England were aware of continental currents of reform. Though there is no background information in the case of Ælfheah, bishop of Winchester, there is no doubt that he had adopted the monastic habit and was known as 'monk and bishop'. The references to Oda and Ælfheah are chance allusions, mentioned in the sources simply because of their association with Oswald and Dunstan, and there is every likelihood that there were many other churchmen in England similarly affected by the new monasticism in their time. In the 930s Ælfheah persuaded Dunstan to take full monastic vows, and it was Ælfheah who ordained Dunstan and Æthelwold priests on the same day. How limited was the viewpoint of the writers of these *Lives* can be seen from the *Life of Oswald*, which represents Oswald's time at Winchester in the 940s as completely unprofitable from the point of view of learning anything of true monastic discipline. The *Life of Oswald* says nothing about Ælfheah, and Oswald was sent (*c.* 950), by his uncle, Oda, archbishop of Canterbury, to be instructed in regular monastic discipline at Fleury.

This is perhaps even more surprising in that by the early 950s Dunstan was well established, according to his *Life*, as abbot of a reformed Benedictine community at Glastonbury. King Edmund made Dunstan abbot of Glastonbury *c.* 943, and Dunstan immediately began a programme of reform, being joined by Æthelwold who received the monastic habit from Dustan. But Oswald, a young priest at Winchester who must surely have known about Dunstan and the reforms at Glastonbury, did not go to Glastonbury. Historians have tended to see Dunstan and his work at Glastonbury out of proportion. There is no doubt that Oda, with his contacts with Fleury, reflected the mainstream of progressive reform in England at this time, and that Oswald was more advanced than Dunstan and Æthelwold in his immediate response to the leading continental centres of monastic reform.

Because he became archbishop of Canterbury, Dunstan's career is generally made the basis of any historical narrative of the monastic revival in England; and certainly the anonymous priest who wrote for Archbishop Ælfric intended to make it appear as if Dunstan were the main leader of the English reform movement in its earliest days. The *Life of Dunstan*, surprisingly so it seems at first, is not so much interested in Dunstan as archbishop as in his relations with the early tenth-century kings of Wessex and his fortunes as a reforming abbot of Glastonbury. Consequently, we know a great deal of Dunstan's early career. He was born near Glastonbury, and educated by the community there, which appears to have been largely composed of clerks. He even lived for some time at Glastonbury after taking the monastic habit but before his appointment as abbot. From *c.* 925, however, Dunstan spent most of his time at the royal court, where he eventually made himself thoroughly unpopular. His appointment as abbot of Glastonbury *c.* 943 by Edmund, reputedly as a royal thanksgiving for the king's miraculous escape from an accidental death, may have been designed rather to remove a troublesome member of the court. Edmund's successor, Eadred (946–55), recalled Dunstan to active court life and evidently made him one of the keepers of the king's treasure. As Dunstan is known to have seen, at some time, the body of St. Cuthbert, he probably accompanied Eadred on at least one of the northern expeditions of that king in 947 and 948. Dunstan again fell out of favour with King Eadwig, and was exiled in 955, at which time he visited the reformed Benedictine monastery at Ghent; he was recalled to England in 957 with the seizure of power in Mercia of Edgar, brother of Eadwig.

It is important to give due prominence to these political events in the life of Dunstan, and to separate them from his monastic interests with which they have no connection. Dunstan's main preoccupations in these early years were political and dynastic, and the fact that he was a Benedictine reformer probably incidental to the kings who supported or opposed him. Dunstan was, so to speak, born to the purple and it was his family connections which propelled him into the forefront of the political scene. This was true of other prominent churchmen too. Though the relationship may in certain instances have been through marriage, Oscetel, archbishop of York, Oda, archbishop of Canterbury, Thurcetel, abbot of Bedford and then of Crowland, and Oswald, bishop of Worcester, were all kinsmen and—what is very important—related to the royal family of Wessex. Oswald had additional family ties with the great lords of East Anglia, Ealdorman Æthelwine (it was Æthelwine who encouraged Oswald's foundation at Ramsey), and his brother, Ealdorman Ælfwold. But the significance of the right family connections can be seen on a particularly impressive scale in the case of Dunstan. Dunstan was the nephew not only of Ælfheah, bishop of Winchester, but also of Athelm, bishop of Wells and subsequently archbishop of Canterbury (914–23). It was Athelm who introduced Dunstan into court circles. Another relative on the episcopal bench was Cynsige, bishop of the important Mercian see of Lichfield. Dunstan is said to have been related to the Lady Æthelflæd, who dwelt at Glastonbury and who was a niece of King Athelstan (924–39). This means that Dunstan, and his episcopal kinsmen, were all related—in varying degrees no doubt but still related—to the West Saxon royal family. It explains his prominence at court—and his unpopularity, for he seems to have been a member of a dynastic family faction. King Eadwig wished to marry the Lady Ælfgifu, probably a relative of the great East Anglian noble family of Ealdorman Æthelwine, and Archbishop Oda forbade it on the grounds that they were too closely related. The sending of Cynsige, bishop of Lichfield, and his kinsman, Dunstan, during Eadwig's coronation feast to drag the king away from his intended bride and back to the feast is clearly symbolic of two opposing branches of the royal family struggling for control of the young king.

Dunstan was expelled for his interference, and Oda's prohibition evidently set at nought. In 957 a rebellion in Mercia, where, of course, Cynsige of Lichfield had great influence, acclaimed Edgar king in opposition to Eadwig. Dunstan was immediately recalled, and from this point in time his rise to power within the Church was both meteoric and unscrupulous. He was made bishop of Worcester in 957 and bishop of London in 958–9, thereby becoming a pluralist, a practice later to be so condemned by the reforming papacy. When Eadwig died in 959, Edgar succeeded to Wessex. Eadwig's recently appointed archbishop of Canterbury, Byrhthelm of Wells, was sent back to his old bishopric—an unprecedented event—and Dunstan appointed in his place.

It is clear that those members of the royal circle who were represented by Cynsige and Dunstan failed to secure control of Eadwig, but succeeded with a vengeance in controlling Edgar. There can be little doubt that in these early years at least Edgar was simply a pawn in a political and ecclesiastical game. Only 13 in 957, he can hardly have played a leading role in events. The appointment of Dunstan to the primatial see was a political appointment which chanced to place a Benedictine reformer in command of the English Church, but Dunstan's early life provided an admirable chance to a biographer to show how a devoted monastic reformer could rise to become archbishop of Canterbury, and it is not surprising that Archbishop Ælfric should have taken such a particular interest in this phase of Dunstan's career.

It is interesting that Æthelwold, who was at Glastonbury when Dunstan was abbot there, was not wholly satisfied with the monastic life at Glastonbury and desired to go to the Continent; he was deflected from this course of action by King Eadred's gift of the ruined abbey of Abingdon to serve as a new reformed house. If Eadred favoured Dunstan, he also favoured Æthelwold, and Æthelwold's *Life* preserves a charming picture of Eadred, actually a sick and failing man at the time, assisting in the measuring out of the new monastic buildings. Once at Abingdon, Æthelwold sent the monk, Osgar, to Fleury to learn the regular monastic life so that Osgar might instruct the brethren and Æthelwold on his return. Osgar became abbot of Abingdon in 963. The *Life of Oswald* records that it was Æthelwold who was entrusted with the education of the young Edgar, son of Edmund. If any single figure was regarded by contemporaries as the leader of a monastic reform party in England, that figure must soon have been Æthelwold of Abingdon. Once appointed archbishop of Canterbury, however, it was Dunstan who was in a position to influence episcopal appointments which could make or break the movement for monastic reform. As it turned out, of some 24 or 25 episcopal appointments in the archiepiscopate of Dunstan (excluding the rather peculiar church of Durham) only five or six are not known to have been monks. The monastic party had triumphed and to have been a monk at one of the major monasteries associated with the reformers or their disciples, provided one's talents were adequate, became a sure road to promotion in the English Church.

Dunstan's own reforming influence was brought to bear, either as abbot of Glastonbury, or subsequently as archbishop, on monastic communities at Malmesbury, possibly Bath, and at Westminster. In 961 Dunstan secured the bishopric of Worcester for Oswald, who had now returned from Fleury. Oswald recalled a fellow English monk from Fleury, Germanus, and established him over a small monastic community at Westbury-on-Trym and then over his larger revived foundation at Ramsey. There may have been a certain harshness involved in the expulsion of clerks from Ramsey, a harshness which is most clearly revealed in Æthelwold's treatment of the canons at Winchester. Æthelwold, possibly the most austere of the three main figures of the reform movement, was appointed bishop of Winchester in 963 and the following year, with the support of King Edgar, took the radical step of expelling what are described in his *Life* as evil-living clerks from the Old Minster, the cathedral church, and from the New Minster. The passions of the monks ran so high that, when Æthelwold was taken ill at Winchester, a clerk was said to have attempted to poison him. Æthelwold went on to revive the fenland monasteries of Ely, Peterborough and Thorney. The interest of Oswald and Æthelwold in the ancient monastic centres in the fenlands is interesting; Oswald's concern with this area developed partly at least out of his family background, but it may be that the survival of so many records from their foundations here results in an undue prominence. Both men, and particularly Oswald, may have been associated with the introduction of monasticism at St. Albans, but for the early history of the abbey of St. Albans material is scanty. It is not easy to define precisely the degree of personal influence of the part of Dunstan, Æthelwold and Oswald in the revival of certain other reformed monasteries with which their disciples were more closely associated; for example, in the 960s Chertsey and Milton; and in the 970s Pershore, Winchcombe and

Evesham. In 971 Oswald became archbishop of York but he appears to have been unable to revive monasticism in Northumbria.

Many of the ancient monastic sites had passed into royal hands by the 960s. Eadred, for example, gave Æthelwold the site of the former monastery at Abingdon, and Æthelwold bought Ely from Edgar. Edgar was liberal in his grants of land to the revived foundations. In addition, the monastery of Thorney seems to have been declared exempt from episcopal control, and a similar exemption seems, on the whole, to have been true of Ely. Such monasteries were subject to the king alone. The emphasis throughout the reform movement was on free abbatial elections, but a vociferous insistence on complete exemption from episcopal control is on the whole a feature rather of the monasticism of the late eleventh- and twelfth-century Church. It is clear that Edgar either came to take or was made to take an interest in monastic reform, and his queen, Ælfthryth, was placed in charge of the welfare of nunneries. It must be emphasised, however, that so little is known in detail of Edgar's reign and the king's secular activities that the distribution of extant source material may yet again introduce a serious element of distortion. Modern historians have tended very much to emphasise Edgar's pious and enlightened qualities; without his earnest co-operation, it has been thought, the monastic reform movement could not have made much headway. To what extent Edgar ever escaped from the formidable influence of Dunstan and his colleagues is unknown. Anglo-Norman historians, drawing on oral tradition now lost to us, emphasised rather Edgar's treacherous, immoral and licentious conduct.

In c. 970 the leaders of the monastic reform movement came together to establish an agreed rule of monastic life, the *Regularis Concordia*, which would provide for uniform observance. Evidently there were still sufficient differences from one house to another to give the purists cause for concern. Dunstan and Æthelwold appear to have been the main architects of the new rule, which drew the basis of its inspiration from the Continent. Ælfric of Eynsham attributes the essential character of the rule to Æthelwold, but Ælfric was Æthelwold's pupil; the predominant influence is not that of Fleury but of Ghent, revealing, no doubt as a consequence of his position as archbishop of Canterbury, the influence of Dunstan. One of the distinguishing features of the rule is the emphasis it places upon praying for the king and royal family. In return Edgar surrendered certain royal rights by freeing the monasteries from the payment of a *heriot*, a tax due to the king on the death of a landowner or nobleman, in this instance an abbot or abbess. The remittance was to deter the religious houses from storing up treasure to pay off these death duties; instead the money was to be used for the needs of the monks and the poor. The principle that cathedral churches should be free to elect a bishop from the cathedral community was also conceded by Edgar.

The monastic leaders aimed at a high standard of monastic discipline. While the Rule of St. Benedict set the minimum standard required for monastic life, the *Regularis Concordia* represents the ideal of the tenth-century reformers. It shows that a monastery of the tenth century would contain, among other buildings, a church, refectory (where meals were served), dormitory, cloister (for study), a room with a fire in cold weather (again for study), a room set apart for the daily meeting or chapter of the community, an auditorium (for conversation and the entertaining of guests), a guesthouse, bakehouse, kitchen, and an infirmary. In such an environment the monks must have led a pleasantly comfortable life by contrast to the outside world. It must not be forgotten that a monk enjoyed a higher standard of life than the peasantry as a whole; in consequence, for a man of fairly humble origins, life in a monastery would be attractive, provided he could discipline himself to the nature of the monastic life. This a great many must have been unable to do. It was, of course, a full and intense life that the monks led. In winter they rose for the first time at 2.30 a.m. and retired at 6.30 p.m. In summer they rose for the first time at 1.30 a.m. and retired at 8.15 p.m. In winter they were provided with one meal a day, in summer with two. Two hours in the morning were set aside for every kind of work. Most of the day was spent in the incessant liturgical round which is so distinctive a feature of reformed Benedictinism on the Continent. The monastic reformers of the twelfth century were to react against the liturgical preoccupations of the tenth, seeing the exaggeration of devotional practice as a danger to the spiritual life. Even in the tenth century, in the heyday of the movement, it is evident that not every monastery was capable of living up to the ideal standard. Ælfric adapted a simplified form of the *Regularis Concordia* for conditions at Eynsham. In his law code of 1014, Æthelred II instructed abbots and monks to live more in accordance with the Rule than they had been in the habit of doing. Many of the monastic houses of Anglo-Saxon England were certainly very wealthy by 1066, and the greater part of their medieval territorial endowment probably complete in most cases before the Norman Conquest, if not by 975. The Anglo-Saxon monasteries controlled one-sixth to one-fifth of the wealth of England by 1066. Glastonbury was the richest house, then Bury St. Edmunds, St. Augustine's Canterbury, Winchester Old Minster, Westminster Abbey and Abingdon. A group of less wealthy, but nevertheless rich, houses included Ramsey, Peterborough, Shaftesbury, Malmesbury, and Thorney. Crowland was among the poorest of the ancient Saxon monasteries. On the other hand, though often rich, there is no reason to doubt that many if not most of the leading monastic communities maintained a high standard of Benedictine life down to the Norman Conquest, nor to suppose that such houses compared unfavourably with any but the most advanced of continental monasteries.

Attention may be drawn to an extremely vital eremetical tradition within the Old English Church. Though precise numbers are unobtainable, the evidence suggests that solitary monks and nuns, claiming as anchorites or hermits to be seeking spiritual perfection even beyond that possible in a monastic community, were common in England in the mid-eleventh century. It was a hermit, Wulfsige, who persuaded Wulfstan to accept the bishopric of Worcester in 1062, and the eremetical tradition is known to have been strong in the Worcester-Malvern area. The ascetic strain which produced Christina of Markyate and Godric of Finchale c. 1100 had roots deep in an Anglo-Saxon past. Finally, just as in the eighth century the healthy condition of the English Church is reflected in the missions to the continental pagan Germans, so in the late tenth and early eleventh centuries the dim but nevertheless detectable influence of the English Church on the Churches of Norway and Sweden is a certain indication of the continuing strength of Anglo-Saxon Christian and missionary zeal.

Chapter three

The Danish Conquest and
the Anglo-Danish State

Æthelred the Unready (*978–1016*)

In 978 the young king of Wessex, Edward, son of Edgar, was assassinated at Corfe (Dorset), and his half-brother, Æthelred, a boy aged between 10 and 12, succeeded as king. Æthelred had the support of a strong Mercian faction, led by Ælfhere, ealdorman of Mercia, and Æthelred's mother, Ælfthryth, was said by many to have been implicated in the murder. There can be no doubt that Æthelred began his reign in inauspicious circumstances. The very next year Edward's body was translated to Shaftesbury from Wareham, and the deed of assassination was evidently so much abhorred by contemporaries that by 1008 at the latest Edward was venerated as a saint, Æthelred being compelled to decree the annual observance of his festival. Æthelred was the first king to come to the throne of Wessex for over two centuries as the direct result of the deliberate murder of a predecessor, in this instance the king's own half-brother. It is hardly surprising that post-Conquest writers attributed to Archbishop Dunstan a violent outburst of prophecy against him.

Æthelred has passed into history as a thorough incompetent. His nickname '*unræd*' ('evil counsel') was a parody on the name Æthelred ('noble counsel'), and in the sixteenth century was again parodied to mean 'unready'—which, oddly enough, seems just as appropriate as the original pun. Though the *Life of Oswald* (*c.* 1000) supplies a picture, albeit conventional, which conveys an impression of Æthelred in his youth as a promising prince, William of Malmesbury in the twelfth century, the first to attempt a complete portrait of the king, describes him as cruel, effeminate, immoral and treacherous. But, almost as an aside, William adds that he has found it hard to reconcile the available historical evidence for Æthelred and his reign with the fact that he had been taught by his elders that Æthelred was neither foolish nor cowardly nor indolent. Here is a trace of an earlier stratum of opinion and tradition more favourable to the king, and it is unfortunate that William did not expand his observations further. What dominates the reign of Æthelred is the renewed Scandinavian attack, beginning almost as soon as he became king. This attack culminated in his flight in 1013, and, despite subsequent restoration and the achievements of Edmund, his son, in the conquest of much of England by the Danes and the ultimate accession of Cnut, king of Denmark, to the West Saxon throne in 1017. No other European Germanic or Celtic state succumbed so completely to the pressure of Scandinavian attack, and few kings and their generals can have acquired a greater reputation for military incompetence than Æthelred and his ealdormen. The reign appears to witness the reversal of trends initiated by Alfred and so successfully continued by Alfred's successors, not least Edgar, father of Æthelred. There must have been more to the Danish conquest of England than the incompetence of one ruler.

What evidence there is suggests that Æthelred was not so much a weak ruler as an unjust ruler. His unpopularity was due in no small measure to his oppressive dealings with his subjects. William of Malmesbury accuses the king of unjustly depriving his subjects of their hereditary possessions without due cause or for suppositious crimes. The annals of the reign do refer to political assassinations and the seizure of property, and it has been suggested that the defensive phraseology of his charters may indicate royal concern to absolve the king from such accusations. It is of great interest in this respect that in 1014, at the time of his restoration, Æthelred had to swear to rule more justly than before, and to reform what the West Saxons hated. This is rather unexpected against the background of the excessive legislation which is one of the distinctive features of the reign, but it seems clear that Æthelred did not observe the Law as he should and that he was surrounded, perhaps partly in consequence, by a web of treachery and intrigue.

Æthelred's personal standing in Wessex may have been slight to begin with, because of the circumstances of his accession. Though West Saxon ealdormen figure prominently in the witness lists of his charters between 983 and 1010, Mercian ealdormen tend to dominate royal councils at the beginning and end of the reign. Æthelred did not marry, so far as is known, within West Saxon aristocratic circles. His first wife may have been a daughter of the Viking, Thored, who died c. 993 after rising to become ealdorman of Deira. Æthelred's second wife, whom he married in 1002, was Emma, the daughter of Richard I, duke of the Scandinavian duchy of Normandy in west Francia. Æthelred had a great many children, some of whom may have been illegitimate, and the careers of the most prominent seem to indicate a northerly orientation of royal policy. It is probable that Æthelred was attempting to bring the West Saxon monarchy into closer contact with the magnates of the more northerly and easterly parts of his realm, for sometimes contact could be very slight indeed. This was the great defect of the administrative legacy which Æthelred inherited from his tenth-century predecessors. There were important regions where royal control was virtually non-existent, and where great men appeared in vice-regal status. Waltheof, earl of Bamburgh from 975 to 1006, is known to have visited the royal court only once: he appears only once, that is, in the witness lists to King Æthelred's charters. It was essential that royal influence should be brought to bear on such men. Consequently, it is significant when one daughter of Æthelred married Ulfcetel, ealdorman of East Anglia, and another married Eadric Streona ('the Acquisitor') in 1006 when Eadric became ealdorman of Mercia. That same year the king created a reunited earldom of Deira and Bernicia for Uhtred, son of Waltheof of Bamburgh, to whom a third daughter was given in marriage. These three great magnates, therefore, became the brothers-in-law of the West Saxon athelings. The will of the atheling Athelstan (c. 1015), oldest of Æthelred's sons, shows the prince with connections in the northern Danelaw, particularly—if the names can be identified correctly—with Morcar and Sigeferth, chief thegns of the Seven Boroughs (the Five Boroughs with the addition of York and Torksey), and with Thurbrand of Northumbria, the man who was eventually to assassinate Uhtred. In 1015, when Eadric Streona assassinated Morcar and Sigeferth and the king ordered their lands to be seized, a classic example of Æthelred's unjust actions, Edmund Ironside, son of Æthelred, married the widow of Sigeferth in opposition to his father's commands and proceeded to take possession of the estates of the dead thegns.

It is clear that there were strong undercurrents of territorial rivalry among these northern magnates in which Æthelred and his sons became involved. The Five Boroughs, for example, still existed in 1013 but by 1015 they had become the Seven. Evidently York was taken from Uhtred's earldom after 1013 and attached to the Five Boroughs. This was a part of the general extension of Mercian influence into Deira at this time. Morcar, for example, was the godfather of the daughter of the Mercian nobleman, Wulfric Spott, the founder of a monastery at Burton-on-Trent and whose estates stretched across nine counties from Gloucestershire to Yorkshire. Wulfric's brother, Ælfhelm, was ealdorman of Deira for several years before his assassination in 1006 by Eadric Streona. It was the slaying of Ælfhelm which enabled Æthelred to give Deira to Uhtred of Bamburgh. Cnut, the son of the Danish king, Swein Forkbeard, took as his first wife Ælfgifu, daughter of Ælfhelm of Deira, and the subsequent assassination by the orders of Cnut of Uhtred and Eadric may not have been unrelated to the events of 1006. In 1013 Uhtred made peace with the invading army of Swein, and it was possibly for this reason that Æthelred, on his restoration, detached York from Northumbria and gave it to the Mercian rulers of the Five Boroughs. In the family disagreement in 1015 over the widow of Sigeferth and the lands of Morcar and Sigeferth, Edmund was able to win the support of Uhtred by returning York to him. A thwarted Eadric Streona now viewed Edmund with such disfavour that he deserted him for Cnut. These hostilities are understandable against a background of struggles for territorial influence along the Mercian-Northumbrian border. They may well have been paralleled elsewhere, along the Mercian-East Anglian border for instance, but what evidence there is relates to Northumbria and Mercia. Such rivalries were probably common to the whole Anglo-Saxon period but they acquired a particular intensity in the reign of Æthelred at a time of disastrous external attack. In 1017 Cnut, as king of England, made Eadric earl of Mercia, confirming his rule over the whole midland region. Eadric is a good example of the over-mighty subject in Æthelred's reign, but he was not alone in this respect. Both Ulfcetel and Uhtred were his equals, though their influence on the king appears to have been less. Eadric's particular power rested on the fact that he was Æthelred's leading counsellor in the last years of the reign. The rivalries of self-seeking, ambitious magnates were clearly an important element in the difficulties of the reign; and it must be emphasised that the northern part-Scandinavian, part-Anglian regions in which they mainly played out their rivalry were but imperfectly integrated into an Anglo-Danish state under West Saxon domination when the Danish attack began. It was evidently very difficult for Æthelred to implement royal authority in the north, but it would appear that he made a positive, if at times misguided, attempt to do so. For this he deserves not a little credit.

It is the Scandinavian attack which is the dominant feature of Æthelred's reign. Most of the records of the period relate to the wars of the time, and in that Æthelred's defeat and the conquest of England was such a striking Danish achievement the viewpoint of contemporaries, preoccupied with the struggle, is a valid one. It is important to emphasise that whereas the Alfredian chronicler was a devoted supporter of King Alfred, rejoicing in his successes, the continuator of the *Anglo-Saxon Chronicle* for the reign of Æthelred was a persistent critic, if not of the king then certainly of those whom he regarded as the king's incompetent, cowardly and treacherous generals. The *Anglo-Saxon Chronicle* provides a remarkably detailed and contemporary narrative for the years *c.* 992–1016, but it is a biased source and must not be taken as necessarily providing a completely reliable account of this period.

The Danish raids began again in 981. Perhaps the best indication of the degree to which the situation worsened over the following years is provided by the sums paid as danegeld to buy peace; 10,000 pounds in 991 (22,000 according to a treaty with the Vikings of that year), 16,000 in 994, 24,000 in 1002, 36,000 in 1007, and 48,000 in 1012. These figures represent what has been described as an appalling level of taxation. On the other hand, for Æthelred and his contemporaries the raids for many years must have appeared sporadic and localised. Certain inland districts rarely if ever saw a Danish army. But new factors did enter into the situation as it existed in Æthelred's time. Æthelred's marriage to Emma yoked him personally to the harsh spirit of a Viking princess whose ultimate sympathies lay with the king's enemies rather than with the king himself. Large tracts of northern and eastern England had already been settled by Danes and Norse, often living at loggerheads with English neighbours and prepared to assist an invading Scandinavian army. The Scandinavians themselves were no longer dividing their attention between England, Ireland, Wales, Scotland and the Continent. The Continent was virtually closed to them by 980 and the tide turning against them in Celtic lands. In the Scandinavian duchy of Normandy the Danes did have a refuge and a base for attack on England. By 991 Pope John XV had mediated peace between King Æthelred and Richard, duke of Normandy, to the effect that neither would receive the other's enemies. In the actual attack on England in the late tenth century the Viking ships of the time must have been superior vessels to those of Alfred's day though to what extent they were larger and able to carry more men is uncertain. The figures for the size of Scandinavian fleets in Æthelred's reign are ill-preserved. The Danish fleet is said to have numbered 94 in 994, a fair-sized expedition. Two figures, however, are given for Cnut's fleet in 1016—340 and 200. The English fleet numbered at least 100 ships in 1009, and must have numbered many more for this represented only a detachment. But whatever the numerical strength of opposing fleets, Swein and Cnut had behind them a united Danish kingdom which their ancestors had not possessed. The creation of new military training fortresses may lie behind the legend of the Jomsburg Vikings, crack Danish warriors taught and trained in the military academy of Jomsburg. The second half of the tenth century also witnessed the beginning of a struggle between Norway and Denmark for mastery of the Baltic, which became the central feature of early eleventh-century Scandinavian history, and the conquest of England though an important was only a dependent part.

The Anglo-Saxon chronicler was constantly critical of the way in which the king and his generals handled the Danish attack. The Danish army went about as it pleased, and the chronicler repeatedly stresses that the English army never came to blows with it. According to the chronicler, the Danes were never fought against because no one dared to challenge them; when the Danish army was in the south, the English was in the north, and when the Danish army was in the east, the English was in the west. Ælfric, ealdorman of Hampshire, is said to have dodged the issue of battle in 992 with the fleet and again in 1003 with the army, and he was regarded by the chronicler as a coward and traitor. The English army is recorded as having avoided the Danes in the years 998, 999, 1001, 1006 and 1010. Administrative inefficiency is also said to have played a part; the chronicler asserts that interminable delays in the development of the English fleet resulted in nothing but the oppression of the English people, the waste of money, and the encouragement of the enemy. The new fleet assembled in 1009 is said to have been destroyed simply through carelessness and mismanagement. In any analysis of the *Chronicle*'s account of the wars with the Danes in Æthelred's reign, Æthelred will be conspicuous by his absence. He never fought decisively with the Danes in the whole of his reign. He did ravage Cumberland (1000) and Lindsey (1014), and he is said to have taken part in a siege of London in the period *c.* 1014, but he never came to grips with the main Danish fleet or army. In 1009 he seems to have deliberately avoided a battle with the Danes on the advice of Eadric Streona. It must be remembered, however, that those local forces which did oppose the Danes were invariably crushed. In 991 Byrhtnoth, ealdorman of Essex, led his men to disaster in a battle against the Danes at Maldon, a battle which passed into Anglo-Saxon epic tradition through the existence and survival of a heroic poem describing the conflict. But even Edmund, son and successor of King Æthelred, when he reverted to fighting pitched battles with the enemy, achieved very limited success. It is important to recognise, on the other hand, that the Danish armies themselves may have been seeking to avoid a battle. They preferred to wear out the English forces by constant manœuvring, and slipped away to sea with such ease that Danish poets contrasted the English 'landfish' with their own 'seafish'. If a Danish poet is to be believed, Æthelred's army was larger than the Danish, which may have indicated evasive action to the Danish leaders, and in 1009, the year in which Æthelred is specifically said to have avoided battle, the Danes in turn avoided his army. Most of the Danish armies operating in England before 1010 were probably relatively small raiding parties, and some of the Danes evidently held Æthelred in awe. Norse tradition described Æthelred as the true friend of warriors, and it was said that men feared England's lord as a god. Æthelred was able to secure the aid of several Viking warriors, among them Thorkell the Tall and two later kings of Norway, Olaf Tryggvason to whom he stood godfather in 994 and whom Edward the Confessor greatly admired, and Olaf Haroldson, subsequently canonised as a saint. Danish mercenary troops, among them the savage *berserks*, were certainly to be found in the armies of Æthelred.

In 1002 Æthelred attempted the assassination of some at least of the Danes settled in England. The massacre of St. Brice's Day cannot have affected more than a small percentage of Danish settlers in England, probably mainly those settled in or resident in West Saxon territory where a massacre is known, for example, to have taken place at Oxford, but among those slain was the sister of Swein, king of Denmark. Later writers considered that Danish determination to conquer England hardened after this event. The period after 1002 witnessed an intensification in the development of the mystique of kingship at the court of Æthelred, which reveals itself in the laws of the period with their emphasis on the king as Christ's deputy on earth. The maintenance of the Christian religion was seen as inseparable from the maintenance of royal authority. Swein Forkbeard of Denmark, for his part, was credited with a vow, said to have been made in the company of the legendary Jomsburg Vikings, to conquer England, but it is not clear when the idea of conquest fully presented itself to him. He may have been involved in the attack on Northumbria in 993, for in the following year he descended on London with the Danish army from the Humber. In 994-5 he ravaged the Isle of Man. In 1004 he defeated the East Anglian army led by Ealdorman Ulfcetel. East Anglia became the main target of attack, and in 1010 a Danish army led by Thorkell the Tall defeated Ulfcetel again and took possession of the province. The events of 1012, the year immediately preceding Swein's great invasion, are unfortunately ill recorded because the Anglo-Saxon chronicler was preoccupied with the martyrdom at the hands of Thorkell's Danes of Ælfheah, archbishop of Canterbury, in that year. But the Welsh annals record that Eadric Streona ravaged South Wales as far as St. Davids in 1012. They note also the shipwreck of Swein and it is not likely that such an episode would have been mentioned had it not happened off the coast of Wales. It is probable, therefore, that Eadric was seeking to frustrate an invasion by Swein directed from the Scandinavian settlements in South Wales. When the invasion did come in 1013 it was not from South Wales but from the Humber. Swein made Gainsborough his headquarters and received, without striking a blow, the submission of Uhtred and the whole of the Danelaw. Crossing Watling Street he began to do as much damage as possible. The new urban communities of Wessex, which had just seen Canterbury sacked, had no desire to go up in flames, and Oxford, Winchester and Bath submitted without argument. Only London held out, for the king was in London together with Thorkell the Tall who had gone over to Æthelred following the sack of Canterbury. When Thorkell's loyalty to Æthelred became suspect, the Londoners did submit and Æthelred fled to Normandy. It seems clear that the men of Wessex withdrew their loyalty to the king at a crucial moment. When Swein died at Gainsborough in February 1015, though his son, Cnut, was accepted as king in the Danelaw, the West Saxons informed Æthelred that no one was dearer to them than their natural lord (Æthelred) if he ruled more justly than before and reformed all that they hated. The negotiator between Æthelred and his subjects for the king's restoration was the king's son, Edward—later the Confessor. Æthelred returned and is said to have been gladly received. Æthelred launched one of his rare expeditions and chased Cnut out of Lindsey, but he had to command the payment of 21,000 pounds to Thorkell's mercenaries now at Greenwich. Æthelred enjoyed no continued success. In 1015 he ordered the assassination of Sigeferth and Morcar, which caused an open breach between the king and his son, Edmund, and between Edmund and Eadric Streona. Consequently, when Cnut invaded Wessex in the same year, Eadric went over to his side and the West Saxons again submitted. Edmund was left to organise resistance as best he could, for Æthelred, more or less permanently stationed at London, seems to have been in failing health and he died in April 1016. The importance of the person of the king at this period is clearly demonstrated when the army refused to fight for Edmund without the presence of his father. Edmund secured the help of Uhtred of Northumbria, but Uhtred had to return to the defence of York and was assassinated through the treachery of Eadric. Edmund succeeded as king of Wessex on Æthelred's death, and, while Cnut besieged London, attacked Danish armies at Penselwood and Sherston. At Sherston, Eadric fought on the Danish side. London proved impregnable and Edmund and Cnut prepared for an open confrontation. Edmund came to terms with Eadric at Aylesford in Kent, but when the opposing armies met at Ashingdon in Essex Eadric deserted to the side of Cnut, Cnut gained the victory, and the *Chronicle* records that all the nobility of England was there destroyed. Among the slain were Ulfcetel of East Anglia, Eadnoth, bishop of Dorchester, and Ealdorman Ælfric of Hampshire, and in 1020 Cnut built a minster there for the souls of the dead. Amazingly, Edmund was still taking advice from Eadric, who is said to have argued that it was impossible to defeat the Danes but that through a treaty Edmund could at least retain half his realm. Edmund, though eager for further battle, reluctantly agreed, and he met Cnut at Alney near Deerhurst. Popular tradition remembered the contrast at this meeting between the diminutiveness of Cnut and the bulkier frame of Edmund Ironside and it was said there was some talk of single combat. The terms of their agreement are not very clear but it is probable that the division was much the same as that between Alfred and Guthrum. Edmund's achievement in rallying Wessex to the degree that he had was considerable, for in 1010 demoralisation is said to have been such that no shire would help another. But his reign was very short; in the

November of 1016 he died. Later legend accused Eadric of the assassination of Edmund, but there is no contemporary evidence for this. In the absence of any leader of Edmund's calibre, the West Saxons accepted Cnut as their king in 1017.

Cnut (1017–35) and his Baltic empire

There is abundant place-name evidence revealing the presence in England by 1017 of a belt of Danish and Norse settlers across northern and eastern England, place-name evidence which is supported by the study of the language and dialect of these regions. Though English and Danish were probably mutually intelligible, there were real differences of phonology and vocabulary and such differences have affected both the development of English dialects in those districts which show a high concentration of Scandinavian place-names and the development of standard English. The accession of Cnut to the throne of Wessex is not known to have brought with it a numerous body of additional newcomers but it did mark a Danish conquest of all England. Cnut set about the creation of an Anglo-Danish state which would integrate English and Scandinavians in a united realm. King Swein had become a Christian in his last years and it was as a Christian ruler that Cnut applied himself to the consolidation of his new position; he ruled on good terms with the English Church, visited Rome in 1027, and was present at the translation of St. Ælfheah, martyred archbishop of Canterbury. Wessex he retained in his own hands, but East Anglia he granted as an earldom to Thorkell the Tall, Mercia to Eadric Streona. Eric of Norway, a mighty Norwegian lord and a supporter of Cnut, was confirmed in possession of Northumbria. Bernicia, however, still seems to have been separate under a line of Bernician earls of the family of Uhtred. Eadric Streona is said to have counselled Cnut to destroy the surviving sons of Æthelred. Eadwig was slain, but Alfred and Edward—sons of Emma, escaped to Normandy, and the children of Edmund to Hungary. In 1020 a certain Eadwig, 'king of the ceorls', was outlawed, but who he was and how he acquired his strange title is unknown. Despite a previous association with Ælfgifu, daughter of Ælfhelm, ealdorman of Deira (to 1006), by whom he had two sons—Swein and Harold, and which was never fully renounced, Cnut married Emma, widow of Æthelred, in the summer of 1017. Emma became the mother of

Harthacnut, son of Cnut. Subsequently she even seems to have opposed Edward, her son by Æthelred. By the end of 1017 Cnut felt secure enough to order the slaying of Eadric Streona on Christmas Day, and with him several other prominent Englishmen. In 1018, 72,000 pounds was exacted in tribute from the nation, and 10,500 pounds from the Londoners, and the *Chronicle* briefly records that the Danes and the English reached an agreement at Oxford. Cnut evidently recognised the legal relationships which had existed in the time of Edgar and which made provision for the variations between English and Danish Law, and in his great law code of 1020–1 Cnut reiterated this traditional Law. And so the great divisions of West Saxon, Mercian and Danish Law survived until the Norman Conquest and beyond. Cnut could hardly have adopted any other course except by wholesale reconstruction on a scale which would have been inconceivable to the men of that age. In the same way William the Conqueror was obliged to accept traditional law and custom though the Normans did attempt to give universal application to West Saxon law. So secure was Cnut that in 1019 he was able to make the first of several visits to Denmark, and internal English differences in 1020 and 1021 did not seriously threaten his position.

Cnut introduced an element of originality into his government of England by addressing letters to his English subjects, quite without precedent, while abroad in 1020 and 1027. The second letter is the best known, written after Cnut had visited Rome and attended the coronation of the Emperor Conrad II, in which Cnut describes the freedom from tolls which he had secured for English travellers and merchants in Italy. These letters were designed to reveal the benefits of his rule to his subjects and they emphasised at the same time the need for continued obedience to the king. For Cnut's hand did not lie lightly on the country. He maintained a large and expensive fighting force or standing army of 'housecarles', in origin at least essentially a royal bodyguard, at the cost of the imposition of an annual heregeld or army tax which replaced the danegeld levies of Æthelred's reign; and an additional levy was required to finance the fleet of 16 warships which Cnut maintained in English waters. The housecarles themselves collected the heregeld, and in the reign of Harthacnut (1040–2) Worcester was ravaged after two housecarles had been murdered. It was estimated by an eleventh-century writer that in all his realms Cnut maintained some 3,000 housecarles, but this figure may be an exaggeration. Military strength, however, was the key to his position in England, together with the placing of Scandinavians in high offices alongside Englishmen. Thorkell the Tall was regent during Cnut's absence in 1019–20. Of Cnut's earls in England, at least in the first half of the reign, the most numerous and the most important were Scandinavians. Although Godwine, earl of Wessex from 1018, was an Englishman he was married to Gytha, sister of Cnut's brother-in-law, so that Godwine's sons, among them Harold, king of England in 1066, were part Scandinavian and often with Scandinavian names. Siward, earl of Northumbria in the latter part of the reign and until his death in 1065, was wholly Danish. Leofric, earl of Mercia also in the last years of Cnut's reign and until his death in 1057, was of English descent but probably with Danish connections, judging from the name of a brother whom Cnut put to death in 1017, Northman. Behind these appointments there may have been a much greater confiscation of the property of English lords and the subsequent granting of it to Scandinavians than the sources would suggest. The great difficulty in the study of Cnut's reign is that, even apart from a deficiency of charters for the period 1026–31, the *Chronicle* entries are particularly brief and unhelpful. Annalistic writing went temporarily into abeyance after the fine flowering of Æthelred's reign, because the moment of crisis had passed. It may be that the absence of annalistic record is a testimony to Cnut's effective control of the country, a control maintained, so far as can be seen, by his undivided command of an efficient army and fleet.

Cnut died at Shaftesbury in 1035. Apart from being king of England, however, and part-resident in this country, he was also king of Denmark and his involvement in Baltic politics had been a major preoccupation. In 1016 Olaf Haroldson, a cousin of Olaf Tryggvason, seized the opportunity afforded by the presence of Eric of Norway in England to take control of Norway. Cnut left his brother-in-law, Ulf, as regent in Denmark when he set out to conquer England, but by 1026 he found himself facing a hostile coalition of Olaf, king of Norway, Ulf of Denmark, and Anund, king of Sweden. He defeated this alliance in a great conflict at Holy River, where the Swedish fleet was concentrated; and two years later Cnut was able to drive Olaf out of Norway. Lord of three kingdoms, Cnut immediately appointed his young son Harthacnut as king of Denmark, and sent first Hakon, son of the late Eric of Norway, and then Swein, son of Ælfgifu, with his mother as guardian to govern Norway. Norway, however, proved very difficult to control and Ælfgifu and her son can scarcely have had the resources to impose their alien régime; they were driven out by 1035 and Magnus, son of Olaf, established as king.

England and Denmark were not to be held together for long, though when Cnut died he intended that his only legitimate son, Harthacnut, should inherit both lands. Harthacnut was accepted as king in Denmark, but he remained in Denmark preparing to resist any attack by Magnus of Norway. A party led by Leofric, earl of Mercia, and most of the thegns north of the Thames, nominated Harold, son of Ælfgifu, as king. Though this was opposed by Earl Godwine and the chief men of Wessex, Ælfgifu and Harold were already in possession of the treasury at Winchester and Harold seized the kingship. The situation was complicated in 1036 by the arrival of Alfred and Edward, the sons of Æthelred and Emma, desiring to visit Emma at Winchester, possibly with a view to bidding for the kingship. Edward did reach Winchester, but Alfred was intercepted by Earl Godwine while on his way to confer with King Harold at London. Godwine, evidently by now a supporter of Harold, mutilated or slew many of Alfred's companions and sent the atheling to Ely. On reaching Ely Alfred was seized and blinded and died of injuries sustained, a crime for which contemporaries held Godwine responsible. Edward fled immediately back to Normandy. The crisis over, Harold set out to master the whole country. Already accepted as king by the Northumbrians and Mercians, Harold now received acceptance in Wessex and expelled Emma, mother of Harthacnut. But Harold's reign was short; on his death in March 1040 the English sent again to Harthacnut. Harthacnut had come to terms with Magnus of Norway whereby if either of them died without an heir the other should succeed to his kingdom. He was able to return to England, therefore, and for his reign of two years England and Denmark were temporarily reunited. Earl Godwine had to make his peace with the king for the slaying of his half-brother, Alfred, and in 1041 it seems that Harthacnut invited Edward to join him in England. Even with the possibility of Norman aid for Edward, it must have appeared rather like a walk into the lion's den, but Edward was bold enough to come and he was honourably received. Harthacnut was a passionate and violent young man who did not shrink from having the body of Harold exhumed and thrown into the Thames, and his rule distinguished itself by the oppressiveness of his taxation. Clearly perceiving the essential need for a strong fleet and army if his father's position were to be maintained, Harthacnut in 1040 exacted a heregeld of 21,099 pounds and then an additional sum of 11,048 pounds to maintain a fleet of 32 ships. While this taxation was not as heavy as the first exactions of Cnut, it probably represented a greater burden than that which had become customary in the last years of his father. Even so, Thorfinn, Earl of the Vikings of Orkney, raided south off the Isle of Man with impunity while Harthacnut was visiting Denmark. Harthacnut died suddenly in 1042, and at his death England and Denmark fell apart. A strong movement in England, led by Earl Godwine, put forward Edward, son of Æthelred, as king, while Swein, son of Ulf and Cnut's nephew, struggled to make himself master in Denmark. Cnut's Baltic empire had disintegrated, but neither Swein, king of Denmark, nor Magnus, king of Norway, and his successor, Harold Hardrada, ever abandoned the idea that England might be re-annexed and that they might one day establish a power like that of Cnut. Edward the Confessor (1042–66) and Harold (1066), and even William the Conqueror (1066–87), lived under the constant threat of Scandinavian invasion and Norwegian kings continued to ravage the coasts of Britain into the mid-twelfth century.

Edward the Confessor (1042–66) and the Norman Conquest (1066)

Edward the Confessor was a man of about 40 when he came to the throne of Wessex after a long exile spent in Normandy. Normandy was the duchy settled in the early tenth century by the Vikings, but by the mid-eleventh century becoming French in culture. It was to an Anglo-Danish kingdom that Edward returned, and the forces and personalities which shaped his reign had been established in the time of the Danish kings. Cnut's recognition of earldoms set the seal on the evolution of the separatist provinces which had been evolving out of the ancient kingdoms during the reigns of Edgar and Æthelred, thereby making the fortunes of the over-mighty subject. Cnut, with his army, fleet and harsh taxation, and his reputation as a victorious warlord, was able to control the situation but Edward proved less capable. The great personalities who dominate the politics of his reign—Godwine, earl of Wessex, in particular, Leofric, Earl of Mercia, and Siward of Northumbria—were appointed to their influential positions in the second half of of Cnut's reign and they survived throughout most of Edward's; Edward came to England virtually as a stranger, bereft of influential friends and relatives, obliged to work as well as he could with the servants of the régime which had overthrown his father and destroyed many of his kinsmen.

The *Anglo-Saxon Chronicle* for the reign of Edward the Confessor survives in several, partly related versions, one of which (the oldest) is anti-Godwine, another pro-Godwine. Interpretations of the reign vary because, even with a relatively detailed chronicle account, many aspects remain obscure; and as early as the twelfth century William of Malmesbury questioned whether Godwine and his sons aimed at equal sovereignty with the king or whether they were the steadfast defenders and supporters of his government, and he records that Norman and English authorities answered this question differently.

Edward married Edith, daughter of Earl Godwine, in 1045, in which year Harold, son of Godwine, became earl of East Anglia. Harold's older brother, Swein, was earl of the *Hwicce* from 1043. There is little reason to suppose, however, that Edward was not his own master in the early years of his reign. In the 1040s he was far from being the monk-like king of later legend. He had a violent temper, loved hunting and admired the Viking warrior, Olaf Tryggvason, king of Norway in the time of Æthelred. There is no reason to suppose that he was the celibate that later generations took him to be. He did not scruple to disinherit his mother, Emma, when he found that she had been intriguing for the succession of Magnus of Norway to the English throne. He appointed his own candidates from Normandy to episcopal vacancies—Robert to London in 1044 and Canterbury in 1051, William to London in 1051 and Ulf to Dorchester in the same year—and both Robert and Ulf were unpopular in English circles. When Magnus was threatening to invade England, probably by virtue of the treaty made with Harthacnut, Edward went out in person with the fleet to oppose him. He was at Sandwich in 1044 with 35 ships and he was again positioned there in 1045. In 1048 he pursued a Viking raiding party and chased it away to Flanders. Not only did Edward refuse to send aid to Swein, king of Denmark and Godwine's nephew by marriage, in his struggle with Magnus of Norway, despite the appeals of Godwine, but in 1049 he supported the Emperor Henry III against Baldwin of Flanders by a naval blockade regardless of Godwine's friendship with the count. These are not the actions of a man dominated by Godwine and the members of Godwine's family. In 1049 it was to Baldwin that Swein, son of Godwine, fled after he had slain his kinsman, Earl Beorn, and there he remained until reconciled to his father and the king. In 1051 Godwine's son, Tostig, married Judith, daughter of Count Baldwin. The action of Edward, therefore, in attacking the count of Flanders is hardly likely to have commended itself to the earl of Wessex.

By *c.* 1050 the situation was changing. The death of Magnus of Norway in 1047 removed the greatest threat to Edward's security, for Magnus's successor, Harold Hardrada, showed no immediate signs of adopting towards England the policies of his predecessor. Edward slowly began to reduce the armed forces on which the strength of the king rested. In 1049 he paid off nine mercenary crews and in 1050 disbanded the remaining fleet; in 1051 he remitted what the chronicler calls danegeld but which was in fact the heregeld of the Danish kings. Though housecarles survived until 1066 and fought at Hastings, by that date many had become very largely country gentlemen, indistinguishable from thegns, and a large, permanent standing army of housecarles can hardly have existed in the years immediately after 1051 because there would no longer be any means of paying it. In so far as Domesday Book (1086) implies that heregeld or danegeld was being at least partially collected before the accession of William the Conqueror, this was possibly a desperate revival measure on the part of King Harold. Edward, himself, made agreements with south-east ports like Dover and Sandwich to supply him with ships when necessary in return for fiscal privileges, but his actions in 1049–51 cut at the very basis of the military and naval power at the disposal of the king of England. Whatever the motives for his actions, Edward left himself vulnerable to attack from any one of his over-mighty subjects, and in the summer of 1051 Earl Godwine did defy the king. Edward's struggle with the Godwines in the period 1051–2 has been seen as a royal attempt to break the power of this influential group which had been dominating him hitherto, but, as has been seen, there is no real evidence for such domination in in the years 1042–51. The struggle was the result of an attempt by an aristocratic family, possibly dissatisfied with royal policies (though which policies in particular it is difficult to say), to resist the king's will; it should be seen as one of several sporadic rebellions against successive Anglo-Saxon kings which invariably ended either in the overthrow of the rebels or the deposition and possibly death of the king under attack. The immediate cause of the opposition of the Godwines to Edward in 1051 was quite petty. Eustace, count of Boulogne and the king's brother-in-law, while returning to the Continent after visiting Edward in England, became involved in a skirmish with the citizens of Dover in the course of which several of his men were slain. Edward ordered Godwine, in whose earldom Dover lay, to ravage the town, which Godwine refused to do, holding Eustace primarily responsible for the incident. Godwine was summoned to a council in early September at Langtree in Gloucestershire. The king sent for Leofric of Mercia and Siward of Northumbria who arrived with small forces to find that Godwine and his sons were assembling a large army from southern England. Reinforcements were speedily sent for. The Godwines assembled at Beverstone, but the royal party refrained from attacking for fear that civil war would endanger the security of the realm. A second council was arranged for late September in London. In the meantime Edward summoned the English army from south as well as from north England, the effect of which was that when the time of the council arrived many of the West Saxon thegns who had previously followed Godwine now adhered to the royal cause. Consequently, Godwine and his sons at Southwark found themselves outnumbered and facing an implacable king. It appears that Edward refused to grant a safe-conduct into his court to enable the Godwines to clear themselves by judicial oath-swearing, and safe-conduct was granted only that they might leave the realm within five days. Godwine, with his sons Swein and Tostig, fled to Baldwin of Flanders; Harold, with another brother, Leofwine, took ship for Ireland. Edward concluded the matter by sending his queen, Edith, daughter of Godwine, to the nunnery of Wherwell. The king had now overthrown his most powerful critics.

Edward's strength rested on the support of Leofric and Siward, and in 1052 he found that they preferred to make peace with the Godwines rather than risk civil war. In that year the Godwines returned in strength, Harold ravaging the Cornish peninsula and joining forces with his father off the coast of Dorset. Together they advanced along the south-east coast, winning the support of the men of Romney, Hythe, Hastings and Folkestone. Edward had stationed 40 small boats at Sandwich, which failed to intercept the Godwines and withdrew to London. It was at London that the opposing forces met for the second time, but now Godwine, with the support of what was left of the English fleet, was in a far stronger position. This time Godwine was prepared to fight, and as the prospect of civil war loomed larger the king's supporters resolved to come to terms. Edward refused peace at first but was prevailed upon by his great men. Clearly, he had no independent striking force. Hostages were given by the Godwines who cleared themselves of the charges against them on oath and who were then restored to their possessions. Swein did not return; he went on a pilgrimage to Jerusalem and died *en route*. Archbishop Robert and Bishop Ulf were forced to flee the country, together with some at least of Edward's Norman soldiers. Godwine died in the April of the following year (1053), when his son Harold succeeded him as earl of Wessex.

The Godwines have often been seen as breaking the influence of the king by the circumstances of their return in 1052, but even in the period 1052–66 Edward never became a mere cipher. He was always the power behind the scenes, even though he left the rigours of military expeditions to Harold. It was Edward himself who went to negotiate peace terms with Malcolm III, king of the Scots, in 1059. Wessex was the only earldom in the hands of the Godwines between 1053 and 1055, for, when Harold succeeded his father, East Anglia was given to Ælfgar, son of Leofric of Mercia; Herefordshire, with Oxfordshire, was given to the king's nephew, Ralph the Timid. In 1055, however, Tostig, Harold's brother, succeeded Siward as earl of Northumbria. Ælfgar was outlawed soon after, unjustly according to the *Anglo-Saxon Chronicle*, but allowed to succeed to Mercia on his father's death in 1057. East Anglia was then given to Gyrth, Harold's younger brother, and when Ralph the Timid died the same year his earldom passed under the control of Harold. When Ælfgar died in 1062, Mercia passed to his young son, Edwin. Gradually, over the years, therefore, the territorial influence of Harold and his brothers grew, and this development was naturally paralleled by their assumption of a leading role in affairs of state. When Ælfgar was exiled in 1055 he secured ships from Ireland and, with the aid of Gruffudd, king of Gwynedd, attacked Hereford, driving back the forces of Ralph and sacking the minster. It was Harold who negotiated at Billingsley in Gloucestershire with the enemy and agreed that Ælfgar be restored. In 1056 Harold negotiated a treaty with King Gruffudd by which the Welsh ruler was to become the under-king of Edward. In 1063 Harold and Tostig launched a major campaign against Gruffudd by land and sea from Bristol and Rhuddlan, which culminated in the betrayal and assassination of Gruffudd by his own men; his severed head was sent to Harold who sent it on to Edward. But these incidents may present a false picture of Harold's power. Leofric of Mercia also took part in the negotiations with Gruffudd in 1056. The expedition of 1063 may have been entrusted to Harold and Tostig alone because of the youth of Edwin of Mercia. Harold was not able to prevent the return of Ælfgar from exile in 1055, nor again after a second expulsion in 1058. Neither was he able to maintain Tostig permanently in Northumbria. Tostig appears to have ruled his northern earldom oppressively; he had prominent Northumbrian lords assassinated, one of them actually at the royal court and allegedly with the connivance at least of Queen Edith. In 1065 the Northumbrians rebelled and invited Morcar, brother of Edwin, to become their earl. Harold met a turbulent Northumbrian army at Northampton and was forced to concede, on behalf of the king, the appointment of Morcar. Tostig departed for Flanders; it was evident that the Godwines could still be displaced.

It is the succession problem which overshadows the reign of Edward the Confessor. The sons of Earl Godwine would live in expectation of being uncles of the next king until it became clear that the marriage of Edward and Edith was to be childless. Edward had neither brother nor son to succeed him so it was important to nominate a successor. Edward's attitude to the succession, however, is shrouded in greater obscurity than historians have allowed. Norman sources claim that he nominated William, duke of Normandy, as his heir and that he sent Robert of Jumièges to Normandy with the news. In early 1051 Robert travelled to Rome as elect of Canterbury for the pallium, and William could have been informed of Edward's intention on this occasion. Indeed, in 1051 between the expulsion and the restoration of the Godwines, William visited England. Historians have tended to see the quarrel between Edward and the Godwines as stemming in part at least from Edward's determination that William of Normandy should succeed him. It is thought that the Godwines were opposed to the succession of William. Norman sources may be interpreted as showing that the price the Godwines had to pay for their restoration in 1052 was their acceptance of the king's wishes respecting the succession. In 1057 Edward the atheling, son of King Edmund Ironside, was brought back from exile in Hungary, and this has been seen as an attempt by Earl Harold to secure instead recognition of the atheling as Edward's heir. The atheling, however, was unable to see the king, for reasons the Anglo-Saxon chronicler knew not, and he died soon after his arrival. Edward, it has been assumed, refused to see him. In about 1064 Harold visited William in Normandy and while there is said to have sworn on sacred relics to support the duke's candidature for the English throne on the death of Edward. Edward may have compelled Harold to make his peace with William. Edward certainly had around him a group of Frenchmen who followed him over from Normandy in the years following 1042, and it is significant that the *Chronicle* states that the French and in particular Robert of Jumièges were responsible for the ill-will between Godwine and the king in 1051. It may even be argued that in reducing his military resources as he did, Edward was seeking to deprive any potential rebel of the effective means by which to oppose the succession of William of Normandy.

There are a number of problems, however, in this reconstruction. Not all the Frenchmen in England were necessarily unpopular. In 1066 one of Harold's supporters was Robert, son of Wimarc, a Norman kinsman of Duke William, who had been established in a castle in England as early as the 1050s. Too much must not be made of the presence of Frenchmen in England in the reign of the Confessor for Lotharingians and Germans had risen to high office under Cnut. A more serious reservation is the heavy bias towards William in the Norman sources and their blatantly propagandist character. It is far from clear how far they may have distorted William's dealings, firstly with Edward and then with Harold. Robert, duke of Normandy, William's father and Edward's cousin, had been Edward's benefactor while Edward was in exile, and Duke William could be seen as Edward's nearest blood-relation. He may have considered himself to be Edward's heir, and Robert of Jumièges may have been attempting to secure his recognition as such. But Edward must have known that the English would not readily accept William, as the events of the Norman Conquest were to show. English sources know nothing of any offer of the throne to William. On the contrary, they are quite explicit that it was King Edward who had the atheling, the son of Edmund Ironside, brought back from Hungary. Furthermore, the events of early 1066 present a strange paradox. Though Archbishop Stigand apparently regarded most of what the dying Edward said as the ravings of a diseased old man, Harold's supporters claimed that he nominated Harold on his deathbed as his successor. Even the Normans seem to have accepted this fact. The great men of Wessex must have been very impressed to accept Harold despite their knowledge—if we accept the Norman account—that Edward had intended since 1051 that William should succeed him. If on the other, hand, they had always been opposed to the succession of William, Edward must have been a very forceful personality indeed to have persisted in what would have appeared to be misguided wilfulness. But it cannot be said that William's own position in Normandy in 1051 was such as to lead the Confessor seriously to consider him as his heir. William was surrounded by disaffection and his control of the duchy at this period was insecure. It is possible that he came to England in 1051 to seek support from Edward for his own position in Normandy.

Edward the atheling was the heir-apparent of the West Saxon royal house, and his son, Edgar, was for a time the figure-head of the English resistance to William of Normandy after the battle of Hastings. King Edward is unlikely to have had the atheling brought back from Hungary unless he intended to recognise him as his successor, and it is clearly stated by an English source that this was his intention. We need suspect no Godwine obstruction to a meeting of king and atheling. The atheling simply died before a royal audience could be arranged. His premature death left the king with no obvious choice of an heir, for Edgar was probably too young and inexperienced—he was still alive in 1125. Harold certainly went to Normandy in about 1064 but the evidence does not permit us to say with any certainty that Edward sent him so that Harold would acknowledge William as Edward's successor. If it were known that William considered that he had a right to the English kingdom, this could have been a preliminary conciliatory move to gauge the duke's reaction before Edward's formal recognition of Harold as his heir. Harold evidently received unpleasant treatment in Normandy and claimed that he had been tricked into swearing on the sacred relics to support William. Edward, therefore, delayed nomination of Harold until the very last possible moment to give William less opportunity to marshal continental support. In view of the swiftness with which Harold was crowned in January 1066, there can be little doubt that his succession was well planned in advance. In the absence of an adult heir of the blood-royal to Edward, Harold, by his experience and leadership in the kingdom, could be the only possible Saxon successor.

After his death, the cult of Edward the Confessor as the patron saint of England was only eclipsed in the fourteenth century by that of St. George. There is no doubt that Edward, like other kings of this period on the Continent, became increasingly preoccupied with religious matters as he grew older. Westminster Abbey was planned by him in the last years of his life and begun at his orders. But there is no reason to suppose that excessive piety was always a primary characteristic, or that Edward was a weak and foolish man. His greatest folly was his apparent reduction of the armed strength of the kingdom, but in so far as

Domesday Book (1086) implies that heregeld or danegeld was being at least partially collected before the accession of William the Conqueror, this was possibly a revival measure towards the end of the Confessor's reign. Edward died on 5 January 1066. The *Anglo-Saxon Chronicle* preserves a glowing tribute to him in verse. On 6 January Edward was buried in Westminster and Harold crowned king by Ealdred, archbishop of York, according to the English evidence, though the Normans maintained Stigand crowned him and so they represented the coronation on the Bayeux Tapestry. Stigand, previously bishop successively of Elmham and Winchester, had been a supporter of Earl Godwine. He was appointed archbishop of Canterbury on the flight of Robert of Jumièges but his position was canonically unsound because of the unlawful expulsion of Robert. For this reason Harold no doubt turned to the archbishop of York.

Harold went to receive separate recognition as king from the Northumbrians, and he married Ealdgyth, sister of Edwin and Morcar. But his position was weak. A comet, later to be viewed by Halley, appeared in April and was regarded as a sign presaging misfortune. His brother, Tostig, was supporting the Norwegian king, Harold Hardrada, in his preparations for an attack on England, while William of Normandy, preparing to invade to make good his own claim, was receiving papal blessing for his venture. Even Swein of Denmark appears to have been claiming that he, too, had been promised the throne of England by Edward, and there was probably every likelihood that he would attack also. Harold, for his part, had only a skeleton fleet in the channel to oppose William. When their supplies were exhausted, the ships departed for home before favourable winds enabled William to cross. It was the winds that kept William at the mouth of the Somme, which blew Harold Hardrada across, first to northern Scotland and then down to the north-east coast of England. If Harold's naval resources were slight, he would lack in addition a strong army of paid mercenaries such as had been the backbone of the military might of the Anglo-Danish kings. He was largely dependent on the *fyrd*, the Old English army recruited primarily from the thegns of the shires, the army of Æthelred and Edmund. This native army was not as out-of-date and obsolete in 1066 as was once thought. The nobility, which formed the essential backbone of the army, may have been trained to fight on horseback, with archers employed to provide support. Cavalry and archers are said in a thirteenth century Norse saga to have been used against the forces of Harold Hardrada at Stamfordbridge, near York, on 25 September; in this battle, Harold won a complete victory and both Hardrada and Tostig perished. Nevertheless, the forces of the northern earls, Edwin and Morcar, had been seriously depleted by the Norwegian attack, and on 29 September William landed at Pevensey; Harold was obliged to make a rapid march south. It may be that Harold intended to take William by surprise by a night attack but the English only reached the Norman camp as dawn broke. It was a defectively organised and possibly exhausted army which was obliged to take up a defensive position on Senlac Hill. Battle was joined before English reinforcements could arrive, and in the battle of Hastings, fought on 14 October, Harold was defeated by those tactics which he is said to have employed at Stamfordbridge: cavalry, archers and possibly the device of feigned flight. Harold, with his brothers, Gyrth and Leofwine, fell around the royal standard of the West Saxon kings. While the defeat at Hastings was probably due to misfortune and faulty strategy as much to as weaknesses in the *fyrd* itself, it is likely that the Old English army ultimately proved as unsuitable for prolonged and intensive fighting as it had done in the last years of Æthelred's reign.

The battle of Hastings is one of the best-known events in English history. Its consequences lie outside the scope of this volume, but a brief word may be said about the impact of the Norman Conquest on English development. This has been the subject of much historical controversy in the past and is still a living issue as historians attempt to assess to what extent the Norman Conquest involved a break with the past in English history. The Normans, of course, were in a minority and, in that the Norman Conquest did not bring with it mass migration from the Continent, the Norman kings were compelled, as Cnut had been compelled, to maintain the fabric of the Old English state. There were changes of some considerable significance. The Anglo-Danish nobility was largely disinherited, Englishmen ceased to hold high administrative or ecclesiastical office, the old earldoms were destroyed, Anglo-Saxon Law was at first modified by and then eclipsed by Anglo-Norman Law, the local administrative and military machinery came to revolve around the fief or feudal estates as well as around the hundred and shire, French displaced Anglo-Saxon as the language of polite society. But it is easier to perceive such changes than to define the fundamental bases of continuity. The rank and file of the English peasantry, though probably more depressed by severe taxation, constituted a solid belt of social and agricultural continuity across the divide of 1066. In the Anglo-Saxon period were laid the foundations of the English language, of English literature, art, government and administration, of English ecclesiastical organisation and of English medieval piety. Against such deeper currents of continuity, the Norman Conquest and its immediate consequences were but ripples on a troubled surface.

Book two

1 GOVERNMENT AND SOCIETY

Chapter one

Social structure and social conditions

Anglo-Saxon society at one and the same time embraced anarchical forces tending to disrupt that society and primitive but influential sanctions and institutions which lent order to social chaos. In a society in which might was often right, violence to person and property widespread, and the criminal difficult to apprehend, the order of the Anglo-Saxon day may well appear to us as having been little but a succession of drunken brawls, murderous family feuds, pillaging robber-bands, suspicious and aggressive villagers, rampaging princes and bloody skirmishes. But it is clear that we must not over-emphasise such aspects of daily living; perhaps the most central fact of Anglo-Saxon social history is that men were able to farm the land successfully on a greater scale than ever before and to develop trade with lands overseas, achievements for which it is essential that the greater part of the population live more or less permanently at peace. There is no doubt that much lawlessness and brutality prevailed throughout the length and breadth of Anglo-Saxon England, but what is particularly striking is that, with so few effective administrative and legal restraints possible, early English society was so stable. If there is one certain fact of Anglo-Saxon society, it is that it was never uniformly the same from the confines of Kent to the borders of Strathclyde. Nevertheless, two social institutions probably contributed most to the relative stability of Anglo-Saxon society, as indeed to that of the Celtic and Germanic societies of west Europe in general: the kindred group and lordship. The kindred group may be defined as the basic unit of Germanic society, the relationship between lord and man the fundamental bond. Though the Anglo-Saxon period appears to have seen the slow waning of the influence of the kindred and the steady waxing of that of the lord, both institutions remained complementary and fundamental to social behaviour until the Norman Conquest.

Kinship and wergeld

It is uncertain how many individuals a single Anglo-Saxon kindred group covered, but all blood-relations within a fairly large but well-defined limit, probably to six degrees (*i.e.* to fourth cousins), would compose a kindred. Originally a man had to belong to a kindred to possess standing in Law for the kindred was the social unit through which the Law at first operated. A man without kin could find himself outside the Law and unable to obtain justice. The kindred not only fed one of its members if he were in prison; it stood surety or guarantee in court for his or her good conduct and saw to the paying of any fine incurred. If circumstances were such that a man had to be ransomed, his kindred paid the price. A man or woman, therefore, received many benefits from belonging to a kindred should he or she become involved in legal proceedings. Conversely, it was the duty of the kindred to see that its members conformed to the legal demands of society. The laws of Æthelberht, king of Kent, decreed that if a homicide escaped his kinsmen had to pay half the *wergeld* of the slain man. Compensation for a death or mutilation depended on the sum at which a man's life was valued, and it was this valuation which constituted his *wergeld* or man-price. The clause in Æthelberht's laws was obviously intended to bring pressure on a kindred to see that one of its members did not evade justice. The kindred itself was a law-enforcing institution. Similarly, the laws of Athelstan (924–39) commanded the kindred of any man without a lord to find him a lord. And in everyday life a family was cosseted and if necessary supported by its kindred. Young heirs were maintained by the kindred, who had a say in the dispersal of the landed estates of one of its members and in the arrangement of marriages. Orphans and widows were provided for by the kindred, and if a woman married and moved to another district she could still call on her kindred to protect and maintain her if necessary. Marriage within the kindred was prohibited. The kindred, therefore, operated its own social service within the limits of the group. If a man in Holy Orders or a stranger suffered robbery or assault the bishop or king would act as his kinsman and protector. In his famous *Sermon* of 1014, Wulfstan II, archbishop of York, expressed forcibly his view that the sense of reciprocal responsibility which held the kindred together was then weakening, kinsman no longer protecting kinsman any more than a stranger. From the earliest times the evolution of new social relationships had corroded the monopoly of the kindred over the daily dealings of its members. The laws of Wihtred of Kent allowed a ceorl to have as compurgators in court three men not of his own kindred but of his own class, and in the time of Ine of Wessex there existed rather mysterious groups of persons called associates, who fulfilled the role of the kindred. From the tenth century tithings, or groups of ten men all responsible for each other's good conduct, came into being as well as urban gilds providing protection and support for their members. In certain instances, the influence of the lord had displaced the kindred from its traditional role. Making allowances for all these developments, however, it would probably be a mistake to regard the kindred, even by the time of the Norman Conquest, as anything other than a powerful social institution.

The most spectacular duty of the kindred was the obligation to pursue the blood-feud or vendetta. If a man were slain, it was the duty of the kindred to exact compensation from the homicide. Only if the slayer was a member of the same kin could no action be taken. If the homicide refused to pay, or if the kindred preferred to exact vengeance, the kindred could take the lives of the offender and a stipulated number of his kin. Such action might well result in retaliatory measures by the homicide's kindred, and a blood-feud would be launched which could affect generation after generation and from which not even the slaves of the persons involved were immune. The blood-feud was allowed free reign in early centuries, though the Church sought to impose penance on participants. A kindred might even seek to avenge a member slain in the course of theft. With the passage of time, kings tried to limit the occasions on which a kindred might resort to the blood-feud and to compel them instead to accept compensation as a general rule. A man who legitimately slew another while defending his lord, for example, was liable to incur the vendetta until King Alfred legislated that he be exempt. There is no doubt that before Alfred's time a kindred could seek vengeance for any of its members slain in battle, and an Anglo-Saxon battle, particularly an internal conflict within a kingdom, must have perpetuated itself in an increasing kaleidoscope of vendettas. But a man had the obligation to avenge his lord if the latter were slain, and Alfred forbade all men to act against their lord. Alfred ordered all men to seek justice in court before resorting to private violence, and sought to impose a interval of 30 days between the apprehending of an offender and the initiation of private vengeance during which time compensation could be offered. Edmund I (939–46) defined further the limits within which the vendetta could be pursued. The homicide alone was to bear responsibility for his actions and he had 12 months in which to pay compensation. If his kinsmen chose to abandon him and refused him shelter they were absolved from the vendetta altogether. It would be such legal pronouncements as this which would contribute to that weakening of the ties of kinship which Wulfstan lamented. Edmund decreed that if compensation were agreed, the paternal kindred should pay two-thirds of the sum involved, the maternal kindred one-third; payment was to be made at regular intervals, and part of the compensation would go to the dead man's kin, part to his lord and part to the king. It is difficult to assess how successful these royal attempts to limit the vendetta were. All that can be said is that the blood-feud was not eradicated. It survived into the reign of William the Conqueror in regions as far apart as Gloucestershire and Northumbria. The feud between the kindred of Uhtred, earl of Northumbria, and his assassin, Thurbrand, and his kindred, lasted from 1016 to 1073. Carl, the son of Thurbrand, slew Ealdred, the son of Uhtred, immediately after planning to go on a pilgrimage to Rome with him, Ealdred being unwise enough to believe that such devout aspirations on Carl's part could in any measure overcome Carl's obligation to avenge Ealdred's slaying of Thurbrand. Waltheof, earl of Northumbria and Ealdred's grandson, massacred the majority of the sons and grandsons of Carl in vengeance for Ealdred in a single surprise attack.

What lay behind the distinction of noble and peasant, behind the different *wergelds* remains obscure, but throughout the Anglo-Saxon period the social standing of men depended not so much on their wealth or possessions as upon their *wergeld* or value. Early English society was divided primarily into two classes, the noble class composed of men of *gesith*—a term which died out after the ninth century—or thegn status, and the peasant class composed of men of ceorl status. A thegn, it has been said, might possess vast estates or none at all, a ceorl might be very wealthy or barely solvent; what divided them was that the ceorl was a *twyhynde* man, a two-hundred man whose *wergeld* was 200 shillings, while a thegn was a *twelfhynde* man, a twelve-hundred man whose *wergeld* was 1,200 shillings. It is evident, therefore, that in value a considerable gulf divided the two classes. In Kent this division was not quite so marked; there the nobleman was only valued at three times that of the peasant, for the ceorl was worth twice as much as his West Saxon counterpart. The possession of a higher *wergeld* brought distinct legal advantages. In Anglo-Saxon courts there was no assessment of evidence but rather an assessment of oaths. A man swore that a charge was true or false and if necessary produced a number of his kinsmen or fellows to support his oath as compurgators or oath-helpers. Oaths were theoretically equated with a specified number of *hides* and related to the seriousness of the offence and the amount of fine involved. If, therefore, the fine for a particular offence was 120 shillings, a man might swear an oath for 120 *hides*. Now there is some evidence that a ceorl could swear an oath to the value of 5 *hides*, a thegn to the value of 30. The effect of this was that a thegn, with noble compurgators, would need far fewer oath-helpers than would a ceorl with peasant compurgators. Consequently, it would be far easier for a thegn to bring a charge against a ceorl than for a ceorl to accuse a thegn, and far easier, of course, for a thegn to refute a charge brought against him by a ceorl than vice versa. Similarly, a ceorl would find it harder to pay the *wergeld* of a thegn than the latter would that of the ceorl. The real grimness of the distinction lay in that the thegn, being worth six ceorls, could be avenged on six ceorls, thereby involving five possibly innocent persons. Some ceorls, however, could look after themselves. King Athelstan had to legislate not only against the kindred of nobles but also those of ceorls who were so powerful in their own districts that they were able to prevert the course of justice.

The value of a Mercian king is known to have been 12 times that of a Mercian thegn, half of which belonged to the kingship and half to the person of the king. Similarly, a Northumbrian atheling or prince was worth six Northumbrian thegns. Such ratios clearly prevailed in Wessex also. Ine exacted a sum of 30,000 *sceattas* from the men of Kent, for the murder of the atheling Mul, brother of King Cædwalla, an amount equal to that of a Northumbrian atheling. East Anglian ratios are unknown, but it is unlikely that they were substantially different. If these *wergelds* are equated with the price of oxen, at a time, for example, when an ox was worth six shillings and there were four pennies in a shilling, a West Saxon ceorl was worth 33 oxen, a *twelfhynde* man 200 oxen, and a king 2,400 oxen. The Anglo-Saxon shilling was a unit of account, at first consisting of four pennies throughout the country, except in Kent where a Kentish shilling, originally a gold coin, was considered the equivalent of 20 pennies. The *gesith* of Ine's time, therefore, the *twelfhynde* man, was worth 4,800 pence, the ceorl 800 pence, and these values remained more or less static in Northumbria and Mercia. In Kent, a nobleman was worth 300 shillings each of 20 pennies, that is 6,000 pence, and the Kentish ceorl 2,000 pence. By the tenth century the West Saxon shilling had come to be a unit of account representing five pennies, so that a *gesith* was now worth 1,200 shillings each of five pennies, that is 6,000 pence. This is when the West Saxon ceorl became worth 1,000 pence, exactly half the value of the Kentish peasant. The change may well date to the annexation of Kent by Egbert (802–39), and it may have been an attempt to establish a common standard for the aristocracy of the two kingdoms. The effect was to increase the value of the West Saxon thegn and ceorl over their Northumbrian and Mercian counterparts. A Mercian nobleman, for example, was now worth the equivalent only of 980 West Saxon shillings. It is not clear whether or not the West Saxons, when they annexed Kent, depressed the Kentish ceorl to the value of the West Saxon ceorl. There is conflicting evidence on this point.

In the regions in which they settled, the Scandinavians brought their *wergelds* into line with West Saxon values. In Northumbria, the unit of account was the *thryms*, equal to three pennies, and the *wergeld* of a thegn in Viking Northumbria became 2,000 *thrymsas*, that is 6,000 pence or 1,200 West Saxon shillings. In the *Law of the North People* the *wergeld* of the king of what must be the Scandinavian kingdom of York was raised to equal that of 15 thegns, that is to 30,000 *thrymsas* which equals 90,000 pence or 18,000 West Saxon shillings. His value, therefore, was now above that of the West Saxon king unless the latter increased his own *wergeld* correspondingly. But probably the greater insecurity of the northern king indicated a higher *wergeld*. It is known that in the later tenth century a breach of the king's peace in the Danelaw carried with it a fine of up to more than nine times that in Wessex. The class of northern society which did not benefit from these Scandinavian readjustments was the ceorl class, for a Northumbrian ceorl continued to be valued in Mercian shillings. This meant that a Northumbrian thegn in the Scandinavian period was worth not six but more than seven times a ceorl. Further, the treaty between Alfred and Guthrum in 886 appears to have raised all Danish freemen to the status of thegns. Only the Danish freedmen (half-free) and ceorls in Danish territory *on gafolland* were to be valued at 200 Mercian shillings. It is disputed whether the ceorl *on gafolland* means a ceorl who occupied rented land and performed labour services, or a free, landowning ceorl who simply paid customary royal dues; if the former view is correct, those among the English peasantry in the Danelaw who were landowners were raised to the thegnage along with Danish freemen, but if the latter they secured no such privilege. Ine's laws refer to peasants as *gafolgelden* or *gebur*, apparently meaning at that time peasants who owned land and peasants who rented land respectively. It seems probable that both groups were included in the term—ceorl *on gafolland*—and, therefore, that in the territories of Guthrum, if not throughout the Danelaw, no English ceorls were elevated with the Danish freemen to noble status. But the nature of the evidence does not permit certainty on this interesting and important point.

Ecclesiastics also had their values which were in proportion to the status of the individual. An archbishop's *wergeld* was the same as an atheling's, while a bishop was four times as valuable as a thegn and a priest the equal of a thegn. From time to time in the laws there appear classes of laymen who do not belong to the major groups of *twelfhynde* and *twyhynde*. In early Wessex a *sixhynde* or six-hundred man, an intermediate class of nobleman not impossibly of British origin, was a *gesith*, one of whose characteristics might be that he owned no land. This class disappears from the records of post-Viking centuries, unless the *radcnihts* (mounted warriors or riders) of the western midlands were *sixhynde* men. In both Wessex and Northumbria peasants of British origin were valued at roughly half an English ceorl, while in Kent a *laet* class, again possibly of British origin, was divided into three groups worth respectively four-fifths, three-fifths and two-fifths of a ceorl. By the late eleventh century even a slave, the lowest of all persons on the social scale, had a *wergeld* of 40 pence allowed him. At the other end of the scale certain privileged members of the Anglo-Saxon nobility were valued more highly than the *twelfhynde* man. Select bodies of thegns around the king, king's thegns, were entitled to swear an oath for 60 *hides*, an oath twice as valuable as that of the ordinary thegn, and by the time of Cnut they paid a very high *heriot* or death duty. Whether or not they had a *wergeld* twice as high as the *twelfhynde* thegn is unrecorded, but when the Scandinavians settled in England they acknowledged their army leaders, the *holds*, as being possessed of a *wergeld* twice as high as a thegn's, 4,000 *thrymsas* or 2,400 West Saxon shillings, thereby creating a highly privileged class among the military aristocracy of the Danelaw. Thurbrand, the man who slew Uhtred, was a *hold* and, when such men became involved in vendettas, compensation figures in terms of oxen would be astronomical. Finally, if *wergelds* could be raised during the Anglo-Saxon period it seems they could also be lowered. An early twelfth century law code, stating ancient custom, records that the *wergeld* of a *villein*, roughly speaking the Anglo-Norman equivalent of a ceorl, was 100 shillings in Mercia and Wessex, only half the traditional figure. This reduction may have been part of what is likely to have been a depression of the peasantry following the Norman Conquest. But one thing is certain. No matter what economic changes took place among the ranks of the peasantry during the Anglo-Saxon period, in 1066 as in 600 a man's *wergeld* was still the crucial determinant of the individual's place and position in society.

Lordship

Lords were men of royal or noble (thegnly) status; their dependants could be either thegns or ceorls. A man swore to be faithful to his lord, to love all that his lord loved and to hate all that his lord hated, promising faithfulness and obedience, and in return the lord promised to protect and provide for his man. If his dependant were slain, the lord exacted *manbot* (man-price), a percentage of the *wergeld*, and the sum may have varied according to the rank of the lord. In court a lord could act as compurgator for one of his men, and his oath would be the valuable *twelfhynde* man's oath. On his man's death, the lord took *heriot*. This was death duty in the form of war-gear, a repayment in a way of the original gift of arms and weapons made to a man by a lord at the time of his becoming the lord's dependant. Horses, helmets, spears and shields formed the *heriot* of a thegn and had to be paid by the widow within a year. For a man of inferior wealth and position, the *heriot* was fixed by Cnut at two pounds.

The gift of arms was ceremonially performed and symbolised the bond of loyalty between lord and man, and subsequent gifts of weapons and treasure were rewards for faithful service. In the earliest period of Germanic history, lordship was essentially the institution which linked together the warrior chief and his war band. Tacitus records that the early Germanic chief fought for victory, his companions for their lord.

Gesith was an Anglo-Saxon term meaning companion, while thegn, which originally meant servant, also came to signify companion. Bede describes how young warriors came from far and wide to serve in the warband of Oswine, king of Deira. The relationship so established between lord and man, chief and companion, was the most honourable of which Anglo-Saxon society could conceive. To the poet nothing was more glorious than to perform valorous deeds in the war band, nothing more grievous than treachery to a lord or exile from the lord's presence, nothing of greater occasion for sadness than the deserted and ruined hall of a dead lord. Such sentiments were common to the Celtic as well as to the Germanic world at this time. They were not always uppermost in practice. King Alfred had to legislate against treachery to a lord at a time when the Danish wars were straining the fabric of society. Not infrequently the shortcomings may have been on the lord's side. Æthelred II had to promise to be a gracious lord in 1014. Æthelbald of Mercia was one of a handful of Anglo-Saxon kings whose unsavoury personality culminated in their assassination by members of their own retinue. But the heroic ideals of the poets were not necessarily far removed from reality. All King Ecgfrith's bodyguard perished with him in 685 at the battle of *Nechtanesmere*, and the followers of both Cynewulf of Wessex and the atheling Cyneheard preferred to die with their respective lords rather than surrender, even to their kinsmen, in 786. For each king who was abandoned or assassinated by one of more of his followers, a great many more were faithfully protected. Edwin of Northumbria escaped assassination when one of his thegns threw himself between Edwin and the dagger of an envoy. In 744 Alchred, king of Northumbria, was accompanied into exile by some at least of his followers, and it was Alfred's personal retinue which stayed at his side in the difficult months of 878. The heyday of the warrior band around its chief must have been the sixth and seventh centuries. As society became more stabilised in the eighth century, and thegns were becoming landlords, royal administrators, patrons of churches and the arts, the profits of peace came to be valued rather more. Nevertheless, the Scandinavian wars stimulated the traditional ideals, and the heroic spirit was still valued in 1066. It was said that the flower of the youth and nobility of England lay dead on the battlefield of Hastings. It is interesting that the epic poem *Beowulf*, though of pre-Viking origin, survives in an eleventh-century manuscript. Beowulf was remembered as a great hero in battle, a prince of thegns, and throughout the poem stress is laid on the loyalty of the followers to their chief. Beowulf was slain because his companions deserted him at the critical moment almost to a man, and there is a pathetically realistic picture of the devoted Wiglaf sitting by the body of Beowulf, trying to revive the hero with water, and at the same time reproaching the cowards for their treachery. The poem on the battle of Maldon (991) shows that such heroic sentiments were still valued in the late tenth century; in this poem the warriors are represented as prepared to die rather than quit the battlefield. The late tenth century, of course, was a time of widespread treachery and cowardice on the field of battle, and poems like that on Maldon may have been a method of exhortation to better conduct. The Scandinavian wars certainly placed the Saxons more squarely on the receiving end of violence and they did not always greatly care for the experience. Fighting was on a much more extended scale than in the period of the Heptarchy, and poets became more sensitive to the destructive nature of conflict. The speedy collapse of English resistance in 1013–16 and again after 1066 does suggest that on the whole men had come to prefer peace to war.

It is easier to describe the relationship between the lord and his immediate retinue, the relationship which so fascinated the poets, than it is to define the lord's dealings with the great mass of his peasant dependants. Very little is known of the process by which peasants were grouped in dependence on Saxon lords. The poem on the battle of Maldon describes how a ceorl refused to abandon the body of his dead lord, asserting that he who wished to avenge his lord would neither waver nor fear for life. Clearly, a ceorl could appreciate the heroic principles behind the relationship between lord and man, and it would seem that a ceorl might be numbered among the companions of a lord. An Anglo-Norman law code, probably of the time of Henry I but stating ancient custom, includes a reference to the *heriot* of a villein. It was the villein's best horse, ox or cow which was given, but it was still seen as *heriot*. It is rarely, however, that a ceorl can be set clearly in a fighting context. No doubt they were always primarily concerned to till the land rather than to wage war, and it is probable that ceorls came together under a chieftain or lord from the earliest days of the Conquest, seeking the military protection of a war band behind which to cultivate their farms. Certainly, the bond between lord and man ran deep through Anglo-Saxon society. By the early tenth century at the latest all men were supposed to have a lord. The laws of Wihtred of Kent refer to the lord of a nobleman, and those of Ine to the free dependants of a *gesith*.

Alfred ordered each man to keep his oath and pledge to his lord, forbidding all ranks, both ceorl and *eorl* (peasant and noble), to plot against their lord's life. The influence of the lord, by stages we can only very dimly perceive, was gradually extended beyond the essentially military nexus into the day-to-day life of his dependent communities. It became necessary for a ceorl to have the support in court of a nobleman, and in the laws of Athelstan the nobleman in question is clearly identified with the man's lord. Freemen, however, had the right to change their lord if they so wished, though no lord was to receive a man as his dependant without making certain that he had fulfilled his obligations to his previous lord. Semi-free dependants or slaves can have had no such freedom. These men were impoverished tenants or labourers, tied to the land they rented and performing labour services on the lord's estates, or merely the lord's chattels. Naturally, the kings, princes and great noblemen formed the families of the greatest landholders, and the prestige and influence of lordship together with the wealth and position of the landed gentry combined to give the aristocracy a crushing mastery of the peasantry on an economic as well as at a personal level. But behind any economic ties between the lord as landlord and the peasant as tenant lay a primary personal bond embedded in centuries of traditional values.

Social standards and manners

Anglo-Saxon society was dominated by an aristocratic minority which dictated social standards. The cultural level of the Anglo-Saxon peasantry, the great bulk of the population, is difficult to discern. What literary evidence survives relates more particularly to the standards and way of life of the nobility, while the archaeological evidence from pagan cemeteries gradually diminishes with the progress of the Conversion.

The Anglo-Saxons were a people of moderate height. Though some males could be almost 7 ft. tall, the average height for men was perhaps about 5 ft. 6 in., for women about 5 ft. o in. Like the Scandinavians of the ninth and tenth centuries, they were predominantly a fair-haired people. William of Malmesbury saw golden strands in the fair hair of King Athelstan when his tomb was opened at Malmesbury in the twelfth century. The dark, stooping Paulinus so impressed one member of his audience in Lindsey that this unique description of him was handed down and included in the pages of Bede. Athelstan and Edgar are said to have been of slender form; later tradition pictured Edmund Ironside as of bulky build; Harold Godwineson is said to have been tall, taller than his brothers, though Harold Hardrada, over 6 ft. in height, considered him a small man. Edward the Confessor is described as a man of outstanding height, distinguished in his old age at least by milky white hair and beard, full face and rosy cheeks. But such descriptions are few. The Anglo-Saxons are generally depicted in early manuscript drawings with full beards and flowing locks. By 1066 beards were shaved but hair and moustaches were still worn long. The French nobility on the Continent beheld with curiosity the long-haired English hostages that William the Conqueror took back with him to Normandy in 1067. Moustaches seem to have been invariably worn by laymen, and the Anglo-Saxons thought the Normans looked like priests because they were so clean shaven. The wearing of tattoos appears to have been very popular. It would seem from a passage in Bede that in the 670s there was not necessarily much difference in personal appearance between an aristocrat and a peasant, for it was possible for a nobleman, captured in battle and admittedly probably not looking his best, to be mistaken at first for a ceorl. In time, however, his countenance, bearing and speech revealed to his captors that he was not of the meaner sort. With the increased refinement that followed greater prosperity, the Anglo-Saxon aristocracy as a whole must have come to enjoy a luxury of coiffure and adornment beyond the reach of any but the richest peasant. In 1061, in Italy, a Northumbrian pilgrim and nobleman, Gospatric, was mistaken for Earl Tostig because of the luxury of his clothes and his distinguished physical appearance.

Among the nobility at least there was a common delight in fine flowing silk, linen, and woollen garments, often of vivid colouring. Bede loved the scarlet dye which, he says, was obtained from cockles, and faded neither with the heat of the sun nor the washing of the rain but became ever more beautiful. Royal robes are known to have been ornamented on occasions with gold. William the Conqueror and his attendants returned to Normandy in 1067 with English garments of gold tissue, enriched with bullion. The gaudy finery of eighth-century courtly dress was criticised by both Boniface and Alcuin, who were concerned at a tendency among clergy to imitate lay fashions. Alcuin regarded the Northumbrian nobility as adopting heathen dress when, in fact, they were copying British fashions. Anglo-Saxon men wore a mantle, fastened by a brooch, over a knee-length tunic and trousers, the lower leg cross-gartered; women wore a long robe, fastened by a brooch, with loose sleeves and occasionally a hood and veil, over a tunic and kirtle reaching to the ground. Leather shoes were worn. Both sexes may have appreciated perfume; Athelstan was sent gifts of rare perfume from Hugh, duke of the Franks. Certainly, both sexes wore head-and arm-bands and took equal delight in fine jewels, brooches and ornamental trinkets. William of Malmesbury says that the arms of the English at Hastings were laden with gold bracelets. Some of their pieces of jewellery, especially those belonging to the royal family, were of considerable value. Colour, particularly bright colour, seems to have had an an intense fascination for the Anglo-Saxons. How the members of Athelstan's court loved the fine emeralds, sent by Duke Hugh, which reflected their greenness in the eyes of onlookers! The pagan cemeteries of the Anglo-Saxon period have revealed thousands of the common brooches of the peasantry of the fifth and sixth centuries, now variously known from their different styles of design as ring and penannular brooches, square-headed, saucer, disc and cruciform brooches. Certain graves, particularly in Kent, have produced some fine examples of brooches, probably from the seventh century, but Kent was an unusually rich province and the majority of the common brooches of the pagan cemeteries of England are cheap and mass-produced. Nevertheless, they must have given a great deal of pleasure to a great many people, a point it is easy to overlook in the arid process of typological analysis. Together with the brooches, necklaces of glass beads, amber and amethyst have been found in considerable numbers. Only a very few pieces of the personal jewellery of the eighth century and after have been preserved. Finger rings, however, of Æthelwulf, king of Wessex, and his daughter, Æthelswith, wife of Burgred of Mercia, were found in the nineteenth century. These rings may have been gift-rings rather than the private possessions of Æthelwulf and Æthelswith, but even so they must have emanated from the royal court. A fine example of later metalwork is the Fuller brooch, dating to the ninth century and portraying the Five Senses.

Objects designed with quite another purpose in mind might be worn as ornaments. Eormenburh, the queen of Ecgfrith of Northumbria, wore Wilfrid's reliquary around her neck; this was probably not meant to be simply an insult to Wilfrid, but a desire to wear a fine object for personal adornment.

The men of the Anglo-Saxon nobility must have enjoyed a boisterous leisure. Training for battle would be a constant daily exercise on the part of young aristocrats. Harold Godwineson is stated to have been well practised in endless fatigues and in doing without sleep and food. Horse-racing was indulged in with enthusiasm by young men who competed against each other when they came upon a suitable stretch of land. Cavalry was used on campaign by Anglo-Saxon kings, and many thegns were probably skilled horsemen. Hunting and hawking were favourite pastimes. Edward the Confessor was noted for his fondness for the chase. Indoors, dicing and a game akin to chess were played. Young and old alike took a delight in the traditional pleasures of eating and drinking on the mead-benches of the lord's hall at times of festivity. The lords took pride in their liberality and generosity, and many a noble thegn must have felt the cold winds of a domestic economy drive after an all-night marathon. Feasting and drinking on a lavish scale undoubtedly took place on occasions in noble establishments or in great monasteries. Usually such bouts ended in a drunken stupor. One of William of Malmesbury's criticisms of the English was that drinking in parties was a universal custom in which they passed whole days and nights; that they were wont to eat until surfeited and drink until sick. This kind of behaviour is corroborated. King Eadred held a feast to celebrate his monastic foundation at Abingdon, actually on the site of the new buildings, and shut the doors so that none might hurry away; the drinking went on all night and the West Saxons seem to have derived considerable satisfaction from out-drinking a Northumbrian delegation. Food was grasped in the hand and eaten with the aid of a knife; it cannot always have been abundant, and it may be that a tendency towards drunkenness was primarily because the amount of food consumed was far less than the amount of drink. But the royal court at least generally dined well as a matter of routine. Henry of Huntingdon, writing in the reign of Henry I, contrasted the royal parsimony of his own day, when only one feast a day was provided at court, with the generosity of Harthacnut who provided four. It must not be thought, however, that the bulk of the peasant population lived at anything like such a level. As Alcuin in the eighth century was moved to comment, the satiety of the rich was the hunger of the poor. At times terrible famines devastated the land. In 1005, for example, occurred a famine in England so severe that no man ever remembered one so cruel. It may be that a general shortage of food was one reason why poets were so fascinated by the great hall and the lavish feast.

A further reason for the close association between poets and feasts is that such festivities were an occasion for poets and musicians to demonstrate their talents. At Athelstan's coronation feast at Kingston-on-Thames a poet described how, as the wine flowed and delicacies were consumed, one made the harp resound and another sang praises while the king observed all with eager eyes. To the accompaniment of harps, often—as in the case of the harp found in the Sutton Hoo ship burial—handed from one to another, songs were recalled of the deeds of heroic warriors of bygone days, the praise of which obscured a little the horrible realities of the battlefield. The Normans held that the English were more intent on feasting and drinking than on thoughts of battle. But, stimulated by mead and song and good cheer, men vowed new deeds of valour equal to those of the greatest heroes. When Byrhtnoth's men faced certain defeat at Maldon they were reminded of the vows they had often made about stern battle when drinking in the hall. Harold's men, probably two nights before the battle of Hastings (for they were on a night march on the eve of Hastings), are said to have passed the night in drinking and singing. King Swein of Denmark was reputed to have vowed to conquer England at a feast. The whole of this milieu of feasting and drinking, heroic song, and valiant and warlike vows had ancient roots deep in the prehistoric past. Heartily enjoyed by Germanic and Celtic peoples alike, there can be no doubt that it remained in fashionable vogue down to the time of the Norman Conquest.

King Alfred's will divides the sexes into the spear-side and the spindle-side. Spinning and weaving are the constant occupations of Germanic goddesses in poetic tradition, and must have taken up much of the time of Anglo-Saxon women of all social ranks. Aldhelm of Sherborne refers to the skill of English women in the art of embroidering with threads of many colours. Edward the Elder is specifically recorded as having had his daughters trained in needlework and spinning as well as in literature. About 912, Queen Ælfflæd, Edward's wife, commissioned the working of a stole and maniple for Frithestan, bishop of Winchester, which was subsequently given to the church at Chester-le-Street for St. Cuthbert's tomb by King Athelstan in 934 and preserved among the relics of St. Cuthbert now at Durham; the surviving pieces, reflecting the influence of Byzantine art, are rare examples of Anglo-Saxon embroidery, revealing, in what has been described as their exquisite needlework and delicate execution, something of the beautiful work which was being produced in England at that time. Like the many tapestries which adorned the households of the wealthy, they were the achievement of hours of patient labour. It was not unknown for mythological scenes and deeds of valour to be depicted on tapestries, as the woven Norse tapestry from the ninth-century Osberg ship and the later eleventh-century Bayeux Tapestry respectively show. The widow of Ealdorman Byrhtnoth, slain at Maldon in 991, bequeathed to the monastery of Ely a fine tapestry on which Byrhtnoth's exploits were depicted. The daughters of the ninth-century Viking, Ragnar Lothbrok, are said to have woven a magic banner for their brothers, reputed to unfurl itself when victory in battle was forthcoming to reveal a flying raven, and a banner known as the 'Raven' was captured from the Danes by the West Saxons in 878. The West Saxon banner is said to have been embroidered with a golden dragon, and that captured by the Normans on the field of Hastings is described as sumptuously embroidered with gold and precious gems in the form of a man fighting.

Apart from spinning and weaving, another traditional role of noble Anglo-Saxon women at least was to take round the hall an ale-cup to feasting guests. Much more exacting must have been the behind-the-scenes management of an aristocratic household, the over-all supervision of catering, brewing, baking, the unrecorded bustle of day-to-day duties. For a man who sought a wife to manage his household there were recognised ways of procedure. Marriage by capture probably died out by the end of the seventh century, though women led away by raiding bands in later centuries may conceivably have found a husband among their captors. Marriage within the degrees of kinship was prohibited by the Church, and hence the clerical opposition to Eadwig and his queen. An offer of marriage had to be acceptable to the kinsmen of the woman in question, and the prospective bridegroom had to be in a position to support a wife. He had to give her both a 'bride-gift' before marriage, and a 'morning-gift' following the nuptials. As early as the time of Ine of Wessex penalties were in force for bridegrooms who did not make the necessary gifts; by the time of Cnut, widows who married again within a year lost their original 'morning-gift'. These payments may have grown out of an older custom of literally buying a wife, but they came to be a means of safeguarding the interests of the woman. The woman, for her part, brought with her a dowry from her parents, which, however, remained in her possession. It is highly unlikely that all marriages followed the customary pattern. A great many appear to have been within prohibited degrees, or against the wishes of the woman, or simply monetary bargains which could be easily broken, judging from recurring legislation against such marriages. Many marriages must have ended in separation and divorce; many liaisons were never solemnised by the Church and were regarded as easily dissoluble. Uhtred, earl of Northumbria, was married first to Ecgfrida, daughter of Ealdhun, bishop of Durham, on condition that so long as he lived he would treat her with honour. Ecgfrida he soon set aside to marry Sigen, daughter of a rich Northumbrian, Styr, son of Ulf, on condition that he slew Thurbrand, Styr's foe, and Ecgfrida herself subsequently remarried. Finally, without having slain Thurbrand, who was, in fact, to slay him, Uhtred went on to receive Ælfgifu, daughter of Æthelred II, in marriage, setting aside (so far as we know) his second wife when Æthelred sought to reward him for military services and to win his loyalty. Ecgfrida, for her part, was eventually sent away by her second husband and returned to her father in Durham, together with part at least of her original dowry in estates. The marital adventures of Uhtred are a useful example of the way in which a career could be furthered thereby and of the ease with which marital relationships, at least in Northumbria, could be broken. It may be that Scandinavian practice led to a weakening of marital bonds in the Danelaw. Though Cnut regarded Harold, son of Ælfgifu, as one of his rightful heirs, he easily set Ælfgifu aside in 1017 to marry Emma, widow of Æthelred II. It was not unknown for marriages to be arranged with a view to ending a blood-feud between two hostile kindreds, not always successfully. On the other hand, there can be no doubt from surviving Anglo-Saxon wills that a great many marriages were entirely satisfactory. The general well-being of the woman was protected by law. Wives could hold property in their own right and transmit it, their estates not being divided among the sons on the death of the father. Further, the woman owned the household goods—furnishings, hardware and ornaments—and she was entitled to a portion of them if divorced. In poor peasant households, of course, such goods would be fewer. But wills survive from only the richer strata of society.

Little is known of the details of family life among the Saxons. On the highest level family relationships were subject to political strains and stresses. Edward the Confessor seems to have found his mother plotting against him for the succession of another to the English throne. The stepmother of Edward the Martyr, ex-queen Ælfthryth, was widely believed to have been directly responsible for Edward's assassination. Athelstan of Wessex was suspected of having had his brother, Edwin, drowned at sea. Edward the Elder prevented his young niece from succeeding her mother in Mercia, and her fate is unrecorded. Æthelwold, Edward's cousin, led a powerful and dangerous revolt against Edward at his accession. Peada of Mercia was said to have been assassinated through the instrumentality of his wife. Egbert of Kent murdered two of his nephews to prevent their opposing his sons in the succession. Such instances are mentioned in the source because they concern the kings and princes of the time. Naturally, unfilial and treacherous conduct must have been found among many families in all social strata. Kings legislated against parricide and incest. But there is no way of knowing to what extent families were likely to encounter brutality or moral degeneracy within the home. There is some evidence, on the other hand, for the ties of affection and devotion which could knit together a family. Asser's picture of the young Alfred with his older brothers around their mother, Osburh, eager to learn to read a beautifully illuminated book of Saxon poems, may rightly be taken as an attractive picture of a little family group, of mother and son. St. Boniface's father placed every possible inducement of pleasure and luxury before his son in a vain attempt to prevent him from leaving home and entering a monastery. A group of women in the Northumbrian hills were prepared to trek some distance carrying a sick youth, probably a relative, on a litter in the hope that St. Cuthbert would bless and perhaps cure him. In one of his visits to a plague-stricken village in the Cheviots, Cuthbert found a woman weeping over her child whom she—mistakenly as it turned out—believed dead. The concern of husband for wife, mother for child, and father for son comes through very vividly in the accounts of healing miracles performed by early saints. Where an Anglo-Saxon family was most likely to quarrel seriously was in disputes over land. In an age when it was not always easy to bring documentary proof to possession of a particular estate in the form of a charter, lengthy proceedings in court—even between mother and son— could follow, as various extant records bear witness.

We are not well informed on the bringing up of children. Those of the nobility and of royalty had nurses and were eventually placed in the care of foster-parents. Athelstan of Wessex was fostered with his aunt, Æthelflæd, in Mercia. Athelstan, the son of Æthelred II, remembered his foster-mother in his will. Cuthbert of Farne long continued to visit his. Discipline within the home was probably very strict for this does not seem to have been an age for sparing the rod. But children in the Anglo-Saxon period were not lacking in high spirits. A colloquy of the time represents them, like boys of ages to come, idling their time away in the absence of the teacher, even posting a look-out to watch for his return. Æthelric, future bishop of Dorchester (1016–34), as a boy with four companions, rang the bells of Ramsey monastery, where he was an inmate, until they cracked. Boys were eager to demonstrate physical prowess, and as a boy Cuthbert was rebuked by a child, whom he had probably frightened, for taking part so enthusiastically in violent wrestling bouts. Children evidently learnt to imitate the cries of birds as a pastime and they would soon come to tell the hours of the day by the position of the sun in the sky. No doubt they fished and hunted for small game and became daily more skilful with a bow and arrow, eventually—as youth approached—with a knife and sword. By their mid-teens they could be recruited into an army or executed for some petty felony.

According to Byrhtferth's *Manual* (1011), the division of the ages of man was as follows: childhood to the age of 14, youth to the age of 28, manhood to 48, old age to 70 or 80. Some Anglo-Saxons are known to have lived to considerable ages. Waltheof I, earl of Bernicia, is said to have been so old in 1006 that he could not fight the Scots, but no precise age is given. Ceolfrith, abbot of Monkwearmouth and Jarrow, who died in 716, is known to have been 74 at the time of his death. Wilfrid, bishop of York, was 75. Æthelberht of Kent must have been at least 70 when he died *c*. 618, while the Northumbrian missionary, Egbert, who converted Iona to the Roman Easter, was 90 at the time of his death in 729. Queens might also enjoy surprising longevity. Werburh, widowed queen of Ceolred, king of Mercia, survived her husband by some 66 years and must have died in her mid-eighties at least. Emma, queen first of Æthelred II and then of Cnut, would be in her seventies at her death. These examples of longevity in Anglo-Saxons are interesting. Pre-Viking evidence indicates the possibility that over 50 per cent of the Anglo-Saxons were dead by the age of 30 and over 90 per cent by the age of 50. Apart from a large infant mortality, however, a peak of Anglo-Saxon deaths occurred between the ages of 15 and 20, possibly representing a young warrior class, and this, of course, affects the averages. Perhaps those who lived beyond 20 could expect a reasonably lengthy life-span. Nevertheless, the history of the West Saxon dynasty affords an example of a high death rate. None of the kings of Wessex from Alfred to Æthelred II lived beyond their mid-fifties. Alfred was 50 when he died, Athelstan in his mid-forties, Eadred in his early thirties, Eadwig in his late teens. Edgar is known to have been 31 at his death, while his daughter, Edith, a nun at Wilton and highly regarded by Æthelwold, was only 23. Cnut can have been barely 40, Harold I probably in his mid-twenties, Harthacnut in his early twenties. Edward the Confessor, who survived until his sixties, was an exception. Such a high mortality amongst kings who enjoyed the height of the luxury of their day may suggest that the peasants were not likely to live to very great ages.

Anglo-Saxon society was at the mercy of disease and malnutrition, on the one hand, and medical ignorance, on the other. Apart from elementary and traditional herbal mixtures, men had no means of treating serious illness. Internal surgery was quite out of the question, though surface operations might be performed. Cynefrith, a physician, operated on Æthelthryth, abbess of Ely, by incising a large tumour under her jaw only three days before her death. The monastic communities seem to have possessed the best physicians, and men and women often came to monasteries to be treated. Perhaps we underestimate these physicians a little. Limbs might be bound, joints set, bleeding performed. In addition, within the monasteries patients were liable to come into contact with individual monks and priests whose reputation for sanctity led to their being regarded as faith-healers, or with the relics of saints of the Church which were believed to possess curative powers. The saints of the early English Church, in common with those of Western Europe generally, all performed healing miracles. Many of their healing miracles can be understood in terms of a determined response on the part of the patient to the powerful personality of the saint or as a perfectly natural recovery from a passing affliction. Neither the faith-healers nor their patients, however, necessarily expected a cure to follow a blessing, and many individuals no doubt died despite the intervention of a saint. It seems that when men and women fell ill the general expectation was that they would die, and a recovery, whether slow or dramatic, was the exception. Death must have appeared inevitably and permanently close to the average Anglo-Saxon family. The Christian concept of heaven offered visions of life in a future paradise to the devout believer, and men like the Northumbrian Dryhthelm in the seventh century gave dramatic accounts of visits to paradise experienced while in a coma. But men also lived in great dread of the Hell of fire and ice which awaited evil-doers and sinners. Bede describes the last days of a Mercian nobleman, racked by pain and afflicted with terrible hallucinations of demons which his contemporaries regarded simply as a penalty for a sinful life.

The Anglo-Saxons did not describe their ailments with any scientific precision, and it is not easy to tell what diseases are being described in early sources. There is no doubt that, at a time when illnesses and diseases had to run their natural course for want of proper treatment, there was an intense amount of suffering. Abbess Hild lived to the age of 66 but was ill for six years before she died. Benedict Biscop, founder of Monkwearmouth and Jarrow monastery, suffered for three years before his death from a slowly advancing paralysis. Abbot Ceolfrith, of the same monastery, was afflicted by an incurable infection of the lungs. Tuberculosis was probably widespread in Anglo-Saxon England. King Eadred suffered from a continual languor, unable in the end to take as sustenance anything other than liquid foods. Alfred the Great was afflicted with illness on and off for most of his adult life, though exactly what ailed him has not been determined with any certainty. Such sufferings must have been multiplied in countless peasant and aristocratic households. Skeletal remains show that teeth were excessively ground down, probably due to mastication of tough and coarse food, and that respiratory ailments were aggravated, no doubt as a consequence of inclement weather and the smoky indoor atmosphere of cramped living quarters. The daily labour of working on the land with primitive equipment is thought to have resulted in widespread rheumatism and arthritis. Injuries sustained from agricultural implements and weapons of war must often have turned septic and gangrenous. A very late source says that Harold Godwineson was suffering from a septic leg before the battle of Stamfordbridge. Hlothere, king of Kent, died while his battle-wounds were being dressed, and Cædwalla's pilgrimage to and death at Rome may not have been unconnected with wounds he is recorded to have received while on campaign. Of course, there is always the possibility in these cases of internal injury.

Cramped living conditions and primitive sanitation must have provided the conditions in which disease and pestilence could easily germinate. The Anglo-Saxons had no idea how to set about combating infection; they did not know its true source. In the same way as they believed that devils possessed people and that elves made men ill with poisonous darts, so they thought that in time of plague the infection

21 King and Witan in judgment (*B.M. Claud. D.IV*)

22 Feasting in April (*B.M. Julius A.VI*)

23 A building scene (*B.M. Harleian 603*)

24 Font—Deerhurst,
    Gloucestershire,
    ninth century

25 Silver chalice—Trewhiddle,
    Cornwall, ninth century

Ecclesiastical objects

26 Tower-shaped bronze
    censer-cover,
    tenth century

27 Head of an ivory pastoral
    staff—Alcester, Warwickshire,
    eleventh century

was in the air and resulted from an excessively dry summer or an excessively wet winter. Bede, in common with his generation, believed that it was impossible to try to combat the plague because it signified the wrath of God and was sent by Him as a punishment for human sin. Bubonic plague was spread by infected fleas from black rats which infest human dwellings if given the opportunity. The severe outbreak of the bubonic plague in 664 destroyed king, monk and peasant alike and a great multitude lost their lives. Many a one then resorted pitifully and vainly to magical incantation. Various kinds of plague, together with dysentery and smallpox, struck repeatedly at the population, particularly in times of famine and undernourishment. A wet summer season could result in the infection of the rye crop and lead to serious outbreaks of St. Anthony's Fire (ergotism). The consumption of unpasteurised cow's milk, it has been said, provided the means of incubating germs of dysentery and enteritis and kept these diseases endemic in the child population, while the lack of winter vegetables and fruit must have resulted in a condition of mild scurvy in the population as a whole. Skin diseases of one kind or another were probably common, not least various kinds of animal-pox among herdsmen. Ælfweard, bishop of London, who died in 1044, was refused admittance to the monastery of Evesham, where he wished to end his days, because he was suffering from leprosy, a term which covered a multitude of different skin diseases.

The Anglo-Saxons can have possessed only a limited appreciation of personal hygiene, though there is little information about their hygienic habits. The English, however, regarded the Scots as verminous, and the Arabs described as lousy those Vikings who settled on the Volga. How the mass of the English peasantry lived is unknown, but there is no doubt that some of the saints rarely washed. Cuthbert changed his clothes once a year. The woman in the plague-stricken village visited by Cuthbert had her sick child wrapped only in rags. Perhaps poverty was a factor here. Beggars were numerous in Anglo-Saxon England, a fraternity not renowned for its cleanliness. On a higher social level, William of Malmesbury records that Ælfhere, ealdorman of Mercia, who translated the relics of Edward the Martyr in 979, was eaten by lice, a statement which could be reflecting a tradition that Ælfhere's clothes were lice-ridden. This is clearly not the whole story, however, and perhaps the Anglo-Saxons should not be underestimated in this matter. Wilfrid of York washed every night until Pope John VI advised him to discontinue the habit out of regard for his age. Hospital clothes at

Lindisfarne in the eighth century were washed in the sea. By the late Saxon period, soap was regarded as a regular item in an aristocratic household. The scrupulous cleanliness of Ælfstan, later an abbot and then a bishop, in the kitchen of Abingdon monastery evidently commended itself to Æthelwold—who wore rags for ascetic reasons—and to Æthelwold's biographer, Ælfric of Eynsham; it may not unreasonably be taken as representing the attitude of the more responsible members of the community to standards of hygiene.

Chapter two

The administration of the
Old English State

Kingship

Just as the kindred was the basic social element in Anglo-Saxon society, so the folk-group was the fundamental unit in the early kingdoms. A kingdom was but a conglomeration of folk-groups over whom a folk-king reigned. It is anachronistic to describe an Anglo-Saxon ruler as king, for example, of Northumbria. These kings were not kings of a territory but of a people, the Northumbrians, the East Angles or the West Saxons. Gradually, however, Anglo-Saxon society became territorialised. By the tenth century, West Saxon kings were coming to be described as kings of Britain and the names of folk-groups were being superseded by those of territorial administrative divisions. Throughout the medieval period the king was the person around whom government and administration revolved. The maintenance of law and order and good government depended almost entirely on the strength of royal authority, which in turn depended to a considerable extent upon the king's strength of character. The ideas of the earliest Anglo-Saxons about kingship were probably vague and imprecise, becoming more defined and complex as the centuries passed. Kingship was known to some of the invading tribes before the Conquest; the Anglo-Saxons celebrated in their literature the deeds of Offa, a fourth-century king of the continental Angles, and of Beowulf, prince of the Geats of South Sweden and the legendary, part historical, kings with whom he was said to have had dealings. Tacitus records that some of the Germanic peoples elected kings in time of war from among the foremost war leaders. The Anglo-Saxons evidently found kingship essential to the co-ordination of folk-groups during the Conquest of Britain. The *Anglo-Saxon Chronicle* preserves a tradition that it was some years after the actual beginning of the conquest of Wessex that Cerdic took the title of king. There is no doubt that kings were a symbol of tribal unity and surrounded with a supernatural aura. They claimed descent from pagan gods and could probably invoke magical powers. They moved amidst a panoply of power. Edwin of Northumbria was preceded by his standard-bearer, and over the shrine of King Oswald hung his banner of gold and purple. The kings appear in historical records primarily as war leaders. In the Anglo-Saxon epic poem, *Beowulf*, the cardinal virtues of the war hero are courage, loyalty and generosity, and the governing passion was the thirst for military fame through deeds of prowess. The war heroes of the Conquest were men like Hengest, Cerdic and Ida, and their successors inherited their principles and standards. The earliest English kings must have been tough, violent men. Certain of them battled their way to the position of *bretwalda*. In the course of time the virtues of the warrior king probably became stylised and traditional, as did chivalrous ideals in the later Middle Ages, but throughout the Anglo-Saxon period a primary duty of the king remained that of defending his territories against aggression and even that of maintaining his dynasty's prestige by military aggression of his own when necessary.

Any temptation, however, to regard the earliest kings as little more than highly placed gangsters, surrounded by their henchmen, must be avoided, for it ignores not only the virtues of loyalty and courage which dominated their ideals but also the fact that when these kings appear in the records of the Conversion they evince an awareness of the responsibilities of their position. Æthelberht of Kent was conscious of his duty to the people he ruled and sensitive to the native traditions of his race. The king told Augustine that he could not easily abandon the traditional faith of the English nation, but because Augustine clearly believed his message to be beneficial he was allowed to preach. The adoption of Christianity involved a tremendous mental upheaval for the kings of the seventh century and they carefully weighed the new faith in the scales with traditional beliefs. In *c.* 653 Sigeberht, king of the East Saxons, who evidently took his Christianity too seriously for the times, was murdered by his own kindred because he was too apt to spare his enemies. The kings had to seek to be as devout as possible, but without jeopardising their political and military responsibilities. The ideal king among the Anglo-Saxons was both a warrior of heroic stature and a devout Christian, as Oswald of Northumbria, for example, was believed to have been. Bede's implied opinion that Oswald would have slain the young sons of Edwin had he caught them suggests that a harsh expediency was not foreign to the saintly benefactor of Aidan.

Claimants to the throne were usually related to the ruling family of the kingdom and kings were normally succeeded by a brother or a son. Both descent from the gods, even in the Christian period, and royal descent were regarded as generally essential to a potential ruler, and kings who were upstarts and without royal blood were viewed with disfavour. This had the naturally desired effect of tending to confine the succession of a kingdom to one family, although that single family could become widely extended with the passage of time. It is possible that any lord up to seven generations removed from a royal ancestor could legitimately claim the kingship. Several of the Northumbrian kings of the eighth century were the seventh generation from Ida of Bernicia; Cenwulf of Mercia and his brothers were the seventh generation from Cenwalh, brother of Penda and Eowa, both of whom were kings. This hereditary principle, if such were the case, would account for the dynastic strife between the princes of the seventh generation which tore Northumbria in the eighth century. An Anglo-Saxon king seems to have possessed the power to nominate his successor, but on the king's death the crucial factor was the support his nominee received from the nobility. Few hazards were more dangerous to the stability of a kingdom than a contested succession. The work of Alfred the Great was threatened in 899 when the succession of his son was disputed by his nephew, and that of Cnut in 1035 by the contest for his realms between his two sons. The number of contested successions in the history of Anglo-Saxon England is quite considerable. Each succession, in fact, could lay the kingdom open to dynastic strife, for some sort of acclamation of the heir-apparent was made by the nobility before coronation and in the case of a divided succession the rival princes would each have their own supporters in the ranks of the nobility. Under Egbert, Æthelwulf and Æthelbald of Wessex the practice was adopted of allowing the heir-apparent to rule in Kent and the south-east. In England, unlike Merovingian or Carolingian Gaul, however, the kingdom was not normally divided among a group of heirs. Though this may have bred disaffection, it meant that once consecrated a king could call upon the whole resources of his kingdom to crush his rivals. The royal bodyguard was expected to be efficient enough to prevent the dangers of assassination though this was not always the case, and the king's person was given added protection by his very high *wergeld* and by the king's peace which heavily penalised any outbreak of violence in the king's presence or on his property. The king had a wealth of land with which he could reward service. From the seventh century kings were making grants of land by diploma or charter, releasing land so granted from public burdens. Such land was known as bookland. The Mercian kings in the eighth century, however, imposed certain burdens on all land, whether bookland or not; these burdens, known as the 'three necessities', were obligations of military service, bridge construction, and fortress maintenance. Another technical term for land was folkland. Historians are not quite sure what was meant by folkland, for there are only one or two references to it. A recent definition has been that it represented land subject to vague and loosely defined burdens of communal obligation.

Kings were usually crowned in their cathedral towns but there were exceptions. Kingston-on-Thames—where the Kingston stone or so-called coronation stone still survives—makes its interesting appearance as one place of the coronation of kings of Wessex as early as that of Athelstan (925) though not all his successors were crowned there. By 1066 the coronation service had developed into a highly elaborate ecclesiastical ritual. The king was anointed and consecrated by his bishops, and probably by the eighth century at the latest swore a coronation oath to protect the Church, preserve the peace, forbid iniquities, and to command in all judgments equity and mercy. A coronation service of the second half of the tenth century described how the king prostrated himself before the altar and swore these oaths. The king was crowned with a diadem and invested with an orb and sceptre. The coronation oath was very important because it expressed the obligations of a king to his people and asserted the implication that the king was subject to the law of God. At the accession of Edmund in 939 both king and people took a reciprocal oath of allegiance, and the Church sought to impress on Edmund his responsibility before God for the good behaviour of his subjects. Kings were instructed not to consider themselves too highly because of earthly power. They must fear God. Anglo-Saxon England knew little of the implications for kingship of Roman Law with its maxim that what pleased the prince had the force of law, and, though the Church was in some doubt as to whether a king who flouted the law of God could be deposed or not, the unlimited authority of the ruler was denied by Teutonic or Germanic customary law. Germanic customary law was the unwritten Law of the folk and the power to declare this Law

lay as much with the folk as with the king. In practice the powers of dec-
laration lay with that section of the nobility with whom the king consulted, but the fundamental principle was present. The laws of Wihtred of
Kent (*c.* 695) state that the decrees have been devised by the leading
men who have added to the lawful usages of the people of Kent, and
Wihtred is not specifically mentioned. A code of Athelstan survives in
which the wise men of Kent drew up a set of decrees and submitted
their draft to the king for his approval. Alfred the Great took care to
consult with his magnates before codifying West Saxon law in a novel
blend of West Saxon, Mercian and Kentish law. And even though the
task of countering the Scandinavian invasions gave a new prestige to
the West Saxon monarchy and the evolution of a Christian view of
kingship made Æthelred II, for example, more a priest-king than a
warrior chief, the Anglo-Saxon rulers remained subject to the Law. A
king, therefore, who antagonised his subjects could be deposed provided
there was a sufficiently strong rival. The great men of a kingdom were
probably generally devoted to their king and ready to die for him, but
several rulers did go beyond the bounds of recognised conduct. In 774
Alchred, king of Northumbria, was deprived of the society of the royal
household and nobles by the counsel and consent of all his people,
which in practice meant the nobility in opposition. In 757 Cynewulf
and the West Saxon *witan* deprived King Sigeberht of his throne which
was seized by Cynewulf. Deposition appears to have taken the form of
the withdrawal of the oath of allegiance sworn at the coronation. In
1013 the great men of the realm turned from Æthelred II and gave
their allegiance to Swein. In the case of Sigeberht, he was deposed because of his unjust acts, and Æthelred was set aside because he had
ruled unjustly. It is clear, therefore, that kings were expected to rule
according to certain just principles and to maintain the oaths sworn at
their coronation.

The precise powers of an Anglo-Saxon king are never defined in the
sources of the period. There is no doubt that they were something more
than great country gentlemen, drawing rents from their estates and
occasionally patronising the arts. The absence of any firm hereditary
principle generally absolved England from the rule of boy kings and,
therefore, of queen-regents. Boy kings are rare in Anglo-Saxon England.
In the seventh century, Seaxburh, wife of Cenwalh, king of the Thames
valley Saxons, ruled for a year by herself on her husband's death, but
queens rarely played a significant part in political affairs, by contrast,

for example, with early Frankish Gaul. Indeed, the very title of queen
seems to have been abandoned in Wessex in the ninth and early tenth
centuries, though used at other periods and elsewhere in England,
queens being known in Wessex during those years simply as the
king's wife or 'Lady'. The king had a proprietary right to *feorm*,
a tax on what would seem to have been all the folkland in his kingdom
except that which he granted as bookland to dependants and lords. The
right to take revenues and tribute was extended to subject territories.
An overlord could reduce the kings of subject lands to the status of mere
nobles. His consent was necessary even for a grant of land, by a sub-
king. The control of the armed might of the kingdom rested in the king.
He had the duty to suppress internal disaffection and to resist external
aggression. Great policy decisions could be taken by the king alone, as
by Oswiu at the Synod of Whitby. The king took a percentage of the
fines imposed in the courts of his kingdom, and could order national
taxation (*e.g.* danegeld) if necessary. He possessed a reservoir of ill-
defined judicial power. He did not have to support his word by a sworn
oath and he could act as judge in all cases of disputed law. A mounting
number of suits to the royal court meant that Alfred had to hear them
even while washing. Edgar forbade men to apply to the king for justice
unless it was absolutely unobtainable at home. It is easy to forget that
the king's daily life was normally spent in a constant round of routine
administration which brought him into contact with all aspects of contemporary life. The successive law codes of the Anglo-Saxons give some
indication of the wide variety of matters with which the king had to
concern himself, from infringements of the peace and problems of
administration to economic and tenurial questions of commerce and
agriculture. Harold I was troubled with litigation matters even on his
deathbed.

Central administration

In Anglo-Saxon England the king was at the very centre of government
and his court embraced all the branches of the administration. The
king's court consisted of his own household, which was always with
him, and those members of the lay and ecclesiastical nobility he
periodically summoned to meetings of the *witan*. The household
managed the mechanics of administration; the *witan* gave advice on
questions of government and policy.

It is important to remember that the king was constantly on the move, remaining only for a short time in any one place. It was by travelling round the kingdom that the king was able to get to know the land and to live off it. His life was spent moving from one royal farm to another or receiving hospitality from one lord or another. Not far behind was the royal household and all the paraphernalia of government. The pending arrival of the royal household on a secular estate or at a monastic centre may often have given cause for alarm both at the amount of provisions needed to supply the king and his household and, in certain instances, the rank indiscipline of the royal party. Anglo-Saxon kings were not infrequently the fathers of illegitimate offspring and a few (e.g. Osred of Northumbria and Æthelbald of Mercia) were said to be ravishers of nuns. The itinerary of Athelstan is quite well known from the places at which his charters were drawn up and which show that he passed through Exeter, Frome, Dorchester, Wilton, Chippenham, Amesbury, Winchester and Abingdon as well as through many other minor centres. Towards the end of his life, Alfred the Great grew weary of the incessant journeying. Like the great noble families, however, the kings tended to have major residential centres to which they repeatedly and regularly returned. Bamburgh was a favourite royal capital in Bernicia, and possibly Catterick in the eighth century in Deira. The Mercian kings held councils at Tamworth. Canterbury was a royal capital in Kent as early as the time of Æthelberht. The West Saxon kings can be traced in particular at the shire towns of Wilton, Dorchester, Somerton and Southampton.

The rudiments of a royal household to assist the king in the burden of routine administration must have existed from the earliest times in however primitive a form. The king would need men to care for his weapons and keep his clothes in order; there must always have been a royal treasure chest to guard and from the Conversion a royal chapel and reliquary to maintain. Such posts rapidly became important honours. Osburh, the mother of Alfred, was Æthelwulf's cup-bearer's daughter, and of aristocratic descent. King Alfred divided his household company into three, each group residing one month in court, on duty day and night, followed by two months at home. An account of the royal household is indirectly provided by the will of King Eadred (955) which mentions the king's seneschals (head stewards), stewards, keepers of the wardrobe (the chamberlains of later centuries), butlers and household priests. The royal treasure was kept partly in the king's bedroom and partly in various deposits throughout the kingdom; Dunstan was one of the keepers of King Eadred's treasure. The king was very rich, and part only of Eadred's treasure, which he bequeathed to his people for dane-geld relief, amounted to 1,600 pounds. Asser provides a most important account of the way in which Alfred divided his revenues, allocating half to secular purposes and half to God. The secular sum was divided into three parts, one for the expenses of his household and retainers, one for the charges of workmen, and one for gifts to foreigners; of the money devoted to God, one quarter was distributed to the poor, another to his own monastic foundations of which there were two, another to the palace school, and a final quarter to churches and monasteries scattered far and wide. These divisions indicate that the royal revenues could be viewed as a whole and dealt with on an annual basis and they imply a trained staff. In the tenth century the levying of danegeld and in the eleventh that of heregeld would require an even more elaborate financial machinery. Danegeld and heregeld were taxes on land without parallel in western Europe. Assessment, as with the older folk taxes, was based on the theory that England was divided into an exact number of *hides* and on each *hide* was imposed a uniform sum, usually two shillings. Sums which have been described as appalling were successfully collected. Though there is no trace of an Anglo-Saxon treasurer, the main treasury came to be established at Winchester from the time of Cnut. One of the first acts of Harold I was to seize the valuables there. Similarly, there is no clear reference to a pre-Conquest chancellor though the existence of an Anglo-Saxon royal writing office is beyond question. Eadred's household priests would serve in the writing office as well as the chapel. Æthelwulf is known to have had a Frankish secretary, Felix, and one charter of Æthelred II's contains reference to Ælfwine, the king's faithful writer. Copies of Edgar's legis-lation were made and circulated in Mercia and East Anglia. But the most substantial body of evidence for the Anglo-Saxon royal writing office is the number of charters and writs. All but a small minority of the charters of Athelstan are composed in an artificial style and have the ap-pearance of having been written by clerks trained in the art of formal composition. The employment of identical formulas in Athelstan's char-ters over a considerable number of years suggests that a writing office was attached to the court in his time. By the time of Æthelred II at the latest copies of charters were being lodged in the king's chapel. Here were the beginnings of a record office. Exactly how the writing office was organised is not known, but organisation was such that by the time of Æthelred II writs were being issued and sent into the country at large. A writ was a short letter on administrative business, naming the sender (the king) and the recipient (an ealdorman, earl, or sheriff), and succinctly stating the king's commands in a specific matter. The language was stylised and formal, and the traditional phrasing of the protocol appears substantially the same as in King Alfred's opening preface to the *Pastoral Care*. The writ may have been evolving, therefore, from the ninth century, and it has been described as Anglo-Saxon England's most notable contribution to the science of government. The king's seal was appended to the writ, confirming that it really was a royal command. King Alfred refers to the letter and seal of a lord, showing that the seal has a very long history. What is called a coin-seal or leaden *bulla* has been preserved of Cenwulf, king of Mercia, which may be genuine. An early seal survives, probably of Æthelwald, bishop of Dunwich, dating to the mid-ninth century, and one of Ælfric who may be the Ælfric, ealdorman of Hampshire, who perished in 1016 at the battle of Ashingdon. Another evidently belonged to Godwine, one of king Æthelred's great men, *c*. 1000. The first writ to survive with royal seal attached is from the reign of Edward the Confessor. Edward's seal was particularly distinctive in that it was a double-faced pendent seal, instead of single-faced and applied to the actual surface of the document, and without parallel in northern and western Europe except at the papal court and the imperial court of Otto III.

When the king needed advice on particular matters or wished to mark a religious festivity with a court gathering as at Christmas, Easter and Pentecost he summoned the *witan* (wise men) and held a *witenagemot*. The *witan* was not an institution but simply those great men whom the king wished to summon to him. Its composition varied from occasion to occasion, and all magnates, bishops and abbots could become members of a *witan*. In the late eighth and early ninth century, the Mercian kings held great synods, meeting with the leading men of Mercia and Mercian subject territories and resolving, probably among much other business, disputes involving Church lands. Such great councils were a feature also of the reign of Athelstan of Wessex (924–39). With the progress towards the unification of England under the kings of the tenth and early eleventh centuries, national *witenagemots* were occasionally held, dealing not only with affairs of general importance but also with local matters on a very wide front indeed.

The ecclesiastical element in the royal councils was extremely important. It is difficult to see how the young Æthelred II can have escaped domination by his bishops, led by Dunstan. Not all episcopal counsels were desirable. In 856 Æthelbald, son of King Æthelwulf, rebelled against his father, largely at the instigation and on the advice of Ealhstan, bishop of Sherborne. Many contemporaries perhaps felt that Sigeric, archbishop of Canterbury, was ill advised when he counselled the payment of danegeld for the first time in Æthelred's reign in 991. The bishops certainly had wide scope to become involved in politics. Lyfing, bishop of Worcester, was accused of having been implicated in the capture and blinding of Alfred, son of Æthelred II, in 1036, and in 1042 he was among those primarily responsible for securing the succession of Edward the Confessor. Several bishops in the Anglo-Saxon period fell into acute disfavour with the king of their day. Eadberht, king of Northumbria, imprisoned Cynewulf, bishop of Lindisfarne, in 750, during the Northumbrian dynastic feuds. King Eadred imprisoned Wulfstan, archbishop of York, for intriguing with the Scandinavians of York in 952. The most famous example of a persecuted bishop is Wilfrid of York in the seventh century; he succeeded in alienating a succession of Northumbrian kings who simply refused to tolerate him. A bishop had little protection against the wrath of a hostile king, or against hostile subjects if the king were weak; in 1052 Edward the Confessor's Norman bishops, Robert of Canterbury, Ulf of Dorchester and William of London, were expelled because of their unpopularity with the English magnates. But bishops could serve the kings in innumerable ways. In the role simply of companions they could play a conspicuous part. Asser was often in the company of Alfred, reading to him and noting matters of interest for him. The education of Edward the Martyr was entrusted to Sideman, bishop of Crediton. In 1052 civil war between Edward the Confessor and Godwine, earl of Wessex, was averted by envoys who included Stigand, bishop of Winchester and later archbishop of Canterbury. In 1049, at the reforming council of Rheims, Duduc, bishop of Wells, represented Edward the Confessor and the English episcopate. In 1054 Ealdred, archbishop of York, was sent on a diplomatic mission to Cologne on behalf of the king, and in the relations between the English king and the king of the Scots the northern bishops played an active diplomatic role. At times bishops were to be found on the field of battle, whither they went to pray for victory if not to participate. A priest of Earl Harold's, Leofgar, who became bishop of Hereford in 1056, is said to have given up his spiritual weapons and taken up his spear and sword against the Welsh, against whom he fell in battle. Two bishops were among the naval commanders of Æthelred II's fleet in 992. Like the bishops, abbots were not strangers to the battlefield. The abbot of Ramsey perished with the bishop of Dorchester-on-Thames at the battle of Ashingdon in 1016, and Leofric, abbot of Peterborough, died after his return from the battle of Hastings. Abbots could be equally as influential as bishops on occasions. Dunstan, while abbot of Glastonbury, is the best example of the way in which an abbot could become prominent among the royal advisers. While abbot of Abingdon, Æthelwold became the tutor of the young Edgar. It was Ælfsige, abbot of Peterborough, who accompanied Queen Emma and her sons to Normandy in 1013. Since appointments to bishoprics in the tenth century were often made from among the abbots, influence at court was no doubt eagerly sought.

A good bishop or abbot could be a fount of wisdom to a young and not necessarily very bright king. King Alfred's relations with his group of scholar bishops show what cultural benefit an intelligent ruler could derive from such men. The ecclesiastical element in the royal councils was a valuable balance to that of the warrior nobility who were inevitably less well educated, less polished. But no Anglo-Saxon king is known to have been completely dominated by ecclesiastics throughout his reign, and the nobility of the land was always well represented at court. Heroic tradition pictured the king's trusted warriors as the leading counsellors in hall. It was an old ealdorman who so impressed King Edwin with his arguments for the acceptance of Christianity. From time to time, magnates in the administrative post of ealdorman appear as the right-hand man of a particular king. Æthelnoth, ealdorman of Somerset, was Alfred's main support in the campaign of 878, he played a prominent part in that of 893, and he was Alfred's envoy to York in 894. In the last four to six years of the reign of Æthelred II, Eadric Streona, ealdorman of Mercia, appears to have been the king's principal counsellor. Cnut relied heavily in England during the early years of his reign on Thorkell the Tall. Godwine and his sons must have dominated the *witenagemots* of Edward the Confessor. The witness lists of royal charters provide an invaluable guide to the lay and ecclesiastical elements of the royal councils, and in the main reveal the frequency or otherwise with which individual great men attended court to advise the king. It is evident that some men, even some bishops, rarely troubled to attend or were rarely summoned, while others were present on almost every occasion and must have been constantly discussing and arguing the issues of the day. The analysis of these lists may well throw light on the regions from which different kings derived most support and from which they received their greatest following.

Local administration

The central government worked in the country at large through the local administration in the primitive folk-groups. The essential local unit was not territorial but personal. Some folk-groups may be traced to very early -*ingas* place-names. Hastings, 'the people of Hæsta', was a folk-group at the time of the Conquest; it was a recognisable entity in 771 when Offa fought the men of Hastings and as late as 1011 the Danes ravaged a district known as that of the men of Hastings. The Domesday Book description of Sonning (Berkshire), from *Sunningas* meaning 'the people of Sunna', corresponds closely to the later medieval 'seven hundreds of Cookham and Bray'. There survives an eighth-century Mercian compilation called the Tribal Hidage which lists several of the folk-groups which made up the kingdom of Mercia and its dependencies. Not all are identifiable, but among the names are those of the *Gyrwe* ('fen dwellers'), *Spaldas* ('the men of the dyke') giving rise to the later district of Spalding, *Cilternsætan* ('men of the Chilterns'), *Pecsætan* ('men of the Peak-district'), *Wreocensætan* ('dwellers around the Wrekin'). The list is not exhaustive for it does not mention the *Magonsætan* ('dwellers around Maund'). The *Elmetsætan*, who are mentioned, go back to the unit of the old British state of Elmet, conquered by Edwin of Northumbria, *c.* 620. Ecgfrith, king of Northumbria, married Æthelthryth of the southern *Gyrwe*. The precise definition of the *hide* need not detain us at the moment; the figures give some idea of relative manpower. Both Bede and the Tribal Hidage agree in assigning 7,000 *hides* to the kingdom of Sussex so the figures may be pretty accurate. 7,000 *hides* are recorded for the *Wreocensætan* and for the *Hwicce* of Worcestershire, 4,000 for the *Cilternsætan*, 1,200 for the *Pecsætan*. The Mercian kingdom was clearly composed of some very large folk-groups, a few large enough to rank as kingdoms. The *Hwicce*, in fact, had their own dynasty, and so for a time did the *Magonsætan*. Others may have done, but no records have survived. Some tribes were much smaller, having as few as 300 *hides*. The *Elmetsætan* had 600. The work of secular and ecclesiastical administration naturally tended to gravitate around such folk-groups. Diuma, bishop of Middle Anglia, died among the *Feppingas* in the 650s. Wilfrid of York died in the province of the *Undulas*, around Oundle, in 709. Many monasteries are known to have been founded in the centres of such folk-groups, the monastery of Oundle being one. Lastingham, where Cedd and Chad built a monastery, signifies 'the homestead of the people of Læsta'; Barking, site of an important East Saxon monastery, 'the people of Berica'; and Repton, great religious centre of the Mercians, 'the hill of the *Hrype*', a folk-group probably related to the *Hrype* among whom Wilfrid built the monastery of Ripon. For the *Hwicce* and the *Magon-sætan*, the bishoprics of Worcester and Hertfordshire were established. Similar folk-groups lie behind other bishoprics.

Gradually in the course of time these natural folk-units were trans-formed by the central government into territorial districts. Certain areas began to be known from quite early times as provinces, and we must not think too exclusively of the shires and hundreds. In a few place-names, *-ge* signifies province and it is found, for example, in *Elge* (Ely), meaning 'eel-province'. Ely is actually called by Bede a region, meaning district, in the province of the East Angles, confirming that Ely formed a recognised subdivision of the East Anglian kingdom. Lyminge and Sturry in Kent contain the same element in their original forms. Chertsey is described by Bede as being in the region *Sudergeona* (Surrey), the southern province. By the seventh century, in fact, regional administrative divisions were beginning to appear. Between Hexham and Carlisle in the seventh century were two regions, *Kintis* and *Ahse*. Dunbar was an administrative centre in Ecgfrith's time, and Eddius Stephanus actually terms Hexham a province. Hexham tradition in the twelfth century alleged that the province of Hexham was given to Queen Æthelthryth by Ecgfrith at their marriage. It may be that medieval Hexamshire represents one of the early territorial divisions of Northumbria, and the same may be true of the medieval shires around Coldingham, an early monastic site, Bamburgh, the Bernician capital, Norham, an estate of the church of Lindisfarne and an important ecclesiastical centre, Bedlington and Richmond. In some instances folk-groups were transformed into territorial administrative districts. In Wessex, *scir* signified a province from the time of Ine at the latest. In 802 the men of what was to become Wiltshire were known as the

Wilsætan, 'settlers on the river Wylye', but by 870 they were the men of *Wiltunscir*, the shire of Wilton. Early *Sumortunsæte*, meaning 'the dwellers at Somerton', became *Sumersætan*, signifying the men of the province known as Somerset. And one of the most important developments in the local administrative history of the tenth and eleventh centuries was the extension of the West Saxon shire system into non-West-Saxon areas. With the exception of the East Anglian divisions into Northfolk and Southfolk, Norfolk and Suffolk, and the regions of Kent, Essex, Surrey and Sussex, all England south of the Tees and the Mersey was divided into shires by 1016. Yorkshire and Lincolnshire were further divided into ridings, signifying a third. The shires were based on the Danish or English fortified strongholds which figure so prominently in the annals of the reign of Edward the Elder. Though the first reference to Oxfordshire as such occurs in 1010, Edward is said in 911 to have succeeded to London and Oxford and all the lands that belonged to them. The first mention of a shire is purely accidental and no guide at all to the date of creation. The shires of west and south Mercia may well date back in origin to the time of Edward and Athelstan. Athelstan is recorded to have fixed the boundary between the Welsh and the Mercians and between the Cornish Britons and the West Saxons, so that the delimiting of shire boundaries may have been a related activity; though shire boundaries were still being determined in the eleventh century. The shires of east Mercia, which developed from Danish army bases, are unlikely to have been modelled on any West Saxon prototype until after 954 and the death of the last Scandinavian king of York. Evidence for the diocesan reorganisation of east Mercia relates to the late 950s. The men who were responsible for the introduction of the shires into Mercia had little regard for the older divisions of the kingdom. Both Shropshire and Warwickshire were artificial units, carved out of the territories of different folk-groups, and the same is probably true of the shires of the east midlands.

The kings were particularly interested, first in the folk-groups and then in the regional divisions of the land, for purposes of taxation. *Geld* or taxation was imposed on a province on the basis of the number of *hides* in that province. The Tribal Hidage is essentially a fiscal document, intended to show an early Mercian ruler the number of *hides* in the various folk-divisions of his realm which could be taxed. For Æthelred the Unready a shire-hidage was prepared, showing the number of *hides* in several of the English shires and indicating, therefore, the

29 Cross-head from Cropthorne,
Worcestershire, ninth century

28 Ruthwell Cross—
Dumfriesshire

30 Viking 'Ringerike' grave-stone
from St. Paul's, London,
eleventh century

Cross-sculpture

31 Part of Offa's Dyke
near Chirk, Denbighshire

32 North Elmham cathedral, Norfolk: interior of the nave looking west
from the transepts

amount of revenue Æthelred could expect to receive from those shires. The regions or provinces of the kingdoms of the Heptarchy, and the shires of Wessex and the later kingdom of England, were administered for the king by a royal official called an ealdorman, who was protected by a high *wergeld* four times that of a thegn, half of which probably belonged to his person and half to his office. Ealdormen were appointed from branches of the royal family itself or from families of great magnates, though no doubt occasionally the fortunes of a lesser family could be made by securing the office. In 851 the name of the ealdorman of Devon was Ceorl which could conceivably imply that he was of peasant stock. The ealdormanry was not hereditary though it sometimes remained in the hands of one family for several generations and at the end of the Anglo-Saxon period the families of Godwine and Leofric seem to have been laying hereditary claim to the earldoms of Wessex and Mercia respectively. The ealdorman may originally have been associated with a folk-group. King Alfred married the daughter of Æthelred, ealdorman of the *Gaini*, an unidentified Mercian tribe. The *Tomsætan* of the river Tame (Warwickshire) had their own ealdorman in the ninth century; in Wessex the *Dornsætan*, men of Dorchester (later Dorset), and the *Wilsætan* of the river Wylye (later Wiltshire) had their individual ealdormen. The ealdorman of Herefordshire was still known in the early eleventh century as the ealdorman of the *Magonsætan*. With the spread of territorial divisions it was usual for an ealdorman to administer one shire, but in the later tenth century combinations of shires in western and central Wessex appear to have been grouped under one man. Mercia was placed as a single ealdormanry under Eadric Streona. East Anglia, Deira and Bernicia were three great ealdormanries. Æthelred II actually reunited Northumbria under Uhtred of Bamburgh. Cnut set the seal on the evolution of these huge units by his creation of earldoms, massive groupings of shires, under an official known by the Scandinavian title of earl. Though always liable to forfeit his ealdormanry and to expulsion or death if he acted treacherously to the king, an ealdorman ruled with semi-regal powers. The chronicler, Æthelweard, himself an ealdorman in the late tenth century, regarded Æthelred, ealdorman of Mercia and brother-in-law of Edward the Elder, as king of Mercia. The ealdorman had the right, like the king, to expect hospitality as he travelled round the shire, presiding at its judicial assemblies and responsible for the maintenance of law and order, and by the eleventh century at the latest was empowered to take for his own revenues one-third of the fines from the courts of shire, hundred and borough.

By *c*. 1000 at the latest the shires were subdivided, in Anglo-Saxon areas into hundreds and in Scandinavian into *wapentakes*. The hundred appears in Wessex for the first time in the mid-tenth-century Hundred Ordinance, usually ascribed to the reign of Edmund, but the laws of Edward the Elder refer to a meeting held every four weeks for the administration of customary law. This seems to be a reference to something very like the hundred court which also met every four weeks. The Anglo-Saxons were acquainted with the hundred as a common denominator from the earliest times. The round figures of the Tribal Hidage show that a hundred was the number used as the basis of assessment, but an administrative area specifically designated a hundred was a later development. Like the shire, the hundred was a territorial rationalisation of ancient folk-groups. The large folk-group of the *Cilternsætan*, for example, was divided into the Chiltern hundreds. In contrast to the rather haphazard hundredal divisions of southern England, the Mercian hundreds are neatly assessed at exactly one hundred *hides*, suggesting that the hundred, like the shire, was artificially imposed on Mercia for administrative convenience. The need for a more up-to-date administrative division of the shire was evidently felt in Scandinavian as well as English districts. The Scandinavian term, *wapentake*, symbolised the flourishing of weapons by which a public assembly signified its decisions, and it first appears in 962.

From the time of the Heptarchy, the lesser local officers of the king were the reeves, who worked with the ealdormen but who were responsible to the king and particularly for the care of royal lands; at first the reeve administered a handful of folk-groups for the king and presided at the folk-court, but with the process of territorialisation the reeve came to preside at the hundred court as the chief official of the hundred. The *wergeld* of a reeve was probably that of a thegn, and a high-reeve twice as much. High-reeves appear in eighth-century Northumbria and eleventh-century Wessex, and would appear to be men with authority over more than one hundred. The essential duties of the reeve were to maintain law and order, punish criminals and supervise the collection of royal dues. Boroughs were placed under their own reeves who were responsible for the efficiency of the borough court and who supervised tolls, exchanges and mints. The reeve of Dorchester was slain by a Viking raiding party in the reign of Beorhtric

of Wessex. With the evolution of the shires and the subsequent group-
ing of several shires under one ealdorman, a percentage of the reeves
became the deputies of the ealdorman in the various shires administered
by him. A reeve who took over the administration of a shire became
known as a shire reeve or sheriff; such an official appears as early as the
laws of Athelstan but it is with the reign of Æthelred II that the county
sheriff emerges clearly. The sheriff came to preside at the shire court
whenever the ealdorman was absent and the writs of Edward the Confessor are often addressed directly to the sheriff. The importance of the
sheriff as the executive agent of the king in the shire in all branches of
the administration was well established before 1066. Sheriffs and reeves
were sometimes regarded as grasping and unscrupulous men. Reeves
were repeatedly urged by successive kings to pronounce just judgments.
The judges criticised by Alfred, whose decisions he questioned, may
have been reeves. Cnut legislated against the reeves who oppressed the
people, and Æthelred II's upholding of the actions of his reeves, despite
criticism, may have been a contributory cause of that king's unpopularity
and reputation as an unjust ruler.

Too much emphasis on royal servants, however, may obscure the
great part played in local government, and particularly in the administration of justice, by local men who held no actual post of responsibility.
The policing of society and the administration of justice were two of
the major and permanent headaches of any Anglo-Saxon ruler. In an
age of undisciplined passions the person needed as much protection as
the state could provide, but this was precious little in Anglo-Saxon
England. Protection was left to the kindred or the lord: policing to the
local officials and those members of the community whom they could
co-opt to their assistance. There can be little doubt that the Danish
wars brought a temporary worsening of social ills. The legislation of the
early tenth-century kings suggest that lawlessness was rampant and
theft in particular on the increase. Apart from theft—murder, rape,
violent assault and arson were common crimes in Anglo-Saxon England.
The lawlessness of the times may have helped to stimulate the administrative reforms of the century, and perhaps led to a development of the
notion that the king ought to take more active responsibility for the
suppression of lawlessness and theft. Athelstan produced law codes
largely concerned simply with the apprehension of thieves and especially
with the pursuit of thieves from one district to another. In his reign the
leading citizens of London established a private insurance association

in which members paid an annual subscription to provide themselves with recompense if they were robbed, and made arrangements to pursue and apprehend criminals. Men of one hundred and of one shire were urged to assist their fellows in adjacent hundreds and shires in the tracking of thieves. Many thieves were simple men who took the stolen goods to their own cottages and were speedily captured, but others operated in bands and covered long distances with their ill-gotten gains to dispose of them in distant markets. Cattle-rustling was rife, and for this reason the sale of cattle had to be carried out in boroughs where royal officials could keep a check. How adequate these crime-prevention measures were it is difficult to say. The laws of Æthelred II in 1008 complained of horrible perjuries and devilish deeds of murder, stealing and spoliation, of evil deeds of many kinds; and it was said, for example, of Northumbria in the mid-eleventh century, that even parties of 20 or 30 men could scarcely travel without being either killed or robbed by the multitude of robbers lying in wait.

The folk-courts of the Heptarchy are very obscure, but from the tenth century justice was dispensed through the courts of shire, hundred and borough. The shire court met twice a year and was an important gathering presided over by the ealdorman and bishop and possibly the sheriff, where judicial and administrative business was transacted. To the shire court went the more complex law-suits and appeals from the hundred court. The hundred court met every four weeks under the presidency of the reeve, a court essentially for lesser men and petty crime. The shire court was paralleled in the boroughs by the borough court, which met three times a year under the presidency of the town reeve. The king reserved certain types of cases, breach of the king's peace, forcible entry and injury to persons in a homestead, ambush, and the harbouring of fugitives, to his own jurisdiction, and there was in addition a constant stream of appeals to the royal court. But there was no idea that the king or the central government should be directly responsible for all justice, and not all royal judgments were regarded as just. Some of King Alfred's were apparently challenged after his death. The king would need considerable legal knowledge for it was naturally only the knottier points of law which came before him, and some of the disputes over land-holding could be incredibly complex. The customary law of the Anglo-Saxons was very complex not simply because it was for the most part unwritten but because it varied from district to district. The Normans recognised three great divisions of Anglo-Saxon law, that of Wessex, that of Mercia and that of the Danelaw. The tenth-century kings of Wessex did not seek to modify regional variations but accepted the laws in force among the Scandinavians. Occasional references to legal experts show that there was a need for men who were well versed in the law and able to determine the custom of the people.

Procedure in court was dictated by formal tradition and would appear very strange to modern eyes. A defendant had to appear in court when accused by the plaintiff or forfeit his suit. The plaintiff swore an oath as to the justness of his accusation, and if the defendant could swear an oath, backed by the requisite number of oath-helpers or compurgators, maintaining his innocence of the charge, the suit was terminated. If the defendant failed to produce the necessary number of compurgators to clear himself, he went to the ordeal. The number of compurgators was determined by the status of the defendant and the seriousness of the accusation. If, however, the defendant was known to be of bad character, or if he had been taken in the act of committing a crime or in possession of stolen property, the plaintiff could bring his compurgators to swear to the defendant's guilt. If this happened, again the defendant went to the ordeal. In the Scandinavian *wapentakes*, by the time of Æthelred II, 12 leading thegns swore to the guilt or innocence of an accused man, an early trace perhaps of the later jury of presentment, and if they swore him guilty he also would go to the ordeal. The ordeal could be variously performed, either by the accused plunging a hand into boiling water to lift out a stone, or by carrying a heated piece of iron a prescribed distance, without sustaining injury if innocent, or by casting the accused bodily into water to see if he floated (guilty) or sank (innocent). The ordeal was regarded as the judgment of God, who, it was believed, intervened directly to expose a perjurer, and it was carried out with elaborate ritual by the Church. If a man were shown to be guilty by the outcome of the ordeal he could suffer the penalty laid down by law, either imprisonment, fining, flogging, mutilation or execution. Anyone over the age of ten was liable to such punishment in the time of Ine; Athelstan raised the age at which a person could be executed from 12, as it was in his day, to 15. Hanging was the most usual method of execution and one Anglo-Saxon poet draws a grim picture of the raven-pecked corpse on the gallows which must have been a common sight, but drowning, burning, beheading and stoning were not unknown. Mutilation was seen in the early eleventh century as a valid alternative to execution, but it never acquired the prominence in Anglo-Saxon England which it did under the Normans. If a defendant fled during court proceedings or resisted the judgment of the court he was outlawed and could be slain by any man unless he received a royal pardon. In 946 King Edmund was slain in a fight with a robber whom he had outlawed. But the most normal outcome of a case involving a member of the nobility was loss of property and particularly the payment of compensation to various parties concerned, the king, the lord, the kindred, the plaintiff. Sentence of death could be commuted by the payment of the defendant's *wergeld*. It is clear that the poor man of peasant or unfree status would come off worst both in the procedural processes of the court and in meeting the requirements of the court. The more serious the charge the greater number of compurgators he would need to swear his innocence, the less likelihood there would be of producing them, the greater probability there would be that the ceorl would be unable to pay the fine. The most striking feature of Anglo-Saxon court procedure to us appears to be that the producing of evidence and its impartial assessment was unknown; but this is probably what went on behind the scenes before the suit ever came into court. Without intimidation and corruption, which was admittedly not unknown, men could not be found to swear to the innocence of a man whom they knew from local knowledge to be guilty. Anglo-Saxon procedure, therefore, attempted in so far as it could to make the local community responsible for good order by its participation in the dispensing of justice.

An important way in which use was made of local men was in the granting of rights to a lord to hold a private court. Lords must always have been in a position to settle petty disputes on their estates, but the first charters which definitely reveal the king granting jurisdictional powers—rights of *sacu* and *socn* (cause and suit)—to landed lords come from the tenth century, though related evidence from the eighth century suggests that such rights have a long history. It has been disputed whether the grant of *sacu* and *socn* conveyed rights of dispensing justice or simply the right to take profits of justice from the popular assemblies, but the weight of evidence suggests the former interpretation. A private court was administered by the lord himself. In the laws of Edgar, the thegns who risked losing their thegnhood if they gave unjust judgments were probably the holders of private jurisdiction. Eleventh-century documents define some of the judicial rights of the lord who possessed such privileges not only as *sacu* and *socn* but also as *toll*, the lord's right to take payment from sales of cattle and goods on his estates, *team*, the right to adjudicate the rightful possession of cattle, and *infangenetheof*, the right to bring thieves taken in possession of stolen goods to justice. It has been thought probable that by 1066 the jurisdiction covered by these terms was possessed by the great majority of men of rank. In addition, there seems to have been a tendency in the first half of the eleventh century for the judicial powers of certain lords to grow at the expense of royal justice. Whole hundreds were granted away into the jurisdiction of a private lord who took over the administration of the hundred courts and united hundred and manorial jurisdiction. By the time of Cnut, rights to hear pleas formerly reserved to the king were also being granted away to private lords. The precise scale on which private courts existed or lords had secured control of the hundred courts by 1066 is unknown, but the indications are that Anglo-Saxon England was riddled with such jurisdictions on the eve of the Norman Conquest. Some historians have seen in this growth of private jurisdiction the great failure of the Anglo-Saxon monarchy to govern the land efficiently. But it can be viewed rather as an effective attempt by the English kings to harness the services of individual members of the nobility for the maintenance of law and order in the countryside at large.

Shires and hundreds or *wapentakes* also served as a military machine. Though the essential bond in an Anglo-Saxon army was between lord and man, the co-ordination of the military resources of the kingdom was the administrative responsibility of ealdormen and reeves. The reeves summoned the military forces from the hundreds and boroughs, and accompanied them on campaign. There are references in the *Chronicle* to reeves fighting in battle; in 1001, for example, a Viking raiding party on the Exe was resisted at Pinhoe by a reeve and a high-reeve. The ealdormen took charge of the assembled forces of their shire or shires. They figure constantly in the forefront of the fighting; the leadership of Ealdorman Byrhtnoth at Maldon may suffice as an example. It was their control of the military organisation which made the loyalty of the ealdormen to the crown so essential in time of war. King Alfred was deserted by at least one ealdorman and Æthelred II by more than one.

It is believed that the basis of recruitment behind the Old English army was that one warrior should be provided by every five *hides* or six *carucates*, though there were naturally regional variations. Similarly, in 1008 every 300 *hides* was made responsible for the provision of one ship for the national fleet.

If a thegn held the five *hides* in question he would serve in the *fyrd* or designate a deputy; if a wealthy ceorl held the five *hides*, similarly, he would be obliged to serve for them. The laws of Ine provide a penalty for the ceorl who neglected *fyrd* duty, and the poem on the battle of Maldon reveals the presence of a ceorl in the thick of the fighting. It is certain that some ceorls performed menial duties behind the battle lines. A passage in Bede shows that ceorls were used to bring supplies to the fighting noblemen. Here, perhaps, the ceorls were serving their military lords. The traditional view, that the great mass of ceorls were liable to conscription for military service, forming a motley host behind the more select *fyrd* from every five *hides*, is now under attack. But in times of crisis, for example in 1016 and 1066, all able-bodied men were probably anxious to protect their lives and possessions; and it is impossible to believe that ceorls were not organised on a military basis up to the point of being able to resist aggression if necessary. All land was theoretically either *inware* or *utware*, meaning that it had to supply men or money for home or national defence. Some royal desmesnes owed no military service and it is probable that certain lords attempted to relieve their own lands of military as well as financial burdens by transferring the whole duty owed on to tenanted land. Certain urban levies were liable to service only within a limited radius of their town. Not all the available resources were summoned for national defence at one and the same time, and the *Chronicle* tells us that Alfred the Great divided his *fyrd* into two, so that half the men were at home, half on service. This was partly to leave men at home for the harvest, perhaps, but by so dividing his forces in this way Alfred also doubled the period when the *fyrd* was at his disposal. It seems that one of these divisions was quite prepared to cease campaigning, however, regardless of circumstances, when its period of service had expired. The *Chronicle* account of the year 893 shows that provisioning and length of service were related, and one division of the English army broke off an aggressive campaign because provisions and period of service had simultaneously run out. One text of the *Chronicle* (C) records that the army and fleet King Harold had stationed along the south coast to intercept William of Normandy were eventually sent home when provisions ran out. There seems no real reason to distrust this statement. It is generally thought that by the first half of the eleventh century the period of *fyrd* service was usually two months. The evidence, however, is slight and has been questioned. What does seem clear from the records of

Æthelred's reign is that the organisation of the military resources of the kingdom for any protracted campaigning had become a major operation by the eleventh century. It is hardly surprising that the key to military strength for an Anglo-Saxon king lay in the employment of paid mercenaries, such as Cnut's housecarles, who would serve indefinitely.

It has been the subject of considerable historical debate as to whether the military system of the Anglo-Saxons by 1066 was such that England can be described as feudal on the eve of the Norman Conquest. Certainly, *cnihts* or knights were not unknown in Anglo-Saxon England. Apart from *radcnihts*, mounted retainers, in western England, there survives evidence for burghal knights at London, Canterbury, Winchester, Cambridge and Exeter. The term signifies a warrior, and these knights were probably mercenaries. In that the number of knights Archbishop Anselm sent to the army of William Rufus from the lands of the Church of Canterbury was said to have been fixed before the Norman Conquest, it is possible that on occasions lay and ecclesiastical magnates were making agreements with the king to send such men as part of their contribution to the royal host. The military organisation of the country does seem to have been subject to some changes as the Old English period drew to a close. Edward the Confessor, for example, allowed certain towns to commute for military service by the payment of a fixed sum. Though, however, it has seemed to some historians that all the basic elements of feudalism were present in the late Anglo-Saxon army, it is essential to clarify what is meant by feudal. Feudalism developed in Gaul in the eighth century under the early Carolingians; it was a development peculiar at first to Gaul and designed to provide the ruler with a great number of military vassals on all of whom there was a personal obligation to perform military service. A substantial part of the territorial endowment of such men was 'secularised' Church land. A feudal society may be most satisfactorily defined as a society in which the fief was the basis of military organisation, a fief being the landed estates held by a lord, himself a vassal, on condition that he provided a specified number of military vassals as warriors for the royal or ducal army. But there is no evidence for parallel secularisation of Church land in England on any scale, and only in so far as the Old English military organisation through the hundred and the shire was replaced by military organisation through the fiefs of vassals under William the Conqueror and his successors can English society be said to have become feudalised.

Chapter three

Culture

Art

The artistic legacy of the Ancient World was Graeco-Roman naturalistic art. The barbarians beyond the frontiers of the Empire either developed a native non-representational style like the Celts, or borrowed from Rome and treated borrowed themes in a non-representational manner like the Anglo-Saxons; that is to say, the barbarian trend was always towards abstract design and pattern in diametric opposition to the artistic values of classical tradition. With the fall of the Roman Empire in the west, barbarian art-forms came to predominate freely over north and west Europe in the lands which the invaders of the fifth and sixth centuries colonised or settled. The artistic traditions of the Ancient World, however, were preserved in the west by the Christian Church at Rome in particular, and pure barbarian art only really lasted until the acceptance of Christianity. As Christianity spread, the Latin Church, if it did not destroy, at least modified the native art. The missionaries brought with them illustrated Gospel Books, paintings and carved reliquaries, all produced in Mediterranean lands. St. Augustine and his companions first approached King Æthelberht bearing a board on which was painted the image of Christ. The first effect of the collision in Britain was the borrowing by Anglo-Saxons of Christian models, the introduction of a new naturalism. In the remoter regions of Scotland or Ireland, the influence of the Roman Church was slower to make itself felt, and barbarian traditions survived and flourished longer, never really dying out. Barbarian art also survived in Scandinavia where there was no seventh-century Mediterranean influence.

The reign of Charlemagne initiated further artistic advances. The culture of the later Merovingian age is generally thought to have been of a low standard, and Charles turned not simply to Germanic art for renewed inspiration but to Rome and the Mediterranean, and beyond to Greece. Naturalism acquired a new lightness and liveliness, and the portrayal of the human form, for example, advanced so far as to enable the Carolingian emperors to be depicted in a lifelike manner. The Carolingian renaissance may have had no popular basis and may have been already passing away by *c.* 880, but it was a striking achievement, a late flowering of ancient civilisation. The artistic history of early Europe, however, does not testify to an easy or even a complete victory of naturalism over non-representational styles. In the tenth century, German Ottonian art drew on Roman, Carolingian and Byzantine models, and it was in the tenth century that Romanesque may really be said to have originated. In Romanesque art, formalisation and love of pattern flourished alongside the naturalism of the revived classical tradition. In the later Anglo-Saxon period, English art reacted to the decorative and naturalistic influences of the art of the Continent and Byzantium, and at the same time brought these influences to bear on the art of the Scandinavian settlers.

It is difficult to say what changes of outlook were involved in the transition among a barbarian people from a purely abstract art to a mixed art containing both abstract and naturalistic elements. The transformation of the primitive and unreal world of native barbarian art could reflect the beginnings of a new approach to the world, a new understanding of life. It is clear that there was an important relationship between the spread of Mediterranean art-forms and the revival of intellectual life under the stimulus of the literary legacy of the Ancient World.

Both Celtic and Germanic art possessed long traditions going back into a prehistoric past, and shared a love of interlace and geometric ornament. By Celtic art is meant in particular the art of all the Celtic regions of the British Isles and, where it can be detected, the British element in Anglo-Saxon art. Anglo-Saxon art in the pagan period tended to break down animal forms in ornamentation until they became mere patterns of intertwined creatures; but with the coming of Christianity, Anglo-Saxon art borrowed from the decorative patterns of the Mediterranean the vine scroll and the inhabited vine, a vine peopled with animals and birds, and this became the most characteristic motive in Christian Northumbrian art.

Attempts to assess the cultural and artistic growth of England in the seventh and early eighth centuries have been confused by a prolonged controversy over Celtic (particularly Irish) and English elements in the art of Northumbria. The fundamental problem is that for the majority of early illuminated manuscripts produced in the British Isles it is impossible to assign a specific home, whether in Ireland, Scotland or England. This is because they are written in an Irish hand known as 'half-uncial', and the decoration of the manuscripts represents a composite blend of Celtic and Anglo-Saxon artistic elements and patterns, known to historians as Hiberno-Saxon. It is impossible to say, for example, whether the important seventh-century illuminated Gospel Book, the Book of Durrow, belongs to an Irish or an English home. Perhaps it is enough simply to be able to place these often beautiful manuscripts within the British Isles. But the question of ultimate origins is important for the artistic development of Celtic Ireland and Saxon England respectively in this period. Some experts would assign the majority of early illuminated manuscripts to Ireland, while others would place them in England, particularly in Northumbria where Irish and Scottish influence is known to have been strong.

Clearly, manuscripts could travel and come to rest far from home in monastic libraries where their styles of ornamentation could be copied. The so-called Lichfield Gospels or Gospels of Chad, dating from the early eighth century, at Lichfield by the tenth century, were probably written at Llandaff; the Book of Kells, so called because it came to rest at Kells, may derive from Northumbria though it has been claimed as a product of Iona; the Echternach Gospels, now at Echternach, with a South Italian text and Hiberno-Saxon illumination, produced in the British Isles, passed over to the Continent. An interesting example of the way in which a manuscript could travel is shown by two late Saxon texts. Erwin, the teacher of Wulfstan, bishop of Worcester, lent Wulfstan a sacramentary and psalter which he had illuminated. Erwin subsequently gave the books to King Cnut, who sent them as a gift to Cologne. In 1054 Ealdred, archbishop of York, visited Henry III at Cologne and received the two books as a parting gift; he gave them to Wulfstan not knowing that Wulfstan had previously had them in his possession.

If manuscripts could travel, so could artists. An Irish scribe, Ultan, is recorded to have been at Lindisfarne in the seventh century. This is particularly interesting because one manuscript in the Hiberno-Saxon tradition which can be placed is that of the Lindisfarne Gospels, written and illuminated—according to a tenth-century colophon— by Eadfrith, bishop of Lindisfarne (698–721). The text is of Mediterranean origin, and the illumination has been influenced to a certain extent by Mediterranean naturalism, but this is fine Hiberno-Saxon work. The text, written out in Irish half-uncial, has been decorated not only with Celtic spirals, Irish illuminated capitals and decorated Celtic 'carpet' page but also with Germanic animal ornament and interlace. The Lindisfarne Gospels are closer to the traditional motifs of Celtic and Germanic art than the Codex Amiatinus, a manuscript evidently based on an Italian model and produced in the first years of the eighth century at Bede's monastery of Monkwearmouth and Jarrow, a centre of strong Roman influence. The naturalism of this manuscript is in no way matched by that of the Hiberno-Saxon group. But native Celtic and Saxon elements could affect art even in such a stronghold of Roman tradition as Canterbury. Though, of course, the classical tradition underwent much less of a transformation in Kent than in the North, traditional influences were still at work as can be seen from the Canterbury Psalter of c. 750. By the early ninth century, however, the influence of Hiberno-Saxon art was fading as the cultural links with Ireland weakened and snapped. After a period of barrenness in manuscript illumination during the Alfredian period, traditional Saxon motifs revived again in southern England in the first half of the tenth century, under Carolingian stimuli, evolving in the second half of the century into what is known as the Winchester style of illumination, from its evidently close association with Æthelwold's church at Winchester. With the monastic reform movement of the period there was evidently a demand for elaborate service books. The earliest group of manuscripts in the Winchester style—including the Durham Rituale, and a manuscript of Bede's *Life of St. Cuthbert*—come from the Wessex of the reign of Athelstan, but the style of decoration is somewhat flat until the peak of excellence was reached in the later tenth century with, for example, the foundation charter for the new minster at Winchester (966) and later the New Minster Gospels. The Winchester style is distinguished for its fresh and vivid blending of naturalism and stylised ornamentation, particularly of leaf decoration, its gracious figures with fluttering drapery, and its delicate colouring. Many Anglo-Saxon artists, again reacting in part at least to continental inspiration, acquired a taste simply for attractive line drawings. In the later tenth century the Winchester style became diffused throughout southern England so that all manuscripts so illuminated do not necessarily come from Winchester, nor was the Winchester school the only centre of individual decorative techniques. A copy of the Gospels from Canterbury, dating to *c.* 1015, shows clearly that Canterbury was the home of a heavier and more solid form of manuscript illumination, and this impression is confirmed by several other late Saxon manuscripts from Canterbury which show a liking for deep colouring and impressive ornamentation.

The collection, preservation, and production of manuscripts in the later Saxon period received the patronage of great laymen and churchmen. Leofric, bishop of Exeter at the time of the Norman Conquest, built up a fine collection of manuscripts, including the famous *Exeter Book* of Old English poetry, which he donated to Exeter Cathedral. Indeed, the development of manuscript art in the later Saxon period can be well illustrated by individual manuscripts associated with particular figures of West Saxon history. Thin line drawing, which is so characteristic a feature of later West Saxon art, and which contrasts, for example, with the thick line drawing of the Book of Cerne, probably from pre-Viking Mercia, is seen for the first time in the surviving contemporary copy of King Alfred's translation of Gregory the Great's *Pastoral Care*, a copy sent to Wærferth, bishop of Worcester, in the 890s; though this copy also shows that the ornamental motifs of West Saxon manuscript art in the Alfredian period were looking back in part to the art of the Mercians—understandably, in view of the Mercian scholars at Alfred's court. The Athelstan Psalter, which appears to have belonged to King Athelstan and to have been given by him to Winchester Cathedral, reflects the beginnings of the emerging Winchester style in its full-page illuminations and delicately drawn illustrations. The fully developed Winchester style is brilliantly represented by the Benedictional of Æthelwold, bishop of Winchester, with its extensive use of gold, its vivacious figures and its ornate border foliage. Here a Carolingian minuscule text is adorned with essentially Byzantine religious scenes and native English decorative pattern. The Sacramentary of Robert of Jumièges, for a time archbishop of Canterbury in the reign of Edward the Confessor, appears to have been produced and illuminated *c.* 1010 and is even more ornate, the figures more agitated, the floral borders perhaps more skilful than in the Benedictional. The Sacramentary, now at Rouen, must have been taken there by Robert when he returned to the Continent in 1051. A lower standard of Old English manuscript art is revealed in the texts of the Gospels known as the Judith manuscript, since it belonged to Judith, wife of Earl Tostig, and was subsequently given by her to the monastery of Weingarten. All the evidence points to a date *c.* 1050–65 for the execution of this manuscript. An additional figure at the foot of the Cross in an illustration of the Crucifixion may be Judith herself. The figures, it has been said, are rather slight and with certain ugly features, and the decoration may represent the less polished style of some East Anglian school. Continental affinities continued to be marked in manuscript illumination in England up to the eve of the Norman Conquest as can be seen, for example, in the Gospel Book of Queen Margaret, wife of Malcolm III of Scotland, dating to *c.* 1060, ornamented in deep colours and drawn in more rigid lines than was common among the manuscripts of south-east England at this time. It reflects the heavier illustration and deeper colouring which was to characterise the art of manuscript illumination in early Norman England.

Individual illuminated manuscripts from the Anglo-Saxon period have received far more attention, because there is more to say about them, than individual pieces of stone sculpture from the same centuries, with the exception of the outstanding Ruthwell and Bewcastle crosses from Dumfriesshire and Cumberland respectively. The fine naturalistic carved figures on these crosses, representing Biblical themes, are adorned with inhabited vine scroll as well as with decorative patterns showing affinities with those of the Lindisfarne Gospels, suggesting a date for the crosses in the first half of the eighth century. Part of the poem, the *Dream of the Rood*, is carved in runic letters on the Ruthwell Cross, and here again the linguistic forms can be approximately dated to the early eighth century. Both the Ruthwell and the Bewcastle monuments belong to a group of crosses known as Northumbrian free-standing crosses, comprising a panelled and ornamented shaft with cross head. Such free-standing crosses evidently characterised the sculptural work of Northumbrian artists, though the vast majority of extant examples now exist only as fragments. Pictland, by contrast, always retained the cross slab, a slab of stone with the form of the cross and other decorative designs simply incised upon it. Mercian artists, in the ninth century at least, favoured sculpture mostly in friezes and relief panels. Indeed, in the field of cross sculpture, in contrast to that of manuscript illumination, marked regional differences are striking. The free-standing crosses of Ireland, Dalriada and Northumbria were never copied by the Picts, and, though the inhabited vine scroll is occasionally found on stone monuments in Celtic lands,

Northumbrian sculptors in the pre-Viking period avoided Irish decorative motifs on their crosses. Neither the Irish nor the Northumbrians ever adopted the so-called disc-faced crosses of Galloway, which resemble in some though not in all features the disc-headed Welsh crosses that had probably evolved by the late ninth century.

From the Celtic north-west of Britain, particularly from Whithorn, survive a number of stone slabs incised with the Chi-Rho symbol. The Chi-Rho monogram was formed of the first two letters in the Greek word 'Christos', set in a circle. The Whithorn stones are generally considered to date from the fifth or sixth centuries and to mark the beginnings of Christian sculpture in Britain as the Roman period drew to a close and the Anglo-Saxon Conquest began. But the subsequent chronology of Celtic and Saxon stone sculpture in the British Isles is extremely hazy. No cross or cross fragment can really be dated closer than to within 50 years either way. Dating depends mainly on the typological analysis of interlace patterns, and on analogies with the ornamentation of more closely dated manuscripts and metalwork, on the whole an insubstantial basis for a chronological approach. Consequently, it is almost impossible to envisage clearly the development of the art of stone sculpture among the various English kingdoms. The crosses of Northumbria have received the most systematic treatment of all, Northumbria affording the most numerous and the finest examples from the pre-Viking period. The origins of Northumbrian cross sculpture appear to derive from Irish influences, but no examples illustrative of continuous development from stones of Irish character at Lindisfarne and Hartlepool to the naturalistic masterpieces of Ruthwell and Bewcastle can now be traced. Possible schools of sculpture have been identified at Hexham and Lancaster, dating to the eighth century. It has been argued that Hoddam in Dumfriesshire emerged as a leading sculptural centre on Northumbria's north-western frontier c. 800, and that a new school at Ripon exercised a marked influence within Northumbria and in Cumbria in the period c. 800–850. The first half of the ninth century seems to have been rather important for Northumbrian sculpture. To this period date the attractive crosses of Easby and Rothbury, Easby in particular being distinguished for its beautiful vine-scroll and its possible reflection of the revived classical influences of the Carolingian renaissance. Mercian sculpture, on the whole, was more backward than Northumbrian, but the new influences of Carolingian art have been detected in the high-quality work of the friezes at Breedon (Leicestershire). A cross-head from Cropthorne (Worcestershire) is a fine example of ninth century West Saxon ornamental styles. In the Viking and post-Viking periods it appears to have been Wessex which emerged as the leading sculptural centre in England, probably by the reign of Alfred the Great, with an advanced sculptural technique that continues through from the ninth-century cross at Codford St. Peter in Wiltshire to the mid- or late-eleventh-century slabs at Chichester, probably from the minster at Selsey. These sculptural pieces parallel in their native ornamentation and Carolingian motifs the manuscript art of the Winchester school. A series of fragments, perhaps of the tenth century, come from Reculver and reveal that Kent shared in this West Saxon sculptural awakening.

Wessex and Kent, of course, escaped the full impact of Viking invasion, nor were they subject to Scandinavian settlement. What is surprising is that northern England produced such an astonishing abundance of sculptural work, which, if of a poor artistic standard in the main, nevertheless testifies to the vigour of the Northumbrian Church in the tenth and early eleventh centuries. The Hiberno-Saxon legacy of older Northumbrian traditions mingled with imported Viking designs. Viking art of this period in England is characterised primarily by what is known as the Jellinge style, so called from objects found in royal burial mounds at Jellinge in Jutland. A secondary phase is known as Ringerike art. The Vikings delighted in elongated animal forms, with spiral joints and backward-looking heads, enmeshed in elaborate interlace and foliage. A remarkable shaft from Sockburn in Co. Durham has the tightly woven mesh of the Jellinge beasts on one face, Hiberno-Saxon animal designs on another, and two full-length sides of fine Northumbrian interlace. For much of their design, indeed, sculptures in Bernicia were turning to ancient manuscript tradition and so kept alive older art-forms, but Anglian treatment of Scandinavian elements in Deira led to the emergence of new barbarian themes. A disintegration of pattern, however, and a lack of coherence appears to be typical of Northumbrian sculpture on the eve of the Norman Conquest, and there can be little question that the Scandinavian influx tended to barbarise the art of the Danelaw and to drown the influence in the north of more advanced artistic circles of southern England.

Anglo-Saxon metalwork ornamentation is characterised essentially by distorted ribbon-like animal forms, interlace and some use of vine-scrolls. It is generally closer to the abstract patterns of barbarian art than to the great naturalism of the best stone sculpture or manuscript illumination, and, though the tenth-century Winchester style did have an effect also in this field, the influence of Scandinavian motifs was much greater. By contrast to the mass-produced brooches of the pagan period, however, relatively little has survived of later Saxon metalwork, in the way of ornaments, ecclesiastical vessels and objects, or figural work. It is correspondingly difficult to form a detailed impression of the development of the Anglo-Saxons in this art-form. It is clear, however, from surviving Kentish jewellery of the sixth and seventh centuries (for example, the Kingston Brooch), the treasures of the Sutton Hoo ship burial and individual pieces like the Cross of St. Cuthbert (which survived inside St. Cuthbert's coffin), that the Anglo-Saxon metalworkers and goldsmiths could produce fine and attractive work, with precious stones, coloured glass, and garnets set on a gold and silver background. The Alfred Jewel, found near Athelney in 1693 and now at Oxford, is of gold and enamel, in the form of a pendant, a crystal plaque covering the portrait of a man holding what appear to be two sceptres. The small object may have been a reading-weight attached to a line-pointer. It is less than 2½ in. in height, terminates in an animal's head and bears the inscription 'Alfred had me wrought'. It possibly belonged originally to King Alfred, and it is likely that the portrait is an allegorical representation of 'Sight'. An important metalwork hoard from much of the same period was discovered at Trewhiddle in Cornwall, the objects decorated with animal interlace and scroll ornament.

The Anglo-Saxons achieved some fine work in whalebone and ivory which can be easily overlooked. The so-called Frank's Casket is a box made of whalebone and carved in a variety of pagan, classical and Christian scenes, ornamented with traditional decorative motifs and inscribed in runes in the Northumbrian language of the early eighth century. It is a unique survival, representative of a more secular art than that of manuscript illumination and cross sculpture. From the later Saxon period come some very attractive ivories, carvings in bone of Christian figures and scenes revealing great mastery of the art. The influence of the Winchester style of illumination is clearly apparent, and more direct Carolingian, even Byzantine inspiration has been detected in several pieces. The depiction of the Crucifixion proved a popular theme of ivory-carving, but functional objects like crosses, portable altars and croziers might also be of ivory. There survives a superb ivory crozier head from the mid-eleventh century, carved with a number of scenes from the Nativity and Passion of Christ.

Valuable sidelights on the development of Anglo-Saxon art are provided in various ways by the coinage of these centuries. Many of the silver pennies of the Anglo-Saxons rank as minor artistic masterpieces. The influence of classical Roman coins is often marked on those of Offa of Mercia, of the art of Ottonian Germany on those of Edward the Confessor. The coinage of the late-ninth-century Danish kings of York, on the other hand, has marked Carolingian affinities.

Architecture

In their construction of fortifications the Anglo-Saxons either requisitioned Iron Age fortresses to serve as *burhs* or built their own rudimentary forts of earthen embankments and wooden stockades at strategic points. The earliest structure at Yeavering in the Cheviots, a palace of King Edwin, revealed relatively recently by excavations, was a large fort enclosed by a double palisade of timber and earth with wooden towers at the corners. Literary references to the architectural features of such sites are virtually non-existent, but Edward the Elder is known to have built a stone wall around his *burh* at Towcester, and archaeological excavation has revealed earthen ramparts with stone facing at Wareham, Cricklade and Lydford. There are a great many references to Bamburgh, which was a township but also a great fortress. Bamburgh is said to have been first encircled with a hedge and then with a wall. It was common practice to encircle monasteries and homesteads in this way. In the eighth century Bamburgh was evidently protected by gates, though conditions must have been primitive inside, for on one occasion a rocky cleft provided the best protected and defensible site. By the eleventh century steps were carved in the rock, ascending in what was regarded at the time as a wonderful manner. It is not until *c.* 1050, however, that references occur to castles as such, erected by King Edward's continental followers in Herefordshire at Hereford, Richard's Castle, and probably Ewyas Harold. These would probably be motte-and-bailey structures such as the Normans introduced in such great numbers into England after the battle of Hastings. It was the absence of the motte-and-bailey castle among the Anglo-Saxons which was held by one twelfth-century writer to account for the relative ease with which William the Conqueror suppressed English resistance.

Domestic dwellings and outbuildings were originally of wood. King

Alfred describes, in his version of St. Augustine's *Soliloquies*, the gathering in the woods of staves, props, bars and beams for the purpose of building a dwelling. Wooden dwellings, of course, were particularly vulnerable to fire. Penda, king of Mercia, attempted to set fire to Bamburgh in the 650s with planks, beams, wattles and thatch taken from the neighbouring villages which he had destroyed. Bede describes the burning of a house in a village on the Mercian-Welsh border; sparks, from a great fire in the middle of the room, flew up and set alight the wattle and thatch roof, and only a solitary post survived the conflagration. Not only individual houses but whole villages might go up in flames quite by accident. When Cuthbert visited his foster-mother, sparks from a blazing house at the west end of the village caught other houses; the heat became so intense that the villagers were driven back and disaster, so it was said, was averted only by the prayers of the saint. In 962 a great and fatal fire is described as having occurred in London, and St. Paul's Cathedral was burnt; in the reign of the Confessor the town of Wilton was ravaged by fire, almost all the houses being destroyed.

Not a great deal is known of Anglo-Saxon dwellings. The sunken hovels at Sutton Courtenay (Berkshire), dating from the pre-Viking period, appear to have been storage pits or working sheds rather than peasant huts. Nevertheless, recurring archaeological traces of small rectangular buildings, which may have been little better than hovels, suggest that such dwellings were common throughout the Anglo-Saxon period. Longer, rectangular buildings, like those at Maxey (Northamptonshire) belonging to the wealthier peasants, would seem to have been a regular feature of the Anglo-Saxon scene. Dwellings of the aristocratic class stood in a court which was surrounded by an earthen or stone embankment. The lord's hall, or, as the poets described it, the mead-dwelling, the wine buildings, the gift hall, appears to have been a long rectangular structure. It was supported by internal posts and external buttresses, surrounded with benches along the walls, and with a fire in its centre. Sleeping quarters or bowers (*burs*) for the lord's family and womenfolk were probably on the whole in separate and smaller rectangular buildings. The poem *Beowulf* provides a valuable poetic description of the hall of Hrothgar, king of the Danes called *Heorot* (Hart), which seems to have been decorated with a gold-adorned roof. Excavations at the royal West Saxon palace at Cheddar (Somerset) revealed a pre-tenth-century long hall, 78 ft. long and 20 ft. wide at its widest point; the main entrances were in the middle of the long sides. The great hall at Yeavering, rebuilt four times in the seventh century, was 100 ft. long.

William of Malmesbury describes the houses of the Anglo-Saxons as mean and despicable. In his *Life of Wulfstan*, bishop of Worcester, he refers to an old house, where the bishop stayed for a while, which literally collapsed on his departure. This unfavourable picture is probably rather unfair in view of the archaeological evidence for the exactness of some Anglo-Saxon carpentry technique. Nevertheless, hanging tapestries in the greater halls were partly designed to exclude draughts, and Alfred's palaces were so draughty that his candle-clocks had to be encased in finely-planed, translucent bone to prevent their being blown out. Alfred began to build more majestic royal houses, both of wood and stone, and stone probably came into increasing use as the period advanced. Earl Harold's hall at Bosham, as depicted in the Bayeux Tapestry, was of stone. But it is important to appreciate how certain at least of the Anglo-Saxons felt about housing; at the time of the rebellion in the north in 1068 against William the Conqueror some of the Northumbrians lived in tents, disdaining to dwell in houses lest they became enervated, on account of which, so we are told by a twelfth-century writer, the Normans thought them savages.

The study of architectural development in Anglo-Saxon England revolves primarily around ecclesiastical architecture; occasionally a nearly complete church survives from the pre-Conquest period, even in rare instances a whole church, while archaeological investigation has revealed the ground plans of many Anglo-Saxon churches on sites where there has been continuous Christian worship from the earliest times to the present day. And fragments, sometimes quite considerable fragments, of pre-Conquest ecclesiastical structures survive in innumerable parish churches throughout England. Not that Anglo-Saxon churches are evenly distributed across all English counties. They are particularly thick in north-east England and noticeably absent from north-west England as far south as a line from the Wash to Cheshire. Though scattered across southern England, they are rare in the south-west peninsula west of Somerset and in the central midland counties of Staffordshire, Derbyshire, Nottinghamshire and Warwickshire. The distribution of surviving fragments of Anglo-Saxon ecclesiastical architecture, of course, is conditioned in part at least by the geological nature of the land, by the suitability of local rock for building purposes. It is important to bear in mind that stone could be transported and is known to have been transported long distances, but on the whole the Anglo-Saxons used local stone. The churches, for example, of Corbridge, Hexham, Bradwell, Brixworth and St. Martin's, Canterbury, to name a few, were built of stone or brick taken from nearby Roman sites. Where Roman stone or brick was not available, flints might be used or suitable local stone. Breamore is a flint church, while the church of St. John the Baptist, Barnack, is built with stone from quarries at Barnack (Northamptonshire). Altogether there are several hundred parish churches and greater minsters containing varying amounts of Anglo-Saxon stonework. But much of this can be easily obscured from the eye of the observer who lacks any extensive architectural knowledge by later building of post-Conquest date.

It was some time, of course, before churches began to be built anywhere in England after the Anglo-Saxon Conquest. There were no churches in Bernicia in the mid-630s when Aidan arrived. It must not be assumed, either, that where a literary reference to the founding of a church survives, as with Brixworth in Northamptonshire, which was founded *c.* 680, or with Bradford-on-Avon, founded by Aldhelm, all or even part of existing Anglo-Saxon work goes back to the actual date of founding, though in some instances it may do. There were four periods of building at Brixworth. The architectural question to be asked is not simply how early a particular phase of construction may be but also how late it could be. In considering the majority of churches, the historian must always reckon with the possibility that the first structure was of wood. At Glastonbury the earliest structure was of wattles, subsequently covered with wooden planks and lead. The original church on Lindisfarne was of hewn oak, covered with reeds, built after the Scottish manner; Eadberht, bishop of Lindisfarne (688–98), first covered the walls and roof with plates of lead. Something of what must have been normal development in innumerable parishes can be seen from findings on the site of the small church of St. Bertelin, Stafford; here there was originally only a wooden cross until eventually a wooden building was put up, possibly in the tenth century, and then finally a stone church in the early eleventh. Even great churches might be built only of wood as late as the Norman Conquest. The church of the important West Saxon nunnery of Wilton was a wooden structure until Edith, the queen of Edward the Confessor, built in stone, and the church of the abbey of Bury St. Edmunds was wooden in 1066. The only example still surviving of an Anglo-Saxon wooden church, albeit heavily restored, is that of St. Andrew, Greensted, Essex, where tree-trunks have been split apart near the centre and arranged in an upright position as the walls of the nave, their flat surfaces forming the inner wall. Excavations have shown that the chancel was originally similarly constructed. It is interesting to note that the north-west corner, part of the original construction, is formed from a single log so cut on the inside that it forms a part of each of the two adjacent sides.

There was a great spate of building in stone in the late tenth and early eleventh centuries. In the main it is traces of building from this period that are found in the parish churches of England; but certain Anglo-Saxon churches contain stonework going back far earlier, even to the seventh century in a few cases. Some of the greater churches and minsters are known to have been of stone from the date of their foundation. The original chancel of the little church of St. Martin, Canterbury, used by Queen Bertha before the arrival of St. Augustine and the seat of a *chorepiscopus* in the early eleventh century, still survives, one of the most fascinating relics of the early Church in England. An important group of seventh-century Kentish churches, including parts of St. Augustine's, Canterbury, and the church of St. Mary, Reculver, throw valuable light on architectural developments in the south-east at that period. In the south-west traces of King Ine's foundation at Glastonbury have been found. In Northumbria Paulinus's church at York is said to have been of stone, re-roofed with lead and fitted with glazed windows by Wilfrid. The basis of our knowledge of Northumbrian architectural styles is derived from the literary references to, and the surviving early portions of, Wilfrid's foundations at Ripon and Hexham as well as those of Benedict Biscop at Monkwearmouth and Jarrow.

The ecclesiastical architecture of the seventh and eighth centuries derived from Gallic and probably to a lesser extent Italian styles of building, introduced into Kent by the Augustinian mission and into Northumbria by men like Wilfrid and Benedict Biscop. Both Wilfrid and Benedict Biscop are recorded to have brought stone-masons from Gaul to direct building operations. The first Kentish churches were rectangular structures, with a nave, side chapels and an apsidal chancel (a chancel, that is, with a semicircular or polygonal ending); the most outstanding churches of the Northumbrian group were evidently distinguished by longer and sometimes aisled naves and by considerably higher walls, being altogether more elaborate than the churches of Kent. Eddius could say of Wilfrid's foundation at Hexham that the like

had not been seen north of the Alps. Not all the northern stone structures would be of Hexham standard for stone-masonry, of course. Excavations have shown that the early stonework at Whitby monastery was
poor. In the course of time even Wilfrid's buildings would come to seem
out of date as new architectural developments in England and the influence first of the Carolingian renaissance and then of Ottonian culture
led to the growth of a liking for towers, sometimes at the east and the
west ends or even in the centre, and for the transepts of the now traditional cruciform church, with altars not infrequently placed both at the
east and west ends. Such new designs had some influence on building,
for example, at cathedral churches like Canterbury and Winchester, at
monasteries such as Ely, Ramsey, Thorney, Peterborough and Glastonbury, and in parish churches like Deerhurst (Gloucestershire) and
Breamore (Hampshire). Many other examples could be given. Financial
considerations, of course, must have dictated the scale of new building.
The richly endowed church of Winchester was lavishly rebuilt by
Æthelwold, in harmony with the latest continental architectural styles.
Sherborne, a less wealthy cathedral church, nevertheless acquired
square western and central towers, transepts, and—a rarer feature in
later Anglo-Saxon churches—an aisled nave. The church of the poorer
nunnery of Romsey (Hampshire) was much simpler in design; it lacked
the aisled nave but was cruciform with small square transepts. The
church of All Saints at Newton-by-Castleacre (Norfolk) consisted of a
nave, tower, chancel and transepts in Anglo-Saxon times, but the transepts have since completely disappeared. It cannot be assumed, therefore, that a church that does not now possess transepts never did so. It
remains likely, however, that churches with towers and transepts were
on the whole a rarity in England before 1066. The Saxon church at
Bosham (Sussex) has a tower but no transepts. The average stone-built
church would probably be a simple structure, a nave and chancel only
and both rectangular in shape, such as can be seen at Boarhunt (Hampshire), of late Saxon date. The chapel of the Holy Trinity which Earl
Odda built at Deerhurst, as we know from a surviving dedication
stone, in 1056, reveals that unsophisticated nave-and-chancel rectangular churches were still being constructed on the eve of the Norman
Conquest, despite continental influences.

The progress of church building in a particular diocese may be
illustrated by the example of the Bernician bishopric, first of Chester-
le-Street (883–990) and then of Durham. The Vikings undoubtedly

destroyed several churches, among them Lindisfarne, which was never
rebuilt in Saxon times, and the churches of the monastery of Monkwearmouth and Jarrow, where considerable rebuilding went on in the
later Saxon period and in the early Norman. The destruction was not
all one-sided for in 947 it was Eadred, king of Wessex, who burnt Ripon
minster. In the later eleventh century many sacred sites were found to
be still in ruin and desolation, though probably as much from the results
of Scottish raids, the Harrying of the North of 1069, and in some cases
neglect as from the effects of the Scandinavian wars. One or two
churches may have survived all vicissitudes more or less intact. Escomb
(Co. Durham) is a fine example of a small parish church with rectangular nave and chancel, said to date from the seventh or eighth century.
Stylistically close to Escomb church are the traces of Anglo-Saxon work
at Seaham and Sockburn (Co. Durham), while it is thought that part of
the surviving fabric of the church of St. Peter, Bywell (Northumberland), may go back to the ninth century. But there was certainly extensive building or rebuilding after the ninth century. The church of St
Mary the Virgin, Norton (Co. Durham), provides an excellent northern
example of a parish church built *c*. 1000 with transepts and a central
tower. Towers were commonly added to existing structures as at
Whittingham and Corbridge (Northumberland), Billingham and the
church of St. Peter, Monkwearmouth (Co. Durham). Staindrop was
given to the church of Durham by King Cnut in 1020, and it was probably at this time that a western extension and a western tower were
built onto what might have been a pre-Viking nave. It is possible that
as soon as land was given to the cathedral church in the tenth or
eleventh centuries a new church was built or an old one modernised.
In the early eleventh century a nobleman, Copsi, gave a church at
Marske (Yorkshire) to the church of Durham, which was immediately
afterwards dedicated by Bishop Æthelric, suggesting that it was a new
foundation. Many Anglo-Saxon structures, of course, have by now
disappeared entirely. There are no churches with Anglo-Saxon fragments surviving at Marske. In the ninth century Egred, bishop of
Lindisfarne, built a church at Norham (Northumberland), an important centre in the Northumbrian church, but the existing fabric of
the church of St. Cuthbert at Norham is post-Conquest. It is, therefore, very difficult to estimate exactly the extent of church building in
the late Old English period. It has been suggested that the episcopate
of Bishop Ealdhun (990–1018) witnessed a great era of church building

in the north. Certainly it was Ealdhun who embarked on the construction of the great white stone church of Durham Cathedral, an object of wonder to the people of his diocese. The old cathedral church at Chester-le-Street was of wood, and remained of wood until the time of Bishop Æthelric (1042–56), a valuable reminder to the architectural historian not to think too exclusively in terms of stone churches even at this date. Ealdhun's new cathedral followed the Carolingian plan favoured in southern England, with a western and a central tower and small transeptal chapels to the north and south of the nave. In design and construction it was probably quite as advanced as its southern counterparts.

The Anglo-Saxons were very impressed by their greater church buildings. Eddius took pride in the columns and side aisles of Wilfrid's foundation at Ripon, and in the remarkably high and long walls, winding passages and spiral staircases of Hexham. York cathedral, rebuilt by Archbishop Æthelberht (786–82), is described by Alcuin as possessing columns and arches, a great number of upper apartments, and 30 altars. Wulfstan the Cantor was rapt in admiration of Æthelwold's new buildings at Winchester, where aisles with side chapels, a central tower, and what seems to have been an elaborate west end and atrium were added by the bishop; Wulfstan was moved to exclaim that there were so many doors one hardly knew how to find the way out. Eadmer described the pre-Conquest cathedral church at Canterbury with its side aisles, small transepts and semi-circular apse at the east end with possibly another at the west. The writer of the *Life of Edward* (the Confessor) describes in glowing words the king's foundation at Westminster; a princely house, its vaulting was lofty and noble, its dressed stone evenly jointed, with spiral staircases, a central tower and side chapels. But Edward's abbey was built in Norman style and was a sign of things to come. Excavations have shown that the internal length of the church was over 320 ft. The size of churches in Anglo-Saxon England varied considerably, but on the whole they were smaller and slighter structures than those that were built after the Norman Conquest, far smaller even than Edward's abbey at Westminster. The only ancient Cornish chapel to survive is that of St. Pieran, near Perranporth, a rectangular structure 26 ft by 13 ft. and not divided into a nave and chancel. The early church at Reculver had a nave 37½ by 24 ft. Escomb church has a chancel 10 ft. square and a nave 43½ by 14½ ft., Boarhunt a chancel 15 by 14 ft. and a nave 41 by 19 ft. Brixworth is an example, a fine example, of a larger church, with a nave 60 by 30 ft., and the nave at

Breamore is 75 ft. long. There were indeed churches of quite considerable dimensions. The transepts of the great eleventh-century church of Stow St. Mary (Lincolnshire) were 23 ft. wide internally from east to west, and their internal span from north to south about 85 ft. For earlier times, however, Wilfrid's church at Hexham, estimated to have possessed a nave 100 by 25 ft., and, with side chapels and passages, a total width of some 65 ft., must have been, as Eddius indicates, strikingly exceptional. On the whole Anglo-Saxon churches, by later standards, remained small. North Elmham (Norfolk) provides the best example of the plan of a Saxon cathedral, probably an average, unpretentious cathedral for the site was abandoned by the bishops of the later eleventh century in favour first of Thetford and then of Norwich. The church has a T-shaped plan, with rectangular transepts crossing the nave at right angles, a shallow apsidal chancel opposite the point of crossing, and a western tower; the nave, however, measures only 66 by 20½ ft. internally, the transept 14½ by 51½ ft. The Normans found the Anglo-Saxon churches generally unattractive and uninteresting, lacking the massive grandeur and more elaborate decoration of their own churches, and they lost little or no time in demolishing those at major monastic and episcopal centres. It must be emphasised that this was not simply the result of inferior workmanship on the part of the Anglo-Saxons but the consequence also of different artistic standards on the part of the Normans.

Because of the great amount of Anglo-Saxon architecture which must have been destroyed, and the corresponding relative absence of early English sculptural monuments, it is by no means easy to date surviving fragments precisely or even to date within a century or so a major structure like Escomb church. The architectural history of the Anglo-Saxon church is still obscure at many points. Many apparently secure dates of key structures may yet be challenged in the light of new theories, new discoveries. The experts are far from being always in agreement. Part at least of the stonework at North Elmham has been dated, on the one hand, to the eighth century, and on the other hand, probably with more reason, the whole has been dated no earlier than *c*. 1020; and similarly at South Elmham (Suffolk), remains of a church there have been variously dated from the pre-Viking to the Norman periods. What has emerged perhaps more clearly than an absolute chronological scheme are some of the more characteristic features of Anglo-Saxon ecclesiastical architecture. Pre-Conquest walls, on average, are about 2½ ft. thick, thinner, that is, than later Norman walling, and often of so-called herring-bone fabric, a decorative pattern found throughout the Middle Ages and produced by laying thin stones in diagonal courses in alternating directions. In the post-Viking period the Anglo-Saxons often decorated and supported their church walls in southern England with vertical stone stripwork panelling known as pilaster-strips, as on the fine tower at Earl's Barton, and with horizontal stone string-courses. They constructed the angles of buildings with quoins, that is with large stones placed generally speaking in alternating horizontal and vertical positions. Their walls tended to be rather high, compared with later standards, relieved by only the smallest windows known technically as either single-splayed or—in the south—double-splayed. The window aperture was placed about the middle of the thickness of the wall and splayed on the inside (single-) or on the inside and outside (double-) to produce an opening in the wall which widens from the window aperture thereby affording the greatest possible amount of light. Doorways were taller and narrower than Norman examples, often with a rounded arch, and similarly in the case of chancel arches. The Anglo-Saxons tended to display a disregard for right-angles, with the result that many of their structures would have had an untidy look, particularly to the precise Normans, and their towers must have appeared a little gaunt. Some of the towers of parish churches reached quite considerable heights. The Anglo-Saxon tower of the church of St. Katherine, Little Bardfield (Essex), is about 50 ft. high, and towers of 60 ft. were not unknown. The only Saxon church to retain its original form of tower roof is that at Sompting (Sussex), the so-called Rhenish helm which developed in the Rhineland in the Ottonian period. The churches of the Anglo-Saxons are not generally depicted in manuscript illuminations; the cathedral of Winchester appears in the Benedictional of Æthelwold and the church of Bosham in the Bayeux Tapestry, but these are stylised illustrations and do not necessarily communicate an exact picture of the pre-Conquest edifice.

Learning

Learning in Anglo-Saxon England was the possession of the monastic houses and occasionally of cathedral communities, and it very largely derived from the intellectual traditions of the Ancient World and from the experience and thought of the early Christian Church. Though the study of Greek was introduced at Canterbury by Archbishop Theodore it never took deep root in England; Latin was the language of Roman literature and of the Church of Rome, and in Dark Age Europe it survived as the primary language of scholarship. Bede's Latin was of a very high standard, and there was nothing in England in the early eighth century to parallel the apparent decline of Latin scholarship at this time in Gaul. Aldhelm of Sherborne, however, though one of the most important of Anglo-Saxon scholars, wrote in an artificially ornate style, and throughout the later Anglo-Saxon period a florid and rhetorical style of writing was generally preferred to plain and simple Latin. But it is important to emphasise that, beginning particularly with the literary activities of Alfred the Great, much significance was attached to the writing of works in Anglo-Saxon and to the translating of Latin works into the same for the benefit of the less educated, the parish priest and the layman with a smattering of knowledge. This systematic attempt to spread the learning of the time far beyond the monastic walls by means of the vernacular has no clear parallel in western Europe.

Two streams of culture flowed into England in the seventh century. Many Anglo-Saxons, from south as well as north England, are said to have flocked to the monastic schools of Ireland. Aldhelm was annoyed that a great number of students were going to Ireland rather than to Theodore at Canterbury. The traditional historical view that the Irish monasteries were important scholastic centres can still be defended against a challenging argument that they were renowned rather for the sanctity of their religious life than for academic strength. It is known that a vernacular literature was evolving in Ireland at this time as well as the ornate Latin style which is so characteristic a feature of much of Anglo-Saxon writing. It is interesting to note, in this connection, that before studying at Canterbury Aldhelm had been a pupil of the Irishman, Maildulf, founder of the community which developed into the abbey of Malmesbury. Aldfrith, king of Northumbria (685–704), brought up in Celtic lands and a pupil of Adamnan of Iona, was known to the Irish as the wise king, the renowned scholar. There is no reason to suppose that Aldfrith received any part of his education in England. Nor are we dependent on Irish opinions of Aldfrith's scholarship. Bede describes him as most learned in the Scriptures and reveals him as a collector of manuscripts. The significance of Irish influence on Anglo-Saxon culture is clearly revealed by the prevailing use in England of Irish minuscule variants of continental handwriting script down to the tenth century.

On the other hand, there can be little doubt that the growth of English scholarship was stimulated primarily by the direct impact of the classical legacy of the Mediterranean world. Even before the arrival of Theodore, Wilfrid and Benedict Biscop from Northumbria were turning to the Mediterranean world for the enrichment of their religious and educational experience. Benedict Biscop made a great many visits to the Continent in pursuit of art treasures and books, and it was the library which he collected at Monkwearmouth and Jarrow monastery, a library of classical authors and Church Fathers, that made possible the work of Bede. If Bede records that Northumbrians flocked to Irish schools, he states also that laity and clergy, men and women, were in the habit of travelling to Rome, and at Rome by the eighth century there was a distinct English colony within the city. Not all Anglo-Saxons, however, went all the way to Rome and not all the books imported into England were necessarily purchased in Rome itself. Bede records that many Anglo-Saxons were accustomed to go to Frankish monasteries in the seventh century, and the evidence indicates that namuscripts were collected from throughout Gaul and, indirectly at least, from Visigothic Spain.

Within Anglo-Saxon England itself, the foundation of monasteries and the establishment of monastic schools by early missionaries made possible the development of scholarship. Augustine of Canterbury may not have been a great scholar, but he possessed, according to Pope Gregory the Great and as we would expect, a good knowledge of the Scriptures; and a school at Canterbury must have been speedily established to account for the appearance by the early 640s of native Saxons adequately trained for the office of bishop. Training for the ministry, of course, was an essential task for the first missionary centres, so that basic libraries of Biblical and Patristic writings must have been indispensable. When Sigeberht, king of East Anglia, succeeded in the 630s he set up a school for youth to be instructed in literature such as he had seen during his exile in Gaul, and he invited Felix of Burgundy to come as bishop together with masters and teachers from Kent. The presence of teachers in Kent by the 630s strengthens the impression that schools were established in that kingdom by the earliest missionaries. Theodore, archbishop of Canterbury, and his companion, Hadrian, abbot of St. Augustine's, attracted a host of disciples to Canterbury, for they were both learned men. Bede says that some of their scholars were still living in his day, as well versed in Greek and Latin as in their own tongue, among whom probably was Tobias, bishop of Rochester, a man learned in the Latin, Greek and Saxon tongues. In Northumbria, as soon as he arrived Aidan began to train ten boys for the ministry. The uncertain beginning of the church of York, however, delayed its appearance as a major centre of learning until the eighth century, but in that period two very able archbishops, Egbert (732–66) and Æthelberht (766–79), built up a fine library and established the flourishing school which produced Alcuin; Alcuin joined the court of Charlemagne in 782 and became one of the leading literary figures of the Carolingian renaissance.

Throughout the Anglo-Saxon period the monastic houses of England remained the major educational and scholastic centres. It was expected by the ecclesiastical authorities that the parish priest would hold schools for the instruction of small children, and such schools, where they existed, must have played a relatively important part in the life of the parochial community; but it was naturally the monastic schools, with their resources both of teaching staff and of books and their ordered way of life, which provided instruction on a higher level, though, of course, essentially for monastic oblates. The basic requirements of literacy had to be obtained, so that the Psalter could be read, and the Litany recited. Monastic education was based on the liberal arts of the ancient world, in theory grouped together, from the ninth century at the latest, as the *Trivium* (grammar, rhetoric and dialetic) and the *Quadrivium* (music, arithmetic, geometry and astronomy). Scriptural study was necessarily a large addition to this traditional framework, but it did not overshadow other subjects. Bede records that the Canterbury school of Theodore and Hadrian taught metre, astronomy and arithmetic as well as the Scriptures and the canonical custom of celebrating Easter. Arithmetic and astronomy were taught so that pupils might be able to calculate the calendar and to work out when the festivals of the Christian year would fall. When Aldhelm was at Canterbury, studying under Theodore and Hadrian, he wrote in a letter that he was engaged in Roman (civil) law, music and metre, astronomy and astrology, and mathematics which he was finding difficult. At this time Roman numerals were used in mathematics, for our familiar arabic figures were unknown in Europe as a whole until the twelfth century. Part of the purpose of Byrhtferth's *Manual*, written in 1011, was to explain mathematics and the calculation of the calendar in simple enough terms for the average parish priest. We can see something also of the studies at Bede's monastery of Monkwearmouth and Jarrow. Roman civil law appears to have been taught, and there existed a grammar and a writing school, a school of music, and school of higher studies, predominantly ecclesiastical in character but including classical and philosophical literature. Alcuin's writings show that at York in the eighth century instruction was given in grammar, rhetoric, the Chant, Roman law, astronomy and arithmetic. Monastic education in England experienced an eclipse in the ninth century, but the traditional educational pattern was fully revived with the reform movement of the tenth. At Glastonbury under Dunstan, for example, Æthelwold learnt the arts of grammar and metre in addition to reading holy books; and at Winchester Æthelwold himself enjoyed teaching the young. Dunstan transcribed a continental treatise on grammar, and his manuscript still exists.

Anglo-Saxon scholars of the pre-Viking period shared a fairly common and restricted literary legacy from the Ancient World and from the fifth and sixth centuries. Their thought was shaped in the field of natural history by the writings of Pliny the Elder in particular, in that of Latin verse by Vergil, in that of history by Eusebius, in that of theology by St. Augustine, St. Ambrose, St. Jerome and Pope Gregory the Great, while the encyclopaedist, Isidore of Seville, determined their knowledge at innumerable points. A scholar at a monastic centre with a particularly well-equipped library, like Bede, for example, would be in a position to draw on an impressively wide range of authors, but those books already listed would form the essential basis of his reading. Alcuin, whose Latin poems are a significant part of the Carolingian renaissance, knew no Latin poet well other than Vergil. In the post-Viking period the influence of the same circle of authors continued to prevail, together with the writings of Carolingian scholars shaped by the same literary tradition. The scholastic activities of early medieval Europe were focused almost exclusively on the understanding and interpreting of the Christian faith, and all studies were directed to the pursuit of Christian knowledge. Latin verse might be written but the Latin poets of the Dark Ages wrote Christian verse and read the pagan writings of Antiquity with dire misgivings. Bede's writings on natural phenomena demonstrate a keen interest in the natural causes of such phenomena, and in this he was unique until Byrhtferth of Ramsey produced his *Manual* in 1011, but even Bede's scientific interests were

33 Escombe, Durham: interior

34 Greensted Essex: the nave walls only are Saxon

35 St. Martin's, Canterbury, Kent

Anglo-Saxon Churches

36 Brixworth, Northamptonshire

37 Sompting, Sussex

38 Earl's Barton,
Northamptonshire

39 Repton, Derbyshire:
crypt

Anglo-Saxon Churches

dominated primarily by problems of Paschal reckoning and coloured throughout by theological preoccupations and metaphysical interpretations. Numbers, for example, possessed for Bede, as for his contemporaries, an intense mystical significance. The average level of Anglo-Saxon academic interest in natural history is revealed by the Old English *Physiologus* or *Bestiary*, consisting of three poems on the panther, the whale and the partridge. In keeping with classical tradition, interest is centred not on the natural characteristics of these creatures but on their mythical traits, with the purpose of establishing moral and religious lessons rather than extracting scientific information. It must be remembered, however, in any consideration of the scientific studies of the Middle Ages, particularly the early Middle Ages, that a rational approach to the world was only very slowly achieved and that for the most part men were unable to distinguish between what might be regarded as natural and what might be interpreted as supernatural. Perhaps the greatest spur to scientific inquiry was the use of mathematics and astronomy in the construction of the Christian calendar.

The two immediate, dominant influences on the thought of Anglo-Saxon monastic communities were the Bible, on the one hand, and the Liturgy of the Church, particularly of the Mass, on the other. Liturgical variety was considerable in the Dark Ages, not simply between the Gallic, Celtic or Roman rite but even within the various kingdoms of Europe. Pope Gregory advised Augustine at Canterbury to adopt the best of both the Gallic and the Roman liturgies. The Gregorian Sacramentary, so called from its association with Pope Gregory the Great, reduced the earlier and more elaborate liturgies of the Roman Church to a new simplicity; and, though it is possible that Greek litanies were finding their way into England in the late seventh and early eighth centuries, the synod of *Clofesho* in 747 imposed the Roman rite or Gregorian Liturgy on the whole Anglo-Saxon Church. Alcuin subsequently played a leading part in Charlemagne's liturgical reforms, when a revised Roman rite was introduced into Gaul to supersede the Gallic, and Alcuin's revision was the basis of supplemented editions of the Gregorian Liturgy which came to prevail over west Europe in the tenth century. The Liturgy, of course, was sung, and it was during the pontificate of Gregory the Great that the liturgical chant of the Roman Church took its definite and typical form, henceforth being known as the Gregorian Chant or Gregorian plainsong. The introduction of Gregorian plainsong into England by the first Roman missionaries can be followed in some detail. Augustine and his companions were singing part of the Litany when they first approached King Æthelberht, and Bede says that Putta, who became bishop of Rochester in 669, derived his knowledge of the Roman Chant, which he subsequently taught to the Mercians, from the disciples of Pope Gregory. Paulinus's helper, James the deacon, is said to have been extraordinarily skilful in music, and to have taught many of the Northumbrians to sing after the custom of the Romans and the men of Kent. Wilfrid took Eddius Stephanus to Northumbria in 669 to teach Gregorian singing, and when Benedict Biscop brought John, archchantor of the church of St. Peter in Rome, to Northumbria all such as had skill in music came to hear him teach. In 747 the synod of *Clofesho* ordered the English Church to adopt the Gregorian plainsong. Providing as it did an ever-varying setting for the Christian cycle, the Gregorian Chant undoubtedly opened up to the Anglo-Saxons a whole new range of musical and religious thought and emotion. With the monastic reform of the tenth century, monks from the Continent were invited to England to re-instruct the Anglo-Saxons in the technicalities of more complex singing to meet the requirements of more elaborate services. Wulfstan the Cantor, a disciple of Æthelwold at Winchester, wrote a work on the *Harmony of Notes*, and he described also the Winchester organ, with its 400 pipes and 26 bellows, an organ which was played by two men at once.

It was against the continuous background of liturgical observance and Gregorian Chant that Anglo-Saxon monastic scholars turned to the study of the Bible in the Latin Vulgate text of Jerome's translation. The Anglo-Saxon scholars are not distinguished for their theological writings. Heresy was rare in the early English Church—though a letter from Egred, bishop of Lindisfarne, to the archbishop of York in the 830s reveals the presence of heresy at that time in distant Bernicia. Anglo-Saxon scholars were content to reflect on the received theology of the Christian Fathers and, with the course of time, on the works of Carolingian theologians. Ælfric of Eynsham sought to explain the doctrine of Transubstantiation, how the bread and wine of the Mass could be changed into the Body and Blood of Christ, but he simply drew on Carolingian writings and contributed no original thought to the subject. Anglo-Saxon scholars were interested in the interpretation of Scripture, so that a great many commentaries on the various books of the Bible were produced, for example by Bede, and in the writing of simple expositions on the meaning of the Lord's Prayer or the Creed. The late tenth century in particular witnessed an important development in the writing of homilies in the vernacular, notably by Ælfric of Eynsham, short religious addresses on an ethical topic or Scriptural passage designed to be read in church on an appropriate day in the Christian calendar. The Incarnation, the Nature of the Trinity, and the Second Coming were three themes, for example, with which homiletic writing was concerned.

It has been rightly said that in the Anglo-Saxon period, and indeed later, ecclesiastical law was a branch of theology. Parallel to the study of the Bible was the study and compilation of Church Law, canon law as it is known. Particularly distinguished in this field in the later Anglo-Saxon period was Wulfstan II, bishop of Worcester and archbishop of York in the early eleventh century. Wulfstan compiled canonist manuscripts and made a formulary of penitential literature. Nevertheless, no canonist manuscripts produced in England at this time exercised an important influence on the study of canon law in Europe. The fact that Anglo-Saxon canonical collections were written in the main in the vernacular probably militated against any widespread influence on their part on the Continent.

Anglo-Saxon learning was distinguished by its long tradition of writing in the vernacular. When the Anglo-Saxons adopted the Latin alphabet rather than their native runes for scholastic pursuits, they did not necessarily sacrifice their own language as a literary vehicle for Latin. Early annalistic notes on current happenings were made in Anglo-Saxon and poets composed their traditional verse in the vernacular. On the whole, the Church in England tended to condemn poetry with a pagan theme. Alcuin criticised Hygebald, bishop of Lindisfarne, for permitting his monks to listen to heathen poetry. But such poetry was certainly enjoyed in Christian times, and a little survives albeit influenced by Christian imagery and sentiments. From the pre-Viking period comes the epic poem, *Beowulf*, which reflects the traditional secular values and supernatural beliefs of an aristocratic and heroic society. It survives in a single manuscript of *c.* 1000, and has been described as the most valuable literary document in an early Germanic language. Bede preserved in Latin the opening lines of an early Christian poem—a hymn of Creation—which Cædmon of Whitby monastery, while a layman, composed in his native language *c.* 660–80. It was said that the poem came to him as inspiration during the night, and that previously (until well advanced in years) he had been unable to make up verses. In this he evidently contrasted with his companions. Many other religious poems by Cædmon followed the hymn of Creation, but these have now perished. Part of an early Saxon poem, the *Dream of the Rood*, has been carved in runes on the Ruthwell Cross. This poem survives in its complete form in the *Vercelli Book* which, with two other late Saxon manuscripts, the Junius manuscript and the *Exeter Book*, preserves fragments of a vast range of Anglo-Saxon poetry from riddles to religious epics. Among these fragments are the poems of the religious poet, Cynewulf—*Juliana, Christ, Elene*, and *Fates of the Apostles*—dating to the late eighth or early ninth century. The *Anglo-Saxon Chronicle* preserves several secular pieces, notably the poem on the battle of *Brunanburh* and another, possibly by Archbishop Wulfstan II, on the banishment of Oslac, earl of Deira, in 975. It does not include the poem on the battle of Maldon, however, which survives in part separately. The Anglo-Saxons of all social levels were fond of their poetry. We know nothing of specifically peasant songs, except that Felix in the eighth century describes them as empty tales and shouts; but if, as seems likely, ceorls appreciated the heroic ideals of thegns, they probably took delight in their own way in the recitation of heroes and dragon-slayers in the taverns which they regularly frequented. Bede implies that Cædmon's companions used to compose secular verse, and Cædmon was a cowherd when he began to compose. Aldhelm, it was said, used to stand on a bridge and sing to the people as they passed, hoping that they would then come and hear him in church. King Alfred loved until the end of his life the Saxon poems he learnt in his youth. Anglo-Saxon poetry, which was recited to the accompaniment of a harp, is characterised by the use of alliteration and short, graphic phrases and metaphors drawn from a common stock of literary motifs. To what extent the poets drew on continental and classical literature for inspiration has not yet been fully explored.

The reign of Alfred witnessed a most impressive flowering of the vernacular culture at a time when Latin learning was rather in abeyance. The decline of the monasteries in England in the ninth century led to a temporary eclipse of Latin culture, which only revived again with the tenth-century monastic movement. King Alfred stated, in a letter or circular which was sent out with copies of his translation of Pope Gregory the Great's *Pastoral Care*, that there were few men in England at the time of his accession (871) who could translate from the Latin.

When Charlemagne found learning decayed in Gaul in the late eighth century he made his court the centre of a revived scholarship, attracting to it learned men from Italy and Spain northwards to Northumbria. Latin letters revived and vernacular literature flourished. In the late ninth century, whether consciously following the Carolingian example or not, Alfred did the same. In the early eighth century, Northumbria appears to us to have been the most advanced cultural realm in England, but it was from Mercia that King Alfred brought scholars to his court, Athelstan and Wærwulf, of whom not much is known, Wærferth, who became bishop of Worcester, and Plegmund, who became archbishop of Canterbury. From the Continent he obtained Grimbald of St. Bertin and John the Old Saxon, and from Wales came Asser of St. Davids. Latin letters were revived—Asser's *Life* of King Alfred was written in Latin *c*. 894—but the emphasis at the West Saxon court was on vernacular literature. Though Alfred learnt Latin he did so more to assist in the translating of Latin works into English for the benefit of non-Latinists than for his own understanding of classical literature. It must not be thought that vernacular translations were something new in England. Alfred himself mentions that though few could understand Latin, many could read books in English, revealing clearly that vernacular works were in existence before his time. Bede, for example, was in the process of translating the Fourth Gospel into English immediately prior to his death. Indeed, it was the fact that men could read English books which gave Alfred the idea of rendering further important works in translation in a systematic attempt to raise the intellectual standards of the Anglo-Saxon clergy.

Alfred is undoubtedly the most attractive secular personality of Anglo-Saxon England. He is, however, the only layman whose thoughts and aspirations it is possible to perceive so clearly; for Alfred, it has been well said, was more than simply a royal warrior of heroic stance. He possessed an approach to life in which he combined both intelligence and the child-like curiosity of his age with an earnest and devout desire to promote the welfare of his subjects in the eyes of God. To this end he planned an important series of translations of literary classics into Anglo-Saxon, at the same time stimulating the writing of contemporary history so that the experiences of the age might be recorded for posterity. He made the effort to understand and translate Latin himself so that he could assist in the work, and it is largely through additions which he made and inserted into the text of the translations that the personality of the king can be discerned. Alfred appears as a very serious and sober man, dominated by his responsibilities and his sense of duty, possessed of a sharp awareness of life around him, searching for a wisdom which would bring him closer to divine truth. According to his own testimony, he did not greatly care for worldly power, but saw himself as a weary pilgrim seeking an eternal home.

The first of the translations to emanate from the royal court was evidently the *Dialogues* of Pope Gregory the Great, a collection of saints' *Lives* and miracles, translated by Wærferth, bishop of Worcester. The first work with which Alfred was associated was Pope Gregory's *Pastoral Care*, a manual for bishops in which Alfred was aided by Plegmund, Asser, Grimbald and John. Then, while Alfred's Mercian scholars translated Bede's *Ecclesiastical History of the English Nation*, Alfred himself was engaged on a translation of Orosius's *Universal History*, a fifth-century work written after the fall of Rome (410) to show that Christianity was not responsible for the catastrophe and containing much historical and geographical material. Alfred cut out a great deal of the original text but added incidental notes drawn from his own military experience and also geographical information which he derived from contemporaries about the countries and peoples of north Europe. In the last years of his life Alfred turned to works of a philosophical nature. He translated the *Consolations of Philosophy* by Boethius, a fifth-century scholar who wrote this particular study while awaiting execution; and Alfred felt himself naturally led on to meditate upon the meaning of life and particularly his own life. The last undoubted work of Alfred is a translation of the *Soliloquies of St. Augustine*, freely interspersed with the king's own thoughts on the meaning of life and the immortality of the soul.

It was King Alfred's intention that the sons of freemen should be sent to school until they could read English, and until those for whom the priesthood was intended could read Latin. The king hoped to ensure that the boys could read and write before hunting and warlike pursuits came to occupy most of their time. But it must have been difficult to establish schools in the country at large. We can see clearly only the monastic school he established at his monastic foundation at Athelney, where John the Old Saxon taught Gallic as well as Saxon boys, including at least one pagan youth, and the more important court school for the sons and daughters of the members of his household. Among those educated at the royal court was Alfred's eldest son,

Edward, later king of Wessex. It is recorded by Asser that Edward, together with his younger sister, Ælfthryth, learnt carefully the Psalms and Saxon books, especially Saxon poems, and that he was continually in the habit of making use of books. It is well worth emphasising that the bellicose Edward, who emerges so successfully as a military commander in the *Chronicle*, was probably a well-educated and cultured man. It was no chance coincidence that his son and Alfred's grandson, Athelstan, indulged a taste for relic- and book-collecting on a grand scale, took an interest in scholarship and encouraged the continuance of the revival of learning. According to William of Malmesbury, Athelstan was remembered by the English as the most learned of all their rulers before the Norman Conquest.

The monastic reform movement of the tenth century was accompanied by the rapid development of Christian literature in the vernacular. Ælfric of Eynsham is the outstanding figure of this literary movement. Born about 955, he was educated at Winchester under Æthelwold, and *c.* 987 sent to the monastery of Cerne Abbas (Dorset) where he translated several books of the Bible and wrote his *Catholic Homilies, Lives of the Saints* and a series of pastoral letters, before becoming abbot of Eynsham in 1005. His contemporary, Wulfstan, bishop of Worcester and archbishop of York, assumed the literary alias 'Lupus', 'the wolf', and among his writings is the important *Sermon of the Wolf to the English*, a fine example of a powerful sermon on the sins of the English by a leading prelate in the last years of the reign of Æthelred the Unready. Wulfstan took a disapproving view of Old English society, riddled as he saw it by disloyalty and treachery and stained by sin and wantonness.

But it must not be thought that the study of Latin was abandoned. Ælfric wrote a *Life of Æthelwold* in Latin, and he prepared a *Colloquy*, quite a well-known literary device at the time, so that boys might practise conversation by question and answer in Latin; the *Colloquy* is in the form of a dialogue, and provides much incidental information on the life of the times. Ælfric's patron, who encouraged him in his work of writing and translating, was Æthelweard, ealdorman of Dorset from *c.* 973 to *c.* 998, and it is a striking testimony to the interest on the part of West Saxon educated lay circles in learning and scholarship that Æthelweard attempted, if in rather poor Latin, a Latin translation of the *Anglo-Saxon Chronicle*.

The writing of history in Anglo-Saxon England is of immediate significance to the historian, for without the fairly continuous interest of the Anglo-Saxons in the recording of the events of their time very little indeed would be known of early England. The greatest of early English historians was Bede, who completed his *Ecclesiastical History of the English Nation* in Latin in 731, dedicating it to Ceolwulf, king of Northumbria. In this work and in an age of few written records, Bede so correlated the fragmentary oral traditions of a group of churches and monasteries scattered across England as to present the appearance of a continuous historical narrative from the landing of St. Augustine down to his own time. Historians have appreciated that Bede was essentially a Christian moralist, that like the writers of *Lives* of saints in early Europe he was primarily concerned to extol virtue, and that in consequence material might be left out of the *History* or included according to its moral worth rather than its historical value. But it has not always been fully appreciated that Bede's powers as a historian were restricted by the limited nature of the oral tradition at his disposal. Oral tradition was dependent for its survival on the continuing interest of a self-perpetuating community, a monastery or royal court; particular traditions about a saint or a king were largely confined to the monastic house or court most intimately associated with that historical figure. It was this localised oral tradition on which the writers of saints' *Lives* primarily depended. For the monasteries of Hexham and Ripon, for example, an early *Life* of Wilfrid of York (d. 709) was written by Eddius Stephanus from materials gathered from Hexham and Ripon, monastic foundations of Wilfrid; at Lindisfarne *c.* 700 an anonymous *Life* of Cuthbert, monk of Melrose, hermit of Farne and bishop of Lindisfarne (d. 687), was written by a monk of Lindisfarne from oral traditions primarily at Lindisfarne. But all the evidence suggests that the monk of Lindisfarne would know very little in detail of Wilfrid's life, and Eddius would know very little of Cuthbert's. Only in so far, therefore, as Bede established contact with a particular monastic house would he discover information about any saint associated with that house. His *Life of Cuthbert*, written *c.* 720, had of necessity to be based on surviving oral tradition at Melrose and Lindisfarne, and on the older Lindisfarne *Life*. This means that the historical writing of the Anglo-Saxons as a whole tends to be based on essentially localised material; such writing does not present a national story, though it may appear to do so, but only an array of local and not necessarily related notices.

This can be seen quite clearly in the vernacular *Anglo-Saxon*

Chronicle. The *Chronicle* reads very much like a national history of England, particularly in its accounts of the wars of the kings of Wessex with the Danes, but in reality it is simply a dynastic chronicle. About 890–2 King Alfred's West Saxon scribes, probably at the king's instigation, put together what they could discover of the early history of the kings of Wessex all the way back to the days of the Conquest, from oral tradition and early written fragmentary annals; such traditions were brought together to form an introduction to the main subject of the chroniclers, the wars of Alfred with the Danes. This first *Chronicle* was continued when the Danish wars began again in 892, not only under Alfred but also under Edward the Elder (899–924), and a very early copy of this *Chronicle* is known to historians as the Parker *Chronicle* (from the name of the Elizabethan archbishop of Canterbury who preserved it and first transcribed it), distinguished by the letter A from the texts of later continuations. When the kings of Wessex perceived how useful the *Chronicle* could be to them as a means of circulating information about their military campaigns, they sent out copies to many of the monasteries of England. As the official continuations became less detailed after 924 (military successes ultimately made them less necessary when the period of crisis had passed), these monasteries began to add their own local notices. Consequently, for the tenth and eleventh centuries more than one different text of the *Chronicle* survives. *Chronicle* A, which tends to peter out in the tenth century, is a Winchester text. *Chronicle* C, which provides the basic text of the later tenth-century annals, appears to be an Abingdon document. *Chronicle* D, closely paralleled by E, is a Northumbrian compilation. From the period following the Norman Conquest *Chronicle* D continues to 1079 after which the text of E (to 1154) alone has survived, first as a copy of a Canterbury chronicle and then as a set of Peterborough annals. At its inception the *Chronicle* was concerned directly with the kings of Wessex, and very pro-royal. As a result other kings and kingdoms received scant mention, reference being made to them only as and when their affairs touched on Wessex. Slight information, therefore, is provided about the eighth-century Mercian kings, virtually nothing about the East Anglian; Northumbrian affairs were generally beyond the ken of the West Saxon chroniclers. Fortunately there survives a set of eighth-century Latin Northumbrian annals in the *History of the Kings*, attributed to Symeon of Durham, which the compilers of the D and E texts of the *Chronicle* also inserted in part and in translation in their version of the

Anglo-Saxon Chronicle. But no such set of annals survives for the East Anglian kingdom, and hence the history of East Anglia both before and after the Danish wars is very obscure. It is vitally important, therefore, for the historian approaching this period to appreciate fully that historical writing was shaped by single-minded devotion to the monastery or dynasty concerned. Those who, like Bede, attempted a wider survey were unavoidably exposed to the limited and localised outlook of their sources, and, though the pursuit of truth might be Bede's avowed ideal, even he was vulnerable to the bias and misinformation of those who provided him with historical material. Devotion to a monastery or dynasty, even to a particular king, naturally led to bias and one-sidedness. The *Chronicle* account of Alfred is clearly very well disposed to the king; that for Æthelred II clearly hostile, at least to the royal ministers. It is very difficult, therefore, to use either account by itself as an authoritative guide to the reigns in question without sound critical analysis. Certainly, Anglo-Saxon historical records must never be taken at face value.

It is easy to exaggerate the amount of historical writing that was undertaken in Anglo-Saxon England. The early *Lives* of Cuthbert and Wilfrid were not followed by a spate of eighth-century English *Lives*, nor those of Dunstan, Æthelwold and Oswald by a spate of early eleventh-century *Lives*. In an age when saints' *Lives* were the easiest of historical accounts to produce, because the writer needed only to tap the traditions of his own monastery for information about a monastic founder, remarkably few historically valuable *Lives* were written. Ælfric complained that no *Life* had been written of Swithin, a ninth-century bishop of Winchester, and William of Malmesbury found his historical researches thwarted by lack of material. Asser's *Life* of King Alfred, written about 894 while the king was still living, is a unique piece of royal biography. Asser's *Life*, unconvincingly criticised quite recently as a later fabrication, is a most valuable source for the reign, containing much otherwise unknown information not only about Alfred himself but also about his military, administrative and educational reforms and about the period in general. Certain chapters in the *Life* may conceivably have been added to Asser's original work, and future criticism may make it possible to say which chapters could have been so added; but that the nucleus of the *Life* is a ninth-century work there is as yet no reason to doubt. A great many other men must have been in a similar position to Asser, that of confidant to a king, but other royal biographies are few. There is, however, a useful *Life of Edward* (the

Confessor), begun possibly in 1066, valuable for the information it provides about the Godwines as well as about Edward. Of course, not all historical writings have survived. A poetical panegyric on Athelstan, king of Wessex, survives only in extracts and paraphrase in William of Malmesbury. Asser's *Life* of Alfred survives in full only in a transcript made before an ancient manuscript containing the *Life* perished almost entirely by fire in the Cottonian Library (Oxford) in 1731. The same fire almost completely destroyed the one ancient text of Æthelweard's translation of the *Chronicle*, which is similarly known to us only from transcripts made before 1731. It is somewhat startling to realise that among the important historical sources for the Anglo-Saxon period which survive only in a single manuscript are the anonymous *Life of Oswald*, William of Malmesbury's *Life of Wulfstan*, bishop of Worcester, the *Life of Edward* (the Confessor), and the *History of the Kings*, ascribed to Symeon of Durham. How much more has been lost by the destruction of single manuscripts it is impossible to assess; but even so there are good grounds for believing that, by contrast with the Norman period, there was on the whole a dearth of historical writing in the late Old English period. The Norman Conquest was followed by an intense interest on the part of several of the greater Benedictine abbeys of England in Anglo-Saxon historical traditions as well as in the writing of contemporary history. While, however, a set of early annals from ninth-century Northumbria survives only in a thirteenth-century chronicle, a systematic analysis of the writings of the chroniclers of the Anglo-Norman period will probably show that they did not possess a great deal more in the way of Anglo-Saxon historical literature than is independently known to us. What they *did* possess was a stock of oral tradition, going back 150 years or so, which has now, of course, entirely disappeared.

2 CULTIVATION AND COMMERCE

Chapter one

Agriculture

It is far from easy to call to the imagination a picture of the natural state of England during the early Middle Ages. Very few tracts of country survive at the present time in anything approaching their original uncultivated state; and the study of the history of the natural history of early England has hardly begun. Similarly, it is difficult to appreciate the unrelenting war with nature which was waged by the Anglo-Saxons in order to so cultivate the land that an adequate crop of grain could be harvested. The Normans said that the English thought of nothing so much as the cultivation of their lands. We know a fair amount about land measurement in Anglo-Saxon England and a little about the social status of the peasant labourers, but almost nothing in detail of the practicalities of farming in this period with only the most basic of implements and no real scientific understanding; while the vast cycle of rural mythology which gave some meaning to the agricultural year for the Anglo-Saxons has largely blown away without trace.

The Land

Climatologists believe that Britain became moister, with cooler summers and milder winters, about 500 B.C., and that such conditions have prevailed fairly constantly since then except that rainfall may have decreased as the Roman period drew to its close. According to Byrhtferth of Ramsey, writing in 1011, winter lasted from 7 November to 6 February and was cold and moist; spring, from 7 February to 8 May, moist and hot; summer, from 9 May to 6 August, was hot and dry; and autumn, from 7 August to 6 November, dry and cold. Anglo-Saxon poets refer to winter storms, torrential downpours, icy hail, frost, fair weather, lightning and summer wild-fire. Extremes of heat and cold seem to be implied. Great significance was attached, particularly when pagan traditions were strong, to the equinoxes. At the time of the vernal equinox the days begin to lengthen and at the autumnal to shorten. The Saxons did not celebrate the equinoxes precisely, but they divided the year into four by the four great days of agricultural tradition; 7 May was summer's day and 7 November winter's day, 24 June midsummer's day and 25 December midwinter's day.

Western society in the early Middle Ages might well be described as a forest civilisation. Much of the surface of early Europe was composed of virgin woodland, scrub and unreclaimed marsh. Luxuriant vegetation and extensive waterlogged tracts in valleys and lowlands must have been conducive to a rather moist and damp atmosphere. It is interesting in this connection that Asser records that King Alfred's clocks were designed to enable him to tell the time in camp when frequent fogs obscured the sun. There is little doubt that oak was the normal forest cover of England, flourishing not only on heavy clay soils—on such tracts as the Kentish weald, for example—but also on the infertile sandy soil of areas like Sherwood, Needwood, and Cannock. Oakwoods permitted a lush undergrowth and were accompanied by ash, elm and yew. Ashwoods in the north and beechwoods at least in the south were probably common. It is not yet possible to plot regional differences in the composition of early woodland with any exactitude, however, and at present botanical science can only give the most general of outlines. Several early woods, it should be noted, have left a description of themselves in place-names, as in Ashwood, Hazelwood, Bircholt and Oakley, while boundary clauses in Anglo-Saxon charters often contain references to trees flourishing in the area to which they relate. Careful local research would make possible for a particular district a clearer idea of the natural environment of the Anglo-Saxons there.

Some of the Old English forests were vast. The forest of *Andredsweald* stretching from Kent to Sussex is recorded to have been 120 miles long and 30 miles wide. Forest expanses were the homes of bears in the pre-Viking period, of wolves (it was said that King Edgar attempted to exterminate wolves), wild boars, wild cattle and horses, wild cats, beavers, deer and, of course, the wild creatures of today. They provided refuge also for false coiners, devotees of pagan cults, robber bands, and outlaws of every description. Cædwalla, before he became king of Wessex, spent some time as an exile in the Chilterns and *Andredsweald*. The Anglo-Saxon forests were not impassable, though there is no doubt that in their thickest and deepest parts they must have been a tangled mass of vegetation; but they were broken up by scrub and heathland, and along their fringes they were exposed to the depredations of man. The precise extent of deforestation between *c.* 600 and 1066 is uncertain, but the great age of deforestation in west Europe was *c.* 1050–1250. The encroachments of the Anglo-Saxons on the woodlands, however, reveal themselves in place-names. For example, one place-name element found particularly in Kent and Sussex, in the region of *Andredsweald*, is Old English *denn*, signifying woodland pasture, usually for swine, though a name such as Cowden clearly means pasture for cows. Old English *leah* and *hyrst*, signifying clearings, usually in a wood, survive as -ley or -hurst in countless modern place-names. There can be little doubt that the Anglo-Saxons took their toll of the woodlands in an age when wood was the only fuel apart from peat, when almost all building was of wood, when utensils, implements, weapons and vehicles required wood, and when charcoal was essential for purposes of smelting metal and for glass-making. Oak was ideal for constructional purposes, ash wood excellent for oars and handles of one sort or another, beech particularly useful for household furnishings. And it was the practice of peasants to take their sheep, cattle, pigs and goats out to graze on the forest verges, so that the incessant chewing and nibbling away of young shoots and seedlings must have played a small part at least in the gradual process of woodland decline. The repeated cutting away of undergrowth for a natural hay crop and for the bedding of stock would similarly tend to the destruction of seedlings. But landowners were aware of the economic value of woodland, and they did not permit indiscriminate felling. Ælfric of Eynsham describes the duties of the manorial official called the woodward in his *Colloquy*. He had the care of his lord's woods, supervising the cutting of timber and underwood, the grazing of animals, and the supplying of the amount of wood needed for building, fencing and fuel. Not least among the assets of the forest to the king and nobility were the pleasures of the chase, for the purposes of which it was essential that considerable stretches of woodland be preserved. Edward the Confessor is said to have spent whole days enjoying the pleasures of hunting in the forests, delighting in his hawks and in the baying of his hounds.

The Anglo-Saxons took delight particularly in the green plains and woods of England. The poet sang of the beauty of the forest grove, where grew pleasant plants and where the trees of the wood tossed and

40   January: ploughing

41   March: digging and sowing

42   May: watching sheep

43   June: cutting wood

Saxon Calendar, (*B.M. Tiberius B.V*)

44 September: hunting, pasturing swine

45 October: hawking

46 November: fencing, keeping warm

47 December: winnowing

Saxon Calendar, (*B.M. Tiberius B.V*)

murmured by the music of running water; he responded to the beauty of spring blossoms and red roses, to the majesty of the salmon in the pool, to the flight of the swallow and the song of the nightingale. An earthly paradise was pictured as a fair field with green forests spread beneath the skies, without mountains, cliffs or rough slopes. To a lesser extent the poet experienced the appeal of the sea-shore, the boom of the sea, the scream of the gull, the call of the curlew, the ice-cold billow, the salt wave. But for the hillier, upland regions of the land the Anglo-Saxons had no love. Bede refers to the Cheviots as craggy, uncouth mountains and admired Cuthbert greatly for entering them on preaching tours; he describes Lastingham monastery in the Clevelands, Yorkshire, as situated among mountains more like lurking places for robbers and wild beasts than habitations for men. The poet of *Beowulf* depicted the moorlands as the home of the shadowy monster, Grendel, the marsh-stepper, the dread fiend. Neither did the Anglo-Saxons have any affection for fenland districts, believing the fens also to be the haunts of demons, and islands were viewed with similar suspicion. Felix, the author of the eighth-century *Life of St. Guthlac*, founder of Crowland (Lincs), describes the great fenland expanse of the Wash basin as a wilderness of marshes, black pools, reeds, thickets, hillocks, islands, and foul streams, a lonely and desolate area. St. Guthlac felt himself sorely tempted by demons in his fenland retreat. In his time Æthelbald, later king of Mercia, was an exile in the fens and became acquainted with the hermit. Occasionally an early monastery developed into a flourishing and wealthy community as at Peterborough and Ely, and a few peasant communities established themselves in the fens in the course of time; but there is little evidence of extensive reclamation before 1066 and the development of the ports of the Wash like Boston and Lynn dates to the post-Conquest period. Another extensive tract of marshland, and one which provided the setting for perhaps the most famous of Anglo-Saxon stories, was that of modern Somerset. These fens almost made an island of the south-west peninsula of England and among them King Alfred took refuge in 878. In his time Athelney was so surrounded by water that it could be reached only by boat or causeway.

It has been estimated that perhaps two-thirds of England was waste and unreclaimed land in the Anglo-Saxon period. Nevertheless, it must not be thought that the country was a complete wilderness. By 1066 the great majority of English villages were within walking distance of each other, and it is important to emphasise that by 1066–86 the area of land under the plough in the country as a whole may not have been much if at all less than the extent of arable land in the early twentieth century—though, of course, there was no great amount of cultivated pasture land. From the seventh century the Anglo-Saxons had been slowly extending the arable land under cultivation and farming as intensively as their methods permitted the richer land of the valleys and plains. Unless, like the Norse settlers in the tenth century, they were to pursue sheep farming in hill territory, the Anglo-Saxons were limited in the extent of land they could cultivate by two constant factors: the nature of the soil and the availability of water. Natural amenities, therefore, dictated where a village could be sited. Not infrequently, a village community once established would move to a more favourable site discovered subsequently, and traces of this process survive in the Great and Little elements in English place-names. Heavy clay soils, often waterlogged and bearing lush vegetation, were of little use to the Anglo-Saxon farmer, and neither were the dry and sandy infertile soils of heathlands. What were desirable were the sandstone, limestone and chalk outcrops among belts of clay, and stretches of loam (clay and sand or gravel) or marl (clay and limestone). Such outcrops were well watered but not waterlogged, and could be easily cleared of natural vegetation. Because they were to be found in relation to the rivers and minor waterways, the pattern of cultivation in England was primarily shaped by the geographical distribution of rivers and streams. Variations in soil type caused sharp contrasts in the pattern of the settlement within quite limited areas. Settlement on the heavy clays of the Northamptonshire heights contrasted unfavourably with the great number on the limestone soils of the Nene valley; in Surrey settlement was on the mixed soils of the northern part of the shire rather than the clays of the Weald; in Middlesex the clays of the northern part of the shire were avoided in favour of the loam and gravel tracts of the south; the claylands of the northern part of the kingdom of Essex permitted settlement because they were interstratified with beds of sand and gravel; in Nottinghamshire settlement was not on the sandy soils of Sherwood Forest but on the loamy clays and gravel patches of the lowlands of the Trent; villages in Leicestershire were usually related to pockets of water-bearing sand and gravel amidst the boulder clay. Such examples could be multiplied. They demonstrate clearly the fundamental importance of geology and soil types in the study of the early agricultural history of any region of Anglo-Saxon England.

The Agricultural Community

The agricultural community of Anglo-Saxon England can be approached through both village and manor. From the earliest days of the Conquest, the majority of Anglo-Saxons lived in village communities, known technically to historians as nucleated villages by contrast with isolated hamlets. The majority of English villages go back to Anglo-Saxon times. The men of the village or *tun* were *tunesmen* or *villani*. The village itself would consist of a group of houses, often with a village green, normally by 1066 around a church. But documentary sources only allude to village communities indirectly and they cannot be closely perceived. Domesday Book, a survey of England as it was in 1086 and as it had been in 1066, describes many of the villages of mid-eleventh-century England but only as parts or part of the estates of one or more lords. As the great landholders possessed land in more than one village, and several would hold land in a single village, only by piecing together a series of scattered references can a picture of an actual village be obtained. Domesday Book, that is to say, describes England from a manorial point of view. Unlike the village, which was a social unit, the manor was an economic institution. The term *manerium* or manor was introduced by the Normans and probably originally signified the lord's hall, but the Normans applied it to the lord's estates. A manorial estate may be described as a group of small estates or manors, widely scattered and probably in more than one shire. The lord of this great manorial estate —though of course they did vary in territorial extent—might be either a king or thegn, and part would be farmed by the lord's personal workers, part rented out to tenants. That which was farmed by the lord himself was known as land in *demesne*. From his estates the lord collected the taxes owing to the king, and there is some evidence that he could transfer the burden of geld on his manor if he so wished entirely on to the land of his tenants and off the *desmesne* land. In 1066 a number of villages in eastern England had no lord and were inhabited by freemen who farmed their own land and paid geld directly to the king. Though, however, such freemen might be found in any village community, the majority of villages formed part of one or more manorial estates by the time of the Norman Conquest, and most of the men of the village worked in varying degrees of personal servitude on the lands of their respective lords.

It is as landlord that the Anglo-Saxon lord has received most attention in recent times, in his relationship, that is, with his peasant tenants. There is no doubt that from the earliest days of settlement an important part was played by landlords. By the laws of Ine, if a nobleman left an estate and moved elsewhere, perhaps to colonise new land, he had to leave a certain proportion of his estates as *gesettes landes*. It is one of the difficulties of Anglo-Saxon social history that the meaning of the term in the seventh century is not understood. It could mean land sown with crops or land occupied by tenants. It is conceivable that the king would be concerned to see that men were left behind to continue cultivation and to prevent a return to waste; but, whatever the meaning of this particular term, the laws of Ine make it clear that tenants did exist in Wessex at this time for they state that a lord who provided a tenant with a house could exact labour services as well. This is important evidence for the existence of a manorial economy at an early date in Anglo-Saxon England.

As well as the lord who commanded the military loyalites of the peasant and answered for him in court, therefore, there developed from the earliest times the person of the landlord. In practice, the two were probably often one and the same, the lord entering naturally into tenurial contracts with his men. But it is important to emphasise that it must have been possible for a peasant to acknowledge one man as his lord and to rent land from two or three other landlords. Members of the nobility often rented land themselves, known as *lænland* or land held on lease for a specified period of time.

It has been a cardinal thesis of early English historical studies for many years that Anglo-Saxon society in the seventh century was essentially a society of free peasants, farming their own land, but that in the course of subsequent centuries, particularly as a result of the Danish wars, economic hardship compelled the majority of peasants to sell out, so to speak, to become the tenants or even labourers of aristocratic landlords. As poor tenants, performing labour services on the lord's *demesne* in addition to paying rent, no longer their own masters with the opportunity to go where they would, sell and buy as they wished, they ultimately became unfree. This depression of a substantial section of the peasant class has been seen by many historians as the dominant theme of Anglo-Saxon social history.

Like all great interpretations of ambiguous and difficult historical evidence, this reconstruction has been subjected to criticism and modification. The trend of historical thought at present is rather to question whether the peasant or ceorl ever was a fully free and respected member of society, except in a few instances. Any view, however, that the mass of ceorls was always in economic subjection to a landed nobility is hardly more capable of proof than the thesis it seeks to displace in view of the complete absence of social statistics before the later eleventh century. It is clear that the Normans were often at a loss themselves to make sense of the various peasant classes, and it is not easy to give precise definition to the terminology they used—*villani* or villeins, *bordarii* or bordars, *coliberti* or freedmen. And evidently they found striking contrasts between one region and another, unless these apparent contrasts be merely variations of terminology which is, on the whole, unlikely. Domesday Book reveals a numerous class of men in the Danelaw called *sokemen*, who were free though not particularly wealthy ceorls. They were to be found mostly in Leicestershire, Nottinghamshire, Lincolnshire, Norfolk, Suffolk and Essex. In Lincolnshire they formed 50 per cent of the total recorded population, and in adjacent counties about 40 to 45 per cent. Their presence is particularly coincidental with those areas which passed under Danish domination in the ninth and tenth centuries, but not completely so, and the reasons for their distribution have been disputed. There is a related problem, that of the peasants described by Domesday Book as '*liberi homines*' or free men: about 96 per cent of the total are placed in Norfolk and Suffolk, a further problem of distribution which has not been completely resolved.

There were probably two opposing and concurrent patterns of change affecting Anglo-Saxon society; one a depression of impoverished peasants—and perhaps also of impoverished lords—into a more servile economic status; the other the advance of prosperous ceorls into the aristocracy. Ceorls were protected by a not inconsiderable *wergeld*, and if a ceorl owned five *hides* of land he could perform military service for them along with the thegns. He or his descendants could then aspire to the thegnhood. This is an aspect of the social scene which has not been adequately stressed. The composition of the Anglo-Saxon thegnhood was probably much more fluid than we may at first imagine.

A fundamental point must be emphasised. It is quite clear that the concept of dividing peasant society in terms of free and unfree is an over-simplification. A peasant could be economically dependent or unfree, but still personally free, paying dues to the Church and possessing a certain standing in Law. There could be an infinite permutation of relationships. A very important tract, the *Rights and Ranks of People*, lists the services and obligations of distinct types of freemen who are also tenants and in varying degrees of servitude, though admitting that regional variations deprive this memorandum of any universal application. The *geneats* or 'companions' performed no servile task, but had rather the honourable duty of riding for their lord as a kind of mounted retainer. With these men may be associated perhaps the *radcnihts* who appear in documents from the west midlands. The *geneats* rented land on a considerable scale. Below the *geneats*, the *geburs* or boors held a quarter of a *hide*, paid rent to a landlord in kind and money, and performed labour services. The lord stocked the land he rented to the *gebur*, and both land and stock reverted to the lord on the *gebur*'s death. The poorer but still free *kotsetlan* or cottager held only five *hides* of land and performed heavy labour services. Such men had no ecomonic freedom left. They could not easily move away for they had no means of support, and if they did they were probably liable to be brought back by their landlord. But they were still personally free. If they lost this personal freedom—if they sold themselves to a lord at a time of acute hardship or if they were captured and sold as chattels—they became slaves. A Durham document of the late tenth century, for example, refers to men and women who sold themselves into slavery for food. Now whatever the social standing and economic position of the ceorl in Anglo-Saxon England, a matter of crucial importance is the number of slaves in England, whether in the seventh or the eleventh century, and the degree to which at any point in time ceorls were being forced into slavery. Once again, we are handicapped for want of statistics. Slavery does not enter as an important factor into the agricultural history of the Middle Ages. It may have been a declining institution by the later eleventh century but, on the other hand, the Normans could be using different words for slave. Domesday Book shows a heavy concentration of slaves in the south-western shires with fewer in the east, showing none at all for Huntingdonshire, Lincolnshire and Yorkshire; but Domesday figures are demonstrably incomplete, for slaves are recorded independently for Huntingdonshire. They must have constituted, therefore, more than the 10 per cent of the population indicated by Domesday Book. In earlier centuries both thegns and ceorls possessed slaves. It is possible that in the Anglo-Saxon period much of the work on greater and smaller estates was done by slave labour. In the mid-680s Wilfrid freed 250 slaves on a South Saxon estate of 87 *hides*. It is not inconceivable that during the wars of the Heptarchy as well as during the Danish wars many ceorls were driven into slavery, nor do we need to look necessarily for times of war as a background to this process. The laws of Cnut imply at one point that lords were known on occasions to have attempted to blur the distinction between ceorl and slave, treating ceorls as slaves in the course of court proceedings. The growth of manorial courts in the later Saxon period must have tended to place tenants at the mercy of landlords and created new opportunities for oppression. As slaves came to cost as much as a pound or the equivalent of a ploughteam of eight oxen by the later Saxon period (perhaps because they were still selling so well on foreign markets), this may have been an incentive to lords to increase the number of slaves at their disposal by depressing their ceorls. On the other hand, it had become a conscious Christian duty by the late tenth century to free slaves by the process known as manumission. Such men became freedmen. A late Saxon document says that slaves were often freed by ceorls, citing this as a parallel process to the way in which ceorls could rise to the thegn-hood.

The Agricultural Scene

The arable land of the Anglo-Saxons was measured in terms which can be difficult to understand today. They assessed their land by basic units called a *hide* in southern England and probably originally in the north, a *carucate* in the Danelaw, and a *sulung* in Kent. It is generally believed that there was a time when, theoretically at least, the *hide* was thought to contain 120 acres, held to be sufficient to sustain a family (kindred) for a year. A quarter of a *hide* was a *virgate* or *yardland* and would amount, again at least theoretically, to 30 acres. It is evident that in practice these acreages could vary considerably, for by 1066 the measurements had been for a long time essentially fiscal in character; that is to say, they tended to reflect the value of a given stretch of land rather than its geographical dimensions.

Over central England, from Durham to the English Channel and from Cambridge to the Welsh border, the arable land was cultivated communally by the villagers, probably from the earliest days of settlement, in vast open fields divided into strips. Each strip was held to be roughly one furlong long and a tenth of a furlong wide, representing an acre, and in theory (though it must have varied in practice) a strip of one acre could be ploughed by one ox-team in a day, a *hide* by one ox-team in a year. The ideal team, though with not all the beasts necessarily engaged in drawing the plough, was eight oxen. In Kent it was customary to divide the *sulung*, a term actually derived from the Old English word for a plough, into four *yokes*, suggesting therefore an eight-ox team. Similarly, in the districts settled by the Danes, men termed the *hide* the *carucate* or ploughland, and divided it into eight *bovates* or *oxgangs*. Such was the system of reckoning which lay behind the rural organisation of Anglo-Saxon England. But there did exist marked regional variations. The East Anglian *tenement* did not resemble in size either the *virgate* or *yoke*. In Kent the compact and rectangular *yoke* was without parallel in the rest of England. In the northern counties and in the Cornish peninsula the large field was found only in certain areas and men tended to follow a system common to Celtic lands, that of *runrig* whereby arable land was only brought under cultivation for a limited period and then allowed to fall back to waste again.

The agricultural system of most of Anglo-Saxon England could be termed the 'two field' system, but the idea of fields numbering two or three is perhaps best set aside; an Anglo-Saxon village may have had any number of fields around it. Though there is still a risk of presenting too neat a picture, it is a little more satisfactory to think in terms of rotations throughout the whole of the arable land, a two- or three-course rotation. If a two-course rotation were the normal practice in Anglo-Saxon England, this would mean that the arable land of the community, 120 acres for example, would be divided roughly into two halves. One half, 60 acres in this case, was left fallow for a year, probably used as pasturage for sheep and cattle, and ploughed in early summer. The other half was divided into two again. One half, in this instance 30 acres, was probably ploughed and sown with a winter crop, and both were harvested in the summer. With successive farming years, land left fallow one year would be sown the next, and in this way a two-course rotation of crops was applied. It is very possible, of course, that the Anglo-Saxons ploughed as much land each year as they could: more than half the available arable, that is, if time permitted, but there would be a limit to the amount of land which could be ploughed in any one year. An ox-team ploughed slowly. In the Middle Ages, horses came to be used in ploughing and more land could be ploughed because horses were much faster; it became common to leave fallow only a third of the land as opposed to a half, placing more land under the plough each year but necessitating a decrease in the length of time a particular piece of land could be left fallow as pasture. The land was rested every three instead of every two years, that is to say, a three-course rotation was in operation. In the Anglo-Saxon period the three-course rotation may not have been unknown, but population had not then entered its period of greatest increase. It is thought that the population of England in 1066 was about one-and-a-half million only, and it seems likely that the three-course rotation was primarily a response to the urgent needs of a soaring population between c. 1050 and 1300. On the whole, though Anglo-Saxon food production must have remained at a lower level than that of the Middle Ages, the Anglo-Saxons probably reaped the benefit of land more frequently fallowed. Even so, by modern standards the yield from the land was low. There is some evidence to suggest that an average yield from an acre of corn may have been about six bushels, approximately a tenth of what would be regarded as a reasonable return today. With the technological limitations of Anglo-Saxon farming, the harvest could be largely ruined by bad weather, and the margin between a successful and a disastrous harvest must have been narrow. Famine would follow a bad harvest, and in the wake of famine, disease. On the other hand though many famines did occur, a great extent of land was under cultivation to support a small population, and the wheat sold in London in the early eleventh century to a Norwegian merchant suggests that a surplus of wheat from the great estates was actually being exported.

The agricultural year began with the essential preliminaries of ploughing and sowing. There were two main types of plough, the light and wheel-less Mediterranean plough, suitable for light soils, and the heavy, wheeled plough of north Europe, suitable for heavier soils. It is generally thought that the heavy plough was used in Roman Britain and subsequently taken over by the Anglo-Saxons, though it remains possible that the lighter variety was used throughout the Anglo-Saxon period on poorer soils. Although the historian would like to know more of the technological aspect of early English farming and the way in which improvements in tools and implements enabled man to farm more efficiently, the archaeological evidence at present does not make possible even a general outline. It has recently been pointed out that no plough and only a single plough-share is known to have survived from the Anglo-Saxon period. We are dependent for our knowledge of Saxon ploughs on early drawings in Old English manuscripts or from the Bayeux Tapestry.

In the Romano-British period wheat and oats are thought to have eclipsed the predominantly barley crop of the Bronze Age. Although wheat was certainly grown by the Anglo-Saxons, it seems to have been a mixture of barley, oats and rye which characterised their husbandry. The first ploughing and sowing took place in October and November, the second (when there was a second) in January and the early months of the new year. The crops were harvested in August. The rye harvest, in fact, gave its name to the Anglo-Saxon equivalent for August, *Rugern*; but the harvest might last into November if the season were very wet. The grain would be threshed and winnowed towards the close of the year and then milled. The spread of the water-mill across England from the eighth century onwards represents an early striking application of power-driven machinery to human requirements. Oats provided porridge and food for horses, rye the 'black' bread of the medieval peasantry, called 'black' in distinction to the lighter wheat-loaf but not all that less nutritious. Barley was a prime ingredient for the brewing of beer. The regular routine of farming devoted itself primarily to the production of cereal crops, but flax was cultivated, sown in the spring and gathered in the summer and providing fibres for linen and wicks for lamps, and woad for dyeing purposes. Some vegetables were grown, particularly beans to judge from the answer of the pupil in Ælf-fric's *Colloquy* to the question of what he ate each day. The Anglo-Saxons no doubt grew their vegetables in their garden plots. Gardens were dug over in February and planted early in the spring. It would be valuable to know more about the vegetable cultivation of the Anglo-Saxons and also about fruit-growing in this period, two essential dietary elements. Select wild fruits and nuts must have provided a constant natural supply but there is no reason to suppose that apple-trees and pear-trees, possibly even plum and cherry, were not common to the country scene.

There was one great defect of Anglo-Saxon agriculture, as of the whole of English agriculture before the eighteenth century: the shortage of a hay crop. The land that they could farm, the Anglo-Saxons preferred to cultivate as arable, using part of it only as pasture in the summer. Natural meadowland along the rivers and streams provided food for cattle and horses but remained in short supply, and there was no systematic cultivation of grassland as in modern agriculture. In the summer, sheep and cattle might even be fed on the leaves of trees, every supply of food being utilised. In consequence of the shortage of food in winter, it was necessary to kill off many beasts in November.

The early English laws indicate a particularly high regard for and interest in cattle. The buying and selling of cattle was regulated by law as early as the time of Ine of Wessex, and it is quite evident from the law codes that cattle-stealing was one of the most practised and presumably most profitable crimes of Anglo-Saxon society. Judging from cattle bones found on Anglo-Saxon sites, the cattle were larger than those of Roman Britain and existed in substantial numbers. It is possible to underestimate the part played by cattle in supplying the Anglo-Saxons with milk as well as meat—Bede knew May as the month when cattle could be milked three times a day—but, nevertheless, a great deal of the milk must have gone into the raising of young stock. It is known that much of the milk produced by Anglo-Saxon dairy farms was sheep's milk, and that butter and cheese were made from sheep's milk. The sheep must have presented one of the soundest of commercial propositions to an Anglo-Saxon farmer, for it could provide milk, wool and meat. Sheep in particular brought increased fertility to land on which they were folded. By 1066 they may have been the most numerous of all animals, and the fact that sheep can tolerate almost any environment made them profitable virtually anywhere. Domesday Book records them particularly thickly in eastern England, but unfortunately does not provide specific sheep figures for the whole country. It is uncertain when exactly sheep farming began to develop on a grand scale in England, but by the late eighth century the export of English wool and cloths was particularly important in the trade with Carolingian Gaul.

Perhaps the most characteristic feature of Anglo-Saxon domestic livestock was the pig, or rather the vast herds of swine which foraged in autumn on the oak acorns and beechmast of the woodlands and in the spring and summer grazed across the more open scrubland. Early illustrations reveal the Anglo-Saxon pig as a long-legged, long-haired, razor-backed creature, almost certainly slow to mature and lean meated. It was, however, for their meat that they were kept, and in herds of up to 2,000 or more. The pig must also have been the poor man's animal, for as foraging beasts they could be more easily fed. In the main, the economy of pig-keeping was based on a plentiful supply of available woodland, and the pig may have suffered some eclipse in popularity with the intensified deforestation after *c.* 1050 and the development of protected royal forests. The prices of cattle, sheep and pigs were naturally scaled. In the time of King Athelstan an ox cost 30 pence, a cow 20 pence, a pig ten pence and a sheep five pence.

Less well documented among Anglo-Saxon livestock are horses and goats. Goats, of value for their milk and for the meat of the kids, are known to have been kept though we cannot say on what scale. Horses were certainly bred in England and a horse cost four times as much as an ox. So far as can be seen, horses were reared for purposes of war, travel and sport. Prohibitions against the eating of horseflesh tended to limit the farming value of the horse, which was not generally used for ploughing purposes in Anglo-Saxon England. King Alfred learnt with surprise that the Scandinavians used plough-horses in Norway. Recent study has stressed that the invention of the horse collar made possible the effective use of the horse in ploughing on the Continent by the ninth century, and a mule is depicted drawing a plough on the Bayeux Tapestry. There is no evidence, however, for the use of the horse for ploughing in Anglo-Saxon England. Hens and geese formed the fowl of the Anglo-Saxon farm, the domestic duck evidently being unknown until the thirteenth century. The farming man faced the usual hazards from vermin. The greatest pests of the time must have been mice and rats, particularly the plague-spreading black rat which infested outbuildings and domestic dwellings. One creature regarded as a modern pest, the rabbit, did not arrive in England until after the Norman Conquest. Dogs were kept to guard the stock; but they were not the domestic pets of today—at least not always—for they were known to have bitten men to death and it was necessary for King Alfred to prescribe against such an eventuality.

Farming produce was naturally sold in all the local markets up and down the country, no doubt together with much that had been gathered from a wild state such as edible berries and nuts. Women sold butter and cheese in London, where it is recorded that live pigs and hampers of eggs and hens were brought.

Two important rural activities deserve to be stressed, firstly the production of drink and secondly the fishing industry. The Anglo-Saxons appear to have been extremely fond of their clear ale, their mild ale, their beer, wine and mead. Beer or ale was made from barley, a certain amount of home-produced wine from vineyards in southern England, and mead from honey. Mead, an expensive drink, is seen very much as the characteristic drink of the Anglo-Saxon nobility, with the survival of many poetic references to the mead-benches around the lord's hall.

Wine or even mulberry juice might be used in the preparation of drinks made with honey. Bee-keeping was in consequence a widespread rural activity. Taxes were not infrequently paid in honey and Alfred legislated against the theft of bees. Honey was, of course, the only sweetening substance known to the Anglo-Saxons. Aldhelm of Malmesbury is said to have been particularly fond of it. Turning to fishing, we find that the coastal communties of England were actively engaged in sea-fishing for whales, dolphins, salmon, sturgeon, plaice, porpoises, crabs, lobsters, oysters, mussels, winkles and cockles. Sea-fishing for herrings is clearly revealed by the renders of herrings in Domesday Book from Southwark and Brighton. The fact that the eating of meat on Fridays was strictly forbidden probably meant that the supply of fish was never quite equal to the demand. It was, however, a costly affair to engage in sea-fishing, for large vessels were expensive. The Anglo-Saxon fishing industry thrived most extensively along the fens and riverways of the country as a whole. Domesday Book, which can have recorded only a fraction of the total number of inland fisheries, shows them scattered thickly along such rivers as the Thames, the Severn, the Trent, the Dee, the Warwickshire Avon, the rivers of Kent, Sussex, Essex, Suffolk and Norfolk. Trout, pike, lampreys, salmon, even minnows, were fished in the rivers. Eels were caught on a prodigious scale. The Anglo-Saxons must have experienced a prominence of eel in their diet. Certain fenland villages produced over 20,000 a year. But fishing may have been an art which the Anglo-Saxons learnt gradually. In the 680s the men of Sussex were so unskilled as fishermen that they could only catch eels, and it was Wilfrid, bishop of York, who taught them to fish in the sea with nets.

Then as now the agricultural year was an incessant round of activity. Tools and implements would have to be maintained and repaired, fences and buildings attended to. Weeding must have been a constantly recurring occupation, for this was a time when weeds would even grow through domestic dwellings. August was known as the month of weeds. The tract, the *Reeve*, enumerates the objects which required the attention of the reeve on a great estate, a list which includes plough-shares, coulters, goads, spades, forks, rakes, scythes, sickles, flails, axes, chisels, churns, cheese-vats, salt-vats, beer-butts, beehives, shears, branding irons, ladders, pans, kettles, loom frames, needles and wool combs. There is no doubt that a large and prosperous manor would employ its own staff of farm labourers and domestic artisans to cope with every aspect of rural life: a swineherd, oxherd, cowherd, goatherd, shepherd, sower, keeper of the granary, bee-keeper, cheesemaker, woodward, woodworker, smith, leather-worker, salter, baker, cook, weaver, seam-ster. We do not know how hard each individual had to work, but Ælfric's *Colloquy* sheds valuable light on the daily or nightly activities of a number of agricultural workers about the year 1000. To the question how hard did he work, the ploughman answered that he worked very hard; going out at daybreak, he drove his oxen to the field and yoked them to the plough and, no matter how harsh the winter, every day he had to plough a full acre or more. The weather was often so bad that the boy with the goad was hoarse with cold and shouting. In the evening the ploughman returned the oxen to shelter, bedding them down, feeding and watering them, and cleaning out their stalls. It may be that in summer some of these duties were performed by the oxherd, who replied to the same question of how hard he worked by saying that he drove the beasts in his charge to pasture during the night, remaining with them to guard against thieves. The shepherd, for his part, drove his flock to pasture and guarded the sheep with dogs for fear of wolves, both in heat and cold; when he led them back to the fold it was his duty to milk them, and this he had to do twice a day, and from the milk he had to make cheese and butter. It is clear, however, that the making of dairy produce was a job frequently given to others. Nevertheless, a pic-ture of unrelenting toil is communicated by these brief replies which are not necessarily complete: the shepherd does not mention sheep-shear-ing, a major task which had to be completed by midsummer. Many a ploughman and many a herdsman must have envied, in an age which loved hunting, the life of the fowler, with his nets, traps and hawks, pro-viding both himself and his master, if he had one, with a constant supply of food in the lean winter months. Perhaps even more envied was the royal huntsman, who describes in the *Colloquy* his life with hounds and nets, taking deer and wild boar and being richly rewarded with horses and bracelets.

The great religious festivals of the year must have loomed particularly large in the lives of Anglo-Saxon peasant farmers for they were the time when church dues had to be paid. Plough-alms had to be paid 15 days after Easter, a tithe of young animals at Pentecost, church dues by Michaelmas (29 September), and a tithe of the fruits of the earth at All Saints (1 November). These were not the only domestic dues but they were the most important. The manorial or royal reeve saw that payments were made on time. But such great religious festivals coincided with holidays. Holy-days of rest were imposed on the laity by the Church, while King Alfred decreed that even slaves were to have the four Wednesdays in the four Ember weeks as rest days. And at certain times of the year on the great estates, feasts were provided by the lord and must have afforded many moments of conviviality among the peasantry: a harvest feast for reaping, a drinking feast for ploughing, a Yuletide feast at Christmas, and an Easter feast. In addition, the cycle of the seasons was marked by ancient festivals at the beginning of the new year, at the beginning of summer, at midsummer and at Hallow-e'en, festivals which gave expression to the rural mythology of men whose horizons were little wider than their village boundaries. It must not be forgotten that behind the great manors and estate economy of Anglo-Saxon England the peasant cultivator retained an awe of the mysteries of nature and was not unknown to incant pagan charms to ensure fertility. He had little or no scientific understanding of seedtime and harvest.

Chapter two

Towns and Industry

The study of the historical geography of Anglo-Saxon England has only just begun. The reasons which caused a kingdom to develop along particular lines of communication, within certain boundaries and around certain select urban communities—or similarly in the case of a shire—have received insufficient attention. Extensive field work still requires to be undertaken before the geographical influences at work on Anglo-Saxon society can be adequately analysed. The investigation of lines of communication and the placing of strategic sites may throw light not only on the forgotten aims of rival rulers but also on the origin of towns; the analysis of town plans may yet reveal the layout of the original Anglo-Saxon settlement, while the putting together of a geographical as well as a legal or historical explanation of the growth of particular boroughs may illuminate further the economic development of early England. This is a field of study which affords a variety of opportunities for research to the local enthusiast. There is much more written on the map of England than has yet been understood or even discerned.

Boundaries and communications

The major riverways of Anglo-Saxon England tended to act as barriers to tribal expansion and as protective frontiers for emerging kingdoms and so they came to be among the most important of early boundaries. Mercia was separated from Northumbria in the north-west by the river Mersey, the name of which means 'boundary river'. The Humber marked the north-east Mercian frontier, the Mercians being originally known as Southumbrians in apposition to Northumbrians. In 829 Egbert of Wessex received the submission of the Northumbrians at

Dore, said to have been on the Northumbrian-Mercian border; Dore is, in fact, just south of the river Sheaf, the name of which also means 'boundary river'. At the period of its greatest extent, the northern frontier of the kingdom of Northumbria was the Firth of Forth. In the early eighth century the river Carron became the frontier and in 1018, after the battle of Carham, the river Tweed. Part of the frontier between Mercia and Wessex was the Bristol Avon, and part the Thames. The kingdoms of East Anglia and Essex seem to have been separated by the Stour. In the early tenth century King Athelstan determined the Wye as the frontier with the South Welsh and the Tamar as that with the Cornish Britons. And the great Anglo-Saxon kingdoms, of course, were but agglomerations of older, smaller units, which in turn had often been marked off from each other by rivers. The two parts of Northumbria, Deira and Bernicia, were separated by the Tees, the North-folk and South-folk of East Anglia by the Waveney, the northern and southern Mercians by the Trent. The *Arosætan* of the Tribal Hidage clearly stood in some relation to the Herefordshire Arrow, the *Tomsætan* with the Warwickshire Tame, the *Wixan* with the Worcestershire Whitsun Brook, the *Gifla* with the Bedfordshire Ivel. If Middlesex reflects the distribution of the Middle Saxons north of the Thames, they were neatly bounded by the Lea, the Colne and the Thames. The Middle Saxons dwelt on both sides of the Thames, and the district of Surrey was their 'southern province'.

Rivers naturally came to form part of the boundaries of later shires. The Tweed continued to divide Northumberland and Scotland, the Tees Durham and Yorkshire. Similarly the Mersey continued to separate Lancashire and Cheshire, the Sheaf Yorkshire and Derbyshire, the Bristol Avon Gloucestershire and Somerset, the Wye Gloucestershire and Monmouthshire, the Tamar Devon and Cornwall, the Stour Essex and Suffolk, the Waveney Norfolk and Suffolk, the Trent Nottinghamshire and Lincolnshire. The Thames formed the southern boundary of Essex and the Mercian shires of Oxford and Buckingham, and the northern boundary of Surrey and West Saxon Berkshire. Within Yorkshire, the East and North Ridings are separated by the Derwent, and the West and North Ridings by the Yorkshire Ouse and the Ure-Nidd watershed, divisions which may go back to pre-Viking times, if not—in the case of the West and North Ridings— to British times and the petty kingdom of Elmet. The river Tyne may have had some significance as an internal Bernician division, for in 867 the Danes set up a king north of the Tyne; the river eventually became recognised as the boundary between Durham and Northumberland. Within Mercia, the river Dove divides Derbyshire and Staffordshire, the Welland separates Northamptonshire from Lincolnshire and part of Leicestershire, the Ouse forms part of the northern boundary of Buckinghamshire. Examples could be multiplied.

Where a frontier or boundary had to be drawn elsewhere than along a river bank, a defensive ditch or dyke might serve. Devil's Dyke, for instance, astride the Icknield Way, divided East Anglia and Mercia, and Grim's Dyke, by Charford, has long served as the shire boundary between Wiltshire and Hampshire at that point. In west Sussex, Marden is a place-name probably signifying originally 'boundary down', a downland boundary between Sussex and Hampshire. Offa of Mercia constructed the earthwork which bears his name, the greatest of all English dykes—Offa's Dyke, to define the Welsh-Mercian frontier of his day. Not only dykes but roads also could serve the same purpose. For 29 out of 40 miles, for example, between High Cross and Cirencester, the Fosse Way forms parish boundaries; and similarly, between High Cross and Tamworth, Watling Street serves as a boundary for 24 out of 29 miles, for 11 of these as a shire boundary. Watling Street figures very prominently in the Danish wars as a frontier between Saxon and Dane. Alfred and Guthrum determined the Anglo-Danish frontier as along the Thames, up the Lea to its source, then in a straight line to Bedford, then up the Ouse to Watling Street. In 940 Olaf of York was recognised as king north and east of Watling Street, and in 1013 Swein and Cnut did no ravaging on their march south until they had crossed it.

A much more intensive study of the growth of English roads is needed before there can be any accurate assessment of the state and importance of Anglo-Saxon communications. Though hardly any direct evidence survives as to the routes used by travellers in the pre-Conquest period, boundary clauses of charters contain a great many references to short lengths of road bordering on the estates with which they deal, and there is every reason to suppose that the present network of long-established roads over most of England is substantially the same as that laid down before the Norman Conquest. The Anglo-Saxons named their roads either by type or individual characteristics; *port*-streets leading to and from market towns, *here*paths suitable for the movements of armies or particularly noted for the same, ridgeways following the high ground to avoid river-crossings and streams, salt ways radiating out from major salt-producing centres like Droitwich, and, of course, a miscellaneous assortment of foul, muddy, clay and green ways. *Straet* or 'street'—and sometimes 'way'—were terms usually applied to Roman roads or made-up roads within a town. Examples of a *here*path are the ridgeway of the Berkshire downs and the Roman street from Winchester to Cirencester. The road from Derby to Leicester, via Loughborough, is believed to be a good example of a *here*path, its direction resulting from the movements of Danish armies between these centres. Ancient ridgeways and streets were the major routes for the movements of armies and commercial traffic, large-scale movements being determined by lines of advance afforded by the hard surfaces of even the most minor of streamless ridges.

The great Roman roads and prehistoric trackways of Anglo-Saxon England provided a certain framework for the evolution at strategic points and important junctions of settlements larger than mere village communities. Watling Street ran from Dover via Canterbury and London to St. Albans, Towcester, High Cross and Wroxeter. The Anglo-Saxon name for St. Albans was *Wæclingacæstir*, the Roman fort of the *Wæclingas*—Wæcel's people—and Watling Street was clearly named from the same folk-group. Ermine Street, *Earninga Street*, was the Roman road of the *Earningas*—Earn's people, and after linking Chichester to London ran north via Royston, Huntingdon, Stamford, Lincoln and York to Corbridge and beyond; a road from Lincoln to York via Doncaster and Tadcaster rather than Auckland was probably the original Ermine Street. The Fosse Way, evidently so named from deep ditches on either side, ran from Lincoln via Newark, Leicester, High Cross, Cirencester and Bath to Ilchester where it forked, one branch going to Dorchester and the other to Axminster. The Icknield Way, a name of unknown origin, stretched from the Wash to Salisbury Plain via Newmarket, Royston, Dunstable, Streatley, and the Berkshire and Wiltshire downs. Another important Roman road was Akeman Street, taking its name from *Acemannes ceaster*, Aceman's Roman fort, otherwise Bath, which ran across the south midlands from Bath via Cirencester and Aylesbury to Tring on the Icknield Way or even to St. Albans. A road known as Ryknield Street linked Caerleon, Gloucester, Worcester, Droitwich, Birmingham, Lichfield, Burton-on-Trent, Derby and York. In Wessex, Winchester and Old Sarum were the centre of a network of Roman roads which joined London in the east to

Dorchester in Dorset and beyond to Exeter in the west. The historian of Anglo-Saxon England must constantly bear in mind what can be discovered about these great highways for they exerted a formative influence on the geographical evolution of the Anglo-Saxon kingdoms and helped to determine to no small extent where the major concentrations of urban development in medieval England would occur.

Though the majority of the population was tied to the land, there was still considerable movement within the country. As early as the reign of Edwin (617–34), the highways in Northumbria were so much in use that the king took the trouble to have stakes fixed by springs to which drinking bowls were attached for the convenience of travellers. Bede refers to a traveller coming to an inn near Oswestry in the 640s. There is no doubt that vast tracts along the sides of ancient Roman roads or primitive trackways were uninhabited in the seventh century and that a traveller might have to go a long way before reaching a village or inn. At 9 a.m. on a winter's day in the 650s, Cuthbert was advised not to continue his journey north from Chester-le-Street in Durham without taking food because there was no house or village on the road ahead which he could reach by sunset. The poem *Beowulf* refers to the 'stone-paved' road, but conditions on many roads, of course, were appalling, particularly in winter. Roads to the south of the Tees were so difficult in the winter of 1069–70 that William the Conqueror had to advance on foot; and some between Pontefract and York so narrow that his soldiers could not march two abreast.

By the late eleventh century, and probably much earlier, the king's peace was extended for the protection of travellers to four major highways—Watling Street, Ermine Street, the Fosse Way and the Icknield Way. Robbers must have been a constant danger to travel on land, and any traveller who unwittingly strayed off the trackway was liable to be regarded by villagers as a thief if he did not repeatedly blow his horn. There survives an Anglo-Saxon charm which, if recited by one about to set out on a journey, was believed to bring protection from all dangers by land and sea. It must not be forgotten, of course, that the sea was an important highway for those travelling from one end of England or Britain to the other. Not a great deal of information survives on this particular aspect of travel, but there is no doubt that the Anglo-Saxons, though they might fear a sea voyage, did not shrink from going by boat if necessary. In the 640s, a Northumbrian nobleman, Utta, going to Kent to fetch Eanflæd, daughter of Æthelburh, as a bride for King Oswiu, travelled south by land but north by sea and was provided with a phial of liquid, guaranteed to quell storms, by St. Aidan. Home waters could be dangerous. Utta did run into a storm and spent some time in fear of shipwreck. One hundred and fifty ships of the Picts seem to have been lost together in 729; and there is a record of the destruction of many ships in a violent storm in 799 in the British Sea (now the English Channel). When the exiled Wilfrid, bishop of York, ran aground in Sussex in the 660s, his ship only narrowly escaped looting by a party of South Saxons. But Æthelburh, wife of Edwin, fled by ship to Kent on the death of Edwin in 634, and more than one later king of Northumbria escaped his enemies by taking to the sea for the land of the Picts. St. Cuthbert sailed on ecclesiastical business from Northumbria to Pictland on at least one occasion, and that in midwinter. Limited sailing such as this, and at all times of the year, may not have been all that uncommon.

The historical geography of Anglo-Saxon England

The names of settlements frequently occur in the records of Anglo-Saxon England, particularly in those of the Heptarchy, which cannot now be identified. These range from the sites of important Church councils such as *Clofesho*, *Pincanheale* and *Aclea*, to those of Northumbrian villages such as *Wulfeswelle* and *Cettingaham* or forts such as *Scythlecester*, somewhere on Hadrian's Wall, and *Aynburg*. It may well be that in certain instances such places have vanished completely from the map, surviving only as deserted village sites now hardly recognisable as such. But this did not necessarily happen in all cases. It deserves to be stressed that it is not unknown for a settlement to have changed its name in the course of the Anglo-Saxon period. An obscure, unidentified name, therefore, could be an archaic name for a settlement which has survived as a village, even possibly as an important urban centre. It has been suggested that *Siddensis*, the site of the bishopric of Lindsey, may have been a suburb of what is now Lincoln. Without the necessary written evidence it would not be known, for example, that *Vortigern's burh* is to be identified with Bradford-on-Avon, that Norham in Northumberland was originally *Ubbanford*, that Redbridge in Hampshire was originally *Redford*, that Whitby was originally *Streoneshalh*, that Derby was originally *Northworthy* but renamed by the Danes. Behind Littleborough lies *Tiowulfingacæstir*, behind Tadcaster lies *Kælcacæstir*, behind Bury St. Edmunds lies *Bædericeswirde*, and behind Newbury in Berkshire *Ulvritone*.

A further point which requires emphasis is that a very important Anglo-Saxon urban centre can go completely unmentioned in the fragmentary source materials for the pre-Conquest period. Leeds, for example, figures in no annal and is mentioned in no Anglo-Saxon source. Situated on the river Aire, however, at the foot of the Pennines and overlooking the plain of York, the convergence of routes across the Pennines from north-west and south-west made the Leeds district, *Loidis*, an important nodal point. Somewhere in its vicinity was probably fought the battle of *Winwæd* (656). The tenth-century continental *Life* of St. Catroe, a pilgrim from Scotland who travelled across England in *c.* 940 *en route* for the Continent, states that Leeds was the border town between the Cumbrian Britons and the Danes; Leeds is rather far to the south to have been on the Cumbrian border, but it is not at all improbable that the writer of the *Life* has made a simple error and that Leeds was actually a border town between the Mercians and the Danish kingdom of York.

A great many of the battle sites of early English history, like *Winwæd*, remain unidentified. Though the site of the great battle of *Brunanburh* is also known by the name of *Wendun* and possibly that of *Vinheath*, it also remains unknown. Only rarely is it possible even to identify tentatively. *Fethanleag*, the battle from which Ceawlin returned in anger to his own country, may be identifiable either with the *Fæh halean*, somewhere by Stratford-on-Avon, of Mercian charters, or with a *Fethelee*, recorded in a later medieval document at Stoke Lyne in Oxfordshire. Where early battle sieges can be identified, they reveal the importance of the roads and communications of the area in which they were fought. The battle of *Fethanleag* took place—if the identification with Stoke Lyne is correct—in the valley of the river Bure, not far from the Roman road north out of Dorchester-on-Thames through Bicester and its junction with an ancient road across Oxfordshire; if the battle is alternatively to be located near Stratford-on-Avon, Stratford is at the crossing of the Warwickshire Avon by a Roman road joining Ryknield Street to the Fosse Way. When Cynric and Ceawlin fought the Britons at Barbury castle they were by an Iron Age hill fort, close to which are traces of what has been described as one of the finest groups of 'Celtic' fields in England cultivated at least into Roman times, on the great

Wiltshire ridgeway at the head of the valley of the river Og, and near Wroughton, where the battle of *Ellandun* was to be fought in 825. This ridgeway was of crucial significance in the military strategy of southern England. After a conflict at Woden's Barrow, Ceawlin was expelled from the kingdom, and in 715 Ine of Wessex fought Ceolred of Mercia there; the site is to be identified with Adam's Grave, near Alton Barnes in Wiltshire. It is located where the Wansdyke, running from near Bristol to near Marlborough and one of the defensive earthern barriers of southern England, is crossed by the great ridgeway of Wiltshire, at the point of descent from the downs into the Kennet valley. Similarly, two battles were fought at Benson or Bensington (Oxfordshire), one in the second half of the sixth century against the Britons and one in 779 between Offa of Mercia and Cynewulf of Wessex in which the Mercians captured the town; Bensington's position on the north bank of the Thames, at the end of a road from Dorchester-on-Thames and just below the crossing of the Thames by the Icknield Way, clearly gave it a particular strategic significance. To study, therefore, in so far as is possible, the recorded events of Anglo-Saxon history with special attention to the places at which they occurred is to see them in a new and valuable perspective. We can infer that Oswald of Northumbria was the aggressor in the campaign that led up to his defeat at the battle of *Maserfelth*, because this site can be identified with the Iron Age hill fort of Old Oswestry on the Mercian-Welsh border. It cannot be assumed that an obscure place-name represents an insignificant and remote site. The record of the assassination of Sigeberht, king of Wessex, in 757 by the stream at Privett, for example, acquires an additional interest when it is appreciated that Privett was not a hidden corner of Hampshire concealing a deposed ruler but a meeting point of important road and ridgeways. Egbert's Stone, where Alfred joined forces with his armies from Wiltshire, Somerset and Hampshire in 878, was probably not in a pathless tract but rather at Kilmington Common at the junction of ancient pathways leading from these shires. Even the saints who went to build their cells in the fenlands of the East Anglian-Mercian border, cells which were to develop into great monastic houses, built them in relation to roads and communications, on or near major thoroughfares; Thorney was at an intersection of Roman roads, Ely on a branch road off Ermine Street, Peterborough a few miles east of Ermine Street and on the river Nene at a point favourable to development as an inland fenland port. The monastic communities of Anglo-Saxon England which thrived as great houses into the Norman period did so not least through their positions in towns and at important junctions of communications.

Settlements at sites where persons following a ridgeway or path were obliged to cross a river by a ford or bridge possessed a natural strategic and commercial significance. Hereford owed its position to the fact that it was by a ford across the Wye. Fords, of course, play a conspicuous part in the military annals of early English history. In 893 the Danes escaped from their English pursuers by crossing the Thames where there was no ford, an achievement which so surprised the West Saxons that a mention of it came to be made in the *Anglo-Saxon Chronicle*. Æthelred and Alfred are said to have escaped from the Danes after their defeat at Reading in 871 only through their knowledge of a ford, unknown to the Danes, over the river Loddon at Twyford. Edward the Elder established a temporary truce with the Danes in 906 at Tiddingford on the river Ouzel, a river which subsequently came to form part of the boundary between Buckinghamshire and Bedfordshire and may have been an Anglo-Danish frontier in 906. Bedford itself developed by a ford over the Ouse, possibly at the point where the river was crossed by a Roman road. Oxford grew up by the junction of a Berkshire ridgeway with a ford across the Thames. To give a few more examples: Cricklade, Walling-ford, Reading, Wilton, Malmesbury and Thetford all developed at the junction of river and ridgeway. Stamford, Northampton, Cirencester and Bath are among the communities which evolved on the important Jurassic ridgeway (so called from its geological composition), which runs across central England from Yorkshire to Somerset. Stamford, for example, is where the Jurassic way crosses the river Welland and where the Welland is fordable, and Northampton where the ridgeway crosses the river Nene.

Occasionally the existence of a bridge gave additional significance to a site, though of course bridges were always likely to be swept away by rivers in flood or by floating ice. An Anglo-Saxon document, probably of tenth-century date, describes the precise burdens on estates which had the responsibility of keeping the bridge over the river Medway at Rochester in a good state of repair; this wooden bridge, however, was often in a state of disrepair from natural forces before it was replaced by a stone construction in the late fourteenth century. Bridge maintenance was an important, universal burden on Anglo-Saxon communities, and there were clearly many more bridges in pre-Conquest England than find a mention in the contemporary records. There is no doubt that the bridge over the Trent at Nottingham, crossed, for example, by Wulfstan, bishop of Worcester, in the mid-eleventh century when he travelled from Worcester to York, was an important factor in the commercial development of Nottingham. The name of Bridgnorth gives significance to the struggle between Danes and Mercians for possession of this site. Bristol, originally *Brycgstowe* ('assembly place by the bridge'), grew up beside a bridge over the Avon. The particular importance of the bridge over the Cam is revealed by the fact that this bridge alone gave its name both to a town and a shire. Oxford owed its importance in the eleventh century not so much to the local ford as to a bridge, in existence by 1004, over the Cherwell. Not every settlement that was by a ford or bridge has preserved the elements *-ford* or *-bridge* in its name—there was a ford and a bridge at Abingdon, for example—but it is interesting that Stamfordbridge, the site of the famous battle in 1066 between Harold of England and the king of Norway, has preserved both elements together. The ford still survives below the bridge.

Because the immediate fate of Roman towns during the Anglo-Saxon Conquest is so obscure, it is difficult to estimate how important a place they occupied in the early kingdoms. It must be remembered that the Britons must have waged war against the Anglo-Saxons from Roman towns and along Roman roads, and the invaders would be naturally drawn to attack these towns. The most outstanding example of an attack on Roman towns is provided by Ceawlin's conquest of Gloucester, Cirencester and Bath. A British poem contains a probable reference to a battle at York. It is generally thought that once the Anglo-Saxons had subdued the Britons they left such urban centres alone. St. Guthlac certainly found Roman *Grantacæstir* (Cambridge) deserted in the second half of the seventh century, and an Anglo-Saxon poem, regarded by most historians as referring to Bath, describes a ruined and abandoned city. But care must be taken not to generalise. Communications tended to bring the Anglo-Saxons back again and again to old Roman towns. Some years after its conquest by Ceawlin, Cirencester was still sufficiently an important focal point to be the scene of a conflict between the Mercians and the West Saxons. It is often thought that a return to Roman towns was dictated by early missionaries conscious of a Roman past, but Paulinus found a royal reeve already resident at Lincoln. At Carlisle, which like Lincoln did not become a bishopric in the Anglo-Saxon period, the citizens showed

St. Cuthbert with pride the Roman fountain built into the old walls. The selection of centres by missionaries was determined not so much by a regard for the traditions of a Roman past, important though this sentiment was, as by considerations in the light of contemporary political conditions. Canterbury, with its Roman history, was the capital of the pagan kings of Kent before the arrival of Augustine, and York may have been an important early centre of the Deiran kings. The Bernician bishopric of Lindisfarne, with no Roman significance, was clearly designed to be near the royal rock-fortress of Bamburgh. On the other hand, the Celtic missionaries should not be regarded as having any aversion to Roman sites. Cedd used the Roman fort of *Othona* in Essex, now St. Peter's Bradwell, as a key missionary centre, and Chad's bishopric at Lichfield was just beside the Roman station of *Letocetum*.

A generalised conclusion is that where a Roman site was attractive and useful to the Anglo-Saxons in the light of their own strategic interests it was developed. Otherwise it was not. What mattered was not simply the relationship of a site to a road or trackway but also its proximity to water. Silchester, though on a Roman road to Winchester, was not on a useful waterway and so remained ruined and abandoned. Occasionally a site might be shifted a little to give better access to water; hence the Mercians abandoned *Uriconium* for nearby Wroxeter, by a ford over the Severn, and *Letocetum* for nearby Lichfield, above the Tame. In many instances the Roman sites continued to be of commercial value to the Anglo-Saxons because their natural advantages remained constant. London, the centre of a network of Roman roads, was at the lowest point at which the Thames could be bridged, and since Anglo-Saxon days the bridge there has been known as London Bridge. Canterbury, apart from being sited at the junction of Roman roads from Lympne, Richborough, Dover and London, was at the highest navigable point on the Stour. Colchester, at the junction of several Roman roads in Essex, was also strategically significant because it was the highest point on the river Colne to which ships could be brought. Cambridge became important not simply because it was at a Roman cross-roads but because it was at the junction of these roads with the river Cam, a main artery for traffic through the fens. The significance of the bridge at Cambridge has already been remarked. Winchester, the great West Saxon centre, was not only at the junction of Roman roads but also where an important Wessex ridgeway crossed the river Itchen. York, on a low plateau between the Ouse and the Foss and dominating the routes across the plain of York, was as useful to the Saxons as to the Romans. Not that the Anglo-Saxons were oblivious to the economic and military advantages of sites which had not been developed by the Romans. The rock of Bamburgh was well chosen as the fortress of the Bernician kings, though it had no Roman significance to commend it. Tamworth was without a Roman past but its situation near the confluence of the Tame and the Anker clearly gave it a strategic value to the Mercian rulers. Wilton, the shire town of Wiltshire, is at a strategic point on the riverways of Wiltshire as well as on a ridgeway and close to the protective barrier of the downs.

It is rarely that a reference survives to the actual founding of a town. The statement in the *Anglo-Saxon Chronicle* that Ine, king of Wessex, built Taunton (*c.* 720) is unique for the early period. Taunton was clearly a strategic West Saxon frontier post, on the Tone and at the head of the gap between the Quantocks and the Black Down Hills, commanding the way to the upper Exe valley.

In the more detailed records of the Anglo-Danish wars under Alfred and Edward a number of military strongholds or *burhs*, many of which subsequently developed into shire towns, are mentioned for the first time. Many must have had a long history in the pre-Viking period but simply escaped mention. Every intelligent Mercian ruler must have appreciated the well-nigh impregnable character of the rocky site of Nottingham long before the Danes captured and fortified it in 867. Bedford, reputed burial place of Offa, by virtue of its position near Watling Street and beside a ford over the Ouse must have been important long before the Alfred and Guthrum treaty made it a border town. Derby, previously *Northworthy*, was sited by the Roman fort of Littlechester on Ryknield Street and on the river Derwent, and guarded the Derwent valley. It must always have been a significant military centre in the Mercian kingdom. Manchester, on the river Irwell and at the junction of several Roman roads one of which led to York, was doubtless a Northumbrian fort before Edward the Elder re-fortified it in 919. Nevertheless, the Danish wars appear to have shaped the map of England by stimulating the development of certain strategically placed centres. And, as the contending armies gravitated by road and river to sites affording the best control over roads and rivers, so these fortified bases were easily open to expansion and development as administrative and commercial settlements. Not that every *burh* necessarily afforded commercial and administrative prospects. The *Burghal Hidage*, a West

Saxon document compiled 911–19, lists over 30 *burhs* in Wessex and south Mercia, a third of which were small military camps of temporary importance which never developed into urban communities. Quite a few of the fortresses of the early tenth century cannot even be certainly identified, as, for example, *Eorpeburnan*, *Bremesbyrig*, *Weardbyrig Scergeat* and *Wingingamere*. It is not impossible that such *burhs* have sometimes developed under another name, but this is not so in every instance. An essential factor was the position of the *burh* in relation to a riverway. Though Eddisbury overlooked the Cheshire plain and Chirbury controlled the main route into central Wales through Montgomeryshire, neither fortress was beside a river-bank. The position of Towcester on Watling Street and on the river Tove made it very important militarily and Edward the Elder built stone fortifications there in 917; but the Tove valley was far less prosperous than the valley of the Nene, and so Northampton at the head of the navigable waters of the Nene ultimately became the shire town of Northamptonshire. In a rather similar way Buckingham rather than Aylesbury became the shire town of Buckinghamshire; though not, unlike Aylesbury, well placed with regard to the main lines of communication by road, its position on a hill, on an easily defensible peninsula, on the river Ouse and in command of the valley of the upper Ouse gave it a greater importance. Hertford developed on the river which figures as a frontier in the Alfred and Guthrum treaty, the Lea, at its junction with three tributaries. Leicester and Huntingdon were two important Danish army bases. Leicester, with its Roman origin, was by a junction on the Fosse Way but derived particular value from its semi-encirclement by the river Soar. Huntingdon developed by Roman Godmanchester and the junction of Roman roads, one of which was Ermine Street, but again it is the river Ouse which is the really significant feature. Torksey in Lincolnshire, probably one of the Seven Boroughs, was at the junction of a dyke joining the river Witham to the Trent and controlling the crossing of the Trent at that point. Gloucester, greatly favoured by Æthelflæd of Mercia, derived its importance not simply from the junction there of Roman roads from Caerleon, Worcester and Cirencester, but also from its position on the Severn which here becomes tidal.

A distinct group of important sites are the coastal ports, and these may be mentioned separately. They developed on peninsulas and along ridges of raised ground by river mouths and beside shallow basins or lagoons affording a sheltered anchorage. Considerable coastal change and erosion often makes it difficult to visualise the Anglo-Saxon settlement and in some instances—as with Selsey and the first Saxon Hastings—the original site has entirely vanished. Many ports the Anglo-Saxons inherited from the Roman period, particularly Richborough at the southern mouth of the Wantsum as it flowed then between Kent and Thanet; but also Reculver, Dover, Lympne, Hythe, Pevensey, Chichester, Southampton and Exeter. As the port of Richborough silted up, the Anglo-Saxons developed Sandwich ('village on the sands') at the mouth of the Stour on newly forming sand flats. By the eleventh century Sandwich was clearly a port of great strategic significance to the Anglo-Saxons, and was used by Æthelred II, Cnut, Harthacnut and Edward the Confessor. Other non-Roman ports in the South-east were Hastings, Romney, Lydd and Folkestone; farther west the non-Roman ports of Portland, Dartmouth and Fowey were probably overshadowed, at least in the later Saxon period, by Exeter. The Danes began their attack in the ninth century by striking at these southern harbours. In 840, for example, battles were fought at Portland and Southampton. In the second wave virtually all the southern harbours were attacked at one time or another, but the Danes found themselves unable to gain a foothold along this coast. The West Saxons fortified many of their harbours as *burhs*, and the *Burghal Hidage* mentions Hastings, Chichester, Portchester, Southampton, Wareham and Exeter. Several references occur to the harbours of the south coast in the reign of Edward the Confessor. Swein Godwineson is found at Bosham and Dartmouth in 1049—Harold sailed from Bosham on the journey which took him to Normandy *c.* 1064—and in 1052 Harold collected serviceable ships from Pevensey, Romney, Hythe, Folkestone and Dover. Along the east coast the Danes made Greenwich on the Thames and Gainsborough on the Trent their main naval bases in the early eleventh century. The name of the port of Grimsby on the east coast reveals its Scandinavian associations, and so too does Whitby in Yorkshire. On the west coast, Chester on the Dee was a major shipping centre; Æthelred the Unready's fleet was stationed at Chester in 1000, prior to a planned attack on Cumbria. Even more so perhaps was Bristol on Avon on a peninsula between the Frome and the Avon, and from here Harold set out by sea to ravage Wales in 1063.

The growth of the borough and of industry

The Anglo-Saxon term for a market town was originally *port*, and each *port* would be under the supervision of a *port*-reeve. The term *burh*, from which derives borough, originally signified a fortified place, be it a *port* or not. By the time of Athelstan, however, *burh* and *port* were interchangeable terms.

Only those *burhs* or boroughs which possessed economic advantages developed as commercial centres. The possession of a thriving market has been seen by some historians as the distinguishing feature of an Anglo-Saxon borough, for these boroughs do not otherwise conform to a common pattern. Not every borough, for example, possessed a borough court. In others, a court was so important an institution that Cnut drew a distinction between borough law and the law of the land. A distinct law for traders was probably essential, and there may have existed experts in borough law in the major towns. The dwellers in the borough, the burghers or burgesses, were distinctive in that they held their tenements in the borough at a fixed rent, generally from the king, according to established customs. They were, for example, subject to separate taxation from the countryside; they did not pay danegeld but they were treated as part of the royal demesne, subject to the same burdens as well as to the same privileges. The crown was careful to retain over-all control of emerging boroughs, remaining the principal landholder and receiver of revenues from rents and taxes, though allocating as a general rule a third of urban dues to the earl by the time of the Norman Conquest. It is clear that for some time before 1066 lay and ecclesiastical lords had been acquiring property in boroughs, treating the property so acquired as a very profitable part of a manor, but despite this trend there is no doubt that boroughs remained essentially royal property.

Placed at sites which offered favourable natural conditions for the development of trade, the growth of urban markets was further stimulated by deliberate royal policy. To minimise the danger of fraud and the sale of stolen goods, Edward the Elder forbade the exchange of goods outside a market town, an injunction repeated by Athelstan with the exception of goods under 20 pence. Though Athelstan subsequently relaxed this prohibition, men still had to trade before trustworthy witnesses and the best place for safe trade must have remained the boroughs where the great markets were held. And it would be in borough courts, known to have been in existence by the reign of Edgar at the latest, that traders would secure the most informed hearing of any suit they wished to bring. Further, what evidence there is suggests that the boroughs were held to be under the king's peace, so that penalties for acts of violence were more severe within the borough than in the countryside and the pursuit of the blood-feud was prohibited. Such conditions would permit the peaceful pursuits of trading and facilitate the steady development of commercial activity. Continuing royal concern with fair exchange in the boroughs is reflected in Cnut's attempt to standardise one borough law of exculpation or oath-swearing.

The *Burghal Hidage* assigns an area of land to each borough roughly proportionate to the extent of wall to be defended. This was on the principle that one *hide* provided one man and four men were required to defend each pole or perch of wall. The 2,400 *hides* assigned to Winchester indicate a tenth-century wall of 3,300 yards, and it is striking that the length of the old Roman wall at Winchester was about 3,280 yards. This shows most vividly that the Saxon *burh* was contained within the existing defences. At Wallingford, counting the river-bank which forms the fourth side of the defences and where the other three earthworks still survive, the rectangular fortress is some 3,030 yards in total length; the *Burghal Hidage* assessment of 2,400 *hides* indicates a wall to be defended of 3,300 yards. Wareham was rather smaller. Not counting the river this time, which forms the fourth side of the fortress, the existing earthworks are about 2,180 yards in length and the 1,600 *hides* of the *Burghal Hidage* in fact allow for the defence of 2,200 yards. Provision was made at Buckingham for a wall of 2,200 yards to be defended, at Oxford and Chichester for one of 2,062, at Cricklade and Wilton for one of 1,925, and at Malmesbury for one of 1,650. Several *burhs* were smaller still and were never to develop into major urban centres. Provision was made at Tisbury or possibly Chisbury in Wiltshire, for example, for the defence of only some 687 yards, and at Lyng in Somerset for that of a mere 137 yards. Even the larger *burhs*, however, were quite small by modern standards. The inhabitants of the boroughs may generally have been unwilling as a consequence of the Scandinavian wars to live outside the fortified walls, and the keeping of cultivated plots within the walls down to the Norman Conquest meant that there could be a serious land shortage. As early as *c.* 680 there was a property boom in London, and the seventh-century kings of Kent legislated to control the buying and selling of property there by Kentishmen. A ninth-century Canterbury document mentions that by customary law 2 ft. had to be left between houses to allow for eavesdrip, so that buildings were evidently close together. A document of 957–8 in which the community of the Old Minster, Winchester, exchanged 12 *hides* of the land in the country for two acres in the city suggests that urban land was indeed very expensive.

Domesday Book (1086) records the number of tenements in the boroughs and in many instances the number given has been complete enough to permit an approximate calculation of the total population. It is generally suspected that the obtainable figures may be a little on the low side, but they do provide an approximation and a guide to relative size. Using statistics in Domesday Book, for example, it has been estimated that the population of York was about 8,000 in 1066, but an eleventh-century writer estimated it at 30,000. Though this figure is certainly too high, it has been rightly pointed out that a contemporary is unlikely to have been quite so wide of the mark as the contrast with 8,000 implies. Bearing in mind, therefore, the approximate nature of these estimates, it may be said that Winchester probably had a population of some 6,000 to 8,000 and may have been one of the three largest cities in England, the two larger being London and York. Domesday Book unfortunately gives no statistics for London, but on the grounds of the size of the Roman city a population of at least 25,000 by the time of the Norman Conquest may be suggested. Other urban centres were diminutive by comparison. Canterbury probably had a population of about 2,500, Colchester probably well over 2,000, Sandwich and Huntingdon about 2,000, Cambridge about 1,600, Northampton about 1,500, Ipswich over 1,300, Southampton at least 1,200, Warwick and Shrewsbury at least 1,000. A few towns were rather larger than the average but not as populous as the three main cities. Norwich, for example, probably numbered about 5,000, Oxford between 4,000 and 5,000. On the other hand some boroughs were minute. Stafford had a population of probably less than a thousand.

A further indication of relative status is provided by the distribution of moneyers in a borough. During the time of the Heptarchy each king minted his own coins if he so desired and even archbishops might mint separately. The tenth-century kings of Wessex confined the minting of coins to specified boroughs and maintained a strict control over the standard of the coinage. Athelstan stipulated that at Canterbury there should be seven moneyers, two of whom were for the archbishop and one for the abbot of St. Augustine's, in Rochester three, one of whom was for the bishop, in London eight, in Winchester six, in Lewes,

Southampton, Exeter, Wareham and Shaftesbury two, and in each of the other boroughs one. Æthelred II decreed that in every principal town there should be three moneyers, in every other town one, but the principal towns are not specified. In the later Anglo-Saxon period there were between 60 and 70 mints operating in the land. By the reign of Edward the Confessor there were 20 moneyers in London producing nearly a quarter of the whole output of coins in England. The ten or so moneyers at York produced about a tenth of the total output, Lincoln and Winchester producing only slightly less. Next in order of importance probably came a group of three boroughs, Chester, Canterbury and Oxford, and then a group of about four, Thetford, Gloucester, Worcester and possibly Norwich and Ipswich. The remaining boroughs were small by comparison.

Not a great deal is known about the layout of an Anglo-Saxon town. Thetford is a rare instance of an urban site which has been intensively excavated to reveal the Anglo-Saxon plan. The Danish town stretched for almost a mile along a cobbled, flint roadway which was 20 ft. wide in one place; the road was flanked by scattered houses, both oval and rectangular and occasionally two-storeyed, but all of wood. By contrast to this kind of ribbon development, excavations at Lydford (Devon) are revealing a regular grid-like arrangement of streets inside the *burh*, with ditches and palisades dividing off property.

A glimpse of a southern town is afforded by the so-called Winton Domesday, a survey of Winchester carried out in the reign of Henry I to determine the revenues from the city in the time of Edward the Confessor. This survey reveals the trades of the town in the names of the streets which bring to life some of the multifarious activities of an early urban community—Tailors' Street and Shield Makers' Street, Tanners' Street and Shoewrights' Street, Fleshmongers' Street and Gold Street. Such names were lost in the course of time as Fleshmongers' Street, for example, became St. Peter's Street and Gold Street became Southgate. Certain towns may well have developed skills in the manufacture of particular products. Canterbury is known to have been producing beer in the later Anglo-Saxon period, and Chester also. A pottery industry existed at *Hamwih*, now a suburb of Southampton, revealed by excavation. Excavations at Thetford have shown that apart from a pottery industry there existed in the town a woollen industry and bronze and iron workings. Winchester was noted for cloth manufacture

What may be described as industrial activity formed a not unimportant part of the economic life of Anglo-Saxon England. In visualising Anglo-Saxon society as essentially agricultural it is easy to overlook the whole range of equipment and commodities required even by an agricultural society which would have to be produced by little groups of industrial workers. Salt, lead and iron were indispensable minerals, and the exploitation or mining of such raw materials was carried out where such activity was possible. We do not know on what scale this was done for lack of evidence, but salt was extracted at numerous centres, either along the coast or inland near brine springs of rock salt, by boiling the water. The Welshman Nennius, writing *c*. 825, numbered the salt works of either Droitwich or Nantwich among the seven wonders of Britain. As an example of inter-dependent industries, the lead mines, of the Mendips and the Peak District for example, would produce the raw material for the manufacture of salt pans to keep the salt workings operative. Lead was used for roofing purposes as early as the seventh century, and weights and measures were of lead. Silver extracted from the lead and from the lead mines would be sent, in part at least, to the various mints of the land. King Æthelwulf was asked to send lead for the roofing of the church of Ferrières in Gaul. Once the art of building in stone began to gain ground in ecclesiastical circles in the late seventh century, suitable stone for building probably came to be quarried locally on a considerable scale: not every new structure can have been put together with stones removed from some ruined Roman edifice. Traces of quarrying occur in Domesday Book. One quarry, for example, at Watton in Nottinghamshire, produced millstones, a necessity as the number of mills multiplied.

Such activity could go back to very early times. Lead mines are mentioned at Wirksworth in Derbyshire in the ninth century, salt workings on the river Salwarp in Worcestershire in the early eighth, an iron mine at Lyminge in Kent in the second half of the seventh. A constant supply of iron must have been required, and iron mines were to be found, for example, in the Forest of Dean and the Kentish Weald. Domesday Book records several iron forges in Lincolnshire, Yorkshire and Northamptonshire, and a thriving iron industry at Gloucester provided—no doubt among many other articles—iron rivets for royal ships. Taxes at Gloucester were paid partly in iron. Smiths are recorded in Domesday Book at Hereford and Glastonbury, for example, and such scattered references suggest that the forges of ironworkers must have been numerous throughout much of England. Smiths must indeed have been valuable members of society. The laws of Ine of Wessex ordered every nobleman moving to new territory to take his smith with him, and many smiths must have catered for very localised markets. In the *Colloquy* of Ælfric of Eynsham, the smith observes that without his craft the ploughman would possess no coulter, share or goad, the fisherman no hook, the seamster no needle. This is the sort of practical day-to-day activity which must be borne in mind in any approach to the social life of early England. Keeping the fishermen of England in fish-hooks or Anglo-Saxon women in needles must alone have been no small undertaking. The mechanics of needle production, for example, both of bone and of iron, and subsequent distribution in Anglo-Saxon England would provide a fascinating sidelight on the industrial organisation of a primitive society, if only the evidence were available.

There must have been some fairly large groups of craftsmen and labourers to be found in Anglo-Saxon England engaged co-operatively in industry and manufacture, in the salt and iron workings, for example, and not least in the production of cloth. Cloth manufacture went on in countless homes throughout the land for domestic consumption certainly, but the cloaks that Offa exported to Gaul, of standardised type and size, and the beautifully embroidered vestments of English production so valued at Rome, imply the existence of major centres of production, associated with which would be fullers, weavers, seamsters, and dyers. The dyeing industry itself must have involved many workers.

Most numerous of all craftsmen must have been the woodworkers in an age when the majority of implements, utensils and dwellings were of wood. Unfortunately for the archaeologist and historian, wooden objects like cloth invariably perish with the passage of time. This is not true to such an extent with household glass and pots of baked clay, which survive in fragments and are the most common relics of a bygone age, particularly, of course, pottery. Glass vessels were probably not common in the houses of the Anglo-Saxons. Bede records that glass-working was an unknown art in Northumbria before Benedict Biscop brought over glass-workers from Gaul in the 670s, at about the same time as Wilfrid of York did likewise. By the 760s the art seems to have been unknown again in Northumbria, for an abbot was obliged to send abroad for a good craftsman. It has been suspected that the manufacture of glass never acquired much importance in the industrial life of

Anglo-Saxon England and that most of the glass used by the Anglo-Saxons was imported. An early centre of production, however, may have been Faversham in Kent, and traces of what may be tenth-century glass furnaces at Glastonbury were uncovered during excavation. It may be that future archaeological discoveries will modify the present knowledge of glass manufacture in England before the Norman Conquest. So far as pottery is concerned, most work has been done on East Anglian fragments and deficient knowledge at present of other regions may set East Anglian pots a little out of perspective. In the course of the seventh century rough, hand-made pottery gave way in East Anglia to wheel-thrown products, but there is some doubt as to how rapidly or extensively the new technique spread beyond East Anglia. At *Hamwih* local pottery was hand-made and wheel-thrown pottery imported. Wheel-thrown pottery is known to have developed in Kent, but the main local centres of wheel-thrown production in the late Saxon period which can be classified by distinct 'wares' are Ipswich, Thetford, Stamford, Torksey, Lincoln, York and possibly Chester. Ipswich 'ware' had a continuous history going back into the seventh century. These bits and pieces of pot provide the historian and archaeologist with their most direct contact with the material culture of an Anglo-Saxon home; they reveal also the existence of flourishing potteries in some at least of the urban communities of early England.

There is no evidence for craft gilds in the towns of Anglo-Saxon England and no reference to an Anglo-Saxon merchant gild, but gilds of a largely undefined nature did exist in many boroughs. A *cnihtengild* or knight gild existed at Canterbury as early as the mid-ninth century, probably a gild of armed retainers though the precise significance of '*cniht*' here is a little uncertain. A thegns' gild existed at Cambridge by *c.* 1000 at the latest. The members of this gild undertook to aid any of their fellow-members, even to engage in a blood-feud if necessary on behalf of a gild-brother. Most of the gilds of Anglo-Saxon England seem to have been mutual-benefit societies, concerned to guarantee protection to their members against legal penalties and other social hazards. In Athelstan's reign, the bishops and reeves who are defined as belonging to London, both nobles and peasants also, joined in a peace-gild to maintain law and order, suppress theft and insure themselves against loss. On the whole, the members of gilds appear to have been men of property and wealth. The gild statutes of Abbotsbury refer to the gift of a gildhall by Urkir, a founder member. The typical gild,

in fact, had a hall or meeting place for meetings and occasional ban-
quets. In large measure the gild-brothers acted to one another as would
the kindred but they still had obligations, of course, to their own individual kindred and to their individual lords.

Chapter three

England and the
wider world

It must not be thought that Anglo-Saxon England was an isolated world, cut off from the Continent and insulated by the sea against European influences. The links between Britain and the Continent were strong as late as *c*. 450. The Anglo-Saxons brought with them their own contacts with their north Germanic and Danish homelands, and with the Franks and the Rhineland. The early English Church was in regular contact with Rome and the continental mission field, and the cultural influence of the Mediterranean world on Anglo-Saxon England was great. Pilgrims from England visited Rome, Constantinople, and Jerusalem. The majority of Anglo-Saxons spent the greater part of their lives bound to the soil, but the researches of economic historians in recent years have stressed the importance of commerce between England and Europe even in the early Middle Ages. Increased emphasis has been placed on constant maritime activity during these centuries and on the continuous development of trade throughout the Anglo-Saxon period, obscured certainly by the usual deficiencies of source material but nevertheless discernible behind political and diplomatic exchanges and in fragmentary but fascinating references to merchants and their dealings.

Diplomatic activity

While not a great many instances of diplomatic contact between Anglo-Saxon England and the barbarian states of west Europe have been recorded, those that have imply the existence of a widely flung diplomatic network.

In *c*. 560–5, apparently before he became king, Æthelberht of Kent was married to Bertha, daughter of the Merovingian king, Charibert of Paris. It is generally held that this marriage symbolises the unique cultural contact at this time between Kent and Frankish Gaul, and it symbolises also the commercial contact. It is significant that one of the earliest groups of Merovingian gold coins found in south-east England and dating to the late sixth century comes not only from the Paris area but from Bordeaux, also a part of Charibert's kingdom. The family link was remembered many years later. When Edwin of Northumbria was slain in 634, Queen Æthelburh, daughter of Æthelberht, sent her youngest sons to the protection of her friend, Dagobert I, king of the Franks.

It was unusual, however, for an Anglo-Saxon prince to marry a foreign princess, even a Celtic princess. Generally they took Anglo-Saxon ladies of noble birth as their queens. An instance is known in which arrangements for the marriage of a prince to a Frankish princess broke down. Offa of Mercia failed to obtain one of Charlemagne's daughters for his son, Ecgfrith. Æthelwulf's visit to Rome in 855 was followed by his marriage, on his way home, to Judith, the flighty daughter of the Emperor Charles the Bald, Charlemagne's grandson, a unique moment in the annals of the West Saxon dynasty and one which says much for Æthelwulf's prestige among the Franks. The only other West Saxon king to marry a foreign princess was Æthelred II, who took as his second wife Emma, daughter of Richard I, duke of Normandy, subsequently the queen also of Cnut. The giving of daughters in marriage on an international level was a two-way process. Offa of Mercia would not give one of his daughters to one of Charlemagne's sons when Charlemagne refused a bride for Ecgfrith. Alfred began a whole series of West Saxon political marriages when he gave one of his daughters, Ælfthryth, to Baldwin II, Count of Flanders, a Frankish buffer-state against Scandinavian attack; it is interesting in this connection that Alfred's stepmother, Judith, had eventually married Baldwin I of Flanders. The marriage of Ælfthryth led to several decades of friendly relations between the counts of Flanders and the West Saxon dynasty, and to an era of similar unions. Edward the Elder gave his daughter, Eadgifu, in marriage to Charles the Simple, king of the west Franks, so that she became the ancestor of the last Carolingians. Athelstan gave one sister to Hugh, duke of the Franks, another probably to the king of Burgundy, and another, Edith, who became the ancestor in the female line of several of the great emperors of the eleventh century, to Otto, son of Henry I, and subsequently the Emperor Otto I.

English intervention in continental politics reached a peak in the reign of Athelstan. Alan, count of Brittany, and Louis, son of Charles the Simple, were both brought up at his court. In 936 Athelstan gave Alan the necessary military support to restore himself in Brittany. Louis, as the son of Charles and Eadgifu, was Athelstan's nephew, and he fled to England on the deposition of his father. In 936 envoys came to the West Saxon court from Hugh, duke of the Franks (since 926 Athelstan's brother-in-law), seeking Louis as king of the Franks. After taking oaths of safe conduct, Athelstan returned his nephew but Louis IV's reign was troubled by external attack and internal rebellion. In 939 Athelstan sent a fleet to aid him against Otto I. The expedition was not a success. According to a continental authority, the protest of Edmund of Wessex to Hugh over the duke's rebellious attitude to Louis IV did bring results, influencing Hugh to make peace with his king. Yet another prince who appears to have been brought up at the court of Athelstan was Hakon, son of Harold Fairhair, king of Norway, with whom Athelstan was on friendly terms and from whom he received gifts. It was customary for diplomatic exchanges to be accompanied by gifts. When Duke Hugh sought the sister of Athelstan in marriage he sent a whole range of precious luxuries and rare relics. It was in accordance with this international practice that Athelstan sent hardly less inferior gifts to Hugh in return.

On such transactions, envoys were necessarily employed. Adelolf, son of Baldwin II and Ælfthryth, negotiated the marriage between Athelstan's sister and Duke Hugh, and he brought Hugh's gifts to the West Saxon ruler. In 936, at the time of the negotiations over Louis, lighted beacons on the clifftops signified the safe arrival of those concerned to watchers across the channel. It is clear that the coming and going of envoys had been a regular feature of the European scene from the earliest period. In the reign of the eastern Emperor, Justinian I (527–65), Frankish envoys visited Constantinople accompanied by a delegation from across the channel, probably from Kent. In 669 Egbert, king of Kent, sent an envoy into Gaul to conduct Archbishop Theodore from Paris to Kent. In 678 Ecgfrith, king of Northumbria, sent envoys to Theodoric, king of the west Franks, and to his mayor, Ebroin, asking them to intercept Wilfrid of York on his way to Rome. When Ebroin discovered that Wilfrid was among the Frisians, he in turn sent envoys to Aldgisl, king of the Frisians, demanding that Wilfrid be handed over. Aldgisl did not surrender Wilfrid, who escaped to the territories of Pectarit, king of the Lombards of north Italy. When Pectarit received letters from England requesting that he detain Wilfrid, he also refused. Pectarit evidently had closer connections with England than are recorded, for in the early 670s, during a temporary exile, he was on the point of sailing to Britain when his restoration was accomplished. So widely did Bishop Wilfrid's diplomatic influence range that in the mid-670s he was able to arrange the return from Ireland of the Merovingian prince, Dagobert II, to his native Gaul via Northumbria. There must have been a constant coming and going of envoys and messengers of one kind or another throughout this period and particularly at the time of the Carolingian Empire. Pepin, ruler of the Franks and first of the Carolingian monarchs, is known to have sent letters to a king as far afield from him as Eadberht of Northumbria (737–58), and in the affairs of this distant kingdom Charlemagne is known to have taken a keen interest. He was shocked by the assassination of Æthelred, king of Northumbria, in 796; and in 806 or 808, when Eardwulf, king of Northumbria, was expelled he sought help from Charlemagne and Pope Leo III. Both pope and emperor were able to effect his restoration, an interesting indication of the degree of influence in England possessed by the great ruler of the Franks.

From the ninth century, Peter's Pence, a papal tax, was paid regularly to the church at Rome. There must have been continuous diplomatic exchange between the English kings and the popes, though only a few papal letters to English rulers have been preserved. Pope Paul I wrote to Eadberht, king of Northumbria, for example, about the secularisation of certain monastic lands in Northumbria. A flurry of diplomatic activity by churchmen and lay princes surrounded Wilfrid's appeals to Rome. Cenwulf of Merica was involved in protracted diplomacy concerning the proposed archbishopric of Lichfield. To give a final example, the papal legate of Pope John XV visited Æthelred II with a view to ending the discord between the king and Richard I, duke of Normandy. Peace terms were arranged, each side undertaking not to harbour the other's enemies.

The Northumbrian royal exiles of the seventh and eighth centuries usually sought refuge among the Picts and Scots. The first Anglo-Saxon ruler known to have fled to the Continent was Sigeberht of East Anglia in the second decade of the seventh century. But what personal connection he had which led him into Frankish territory is unrecorded. Before he became king of Wessex, Egbert found refuge during his exile in Gaul, and quite probably at the court of Charlemagne. As early as the 790s, Charlemagne wrote to the archbishop of Canterbury and the bishop of Lindsey maintaining that he had sheltered certain exiles from England, whose lord had died, not out of enmity to Offa but from the hope that, through the archbishop's intercession, they might be allowed to return in peace to their native land. An interesting aspect of relations between England and the Continent in the tenth and eleventh centuries is the continuing close contact between England and Flanders and the asylum given in Flanders to English political refugees. Dunstan spent some time at Ghent. When the atheling Alfred, son of Æthelred II, intended visiting England, he endeavoured, though unsuccessfully, to obtain military aid from Baldwin V. It was to Bruges that Emma, the mother of Harthacnut by Cnut, sailed in 1037 when she was expelled from England by Harold I; and from Bruges that Harthacnut set out in 1040 to claim the English kingdom on Harold's death. Earl Godwine fled to Bruges in 1050, and in 1065 his son, Tostig, was married to Judith, half-sister of Baldwin V. Judith was Edward the Confessor's second cousin through her kinship with the ducal house of Normandy, but relations between King Edward and Baldwin were strained even before the latter's reception of Godwine. Baldwin had given refuge in 1048 to a fleet of Viking raiders who had been chased away from the shores of Essex by Edward. But Baldwin was also at war with the Emperor Henry III, and when Henry requested Edward to blockade the count of Flanders at sea to prevent the movement of Flemish ships, Edward obliged. Baldwin was forced to submit, but it must have afforded him a measure of satisfaction to offer sanctuary to the Godwines. There is nothing to show that William of Normandy received any official help from Baldwin in the events that led up to the defeat of Harold Godwineson at Hastings, but, on the other hand, Baldwin did give shelter to some of Harold's family after 1066.

Treaties were not infrequently arranged during the Anglo-Saxon period between the rulers of different states. Archbishop Theodore mediated the terms of a settlement between Æthelred of Mercia and Ecgfrith of Northumbria in 679. Edmund of Wessex gave Cumbria to Malcolm I, king of the Scots, in 945 on condition that Malcolm became his helper by sea and land. Similar but less spectacular agreements with the Scots overlords in Lothian were made later in the tenth century.

Before he became king of England, Harthacnut made his treaty with Magnus of Norway, that if either of them died without heir the kingdom should pass to the survivor. In 1063 Edward the Confessor made what must have been a treaty with the two Welsh princes, Bleddyn and Rhiwallon, on much the same lines as Edmund's with Malcolm I, namely that they would be faithful in all things to Edward and that they would serve him everywhere by land and sea.

Travelling routes

With the survival of written records from the seventh century onwards several references occur to harbours and ports which were on important routeways to the Continent or to Ireland. Such references provide a valuable if partial framework for the system of cross-Channel and transmaritime communications behind Anglo-Saxon commercial activities.

For the Britons crossing from Fowey to Brittany, the English Channel was known alternatively as the British Sea or the Southern Sea. The North Sea was thought of by those nations which bordered it as a dangerous sea. It took three days to cross it from Denmark to south-east England, even with a favourable south-east wind. Most of the traffic to the Continent from England appears to have gone from south-east ports. Perhaps the most important Channel crossing in the pre-Viking period was from a Kentish port to *Quentovic*, near Étaples at the mouth of the river Canche and at the head of a network of Roman roads across Neustria. In 678 Wilfrid of York was believed by his enemies to be crossing to Étaples because it was the most direct route to Rome. Coins found in south-east England from the sixth century show that many came from the mint at *Quentovic*, and that the link with this port was close even then. Archbishop Theodore sailed from there to Kent in 669, and in 718 St. Boniface sailed from London to *Quentovic*. A longer crossing was adopted by St. Willibald, a cousin of St. Boniface, in 720 when he sailed from *Hamwih* (Southampton), described as an emporium or trading centre, to Rouen on the Seine. It was possible also to sail from Wareham in Dorset. The Seine was obviously well travelled by Saxon merchants for in 634 Dagobert I established the Fair of St. Denis at Paris, held annually and attended by traders from England.

Wilfrid of York, whether by accident or design, fooled his enemies in

678 by crossing not to Gaul as expected but to Frisia. By the late 670s the Frisians had already emerged as influential traders. Boniface sailed from London in 716 to the great Frisian port of Wijk bij Duurstede—Dorestad—on the Lek (Rhine). There is little doubt that Dorestad and *Quentovic* formed the most important commercial centres on the north coast of Europe in the pre-Viking period. But more protracted sea voyages than those simply from south-east England to north Gaul were made in the seventh and eighth centuries. As early as the late sixth century, Irish merchants were to be found in Gaul. Ceolfrith, abbot of Monkwearmouth and Jarrow, sailed to Gaul from the mouth of the Humber. In the late eighth century Frisian merchants must have travelled regularly from Frisia to York, where there was a Frisian colony, and Alcuin despatched wine and tin to York from Gaul. It is clear that all Britain was accessible to merchant ships—Columba is said on one occasion to have been awaiting the arrival of a Gallic merchant ship on Iona—even though, in the main, most traffic would be to the nearest ports in the most prosperous regions. Similarly, much of west Europe was probably open to English merchants. In the second half of the eighth century the name of an Anglo-Saxon merchant, Botta, is recorded at Marseilles. At that time Marseilles on the Rhône was the great southern commercial outpost of Merovingian Gaul and one of the most important centres of Mediterranean trade. Exactly how far afield a merchant might roam is difficult to say. Probably few if any Anglo-Saxon merchants ever ventured beyond Rome and Italy. The great trade routes of the world, from Britain and beyond in the west to India and China in the east, converged on Constantinople, capital of the Byzantine Empire, but through legions of middlemen. Luxury goods were not brought direct from the far corners of the world nor did Anglo-Saxon merchants sail the Seven Seas. In the early seventh century a Byzantine ship carrying wheat was blown by a storm into what were regarded as strange and distant waters, finding itself eventually off what could have been the Cornish coast. It is quite clear that even Byzantine vessels did not make a practice of sailing such distances.

In the ninth and tenth centuries new patterns of communications appeared, and by *c.* 1000 merchants do seem to have been sailing on more extended voyages than in the pre-Viking age. The Vikings discovered Greenland and *Vinland*, the latter generally believed to have been located in North America; they explored the Arctic circle. The Danes possessed a great trading centre at Hedeby which was well frequented by western merchants. King Alfred was even interested in the Norse routes to the White Sea, and received an account from an Englishman, Wulfstan, of a voyage he had made from Hedeby to Truso at the mouth of the Vistula. Nevertheless, most merchant shipping must still have been carried on between old ports and newly emerging centres in the north-west of Europe. Dorestad was destroyed by the Vikings in 863 and subsequently eclipsed by Tiel. As the mouth of the Canche silted up, cross-Channel traffic to Gaul tended to go not to _Quentovic_ but to Wissant, north of Boulogne. This it continued to do until Wissant was itself eclipsed in the eleventh century by Calais. Boulogne, an ancient Roman port, reappears in the records of the ninth and tenth centuries. In 892 the great Danish army, as it was known, crossed to the estuary of the Lympne from Boulogne, and _c._ 940 Catroe, a pilgrim from Scotland, went from Lympne to Boulogne. In 936 Louis IV landed at Boulogne, and in 1036 the atheling Alfred crossed from there on his ill-fated expedition to England. Boulogne was in the countship of Flanders, which, in the later Anglo-Saxon period, witnessed the growth of great commercial centres like Ghent, Bruges, St. Omer, Cambrai and Tournai, linked to England by vital trading interests particularly in cloth.

Not all travelling round the Continent was by sea. Many English pilgrims and merchants also went overland through Gaul to reach the Mediterranean. Archbishop Theodore, on his way to England, travelled overland through Gaul via Paris and _Quentovic_. When Tostig, son of Earl Godwine, visited Rome in the 1060s he went down the Rhineland and through Saxony. By the late eighth century merchants were passing through Gaul with pilgrims _en route_ to Rome and attempting to dodge Frankish tolls by passing themselves off as pilgrims. In 1027 Cnut travelled to Rome to attend the coronation of the Emperor Conrad II, and while doing so obtained from the emperor and from Rudolph, king of Burgundy, the concession that English and Danish merchants and pilgrims be permitted to journey to Rome through their lands free from tolls and other hindrances. The overland routes across Europe, in fact, were probably the main thoroughfares of trade in the west throughout the early Middle Ages. No doubt, as Saracen and Viking pirates infested the seas, the land was a safer place; but many Anglo-Saxon pilgrims to Rome were slain by Arabs in the alpine passes in the early tenth century. Thieves, of course, were an additional menace. When Harold's brother, Tostig, and his retinue were robbed on their way home from Rome a common criminal act became a diplomatic incident. Tostig had to be placated with rich papal gifts.

Of established routes of commercial contact between England and the Celtic world less is known; but Bristol and Chester clearly developed as ports on the western seaboard of England to cope with Irish trade from Dublin and Limerick. Harold, fleeing from Edward the Confessor, sailed to Ireland from Bristol in 1050.

Coinage and trade

Numismatics is still a young science and it is only in recent years that the history of coinage in Anglo-Saxon England has grown clearer. There are still unresolved problems, but the main stages of development can be traced in outline. From the point of view of commercial activity, a most important feature of Anglo-Saxon coinage is the close dependency on Frankish coinage and the association of reform in Gaul with reform in England. The Celtic kingdoms of the British Isles, by contrast, appear to have possessed no continuous coinage.

Romano-British coinage ceased *c*. 430, and the Anglo-Saxons were some time before minting their own. From *c*. 575 Merovingian gold coins, entering Britain in growing quantities, were used as currency by Anglo-Saxons as well as by Franks. These coins have been found primarily in Kent and to a lesser degree in the Thames valley, but outliers have been found in East Anglia and even in Yorkshire. The Sutton Hoo ship burial contained a hoard of Merovingian gold coins dating to the seventh century. It was the presence of these coins which made possible the approximate dating of the burial of the ship and its treasures. Once the importation of gold coins was under way it was but a matter of time to the beginning of production in England, probably *c*. 675. By *c*. 680 the Franks were switching from a gold to a silver currency, a step which has been described as the beginning of a new age of commercial activity in the west, for silver is believed to have been a much more serviceable metal for day-to-day exchange in western Europe at this time than gold, essentially the symbol of a more luxurious Byzantine commerce. The Anglo-Saxons were following the Franks in the minting of silver coins by *c*. 690, coins known to numismatists as *sceattas*. When the advent of the Carolingian dynasty to power in Gaul saw a reform of the Frankish silver coinage *c*. 755, the coin now known as the Anglo-

Saxon silver penny followed in Kent *c.* 775–80. Such pennies normally have the name of the ruler for whom they were struck on the obverse side, and the name of the moneyer, the craftsman responsible for their quality, on the reverse. The name of the place where the coins were minted might also be given. Offa of Mercia gained for the silver penny a wide circulation in the south of England when he adopted it as his coin. The silver penny henceforth remained the standard coin of English commerce and gold pieces were rarely struck. The kingdom of Northumbria, however, retained the *sceatta* until almost the end of the eighth century when *sceattas* were replaced not by silver pennies but by copper *stycas*. The *styca* coinage survived in Northumbria until *c.* 855. The Northumbrian and Mercian currencies during this period appear to have existed in complete separation from each other, no pennies having been found in Northumbria and no *stycas* in the circulation area of the penny. The Scandinavian settlers in Northumbria and the Danelaw adopted a silver coinage in the late ninth century which was maintained until the end of the Scandinavian kingdom of York in the mid-tenth century. The West Saxon kings in the tenth century always kept a watchful eye on the standard of their own coinage and on weights and measures, and they took over the Danish mints as Danish territories fell under their control. In the second half of the tenth century, shillings came to be regarded as the value of 12 pence. Under a system established probably in 973 in the reign of Edgar, the coinage was recalled regularly every six or seven years and reissued. Edgar ordered that one coinage should be current throughout the whole country. Apart from differences in the name of the moneyer and the mint, the design and legend of the obverse and reverse sides of a coin became standardised and uniform. Æthelred II legislated against those who minted false coins and imposed stringent measures to ensure that coins were pure and of the correct weight. Following the heavy monetary exactions of the Danish period, the silver coins of Edward the Confessor were weightier than their predecessors, a sign probably of increasing prosperity. By manipulating the weight of the coins and by occasional devaluation in relation to continental coin weight, the Anglo-Saxon kings of the late Old English period actually sought to discourage imports and to encourage exports, and it was as a result of such measures that England possessed so sound and stable a silver currency on the eve of the Norman Conquest.

Few fields of Dark Age history have been so fruitful of scholarly debate in recent decades as the economic. Attention has been focused on three basic problems: firstly, whether the barbarian invasions of the fifth century seriously dislocated the commercial and economic life of west Europe; secondly, whether in fact it was not the advance of the Arabs, spreading out from Arabia and shattering the economic unity of the Mediterranean in the seventh and eighth centuries, which caused a real break in the commercial development of Europe; and thirdly, as a consequence of the second, whether Carolingian Gaul was deprived of foreign trade, thrown back on a natural economy and therefore so much poorer than Merovingian Gaul. Europe has been seen as reduced to an economic backwater by the ninth century from which it only began to emerge in the tenth. Few definitive conclusions have been reached as yet, and it may be a long time before they are. The weight of historical opinion at present seems to be that neither the barbarian invasions nor the Arab advance seriously dislocated western economy, that if recessions occurred they were of a temporary and probably often of a local nature, and that Carolingian Gaul in the ninth century at least appears to have enjoyed the traditional luxury trade with the lands around the Mediterranean. On the other hand, western economy was already in a chaotic and impoverished condition in the later years of the Roman Empire, and it is hard to see how the barbarian invasions can have automatically improved matters. The re-establishment of Mediterranean economic unity in the second half of the sixth century by the Emperor Justinian must have been an important element in the commercial development of Merovingian Gaul. And, though it is true that the trade in luxury goods in the Mediterranean never seems to have completely dried up, numismatic evidence reveals no vast commerce on the part of Carolingian Gaul with foreign lands but, on the contrary, a creeping localisation of trade in the course of the ninth century.

The difficulty in the study of the economic history of the early Middle Ages is that Dark Age sources provide little economic information. Furthermore, the limitations of what is recorded have not always been appreciated. The fragmentary nature of the literary evidence means that it cannot be used to provide a continuous narrative of commercial activity but can only illuminate certain aspects at certain moments in time. The same is true of the archaeological material. The port of *Hamwih* is not so much an exceptional example of urban development in the pre-Viking period as an exceptional example of an excavated urban and maritime site. And the total absence of statistical information makes it virtually impossible to compare and contrast the prosperity of one region with that of another, or the volume of trade between one century and another. In so far as coin evidence can be used to show the scale and extent of trade, it must be emphasised that throughout the early Middle Ages most of the day-to-day commercial activity was by a haphazard process of barter; and the bartering of goods rather than their selling for coined money is true also of the international market. We may not yet appreciate, therefore, the precise relationship between the distribution of coins and the actual lines and limits of trade within Dark Age Europe. Literary references may reveal the passing of goods through established portals of commerce and exchange along sea-coasts, at the mouths of great rivers, at the junction of roadways and at the confluence of minor tributaries, but on what scale and with what varying fluctuations we know not.

Many areas of Britain in the seventh century cannot have been greatly affected by foreign commerce, even though Columba awaited a Gallic merchant ship on Iona in the late sixth, and luxury objects were coveted by all royal courts. Kent, East Anglia, Wessex and probably Deira received a variety of continental goods from Rhenish swords to Mediterranean trinkets, even Byzantine silver in the case of East Anglia. Oswald of Northumbria possessed a great silver dish, which may have been imported, which he ordered to be broken up and the pieces given to the poor. How the regions of the hinterland fared archaeology does not yet show. It is important to remember, however, when dealing with these early centuries, that a number of goods changed hands not in the process of trade but as gifts or as the result of war. Pope Boniface V sent Æthelburh, queen of Edwin of Northumbria, a silver looking-glass and a gilt ivory comb, but should these particular articles ever be recovered during the excavation of a Northumbrian site it might easily be concluded that they reached Northumbria through commercial activity, especially if we did not possess the literary reference just quoted. Similarly, in 656, for example, Oswiu of Northumbria attempted to buy off an attack by Penda of Mercia by a gift of riches which Penda then distributed among his British allies. In such a way a piece of jewellery which had chanced to reach Northumbria from distant lands might turn up in North Wales, but naturally there would be no means of deducing this history from the object itself.

The practice of exchanging gifts continued throughout the Anglo-Saxon period, but as time went on merchant activity became a more constant and widespread phenomenon and the dispersal of goods as a consequence of trade more common. The early English law codes contain several references to trading activities. In Kent by *c.* 680 a man who gave hospitality to a trader from over the border for three days was responsible for bringing the trader to court if he committed a wrong. By the laws of Ine, a trader making his way inland has to carry out his transactions before witnesses. By Alfred's time, merchants were responsible for the actions of their men who accompanied them upcountry. Alfred and Guthrum agreed on the giving of securities before Danes and Englishmen traded with each other in cattle or goods. Bede's reference to a Frisian trader in London *c.* 679 shows that Frisians were to be found in England at an early date, and a colony of Frisian traders was established in York by the late eighth century. When Asser describes the lordship of Alfred as accepted by Frisians and Bretons, perhaps he was referring to Frisian and Breton communities in England. William of Malmesbury says that many foreigners were attracted to England by the fame of King Edgar, with results often prejudicial to the natives in William's view; for, according to William, from the Saxons the English learnt ferocity of mind, from the Danes drunkenness and from the Flemings effeminacy. Described by Bede, in the early eighth century, as the mart of many nations, it was said of London in the mid-eleventh century that abundant merchandise was brought there of every kind for sale from the whole world. A valuable document, probably of *c.* 1030, enumerates the merchants who visited London: the men of Flanders, of Lorraine (which embraced ancient Frisia), of Germany (which would include the Saxons), of Ponthieu, of Normandy, of the Isle de France and of Rouen. This particular document is the fundamental literary source for the extent of Anglo-continental trade by the early eleventh century, though it cannot be complete. It omits mention of Scandinavian traders. The trading ships of a Viking merchant of Limerick are recorded to have visited England in the tenth century, nor was he alone. Scandinavian merchants must have traded in London and all the major towns. Irish traders are found at Cambridge in the tenth century, and about the same time Welsh merchants at the mouth of the Wye. There is some evidence for the concern of the English government for the protection of merchants trading in England. In 964 King Edgar punished the men of Thanet for attacking and robbing a party of merchants from York.

The Anglo-Saxon kings had a well-developed interest in tolls and customs duties. The relief from tolls which Cnut secured for English merchants on the Continent, particularly in Germany and Burgundy, was at the cost of concessions to merchants in London from German imperial lands. The imposition of tolls at trading centres was in force from the earliest days of commerce going back to Roman times. Privileged exemptions soon came to be granted, by Æthelbald, king of Mercia, for example, on two ships belonging to the bishop of Worcester in the port of London, and by Eadberht, king of Kent, on ships belonging to the bishop of Rochester, the abbess of Minster in Thanet, and the monastery of Reculver on some of their ships at the ports of Fordwich and Sarre in Kent. Domesday Book contains several references to exemptions from tolls, at Dover, for example, and at Hythe, Romney and Sandwich, but the most exhaustive catalogue of particular tolls imposed is to be found in the document of c. 1030 which describes London trade. This document mentions by name Aldersgate, Cripplegate and Billingsgate. On small ships at Billingsgate half a penny was paid in toll, and on a larger ship with sails, one penny. In addition tolls were paid on the actual goods unloaded, and in one case, that of cloth, the unloading and payment of tolls took place on specified days of the week.

From the concern of communities such as the nunnery of Minster in Thanet and the monastery of Reculver with exemption from tolls on their ships it is clear that commercial activity interested a far wider range in society than simply a restricted merchant class. At a very early period the importance of trading activity to the Anglo-Saxons is shown by the form the quarrel between Offa and Charlemagne took. So enraged was Charlemagne over Offa's attitude to marriages within the two royal families that he closed the ports of his territory to English ships. Writing in 790, Alcuin refers to the recent dissension between the two kings and it is clear from his account that Offa had retaliated by closing English ports to continental merchants. It appears to have been largely through the diplomacy of Alcuin that harmonious relations were eventually restored; but for such action to have been worth taking trade between the Anglo-Saxons and the Franks must already have reached significant proportions. There can be no doubt that by the time of the Norman Conquest England was a very rich land indeed.

A few non-perishable objects of trade have survived in quantities from archaeological sites sufficient to permit certain generalised statements regarding their distribution and the light thereby thrown on commercial activity. Glass was imported into south-east England in the sixth and seventh centuries from the Rhineland and north Gaul, and Merovingian glass has been found at *Hamwih*. It is also possible that some glass reached Britain from Egypt and Syria. By the Viking period, the Rhineland was an important centre for the production of fine swords which were imported into England and used by the Vikings in west Europe. From the lower Rhine, through Frisia and the port of Dorestad, passed pottery which is found as far north as Whitby. From *c.* 500–700 the Celtic regions of the British Isles possessed their own trading connections with the Rhineland pottery kilns. Later Rhenish ware has been found only in south-east England, however, and it is thought that there might have been a complete shift in this trade in the course of the eighth century, probably not unrelated to the Mercian ascendancy. In and after the eighth century the bulk of imported pottery seems to have come from the middle Rhine, between Bonn and Cologne; and fine quality glazed home-made ware, found over a considerable part of eastern England as far north as York in the post-Viking period, may have been influenced by glazing techniques first developed in Frisia in the mid-ninth century.

But most objects of trade are perishable and leave no archaeological trace. The cloths exported in the eighth century from England to Gaul via Frisia, for example, are naturally known only from literary references and without the literary evidence there would be no knowledge of the trade, let alone of its scale. Charlemagne asked Offa of Mercia to see that the cloaks sold to the Franks were of the same length as previously; he is known to have complained that knee-length cloaks—being sold by the Frisians at the same price as full-length garments—were no use either for cover in bed or protection against the elements when riding horseback. Ælfric describes in his *Colloquy* a merchant who traded in purple robes and silk, rare apparel, precious stones, gold and spices, wine and oil, ivory, copper, brass, tin, sulphur and glass. Fine carvings were done in ivory in the later Anglo-Saxon period but, while ivory carvings might survive and in a few instances have survived, fabric and other raw materials have vanished almost without trace. Goods changing hands on the London market included planks, wool, melted fat, cloth, gloves, pepper and vinegar; Irish merchants at Cambridge in the tenth century traded in cloth, and a Norwegian merchant in the early eleventh century exchanged furs and skins for wheat and cloth. Trade in livestock must have gone on continuously but such trade is rarely recorded. Athelstan found it necessary to prohibit the sale of horses overseas, and hence a brief allusion to the horse trade survives in his legislation. Occasionally articles associated with perishable goods do survive to give evidence of a particular trade. Archaeological traces of pot wine-vessels suggest that the bulk of imported wine came from the Rhineland. It is clear, however, from the description of the trade at London *c.* 1030, that merchants from Rouen, apart from importing fish, dealt also in wine.

One of the most important items of Dark Age trade, which has similarly left no archaeological traces, was the slave trade. A fair amount can be deduced about this particular trade for it is mentioned repeatedly in the written records. Slaves were traded throughout the British Isles and across Europe and Asia, to Spain, Byzantium, Arabia and beyond. Jewish merchants figured quite prominently among slave-traders on the Continent, but it is not known if any operated in England. By 679 a Frisian merchant was dealing in slaves at London. Even earlier, slaves from the kingdom of Ælle of Deira (*c.* 558–88) were on sale in the markets of Rome, possibly despatched there by some rival Anglo-Saxon ruler. Slavery and slave-trading must have been one of the economic foundations of emerging Anglo-Saxon kingdoms. Gildas says that many Britons were enslaved, and the wars not only with the Picts, Scots and Britons, but also between kingdoms, must have furnished a copious supply. Men captured in battle might be sold into slavery. Ine of Wessex attempted to forbid the selling of men overseas, but as slaves were worth three to six times more on the Continent than in England export was a profitable venture. Rich Franks in the seventh century took it upon themselves as a Christian duty to redeem boatloads of slaves. One English slave, Balthild, was fortunate enough to become the queen of Clovis II, king of the Franks (639–57), and subsequently queen-regent, but few can have enjoyed anything approaching such a fairy-tale adventure. Some may have been offered as pagan sacrifices. The Vikings, of course, stimulated the slave trade which they operated from Ireland to the Black Sea. Æthelred II ordered that men be not sold out of the land, least of all to the heathen. The trade in slaves was still thriving in the mid-eleventh century. Wulfstan, bishop of Worcester, endeavoured to suppress the trade from Bristol to Ireland. The sources of supply deserve some consideration. Border warfare was still a feature of Anglo-Saxon life, and would provide a regular quota of slaves. William of Malmesbury states that the Anglo-Saxons were accustomed to selling their domestic female slaves into prostitution or foreign slavery when they became pregnant. There is some evidence that even relatives of the royal family had a commercial interest in the traffic. It was said of Gytha, sister of Cnut's brother-in-law and mother of King Harold II, that she used to purchase companies of slaves in England, particularly girls whom beauty and age rendered more valuable, to be shipped to Denmark, there to be sold. Here we gain a glimpse of one of the grimmer aspects of life in Anglo-Saxon England.

*   *   *

We do not possess statistical information for Anglo-Saxon sociological studies of great depth, nor do we know enough to integrate scattered references to dress or hygiene, for example, into a thoroughly coherent social and historical picture. It is, of course, important for the historian to appreciate that what mattered to most men and women then as now was good health, adequate food, essential clothing, and reasonable accommodation; the normal preoccupations, in fact, of family life. These factors are constant. If we remember that most men saw life in the main over the furrow of a ploughed field, across the bench of a tavern, and through the black smoke of their own hearthside, we will possess a perspective on the history of early England rooted in the realities of daily living. There is nothing in this whole field of social study which is too trivial to be entirely without interest, nothing which is too commonplace to be without a place in the fabric of our history.

6 *Victoria County Histories*

The Victoria County Histories have been appearing since 1900 and are now published under the auspices of the Institute of Historical Research. All English counties are at least partially covered with the exception of Cheshire and Northumberland. These volumes are a mine of information and provide an immediate introduction to the early development of a particular region. R. R. Darlington's account of Anglo-Saxon Wiltshire (*V.C.H. Wilts.*, II) is a model for all future regional surveys of early English development. *A History of Northumberland*, the later volumes of which were edited under the direction of the Northumberland County History Committee, has been published in fifteen volumes (Newcastle, 1893–1940).

7 *Sources*

The historian of Anglo-Saxon England is well placed in the main for editions of sources. Gildas and Nennius are fundamental for the British background. Gildas, *The Ruin of Britain*, fragments from lost letters, the *Penitential*, together with the *Lorica* of Gildas, ed. and translated H. Williams, 2 vols., *Cymmrodorion record series*, 3 (London, 1899–1901), brings the writings of Gildas together and includes explanatory notes. The Latin text of Nennius's *Historia Brittonum* is edited by T. Mommsen, *Monumenta Germaniae Historica: Auctores Antiquissimi*, XIII (pt. I) (Berlin, 1894), and a translation, together with a set of early British genealogies, is provided by A. W. Wade-Evans, *Nennius, History of the Britons* (London, 1938) (the notes to this translation must be used with extreme caution). The Latin text of Bede's *Historia Ecclesiastica* may be consulted in C. Plummer's important edition, equipped with a volume of notes, *Venerabilis Baedae Opera Historica*, vol. I (text) and II (notes) (Oxford, 1896, reprinted 1960), and there is a recent translation by L. Sherley-Price, *Bede's Ecclesiastical History of the English People* (Penguin Classics, 1955). The *Anglo-Saxon Chronicle* has been edited, with translation, by B. Thorpe, *The Anglo-Saxon Chronicle*, 2 vols. (Rolls series, London, 1861). A valuable edition of two texts of the *Chronicle*, again equipped with a volume of notes (but no translation) is C. Plummer, *Two of the Saxon Chronicles Parallel*, I (text) and II (notes) (Oxford, 1892: 1952 edition). Translations of the *Chronicle* include G. N. Garmonsway, *The Anglo-Saxon Chronicle* (Everyman's Library, 1953), and, more recently, D. Whitelock, D. C. Douglas and S. I. Tucker, *The Anglo-Saxon Chronicle* (London, 1961). Æthelweard's Latin text of the *Chronicle* is edited and translated by A. Campbell, *The Chronicle of Æthelweard* (Nelson's Medieval Texts, London etc., 1962). Asser's Latin *Life* of Alfred, which contains a variant text of the *Chronicle*, was edited by W. H. Stevenson, *Asser's Life of King Alfred* (Oxford 1904: 2nd impression, 1959) (with additional introduction by D. Whitelock). Of the many translations see L. C. Jane, *Asser's Life of King Alfred* (London, 1908). A. Campbell, *Encomium Emmae Regina* (Royal

Historical Society, 1949), includes text, translation and notes. F. Barlow, *The Life of King Edward the Confessor* (Nelson's Medieval Texts, London etc. 1962) is very important. The Latin texts of the Anglo-Norman historians have been edited in the Rolls series. Mention may be made in particular here of *The Memorials of St. Dunstan*, ed. W. Stubbs (London, 1874); *Historians of the Church of York and its Archbishops*, ed. J. Raine, 3 vols. (London, 1879–94); the two great works of William of Malmesbury, *Gesta Pontificum*, ed. N. E. S. A. Hamilton (London, 1870), and *Gesta Regum*, ed. W. Stubbs, 2 vols. (London, 1887 and 1889); and the writings of *Symeon of Durham*, ed. T. Arnold, 2 vols. (London, 1882 and 1885). Series of translations were published in the last century in *Bohn's Antiquarian Library* and in J. Stevenson's *The Church Historians of England;* these include the majority of the Anglo-Norman historians, for example, *William of Malmesbury's English Chronicle*, translated J. A. Giles (Bohn's Antiquarian Library, London, 1847), and *The Historical Works of Simeon of Durham*, translated J. Stevenson, *The Church Historians of England*, vol. II (pt. II) (London, 1855). Such translations, though helpful, are not always absolutely reliable, partly because of the scarcity at that time of satisfactory editions of the Latin texts.

B. Colgrave's editions of early saints' *Lives* have been of great value for the study of the early Church: *Eddius Stephanus, Life of Bishop Wilfrid* (Cambridge, 1927), *Two Lives of St. Cuthbert* (Cambridge, 1940), and *Felix's Life of St. Guthlac* (Cambridge, 1956). C. H. Talbot, *The Anglo-Saxon Missionaries in Germany* (London and New York, 1954), includes translations of the lives of a group of missionaries, including that of Boniface by Willibald, and a selection of the correspondence of Boniface. E. Emerton, *The Letters of St. Boniface* (Columbia University Records of Civilisation, XXXI, 1940), gives a translation of all his letters, the Latin texts of which may be found in *Monumenta Germaniae Historica, Epistolae Selectae*, I (Berlin, 1916), ed. M. Tangl. S. H. Gem, *An Anglo-Saxon Abbot* (Edinburgh, 1912), provides a translation of Ælfric's *Life of Æthelwold* (and of Ælfric's *Colloquy*), and the agreed rule of the monastic reformers is edited and translated by T. Symons, *Regularis Concordia* (Nelson Medieval Classics, London, 1953). From the later Saxon period, *Byrhtferth's Manual*, edited and translated by S. J. Crawford (Early English Texts Society, vol. 177, London, 1929), contains much of interest. R. R. Darlington's edition of William of Malmesbury's *Vita Wulfstani* (Camden Society, vol. XL, 1928) may be supplemented by *William of Malmesbury's Life of St. Wulstan*, translated by J. H. F. Piele (Oxford, 1934). Of the monastic chronicles, several are to be found in the Rolls series, for example *Chronicon Abbatiae Rameseiensis*, ed. W. Dunn Macray (London, 1886). The important *Liber Eliensis* has been edited by E. O. Blake (Camden Society, vol. XCII, 1962). W. T. Mellows edited and translated *The Chronicle of Hugh Candidus: A Monk of Peterborough* in two volumes (London, 1941 and 1949). For a Latin edition of William of Malmesbury's account of Glastonbury Monastery, refer to *Adami de Domerham, Historia de rebus gestis*

Glastoniensibus, ed. T. Hearne (Oxford, 1727); F. Lomax, *The Antiquities of Glastonbury* (London, 1908), provides a translation.

B. Thorpe, *Ancient Laws and Institutes of England*, 2 vols. (London, 1840), was a monumental achievement. A number of important volumes have been concerned with particular classes of documents. These include F. L. Attenborough, *The Laws of the Earliest English Kings* (Cambridge, 1922), A. J. Robertson, *The Laws of the Kings of England from Edmund to Henry I* (Cambridge, 1925), D. Whitelock, *Anglo-Saxon Wills* (Cambridge, 1930), A. J. Robertson, *Anglo-Saxon Charters* (Cambridge, 1939), and F. E. Harmer, *Anglo-Saxon Writs* (Manchester, 1952). Documents and charters are brought together by A. W. Haddan and W. Stubbs, *Councils and Ecclesiastical Documents Relating to Great Britain and Ireland*, vol. III (Oxford, 1871; reprinted 1965), J. Kemble, *Codex Diplomaticus Aevi Saxonici*, 6 vols. (London, 1839–1848), and W. de Gray Birch, *Cartularium Saxonicum*, 3 vols. (London, 1885–93; reprinted 1965). Two important volumes of documents are *The Crawford Collection of Early Charters and Documents*, ed. A. S. Napier and W. H. Stevenson (Oxford, 1895), and F. E. Harmer, *Select Historical Documents of the Ninth and Tenth Centuries* (Cambridge, 1914). Many but by no means all charters are translated in the transactions of local archaeological societies. Guides to the charters of prescribed regions are provided by H. P. R. Finberg, *The Early Charters of Devon and Cornwall* (Leicester, 1953), *The Early Charters of the West Midlands* (Leicester, 1961) and *The Early Charters of Wessex* (Leicester, 1964).

Translations of prose and verse literature are numerous. Mention may also be made here of A. S. Cook and B. Tinker, *Select Translations from Old English Poetry* (Boston, 1902), N. Kershaw, *Anglo-Saxon and Norse Poems* (Cambridge, 1922), R. K. Gordon, *Anglo-Saxon Poetry* (Everyman's Library, 1926), M. Williams, *Word-Hoard* (London, 1946), K. Crossley-Holland and B. Mitchell, *The Battle of Maldon and Other Old English Poems* (New York, 1965: London, 1966), and C. W. Kennedy's *The Poems of Cynewulf* (London, 1910), *The Cædmon Poems* (London, 1916) and *Early English Christian Poetry* (London, 1952). G. F. Browne, *King Alfred's Books* (London and New York, 1920), includes extracts in English from King Alfred's translations; other English translations of Alfred's Anglo-Saxon works include H. Sweet, *King Alfred's West Saxon Version of Gregory's Pastoral Care* (Early English Texts Society, 1871, vols. 45, 50), W. J. Sedgefield, *King Alfred's Version of the Consolations of Boethius* (Oxford, 1900), B. Thorpe, *King Alfred's Anglo-Saxon Version of the History of Paulus Orosius* (Bohn's Antiquarian Library, 1878: reprinted, 1900); and H. L. Hargrove, 'King Alfred's Old English Version of St. Augustine's Soliloquies', *Yale Studies in English*, XXII (1904). For the writings of Ælfric, see *The Homilies of the Anglo-Saxon Church*, pt. I, ed. B. Thorpe, 2 vols. (London, 1843–6), and *Ælfric's Lives of the Saints*, ed. W. W. Skeat (Early English Texts Society, vols. 76, 82, 94, 114, 1881–1900). Finally, there are a number of useful collections of translated sources.

R. W. Chambers, *England Before the Norman Conquest* (London, 1928), is a helpful little volume, but it has been superseded by D. Whitelock, *English Historical Documents, c. 500–1042* (London, 1955), and D. C. Douglas and W. Greenaway, *English Historical Documents, 1042–1154* (London, 1953). A more limited collection is M. Ashdown, *English and Norse Documents of the Reign of Ethelred the Unready* (Cambridge, 1930).

8 Book One, Part I, The Pre-Viking Period

Archaeological, place-name and literary material must all be used in the reconstruction of the history of this age, but F. T. Wainwright, *Archaeology and Place-Names and History* (London, 1962), emphasised that the evidence of any one of these disciplines need not necessarily have a bearing on that yielded by another. His little book is a most stimulating, if cautionary, statement of the problems of evidence facing the historian of the Dark Ages.

The British background to the Anglo-Saxon Conquest has attracted considerable interest. C. E. Stevens, 'Gildas and the Civitates of Britain', *English Historical Review*, LII (1937), and the same writer's 'Gildas Sapiens', *ibid.*, LVI (1941), remain essential reading. A. D. White, *Litus Saxonicum* (Wisconsin, 1961), considers the role of the Saxon Shore in British defence. J. D. Bu'Lock, 'Vortigern and the Pillar of Eliseg', *Antiquity*, XXXIV (1960), attempts to make historical sense of Vortigern and his alleged dealings with Germanus of Auxerre. Mrs. Chadwick presents valuable studies of Germanus of Auxerre and the intellectual contacts between Britain and Gaul in the fifth century in *Poetry and Letters in Early Christian Gaul* and *Studies in Early British History*. J. N. L. Myres, 'Pelagianism and the End of Roman Rule in Britain', *Journal of Roman Studies*, 50–1 (1960–1), offers a challenging interpretation of an obscure period. On Celtic matters, the writings of K. H. Jackson are outstanding; 'Once Again Arthur's Battles', *Modern Philology*, 43 (1945–6), shows how difficult it is to place Arthur geographically, while 'The Gododdin of Aneurin', *Antiquity*, XIII (1939), and 'The Britons in Southern Scotland', *Antiquity*, XXIX (1955), investigate the northern scene. The same writer's *Language and History in Early Britain* (Edinburgh, 1953) is primarily concerned with linguistic development, but contains an historical introduction. R. Bromwich, 'The Character of Early Welsh Tradition', *Studies in Early British History*, ed. N. K. Chadwick, is useful for the poems of the British bards, and the influence of the North Britons on Welsh culture and literature is discussed by I. Williams, 'Wales and the North', *Trans. of the Cumberland and Westmorland Antiq. & Archaeol. Society*, LI (1952).

On the Saxon side, the pioneer studies by E. T. Leeds of early archaeological material have not been entirely superseded. Among his many writings, mention may be made of *The Archaeology of the Anglo-Saxon Settlement* (Oxford, 1913), *Early Anglo-Saxon Art and Archaeology* (Oxford, 1935), and 'The Distribution of the Angles and Saxons Archaeologically Considered', *Archaeologia*, XCI (1945). These may be read together with N. Åberg, *The*

Anglo-Saxons in England (Cambridge, 1926), and J. N. L. Myres, 'The Present State of the Archaeological Evidence for the Anglo-Saxon Conquest', *History*, XXI (1937). One or two regional surveys have been attempted which deal also with the prehistoric and Roman periods, in particular C. Fox, *The Archaeology of the Cambridge Region* (Cambridge, 1923), and, more recently, L. V. Grinsell, *The Archaeology of Wessex* (London, 1958), and C. J. Copely, *An Archaeology of South-East England: A Study in Continuity* (London, 1958). V. I. Evison, *The Fifth-Century Invasions South of the Thames* (London, 1965), is a controversial archaeological and historical study which has proved far from acceptable to many scholars. Examples of recent art and archaeological studies are E. Bakka, *On the Beginnings of Salin's Style I in England* (Bergen, 1958), S. C. Hawkes, 'The Jutish Style A: A Study of Germanic Animal Art in Southern England in the Fifth Century A.D.', *Archaeologia*, XCVIII (1961), and J. N. L. Myres, 'Romano-Saxon Pottery', *Dark Age Britain*, ed. D. B. Harden. On early pottery see also J. N. L. Myres, 'Some Parallels to the Anglo-Saxon Pottery of Holland and Belgium in the Migration Period', *L'Antiquité Classique*, XVII (1948). A. Meaney, *Gazetteer of Early Anglo-Saxon Burial Sites* (London, 1964), provides a valuable survey for the whole of England.

Place-names ending in -*ing* are reviewed by A. H. Smith, 'Place-Names and the Anglo-Saxon Settlement', *Proc. of the British Academy*, XLII (1956), but J. M. Dodgson, 'The significance of the distribution of the English place-name in -*ingas*, -*inga* in south-east England', *Medieval Archaeology* 10 (1966) suggests that such place-names may be rather later than the earliest phase of pagan immigration, belonging rather to an epoch of territorial expansion and social consolidation. An example of the way in which the evidence of place-names and dialect may reveal early patterns of settlement is provided by K. Cameron, 'An Early Mercian Boundary in Derbyshire', *The Anglo-Saxons*, ed. P. Clemoes.

The origins of the various kingdoms of the Heptarchy are complex. With particular reference to Kent, see J. N. L. Myres, 'The Adventus Saxonum', *Aspects of Archaeology*, ed. W. F. Grimes, and C. F. C. Hawkes, 'The Jutes in Kent', *Dark Age Britain*, ed. D. B. Harden. Reference may also be made to V. I. Evison, *op. cit.*, who discusses both Kent and Wessex. On Wessex, E. T. Leeds expressed his controversial views on the origins of the kingdom in 'The West Saxon Invasion and the Icknield Way', *History*, X (1925), and this may be read together with C. J. Copley, *The Conquest of Wessex in the Sixth Century* (London, 1954), and D. P. Kirby, 'Problems of Early West Saxon History', *English Historical Review*, LXXX (1965). Important studies of the Wansdyke in Wessex are as follows: A. and C. Fox, 'Wansdyke Reconsidered', *Archaeological Journal*, CXV (1958), A. Clark, 'The Nature of Wansdyke', *Antiquity*, XXXII (1958), and J. N. L. Myres, 'Wansdyke and the Origin of Wessex', *Essays in British History Presented to Sir Keith Feiling*, ed. H. R. Trevor-Roper (London, 1964). On Northumbria, see J. N. L.

Myres, 'The Teutonic Settlement of North England', *History*, XX (1935), Peter Hunter Blair, 'The Origins of Northumbria', *Archaeologia Aeliana*, XXV (1947), and 'The Northumbrians and their Southern Frontier', *Archaeologia Aeliana*, XXVI (1948), and D. P. Kirby, 'Bede and Northumbrian Chronology', *English Historical Review*, LXXVIII (1963). An important study of the early British material for Northumbrian development is K. H. Jackson, 'On the Northern British Section in Nennius', *Celt and Saxon*, ed. N. K. Chadwick. Mercia has received less attention, so little being known about its origin. T. Barns, 'The Making of Mercia', *North Staffs. Field Club*, 46 (1912), is interesting. A. Ozonne, 'The Peak Dwellers', *Medieval Archaeology*, 6 (1962), presents an archaeological approach to a known early folk-group within the Mercian kingdom. By contrast, East Anglia has been much studied because of the Sutton Hoo ship burial. A Sutton Hoo bibliography will be found in *Speculum*, XXIX (1954), and XXXIII (1958). Of this important excavation, R. L. S. Bruce-Mitford published a preliminary survey, *The Sutton Hoo Ship Burial, A Provisional Guide* (British Museum, 1947: reprinted 1951). Among subsequent writings, special mention may be made of R. L. S. Bruce-Mitford, 'Saxon Rendlesham', *Proc. of the Suffolk Institute of Archaeology*, XXIV (1948), 'The Sutton Hoo Ship Burial', *ibid,*. XXV (1949), and 'Excavation at Sutton Hoo in 1938', *ibid.*, XXX (1964); P. Grierson, 'The Dating of the Sutton Hoo Coins', *Antiquity*, XXVI (1952), C. Green, *Sutton Hoo: The Excavation of a Royal Ship Burial* (London, 1963), important for a study of navigation and shipping in the Migration period, C. F. C. Hawkes, 'Sutton Hoo: Twenty-Five Years After', *Antiquity*, XXXVIII (1964), which contains information of a new dating for the burial, and J. N. L. O'Loughlin, 'Sutton Hoo—The Evidence of the Documents', *Medieval Archaeology*, 8 (1964), dealing with the Scandinavian links of place and personal names in East Anglia.

On the problems of continuity across the Conquest period, see J. N. L. Myres, 'Archaeology and History: Britons and Saxons in the Post-Roman Centuries', *Council for British Archaeology, Report 11* (1961). H. P. R. Finberg, 'Continuity or Cataclysm', *Lucerna*, favours continuity, and in 'Roman and Saxon Withington', now to be seen in *Lucerna*, he seeks to demonstrate continuity from a Romano-British villa to an Anglo-Saxon estate. Reference should be made to R. Lennard, 'From Roman Britain to Anglo-Saxon England', *Wirtschaft und Kultur* (Festschrift zum 70. Geburstag von Alfons Dopsch, Leipzig, 1938), for the argument that something in the nature of a real break did occur. N. K. Chadwick, 'The British or Celtic Part in the Population of England', *Angles and Britons*, attempts to assess the strength of the survival of a British population within the Anglo-Saxon kingdoms. Important work on settlement problems has been published recently by G. Jones, for example, 'Settlement Patterns in Anglo-Saxon England', *Antiquity*, XXXV (1961).

The political history of the Heptarchy has received uneven attention. On

Wessex, F. M. Stenton, 'The Foundations of English History', *Trans. of the Royal Historical Society*, IX (1926), discusses the early source material, and H. P. R. Finberg, 'Sherborne, Glastonbury and the Expansion of Wessex', in *Lucerna*, the attack on the Britons of the south-west. Northumbrian development has attracted a number of research projects not yet in print, some still in progress; but Peter Hunter Blair, 'The Bernicians and Their Northern Frontier', *Studies in Early British History*, ed. N. K. Chadwick, W. R. Kermack, 'Early English Settlement in South-West Scotland', *Antiquity*, XV (1941), and K. H. Jackson, 'Edinburgh and the Anglian Occupation of Lothian', *The Anglo-Saxons*, ed. P. Clemoes, deal with expansion and settlement on the Northumbrian frontier. N. K. Chadwick analyses the sources for the battle of Chester in *Celt and Saxon*, ed. N. K Chadwick. Light is shed on dynastic history in two studies by F. M. Stenton, 'Lindsey and its Kings', *Essays in History Presented to R. L. Poole*, ed. H. W. C. Davis (Oxford, 1927), and 'The East Anglian Kings of the Seventh Century', *The Anglo-Saxons*, ed. P. Clemoes. Stenton's 'The Supremacy of the Mercian Kings', *English Historical Review*, XXXIII (1918), and C. Fox, *Offa's Dyke* (London, 1955), illuminate different aspects of Mercian history.

It is the ecclesiastical history of the Heptarchy in the seventh and eighth centuries which has attracted the bulk of specialist interest, though some of what has been written seems superficial. E. O. G. Turville-Petre, *Myth and Religion of the North* (London, 1964), though primarily concerned with Norse paganism is useful for the paganism of the Anglo-Saxons. On the place-name evidence for Anglo-Saxon paganism, see F. M. Stenton, 'Anglo-Saxon Heathenism', *Trans. of the Royal Historical Society*, XXIV (1942). On the conversion, W. Bright, *Chapters in Early English Church History* (3rd edition, Oxford, 1897), continues to be useful. The Celtic Church is well covered by J. Ryan, *Irish Monasticism* (Dublin, 1931), J. A. Duke, *The Columban Church* (Oxford, 1932), L. Gougaud, *Christianity in Celtic Lands* (London, 1932), N. K. Chadwick, *The Age of the Saints in the Early Celtic Church* (London, 1961), and K. Hughes, *The Church in Early Irish Society* (London, 1966). On some aspects of the Celtic Church there is a mass of material, but most of it lies beyond the scope of this bibliography. A group of studies on St. Ninian, however, will be found in the *Trans. of the Dumfriesshire and Galloway Antiq. Society*, XXVII (1950), and Ninian is the subject of a little study by J. D. MacQueen, *St. Nynia* (London and Edinburgh, 1961). Surveys of the Anglo-Saxon Church throughout the whole period to 1066 are presented by M. Deanesly, *The Pre-Conquest Church in England* (2nd edition, London, 1963), and C. Godfrey, *The Church in Anglo-Saxon England* (Cambridge, 1962). M. Deanesly, 'English and Gallic Minsters', *Trans. of the Royal Historical Society*, XXIII (1941), is fundamental. N. K. Chadwick, 'The Conversion of Northumbria', *Celt and Saxon*, ed. N. K. Chadwick, deals in detail with a particular problem, the conversion of Edwin.

D. P. Kirby, 'Bede's Native Sources for the *Historia Ecclesiastica*', *Bulletin of the John Rylands Library*, XLVIII (1966), considers Bede's practical difficulties in writing his *History* and the limitations of oral tradition. Much information is to be found in B. Colgrave, *The Venerable Bede and His Times*, Jarrow Lecture 1958, in Peter Hunter Blair, *Bede's Ecclesiastical History of the English Nation and Its Importance Today*, Jarrow Lecture 1959, and in D. Whitelock, *After Bede*, Jarrow Lecture 1960. The complexities of the Easter Controversy are explained by C. W. Jones, *Bedae Opera de Temporibus* (Cambridge, Mass., 1943), and D. J. V. Fisher, in a very useful article, surveys 'The Church in England from the Death of Bede to the Danish Invasions', *Trans. of the Royal Historical Society*, II (1952). S. J. Crawford, *Anglo-Saxon Influence on Western Christendom* (Oxford, 1933), and W. Levison, *England and the Continent in the Eighth Century* (Oxford, 1946), consider the continental background. On papal interest in missionary work, see R. E. Sullivan, 'The Papacy and Missionary Activity in the Early Middle Ages', *Medieval Studies*, XVII (1955).

9　Book One, Part II, The Post-Viking Period

There are several volumes describing the Scandinavian background and the Viking attack on Europe. Mention may be made of T. D. Kendrick, *A History of the Vikings* (London, 1930), J. Brøndsted, *The Vikings*, trans. K. Skov (Pelican, 1965), H. Arbman, *The Vikings*, trans. A. Binns (Ancient Peoples and Places, 21: London, 1961). P. H. Sawyer's stimulating book, *The Age of the Vikings* (London, 1962), attempts to demonstrate that contemporaries greatly exaggerated the Viking menace.

The best biography of Alfred the Great remains C. Plummer, *Alfred the Great* (Oxford, 1902); B. A. Lees, *Alfred the Great, the Truth Teller* (New York, 1915), may be consulted, and E. S. Duckett, *Alfred the Great and His England* (London, 1957). The new biography by Professor D. Whitelock is eagerly awaited. J. M. Wallace-Hadrill, 'The Franks and the English in the Ninth Century', *History*, XXX (1950), is sceptical about Alfred's greatness, though perhaps on inadequate grounds. D. P. Kirby considers 'Northumbria in the reign of Alfred the Great', *Trans. of the Architectural and Archaeol. Soc. of Durham and Northumberland*, XI (1965). F. T. Wainwright was particularly interested in the reign of Edward the Elder, and his articles on the period are important; they include 'North-West Mercia, A.D. 871–924', *Trans. of the Historic Soc. of Lancs. and Cheshire*, 94 (1942), 'The Submission to Edward the Elder', *History*, XXXVII (1952), and 'Æthelflæd, Lady of the Mercians', *The Anglo-Saxons*, ed. P. Clemoes. In addition to an edition of the text of the poem, A. Campbell's *The Battle of Brunanburh* (London, 1938) contains a valuable historical study of the battle and its site. Specialist studies on the reconquest of the Danelaw include A. Mawer, 'The Redemption of the Five Boroughs', *English Historical Review*, XXXVIII (1923), A. Campbell, 'Two Notes on the Norse Kingdoms in Northumbria', *English Historical Review*

LVII (1942), D. Whitelock, 'The Dealings of the Kings of England with the Northumbrians', *The Anglo-Saxons*, ed. P. Clemoes, and A. Binns, 'The York Viking Kingdom', *The Fourth Viking Congress*, ed. A. Small (Edinburgh and London, 1965). There is no good specialist study of the reign of Æthelred II, but L. M. Larson, *Canute the Great* (New York, 1912), deals with the Danish Conquest of England. A new study of the reign of Cnut is much needed. D. Whitelock discusses the work of the great legalist of this period, Archbishop Wulfstan, in 'Archbishop Wulfstan, Homilist and Statesman', *Trans. of the Royal Historical Society*, XXIV (1942), and 'Wulfstan and the Laws of Cnut', *English Historical Review*, LXIII (1948). R. R. Darlington, 'The Last Phase of Anglo-Saxon History', *History*, XXII (1937), reviews that later period as a whole. B. Wilkinson's two studies of the politics of the reign of the Confessor, 'Freeman and the Crisis of 1051', and 'Northumbrian Separatism in 1065 and 1066', may be read in the *Bulletin of the John Rylands Library*, XXII (1938), and XXIII (1939), respectively. More recently, D. C. Douglas sets out his views on the reign of Edward the Confessor in *William the Conqueror* (London, 1964), while F. Barlow, 'Edward the Confessor's Early Life, Character and Upbringing', *English Historical Review*, LXXX (1965), offers a cautious analysis of the political situation. The whole series of events leading up to the Norman Conquest has been reinterpreted by S. Körner, *The Battle of Hastings: England and Europe 1035–66* (Lund, 1964). While not every historian of the period has agreed with his conclusions, this is one of the most stimulating and valuable pieces of work on the subject in recent years.

The ecclesiastical history of the later Saxon period is well covered. D. Whitelock, 'The Conversion of the Eastern Danelaw', *Saga Book of the Viking Society*, XII (pt. III) (1941), deals with an obscure process, and W. Angus does what he can with 'Christianity as a political force in Northumbria in the Danish and Norse Periods', *The Fourth Viking Congress*, ed. A. Small. M. D. Knowles, *The Monastic Order in England* (2nd edition, Cambridge, 1949), provides the fundamental survey of the tenth-century monastic reform movement. M. Deanesly, *Sidelights on the Anglo-Saxon Church* (London, 1962), is very largely concerned with the tenth-century reformation and late Saxon ecclesiastical development. E. S. Duckett, *St. Dunstan of Canterbury* (London, 1955), may be read together with the weightier volume by J. A. Robinson, *The Times of St. Dunstan* (Oxford, 1923). Specialist articles on the tenth-century reform movement include T. Symons, 'English Monastic Reform of the Tenth Century', *The Downside Review*, 60 (1942), P. G. Caraman, 'The Character of the Late Saxon Clergy', *The Downside Review*, 63 (1945), and E. John, 'The King and the Monks in the Tenth-Century Reformation', now to be seen in *Orbis Britanniae*. E. Miller, 'The Abbey and Bishopric of Ely', *Cambridge Studies in Medieval Life and Thought*, new series, I (Cambridge, 1951), sheds light on the economic aspect of the reform movement, and this may be read together with D. J. V.

Fisher, 'The Anti-Monastic Reaction in the Reign of Edward the Martyr', *Cambridge Historical Journal*, 10 (1952). F. R. H. Du Boulay, *The Lordship of Canterbury* (London, etc., 1966), traces the growth of the territorial endowment of the archbishopric of Canterbury from Anglo-Saxon times. A valuable study of archdeacons is by M. Deanesly, 'The Archdeacons of Canterbury under Archbishop Ceolnoth', *English Historical Review*, XLII (1927), and R. A. L. Smith traces the history and secular origin of 'The Early Community of St. Andrew at Rochester, 604–*c*. 1080', *English Historical Review*, LX (1945). R. R. Darlington's 'Ecclesiastical Reform in the Late Old English Period', *English Historical Review*, LI (1936), has always been a source of inspiration. F. Barlow, *The English Church 1000–66: A Constitutional History* (London, 1963), is concerned primarily with the administration of the late Old English Church and its relations with the Crown. On the Scandinavian mission field, see C. J. A. Opperman, *The English Mission in Sweden and Finland* (London, 1937).

10 Book Two, Part I, Government and Society

A description of social developments in Anglo-Saxon England will be found in H. R. Loyn, *Anglo-Saxon England and the Norman Conquest* (Oxford, 1962), which forms volume I of *A Social and Economic History of England*, ed. Asa Briggs. This is a most useful guide to the problems of early social history. Rather more controversial and unorthodox approaches to social and administrative history will be found in H. G. Richardson and G. O. Sayles, *The Governance of Medieval England* (Edinburgh, 1963), and *Law and Legislation* (Edinburgh, 1965), and in the writings of Eric John, *Land Tenure in Early England* (Leicester, 1960) and *Orbis Britanniae* (Leicester, 1966).

H. M. Chadwick, *Studies on Anglo-Saxon Institutions* (Cambridge, 1905), continues to be rewarding, not least for its analysis of *wergelds*. On the nobility, see H. R. Loyn, 'Gesiths and Thegns in England from the Seventh to the Tenth Century', *English Historical Review*, LXX (1955). Much of the social background, of course, remains obscure. J. E. A. Joliffe contributed two important studies: *Pre-Feudal England: the Jutes* (Oxford, 1933), and 'Northumbrian Institutions', *English Historical Review*, XLI (1926). Perhaps the most convenient survey of the social scene is D. Whitelock's *The Beginnings of English Society* (Pelican History of England, vol. II, 1952). F. M. Stenton approaches through place-names 'The Place of Women in Anglo-Saxon Society', *Trans. of the Royal Historical Society*, XXV (1943). D. Whitelock considers *The Audience of Beowulf* (Oxford, 1951), and R. J. Cramp, '*Beowulf* and Archaeology', *Medieval Archaeology*, I (1957). D. M. Wilson, *The Anglo-Saxons* (Ancient Peoples and Places, 16: London, 1960), presents an archaeologist's view of society. W. Bonser, *The Medical Background to Anglo-Saxon England* (London, 1965), attempts to survey the evidence for the health of the Anglo-Saxons. A. E. W. Miles, 'Assessment of the Ages of a

Population of Anglo-Saxons from their Dentitions', *Proc. of the Royal Society of Medicine*, 55 (1962), is a most important paper, and there are many points of interest for the Anglo-Saxon historian in C. Wells, *Bones, Bodies and Diseases* (Ancient Peoples and Places, 37: London, 1964).

Aspects of Anglo-Saxon government and institutions are covered in many works. C. N. L. Brooke, *Saxon and Norman Kings* (London, 1963), may be read together with P. E. Schramm, *A History of the English Coronation* (Oxford, 1937). F. Pollock and F. W. Maitland, *The History of English Law*, vol. I (2nd edition, Cambridge, 1923), begins with the Anglo-Saxon period, as does S. B. Chrimes, *An Administrative History of Medieval England* (2nd edition, Oxford, 1959). In an important article H. R. Loyn considers 'The King and the Structure of Society in Late Anglo-Saxon England', *History* 42 (1957). L. M. Larson, *The Kings' Household in England before the Norman Conquest* (Wisconsin, 1904), and T. Oleson, *The Witenagemot in the Reign of Edward the Confessor* (Toronto, 1955), are specifically concerned with Anglo-Saxon institutions, and Oleson's volume is important for the reign of Edward the Confessor. F. M. Stenton, *The Latin Charters of the Anglo-Saxon Period* (Oxford, 1955), sheds light on Anglo-Saxon royal writing offices. C. S. Taylor's 'The Origin of the Mercian Shires' (which first appeared in 1898) is reprinted by H. P. R. Finberg, *Gloucestershire Studies* (Leicester, 1958), and is a first-class study. W. A. Morris described 'The Office of Sheriff in the Anglo-Saxon Period', *English Historical Review*, XXXI (1916). Helen Cam's studies of the hundred deserve particular attention, for example, *Liberties and Communities in Medieval England* (Cambridge, 1944). On the military organisation of early England, C. W. Warren Hollister, *Anglo-Saxon Military Institutions* (Oxford, 1962), is the fundamental survey, but certain of the author's conclusions have been challenged by Richardson and Sayles, *op. cit.*, and by E. John, for example, in 'English Feudalism and the Structure of Anglo-Saxon Society', now to be seen in *Orbis Britanniae*. R. Glover, 'English Warfare in 1066', *English Historical Review*, LXVII (1952), is stimulating. J. O. Prestwich reviews 'Anglo-Norman Feudalism and the problem of continuity', *Past and Present* 26 (1963) and puts forward his own conclusions regarding military developments.

Anglo-Saxon culture has been unevenly treated. There is a great deal of material on the artistic history of the Anglo-Saxon period but less on the intellectual history. N. Åberg, *The Occident and the Orient in the Art of the Seventh Century*, vol. I (Stockholm, 1943), is fundamental. T. D. Kendrick provides the basic guides to the artistic development of early England in two volumes, *Anglo-Saxon Art to A.D. 900* (London, 1938) and *Late Saxon and Viking Art* (London, 1949), and the latter volume may be read together with D. Talbot Rice, *English Art 871–1110*, *Oxford History of English Art*, vol. II (Oxford, 1951). Talbot Rice emphasises the importance of Byzantine influence on English art. The influence of Mediterranean models as a whole is indicated by W. Oakeshote, *The Sequence of English Medieval Art* (London, 1950) and

Classical Inspiration in Medieval Art (London, 1959). D. M. Wilson and O. Klindt-Jensen, *Viking Art* (London, 1966), is important. Irish art and Hiberno-Saxon culture is well described by F. Henry, *Irish Art in the Early Christian Period* (London, 1940: revised ed., vol. I (to 800), London, 1965). The most extensive over-all survey of early English antiquities is G. Baldwin Brown, *The Arts in Early England*, 6 vols. (London, 1903–37).

There are a number of specialist studies. *The Relics of St. Cuthbert*, ed. C. Battiscombe (Oxford, 1956), is a mine of information on a wide range of objects. J. Brønsted, *Early English Ornament*, trans. A. F. Major (London and Copenhagen, 1924), unravels the development of barbarian motifs. R. Jessop, *Anglo-Saxon Jewellery* (London, 1950), deals with particular pieces, and H. R. E. Davidson with *The Sword in Anglo-Saxon England* (Oxford, 1962). E. Bakka, 'The Alfred Jewel and Sight', *The Antiquaries Journal*, XLVI (1966), offers the most recent interpretation of this particular object. On metalwork, see D. M. Wilson, 'The Trewhiddle Hoard', *Archaeologia*, XCVIII (1961), and *Anglo-Saxon Ornamental Metalwork, 700–1100* (British Museum, 1964). See above (p. 286) for Sutton Hoo. L. Stone, *Sculpture in Britain: The Middle Ages* (Pelican History of Art, London, 1955), discusses Anglo-Saxon sculpture. W. G. Collingwood's *Northumbrian Crosses of the Pre-Norman Age* (London, 1927) was a pioneer work, which has not been entirely superseded. Systematic studies of the cross-sculpture of other English kingdoms have not yet appeared in print but A. R. and P. M. Green, *Saxon Architecture and Sculpture in Hampshire* (Winchester, 1951), is useful. For the sculpture of the Celtic lands and bordering territories, see W. S. Calverley, 'Notes on the Early Sculptured Crosses, Shrines and Monuments in the Present Diocese of Carlisle', ed. W. G. Collingwood, *Cumberland and Westmorland Antiquarian Society*, extra series, XL (Kendal, 1899), J. Romilly Allen, *The Early Christian Monuments of Scotland* (Edinburgh, 1903), and V. E. Nash-Williams, *The Early Christian Monuments of Wales* (Cardiff, 1950). Manuscript art has attracted a great deal of interest. M. Rickert, *Painting in Britain: The Middle Ages* (Pelican History of Art, London, 1955), presents a general survey. C. Nordenfalk, 'Before the Book of Durrow', *Acta Archaeologia*, 18 (1947), tackles problems of origins. Longer studies include J. A. Herbert, *Illuminated Manuscripts* (London, 1911: revised ed., New York, 1959), E. G. Millar, *English Illuminated Manuscripts from the Xth to the XIIIth Century* (Paris and Brussels, 1926), D. E. Saunders, *English Illumination*, 2 vols. (Florence, 1928), and F. Wormald, *English Drawing of the Tenth and Eleventh Centuries* (London, 1952). There are a few valuable facsimile editions: A. A. Luce *et al.*, *Evangeliorum Quattuor Codex Durmachensis* (Durrow) (Urs Graf, 1960), T. D. Kendrick *et al.*, *Evangeliorum Quattuor Codex Lindisfarnensis*, 2 vols. (I, facsimile; II, text) (Olten-Lausanne-Fribourg, 1956, 1960), and F. Wormald, *The Benedictional of St. Æthelwold* (London, 1959). For the Bayeux Tapestry, see F. M. Stenton *et. al.*, *The Bayeux Tapestry* (London, second edition, 1965).

There are a great many architectural studies of ecclesiastical sites. The
standard account is A. W. Clapham, *English Romanesque Architecture Before
the Conquest* (Oxford, 1930: reprinted 1966), while G. Webb, *Architecture in
Britain: The Middle Ages* (Pelican History of Art, London, 1956), includes
the Anglo-Saxon period. E. A. Fisher, *Introduction to Anglo-Saxon Architecture and Sculpture* (London, 1964), gives a partial account of basic features;
the same writer's *The Greater Anglo-Saxon Churches* (London, 1962), though
criticised for its exclusion of towerless churches, contains much of interest
and many attractive plates, but it has been eclipsed by H. M. and J. Taylor,
Anglo-Saxon Architecture, 2 vols. (Cambridge, 1965). The nature of the
technicalities of architectural problems and the divergence of interpretation possible is indicated, for example, by the debate over the date of the
church at Bradford-on-Avon: E. D. C. Jackson and E. G. M. Fletcher, 'The
Saxon Church at Bradford-on-Avon', *Journal of the British Archaeological
Association*, 16 (1953); E. Mercer, 'The Alleged Early Date of the Saxon
Church at Bradford-on-Avon', *ibid.*, 29 (1966); and E. D. C. Jackson and
E. Fletcher, 'Bradford-on-Avon: A Reply to Mr. Mercer', *ibid.*, 29 (1966).
Recent architectural articles of interest and importance include S. E. Rigold,
'The Anglian Cathedral at North Elmham', *Medieval Archaeology*, 6 (1962),
E. Fletcher, 'Anglo-Saxon Architecture in the Seventh Century', *Trans. of
the London and Middlesex Archaeological Society*, XXI (pt. 2) (1965), and the
same writer's 'Early Kentish Churches', *Medieval Archaeology*, 9 (1965).
For a report of important excavations at Whitby, see C. Peers and C. A.
Ralegh Radford, 'The Saxon Monastery of Whitby', *Archaeologia*, LXXXIX
(1943). The complex structures at Winchester are discussed by R. N. Quirk,
'Winchester Cathedral in the Tenth Century', *Archaeological Journal*, 114
(1957), and 'Winchester New Minster and its Tenth-Century Tower',
Journal of the British Archaeological Association, 24 (1961). A recent report on
excavations at Winchester by M. Biddle is to be seen in *The Antiquaries
Journal*, XLVI (1966). On secular architecture, see E. T. Leeds, 'A Saxon
Village Near Sutton Courtenay, Berkshire', *Archaeologia*, LXXIII (1923),
LXXVI (1927), XCII (1942), C. A. Ralegh Radford, 'The Saxon House:
A Review and Some Parallels', *Medieval Archaeology*, 1 (1957), P. Rahtz,
'The Saxon and Medieval Palaces at Cheddar, Somerset', *Medieval Archae-
ology*, 6 (1962) and P. V. Addyman, 'A Dark Age Settlement at Maxey,
Northants.', *Medieval Archaeology*, 8 (1964). There is a brief report of the
excavations at Yeavering, *sub* 'Medieval Britain in 1956, I. Pre-Conquest:
Northumberland', *Medieval Archaeology*, 1 (1957), and on old Windsor, *sub*
'Medieval Britain in 1957, I. Pre-Conquest: Berkshire', *Medieval Archae-
ology*, 2 (1958).

Specialist studies on the learning and scholarship of the Anglo-Saxons are
not all that numerous. M. L. W. Laistner, *Thought and Letters in West
Europe, 500–900 A.D.* (2nd edition, London, 1957), deals primarily with continental scholarship. P. F. Jones, 'The Gregorian Mission and English

Education', *Speculum*, III (1928), contains much of interest, while J. M. Wallace-Hadrill, 'Rome and the Early English Church: Some questions of Transmission', *Settimane Di Studio Del Centro Italiano Di Studi Sull'Alto Medioevo*, VII (1960), critically re-examines the debt of English scholarship to Rome and the Continent. R. B. Hepple, 'The Monastic School of Jarrow', *History*, VII (1922), R. Davis, 'Bede's Early Reading', *Speculum*, VIII (1933), and R. W. Chambers, 'Bede', *Proc. of the British Academy*, XXII (1936), fill in the background to Bede's scholastic pursuits, and the varied aspects of Bede's life and work are reviewed in a set of important studies, *Bede, His Life, Times and Writings*, ed. A. H. Thompson (Oxford, 1935). Aldhelm's career and literary activity are described by G. F. Browne, *St. Aldhelm, His Life and Times* (London, 1903), and M. R. James investigates *Two Ancient English Scholars: St. Aldhelm and William of Malmesbury* (Glasgow, 1931), essential reading on Aldhelm. There are two biographies in English of Alcuin: G. F. Browne, *Alcuin of York* (London, 1908), and E. S. Duckett, *Alcuin, Friend of Charlemagne* (New York, 1951). J. D. A. Ogilvy reviews the literary background to the scholars of pre-Viking England in two studies, *Books Well Known to Anglo-Latin Writers from Aldhelm to Alcuin (670–804)* (Cambridge, Mass., 1936) and *Anglo-Saxon Scholarship, 597–780* (Colorado, 1935). Similar studies are badly needed for the post-Viking period. F. P. Magoun, 'King Alfred's Letter on Educational Policy', *Medieval Studies*, 11 (1949), is interesting and P. Grierson's 'Grimbald of St. Bertin's, *English Historical Review*, LV (1940), is a first-class study of one of Alfred's court scholars. On Ælfric, see C. L. White, *Ælfric: A New Study of His Life and Writings* (Yale Studies in English, 1898), and K. Sisam, 'MSS. Bodley 340 and 342: Ælfric's Catholic Homilies', now to be seen in his collected *Studies in the History of Old English Literature* (Oxford, 1953). P. Clemoes clarifies 'The Chronology of Ælfric's Works', *The Anglo-Saxons*, ed. P. Clemoes, and on Wulfstan, see D. Whitelock, 'Archbishop Wulfstan, Homilist and Statesman', *Trans. of the Royal Historical Society*, XXIV (1942). The liturgical background to Anglo-Saxon scholarship is outlined, for example, by G. Dix, *The Shape of the Liturgy* (Glasgow, 1943), and A. Baumstark, *Comparative Liturgy* (1939), revised by B. Botte and translated into English by F. L. Cross (London, 1958). Reference may be made also to E. Bishop, *Liturgica Historica* (Oxford, 1918). On the Gregorian Chant, see *Early Medieval Music to 1300*, ed. A. Hughes (New Oxford History of Music, vol. II, London, 1954), and on the study of the Bible, B. Smalley, *The Study of the Bible in the Middle Ages* (2nd edition, Oxford, 1952).

The prose and verse beginnings of English literature have produced by contrast a vast number of studies, so that selection becomes very difficult. S. B. Greenfield, *A Critical History of Old English Literature* (New York, 1965: London, 1966), and *Continuation and Beginnings: Studies in Old English Literature*, ed. E. G. Stanley (London, 1966) present recent surveys, but mention must also be made of K. Malone, 'The Old English Period to

1100', *A Literary History of England*, ed. A. C. Baugh (New York, 1948). C. E. Wright, *The Cultivation of Saga in Anglo-Saxon England* (London, 1939), and R. M. Wilson, *The Lost Literature of Medieval England* (London, 1952), provide fascinating background. C. W. Kennedy, *The Earliest English Poetry* (Oxford, 1943), deals with Anglo-Saxon verse. On *Beowulf*, R. W. Chambers, *Beowulf: An Introduction* (3rd edition, ed. C. L. Wrenn, Cambridge, 1959), and also D. Whitelock, *The Audience of Beowulf*, are essential reading. Of the writings of K. Sisam, attention may be drawn to 'Cynewulf and His Poetry', now to be seen in *Studies in the History of Old English Literature*, and *The Structure of Beowulf* (Oxford, 1965). D. Whitelock, 'Anglo-Saxon Poetry and the Historian', *Trans. of the Royal Historical Society*, XXXI (1949), deals with the historical value of verse literature.

There have been some important studies of the historical literature of the Anglo-Saxons. Some of these have accompanied editions of texts and have been cited *supra* (p. 281f.). In addition, mention may be made here of the following: B. Colgrave, 'The Earliest Saints' Lives Written in England', *Proc. of the British Academy*, XLIV (1958); B. Colgrave, 'The Earliest Life of St. Gregory the Great, Written by a Whitby Monk', *Celt and Saxon*, ed. N. K. Chadwick; V. H. Galbraith, 'Who Wrote Asser's *Life of Alfred*?', *An Introduction to the Study of History* (London, 1965) (arguing that the *Life* is not genuine); M. Schütt, 'The Literary Form of Asser's *Vita Alfredi*', *English Historical Review*, LXXII (1957); R. Vaughan, 'The Chronology of the Parker Chronicle, 890–970', *English Historical Review*, LXIX (1954); F. T. Wainwright, 'The Chronology of the Mercian Register', *English Historical Review*, LXIX (1954); D. Pontifex, 'The First Life of St. Dunstan', *Downside Review*, LI (1933); D. J. V. Fisher, 'The Early Biographers of St. Ethelwold', *English Historical Review*, LXVII (1952); and Peter Hunter Blair, 'Some Observations on the "Historia Regum" Attributed to Symeon of Durham', *Celt and Saxon*, ed. N. K. Chadwick, which is important for Asser and the whole series of early Northumbrian annals.

11 *Book Two, Part II, Cultivation and Commerce*

A. G. Tansley, *The British Isles and Their Vegetation*, 2 vols. (Cambridge 1939: 1965 impression), is the fundamental study of the early flora of Britain. Mention may be made also of H. Wilcox, *The Woodlands and Marshlands of England* (London, 1936), and H. Goodwin, *History of British Flora* (Cambridge, 1956). D. Justin Schove discusses a new historical science, that of dendrochronology, in 'Tree-rings and Medieval Archaeology', *Medieval Archaeology*, 1 (1957).

The population of early England is analysed by J. Russell, *British Medieval Population* (Albuquerque, 1948). Studies of settlement include *An Historical Geography of England before 1800*, ed. H. C. Darby (London, 1936), H. C. Darby, *The Medieval Fenland* (Cambridge, 1940), H. P. R. Finberg, *Gloucestershire: An Illustrative Essay on the History of the Landscape* (London,

1955), and two by W. G. Hoskins, 'The Landscape Before the English Settlement', and 'The English Settlement', in his book, *The Making of the English Landscape* (London, 1955: 1960 impression). H. Thorpe, 'The Green Village in Its European Setting', *The Fourth Viking Congress*, ed. A. Small, is stimulating. The series of Domesday Geographies, edited by H. C. Darby and others, is extremely important and helpful, and has added a new dimension to eleventh-century English history: *The Domesday Geography of Eastern England* (Cambridge, 1952), *The Domesday Geography of the Midland Counties* (Cambridge, 1954), *The Domesday Geography of South-East England* (Cambridge, 1962), and *The Domesday Geography of Northern England* (Cambridge, 1962). These volumes are as essential to the study of the agricultural community as to that of settlement patterns.

Some of the greatest names of early English historical study have written on the agricultural community. F. W. Maitland, *Domesday Book and Beyond* (Cambridge, 1897: reprinted London, 1960), is a classic. It should be read together with F. Seebohm, *The English Village Community* (4th edition, London, 1905), and the fundamental studies by P. Vinogradoff, *Villainage in England* (Oxford, 1892), *Growth of the Manor* (2nd edition, London, 1911), and *English Society in the Eleventh Century* (Oxford, 1908). Volumes I (ed. J. H. Clapham and E. Power, 1941) and II (ed. M. M. Postan and H. J. Habakkuk, 1952) of the *Cambridge Economic History of Europe* are valuable. R. Lennard, *Rural England, 1086–1135* (Oxford, 1959), though concerned with the post-Conquest period, contains much to interest the Anglo-Saxon historian. F. M. Stenton's interpretation of the social evidence may be seen in *Anglo-Saxon England*. Challenging views are put forward by R. H. C. Davis, 'East Anglia and the Danelaw', *Trans. of the Royal Historical Society*, V (1955), T. H. Aston, 'The Origins of the Manor in England', *Trans. of the Royal Historical Society*, VIII (1958), and H. P. R. Finberg, 'Charltons and Carltons', *Lucerna*. H. R. Loyn, *Anglo-Saxon England and the Norman Conquest*, to which attention has already been drawn, presents a conservative approach to the problems associated with the agricultural communities of early England.

B. H. Slicher van Bath, *The Agrarian History of West Europe, 500–1850* (London, 1963), deals briefly with the early period and may be supplemented by R. Trow-Smith, *English Husbandry* (London, 1951) and *A History of British Livestock Husbandry to 1700* (London, 1957). K. Jessen and H. Helbæk, *Cereals in Great Britain and Ireland in Prehistoric and Early Historic Times* (Copenhagen, 1944), is a first-class pioneer study. H. L. Gray, *English Field Systems* (Cambridge, Mass., 1915: reprinted London, 1959), and C. S. Orwin, *The Open Fields* (Oxford, 1938), describe the various patterns of cultivation in early England. E. Barger, 'The Present Position of Studies in English Field-systems', *English Historical Review*, LIII (1938), is helpful. On the history of the plough, see F. G. Payne, 'The Plough in Ancient Britain', *Archaeological Journal*, 104 (1947), and 'The British Plough: Some Stages in

Its Development', *Agricultural Historical Review*, V (1957). Among the studies of the plough-team may be mentioned: H. G. Richardson, 'The Medieval Plough Team', *History*, XXVI (1942), and R. Lennard, 'Composition of Domesday Caruca', *English Historical Review*, LXXXI (1966). Lynn White, Jr., *Medieval Technology and Social Change* (Oxford, 1962), contains a great deal of interest on the technological development of the early Middle Ages and after, but needs to be used with caution: see, for example, R. H. Hilton and P. H. Sawyer, 'Technical Determinism: The Stirrup and the Plough', *Past and Present*, 24 (1963).

The historical geography of England may be approached through the Victoria County Histories. In addition there have been some important regional studies in recent years, published by the British Association for the Advancement of Science, which include an historical-geographical description of the regions in the Anglo-Saxon period; these include: *The Oxford Region*, ed. A. F. Martin and R. W. Steel (London, 1954), *Bristol and Its Adjoining Counties*, ed. C. M. MacInnes and W. F. Whittard (Bristol, 1955), *Sheffield and Its Region*, ed. D. L. Linton (Sheffield, 1956), *Norwich and Its Region*, ed. F. Briers (Norwich, 1961), *Manchester and Its Region*, ed. C. F. Caster (Manchester, 1962), *Southampton and Its Region*, ed. F. J. Monkhouse (Southampton, 1964). A. E. Smailes, 'North England', *Regions of the British Isles*, ed. W. G. East (London, 1960: 1961 impression), is an impressive first volume in this series. E. M. Jope, 'Saxon Oxford and Its Region', *Dark Age Studies*, ed. D. B. Harden, is important and there is a good deal of interest in R. R. Clarke, *East Anglia* (Ancient Peoples and Places, 14: London, 1960). I. D. Margary, *Roman Roads in Britain*, 2 vols. (London, 1955 and 1957), is a standard work. R. Hippisley Cox, *The Green Roads of England* (2nd edition, London, 1948), is an attractive little book, and a recent study of a major ridgeway is W. F. Grimes, 'The Jurassic Way Across England', *Aspects of Archaeology*, ed. W. F. Grimes. G. B. Grundy reconstructed vanished landscapes from the evidence of charter boundary clauses: see, for example, 'The Ancient Highways and Tracks of Wiltshire, Berkshire and Hampshire, and the Saxon Battlefields of Wiltshire', *Archaeological Journal*, 75 (1918), and 'The Ancient Highways of Dorset, Somerset and South-West England', *Archaeological Journal*, 94–5 (1938–9), which may now be supplemented by H. W. Timperley and F. Brill, *Ancient Trackways of Wessex* (London, 1965). A first-rate discussion of the history of the roads of Leicestershire by P. Russell will be found in the *Victoria County History of Leicestershire*, vol. 3. More studies like this are needed. A great many writers have investigated the history of their local towns and it is difficult to single out individual studies, but no bibliography can fail to mention J. W. Hill, *Medieval Lincoln* (2nd edition, Cambridge, 1965), and C. S. Taylor, 'The Genesis of the Gloucestershire Towns', now to be seen in *Gloucestershire Studies*, ed. H. P. R. Finberg (Leicester, 1957). An archaeological approach to early London is provided by R. E. M. Wheeler, *London and the Vikings* (London, 1927) and *London and the Saxons* (London, 1935).

On the growth of towns as a whole, see F. W. Maitland, *Township and Borough* (Cambridge, 1898), A. Ballard, *The Domesday Boroughs* (Oxford, 1904), and in particular J. Tait, *The Medieval English Borough* (Manchester, 1936). R. R. Darlington, 'The Early History of English Towns', *History*, XXIII (1938), reviews conflicting interpretations. N. Brooks considers 'The Unidentified Forts of the Burghal Hidage', *Medieval Archaeology*, 8 (1964). L. F. Salzman, *English Industries of the Middle Ages* (2nd edition, Oxford, 1923,) provides a general outline of industrial development. On a particular industry, see E. M. Jope. 'The Saxon Building-stone Industry in Southern and Midland England', *Medieval Archaeology*, 8 (1964). F. L. Gross, *The Gild Merchant*, 2 vols. (Oxford, 1890), is useful for Anglo-Saxon gild origins.

A source of continuing inspiration to historians engaged on the study of medieval trade and commerce has been H. Pirenne, *Mahomet and Charlemagne*, translated B. Miall (London, 1939: 1958 impression), and A. F. Havighurst, *The Pirenne Thesis: Analysis, Criticism and Revision* (Boston, 1958), includes extracts from Pirenne's book and from the writings of economic historians on Pirenne's interpretation of the evidence for Dark Age trade. In addition to studies quoted by Havighurst, mention must be made of several important articles which bear directly or indirectly on English commercial activity: P. Grierson, 'Relations Between England and Flanders Before the Norman Conquest', *Trans. of the Royal Historical Society*, XXIII (1941); D. Jellema, 'Frisian Trade in the Dark Ages', *Speculum*, LV (1955); G. C. Dunning, 'Trade Relations Between England and the Continent in the Late Anglo-Saxon Period', *Dark Age Britain*, ed. D. B. Harden; P. Grierson, 'Commerce in the Dark Ages', *Trans. of the Royal Historical Society*, IX (1959); and P. H. Sawyer, 'The Wealth of England in the Eleventh Century', *Trans. of the Royal Historical Society*, XV (1965). F. M. Stenton, *York in the Eleventh Century*, York Minster Historical Tracts no. 8 (1927), discusses trading in York. Specialist studies of particular objects of trade include: D. B. Harden, 'Glass Vessels in Britain and Ireland, A.D. 400–1000', *Dark Age Britain*, ed. D. B. Harden; C. Thomas, 'Imported Pottery in Dark Age Western Britain', *Medieval Archaeology*, 3 (1939); G. C. Dunning, J. G. Hurst, J. N. L. Myres, and F. Tischler, 'Anglo-Saxon Pottery: A Symposium', *Medieval Archaeology*, 3 (1959); and J. G. Hurst, 'Late Saxon Pottery', *The Fourth Viking Congress*, ed. A. Small.

Few new historical sciences can have developed so quickly as that of Anglo-Saxon numismatics. *Anglo-Saxon Coins: Historical Studies Presented to Sir Frank Stenton*, ed. R. H. M. Dolley (London, 1961), contains important articles by a group of leading numismatists and historians, including, for example, J. P. C. Kent, 'From Roman Britain to Saxon England', C. E. Blunt, 'The Coinage of Offa', H. R. Loyn, 'Boroughs and Mints', and R. H. M. Dolley and D. M. Metcalfe, 'The Reform of the English Coinage

Under Eadgar'. In addition, particular mention must be made of the following studies: C. H. V. Sutherland, 'Anglo-Saxon Sceattas in England: Their Origin, Chronology and Distribution', *Numismatic Chronicle*, 11 (1942); C. H. V. Sutherland, *Anglo-Saxon Gold Coinage in the Light of the Crondall Hoard* (Oxford, 1948); P. V. Hill, 'Saxon Sceattas and Their Problems', *British Numismatic Journal*, XXVI (1949–51); R. H. M. Dolley and D. M. Metcalfe, 'Two Stray Finds from St. Albans of Coins of Offa and Charlemagne', *British Numismatic Journal*, XXVIII (1955–7); C. E. Blunt, 'Anglo-Saxon Coinage and the Historian' *Medieval Archaeology*, 4 (1960); R. H. M. Dolley, *Anglo-Saxon Pennies* (British Museum, 1964); R. H. M. Dolley, *Viking Coins of the Danelaw and of Dublin* (British Museum, 1965); and J. J. North, *English Hammered Coinage* (London, 1963). The fascicules of the British Academy's *Sylloge of Coins in the British Isles* are a series of major importance, and parts have appeared of the volumes covering the Fitzwilliam Museum, Cambridge (London, 1958), the Hunterian and Coats Collection, Glasgow (London, 1961), the National Museum, Copenhagen (London, 1964), the Grosvenor Museum, Chester (London, 1964), and the Hiberno-Norse coins in the British Museum (London, 1966).

INDEX

Index